CAMUS,
A ROMANCE

Alger — A travers les Oliviers

CAMUS,
A ROMANCE

Elizabeth Hawes

Grove Press
New York

Published simultaneously in Canada
Printed in the United States of America

FIRST EDITION

ISBN-13: 978-0-8021-1889-9

Grove Press
an imprint of Grove/Atlantic, Inc.
841 Broadway
New York, NY 10003

Distributed by Publishers Group West

www.groveatlantic.com

09 10 11 12 13   10 9 8 7 6 5 4 3 2 1

For Elizabeth Whitney Dodge, my mother and my first reader

Contents

Prologue: From the Beginning   1

1. Young in Algeria   15
2. Moving On   25
3. To France   51
4. Paris 1943   69
5. New York 1946   99
6. Back to Europe   125
7. TB   149
8. *L'Homme Révolté*   163
9. Friends   181
10. Pursuing Char   199
11. The Company of Women   213
12. War in Algeria   235
13. Fans   259
14. *Le Premier Homme*   271
Epilogue   289
Acknowledgments   291
Permissions   293
Photo Credits   295
Notes   297
Selected Bibliography   315

Works By
Albert Camus

Awarded the Nobel Prize for Literature in 1957

The Stranger, 1946 (*L'Étranger*, 1942)

The Plague, 1948 (*La Peste*, 1947)

The Rebel, 1954 (*L'Homme Révolté*, 1951)

The Myth of Sisyphus and Other Essays, 1955 (*Le Mythe de Sisyphe*, 1942)

The Fall, 1957 (*La Chute*, 1956)

Exile and the Kingdom, 1958 (*L'Exil et le Royaume*, 1957)

Caligula and Three Other Plays, 1958: *The Misunderstanding, State of Siege, The Just Assassins* (*Caligula*, 1943; *Le Malentendu*, 1944; *L'État de siege*, 1948 *Les Justes*, 1950)

The Possessed, 1960 (*Les Possédés*, 1959)

Resistance, Rebellion and Death, 1961

Notebooks 1935–1942 (*Carnets mai 1935–février 1942*), 1963

Notebooks 1942–1951 (*Carnets janvier 1942–mars 1951*), 1965

Lyrical and Critical Essays 1968 (*L'Envers et l'endroit*, 1937, *Noces*, 1939, *Été*, 1954 and literary essays)

American Journals, 1987 (*Journaux de Voyage*, 1978)

A Happy Death, 1972 (*La Mort Heureuse* 1971)

The First Man, 1997 (*Le Premier Homme* 1996)

Notebooks 1951–1958, 2008 (*Carnets mars 1951–décembre 1958*, 1989)

CAMUS,
A ROMANCE

Prologue:
From the Beginning

During my last college years, I had a photograph of Albert Camus prominently displayed above my desk—the famous Cartier-Bresson portrait with the trench coat and dangling cigarette. He was a celebrated and sophisticated writer; I was a young and serious French major at one of the eastern academic establishments then known as the Seven Sisters. I was writing an honors thesis on Camus's work, and in the process I had fallen in love with him. Not romantic love in the only sense I had experienced it in those days, an overheated yearning mixed with perpetual daydreaming, but something deeper, like the bonding of two souls.

In addition to the photograph, I had posted quotations from Camus's work around my dormitory room—stuck in the frame of a mirror, propped up against a can of hair spray, sharing a thumbtack with a Picasso print on the wall. They were inscribed on index cards in a careful script: "*Pour devenir un saint, il faut vivre*," "To become a saint, you need to live." "*Si le monde était clair, l'art ne serait pas*," "If the world were clear, art would not exist." This display—the photo, the words, together with a large poster of the grand Pont Neuf in Paris, which I had never seen, and the stack of Edith Piaf records I played every night—was my testimonial. It was everything that mattered then; in its way, it summed up who I was. Even the hair spray had its significance as a weapon against the naturally curly hair that did not fit my image of the intellectual I wanted to be.

If writers only knew, or at least remembered in their solitary travail, what an impact they can have on the psyche of a reader, how with just a

1

random insight or a phrase or even a prose style they can change the course of someone's life, alter thinking forever. Perhaps Camus, struggling with his admitted desperation to produce what would be his last novel in a study on the rue de Chanaleilles in Paris, might have been at least amused to know that in a room full of stuffed animals and drinking mugs in the backwater of western Massachusetts, there was a very unworldly young woman who was being transformed by his work. I, of course, did not appreciate the extent of his influence then, but I knew that as I read his words I felt both grounded and empowered by the simple fact that I understood exactly what he meant. I accepted his basic message—that in a world that was absurd, the only course was awareness and action.

In my innocence, I was confident that one day I would arrange to meet Camus. After I graduated, I planned to go to Paris, and I imagined that somehow we would have a drink at the Café Flore or one of the other Left Bank establishments I had heard about, and that over a *café filtre* or a *vin blanc,* we would talk for hours. Then, on January 4, 1960, Camus died in a car crash outside Paris. He was only forty-six. I had just turned nineteen. I was still on Christmas vacation with my family, so I did not hear the news until I returned to school. Only then did I see the awful headline and the picture of the Facel Vega wrapped around a tree. I felt bereft, and I was also more helplessly involved with him than ever.

I have unearthed a copy of the thesis I completed after Camus's death, entitled "*La Notion de Limite dans l'Oeuvre d'Albert Camus,*" "The Idea of Limit in the Work of Albert Camus." It is a period piece now, yellowed and brittle, typed on the newly invented "corrasable" paper on a heavy-duty Royal portable that I had customized with French accents. I remember the weeks of all-nighters I spent physically producing this manuscript, working in the bright lights of the dorm's dining room while my roommate slept undisturbed upstairs. I used two sheets of carbon paper for copies and an ink eraser or white-out for errors, staving off exhaustion with coffee, No-Doze, and an incipient and exhilarating sense of accomplishment. I also remember the great sadness that came with the knowledge that my affair with Camus was ending. I had never before experienced such an intimate relationship with a writer, poring over his prose and filling up with his rhythms, thinking his thoughts, trying to crawl under his skin. Inadvertently, my kinship with Camus had progressed far beyond academic interest. However unlikely it seemed, I had come to identify with Camus, the courageous expatriate from Algeria, and for my own sake, I needed to know more about the man than his public pronouncements and his published work.

Thus began what has become a forty-year quest that effectively connects my past to my present. My pursuit of Camus has been neither always constant nor even conscious, but our relationship has endured. In the mid-1960s the pursuit was active, for I was at last living in France, and I expected to find Camus at every turn. But it was already a different era, and his death seemed to have been one of those turning points that divide time into then and now. In Paris, a new wave of writers was the rage, Nathalie Sarraute, Alain Robbe-Grillet, Roland Barthes, Michel Foucault. The multicultural Algeria that Camus had labored to preserve was a lost cause and the FLN leader Ahmed Ben Bella had been elected president of the newly independent Arab country. Dutifully, I collected some of the many volumes of homage that were issued after Camus's death and studied the photographs in them—Camus at the lycée in Algeria, Camus with Sartre and Beauvoir, Camus directing the actress Maria Casarès in his play *Le Malentendu* (*The Misunderstanding*). The images still had that beautiful presence. I bought the impressive leather-bound Pléiade edition of his complete works, which had just been issued by Gallimard, edited and annotated by Roger Quilliot, a critic I had admired in college and had also hoped someday to meet. To have your complete works issued in the Pléiade series was a distinct honor in France, often awarded posthumously and reserved for fine writers of enduring interest, but in Camus's case it also seemed to be a confirmation of his death. A professor at the Sorbonne told me that scholars from all over the world—Swedes, Germans, Americans, Chileans, and Libyans—were preparing doctoral theses on Camus: on Camus the Hellenist, Camus the pagan, or Camus the picaresque saint. Camus was being consecrated, I thought; his tomb was being sealed. Other than in an academic way, it was too late to know him.

During the 1970s and 1980s, my investigation of Camus was sporadic. For long periods of time, I completely forgot him. He still qualified as a literary hero, but as a subject he had proved difficult—and impenetrably private, even in his journals. The two volumes that had been published in the 1960s revealed the struggling human being that was intimated in the work, but made no reference to events and people, to the life behind the writing. For better or worse, I had to be content with the identity that I had created for Camus on my own. The moral positions of his characters, for example, their pathos and stoicism, suggested that Camus's own life was also about the importance and pathos of moral position. The austerity of his message—that in a world without hope we must still struggle to survive—spoke to his own despondency and courage; his prose style, direct and unadorned, to his honesty. These qualities, together with the sensuality, passion, and yearning that I had found in his early Algerian essays, and the unwavering principle of essays such as "Reflections on the Guillotine," which made the case against capital punishment, matched up with the Camus of my photos: the handsome young loner with the cigarette, the high furrowed forehead, and the sad Mediterranean eyes; the Camus who inspired uncommon devotion.

It now seems ironic and probably fortunate that I was not able to confront the private Camus until a time when I could better relate to and understand his life, when I had grown up and was effectively on more equal terms. I am older now than Camus was when he died, and the original gaps between his world and mine have narrowed. I have lived in France, visited North Africa, had love affairs, joined protest movements, married and had children, become a writer and a literary person. I know writers who knew the Paris of the 1940s and 1950s, writers who met Camus, even Camus's literary agent. Along the way, I have acquired other literary heroes and have felt a pressing curiosity about their journey through the world, their "life and letters"—but never the sort of attachment I had to the passionate young man from Algeria.

Camus resurfaced in my life with primal force in 1994, the year that his daughter and literary executor decided to release for publication the long-withheld manuscript of *Le Premier Homme* (*The First Man*), the unfinished novel he was working on at the time of his death. Reading that book, which, as it stands, is patently autobiographical and tells the story of Camus's childhood in poverty and his search for an identity, I was struck by the uncanny sense that I had anticipated its message. The voice was Camus's as I heard it in the truthful essays of his youth. Although told in the third person, the chronicle was unmistakably Camus's own. Here was the absent father, the beloved silent mother, the honesty, the self-doubt and self-determination. With both astonishment and a sense of gratification, I read *The First Man* as the beginning of an autobiography that was long overdue. I reveled in its spontaneity, its transparency, its sense of immediacy and purpose, as well as in my own intense response to a resurrected mentor. Camus had originally entitled his novel *Adam*. Coming, as it did, several years after the confessional novel *La Chute* (*The Fall*) and at a time of personal decline and depression, it represented a new beginning for him. It was also a new beginning for me and Camus.

For many years, I had thought about Camus only indirectly, when I read about new violence in Algeria, or learned that after his brother's death, Bobby Kennedy turned to Camus for his thoughts on fate and suffering, finding support in his message that the apparent meaninglessness of the world is not an end but a beginning. (Kennedy, too, kept his favorite Camus quotes on index cards, and in his journal he wrote down Camus's line "Knowing that you are going to die is nothing.")[1] Occasionally, working in my study, I would glance up at the shelf full of yellowing paperback editions of his work and feel a particular, rather possessive pleasure. But reading *The First Man* brought Camus dramatically into the present. Again he was relevant and again he was real. In fact, his voice in that book was so real that it affected me like a visitation. All the old feelings came flooding back, all the drive of my original mission, and then, perhaps most strongly, a profound pride in Camus simply because he was still the Camus I knew him to be. It struck me that it was ironic but not out of character that in what would be his final work, he had at long last relinquished his privacy, climbed down from his pedestal, and faced up publicly to his real self. In effect, he was asking for understanding. And I was quite helplessly engaged anew.

I spent a long time looking at the cover of *The First Man*, which shows a thirteen- or fourteen-year-old gamin-like Camus grinning shyly at the camera. He radiates the mischief and innocence of boyhood, but he also looks unmistakably and irresistibly like himself, the man as child. On an inside page of the volume, I studied a reproduction of a page from his original manuscript, written in a tiny, tight, almost indecipherable script. I had not seen Camus's handwriting before, and trying to recognize words and read beneath the cross-outs, I could imagine his hand moving across the page. That is why I resumed the pursuit: I felt a flicker of his living presence, and beyond the work I wanted to find the man.

There is more to know about Camus today than when I was a student and he was in large part a mythic figure. The final volume of his journals and an assortment of youthful writings, including a novel, have been published. Most of his essays from the Resistance newspaper *Combat* have been translated into English. Friends of Camus's have written memoirs; an American and a Frenchman have written compelling biographies. The appearance of *The First Man* added Camus's own direct voice to the mix; it created a literary sensation in France, and he became the focus of magazine articles and television shows. He is again a popular and provocative subject there. In America, he is material for book clubs, and his relationship with Sartre is the focus of seminars at important universities. Yet after all these years, I still think of Camus as my subject. He has proved himself to be at the very least a good man and a credible hero. His beliefs have taken on the added weight of prescience; his thoughts on violence and terrorism are timely; his humanism and honesty, sometimes astonishing, are more admirable than ever. As an independent thinker in difficult times, he provides a model that is very relevant in our current day. But my reaction derives from more than all this. Ultimately, it is personal. To my way of thinking, Camus would not have existed without me or I without him. Our relationship is about both of us, about who he was and who I was and still am. If he is my writer, I am his reader.

Last night I found myself thinking about Camus's life during the Resistance. I was alone at home with the radio and the dog, and I had been reading an article in *The New York Times* about France's latest *crise de conscience* over national behavior during the Vichy years. This brought to mind a story I had read about one of Camus's encounters with the police at that time. He was carrying copy for the underground newspaper *Combat* and was in the company of Maria Casarès, the beautiful young Spanish actress with whom he was having a passionate affair, when they were caught in a roadblock in the center of Paris and shaken down by a commandant. Camus, however, had quickly passed Maria the incriminating papers to hide in her coat, and they were released. Like the other small dramas that were then his daily fare—sheltering dangerous friends, changing apartments under the cover of night, a hasty exodus from Paris by bicycle—this story had made me proud of Camus and his unhesitating engagement, and also pleased with myself, because by the sheer force of knowing about this event I was in a way associated with it. But this feeling of complicity, however natural to the subject-mentor relationship, was objectionably shallow, for even now, enlightened by biographies, war histories, and documentaries, I have no way of understanding what it meant to suffer a long war and live under an occupation, no way to shed my Americanness, my time line, or my innocence. As if to confirm my situation, I suddenly became aware of a song on the radio, which the announcer was introducing as number two on the 1963 hit parade. As I listened to "Don't Hang Up," I realized that I knew the words in French ("*Ne Raccroche Pas*") as well as English, because in 1963, as a young graduate student in France, I was as caught up with pop singers—Sheila and Sylvie Vartan and Johnny Halliday—café life, bistro food, and the purchase of a bikini as I was with deconstructing Camus.

In 1963, I did not know how much I didn't know about Camus. I had read everything he had written that had been published then: three novels, three volumes of lyrical essays, two volumes of philosophical essays, four plays, a volume of short stories, a collection that included the "Algerian Chronicles," his "Letters to a German Friend," "Reflections on the Guillotine," and his Nobel Prize acceptance speech. I was involved with his words rather than his life, and our relationship had an enviable purity, a desert-island quality of privacy that had to be compromised once I became more than a mere reader and imaginary sidekick and began to accumulate facts. Facts, with their cool and incontestable authority, have a way of sabotaging understanding, clouding perspective, and shattering the intimacy one has enjoyed with a subject. Once I had taken a footstep into his past, I would be caught in the impossible task of playing catch-up with an era with which I had only the most tenuous connections. I would be alternately exhausted and exhilarated by Camus, but as his life unfolded in bits and pieces and a tentative narrative emerged, I began to feel that I knew him, and this feeling was the beginning of understanding and a new kind of love.

★ ★ ★

I am not sure what initially attracted me to Camus as worthy of more than the usual academic attention granted to the writers of western classics. I read *The Stranger* in high school along with *Vanity Fair, Anna Karenina,* and *Crime and Punishment,* a first introduction to the literature of Europe, a place I knew only through the movies at the new local "art theater." I was impressed by the slimness of *The Stranger* and its simple uncadenced prose, in direct contrast to the girth and the convoluted rhythms of Thackeray, but I don't think this tale of a random murder of an Arab on a hot beach in Algiers registered in my consciousness as more than a strange adventure story of peculiar and disturbing obliqueness. Nonetheless, I was close to tears at its end when the protagonist, Meursault, facing execution, is suddenly filled with the sounds and smells of the earth, Camus's equivalent of redemption. "For the first time," Meursault says, "in that night alive with signs and stars, I opened myself to the gentle indifference of the world. Finding it so much like myself—so like a brother really—I felt that I had been happy and that I was happy again."[2] I suppose that this small well of emotion meant that something of Camus's thinking had registered on me, although the days when I would talk about "existentialism" or read Nietzsche late into the night were still far in the future. I think I recognized that Camus was "modern" and was addressing the postwar generation of which I was among the youngest members.

The process by which writers become real men or women in a reader's mind is subconscious and stealthy until that moment when something suddenly registers with a warm, almost audible buzz. I read all of Camus's major work without feeling anything more provocative than admiration. *La Peste (The Plague)* was a morality tale about a small town under the siege of an epidemic; *La Chute (The Fall)* was a lawyer's bleak confessional about judgment and guilt, which intrigued but ultimately eluded me; *Caligula* was a play about the young emperor's quest for the impossible. I was arrested by the primary question in *Le Mythe de Sisyphe (The Myth of Sisyphus)*—whether in the face of the silence of the world life is worth living—and reassured by its answer: "The struggle toward the summit itself suffices to fill a man's heart. One must imagine Sisyphus happy." But this work did not strike me as a personal lesson in lucidity and courage the way it would later.[3] I labored to follow the convoluted thinking on revolt in *L'Homme Révolté (The Rebel)*, which was Camus's prescription for action in an absurd world. Nonetheless, I had entered Camus's force field and was beginning to feel intimations of his presence. Camus was famous—Camus and Jean-Paul Sartre were the kingpins in postwar French letters, and Camus was awarded a Nobel Prize in 1957—and I was drawn closer to him by his celebrity, which magnetized him in the way celebrity does. He was also very appealing. He was a very young laureate—only Kipling, at forty-three, had been younger—he was handsome and manly in a casual way, and surprisingly modest. His acceptance speech when he received the Nobel Prize reflected his habit of solitude, his self-doubt, his "panic" at being thrust into the limelight. In a photograph of the ceremonies, his eyes were cast downward and his incipient smile was shy. Formal, almost disembodied in much of his work, Camus was accessible in his photographs: boyish, earnest, disarming.

I did not begin to study the photographs for clues to Camus until after the moment, clearly recollected now, when I first identified with him, first heard the buzz that, when it came, was like the roar of a jet engine. As it happened, the words that turned me on to Camus came from a later work, *L'Été* (*Summer*), which he wrote in his late thirties in the lyrical and more personal style of his youth. I still have the three-by-five index card on which I wrote, "*Au milieu d'hiver, j'apprenais enfin qu'il y avait en moi un été invincible*," "In the depths of winter, I finally learned that within me lay an invincible summer." As I would come to know, it describes a moment in which Camus, in despair over events provoked by *The Rebel,* and seeking solace in the beauty of the Roman ruins at Tipasa, a seaside village outside Algiers, discovers that he has within himself an unquenchable source of joy.[4] Nearing the end of sophomore year, I had been in the throes of my own melancholy, a result of my first serious questioning of life in combination with a bout of homesickness, when I encountered that line of Camus's. In a moment I still remember, I suddenly identified so strongly with Camus that my heart began to thump and swell with a feeling of connection, compassion, and love for all of mankind—a rather Camusian moment, it now seems. I was almost giddy, because I knew that however small my own depression, at least in contrast to Camus's profound disillusion with the workings of love and justice, however different my own experience, however undeveloped my thinking, Camus was writing directly to me.

Henceforth, Camus was my guide and mentor. I selected my thesis topic and spent many hours a day alone with him in a carrel tucked away deep in the recesses of the library stacks. During these hours, I had my first true private life and my first room of one's own. Ironically, in experiencing a deep connection to Camus, I began to experience a new kind of solitude, to feel different from my friends and interested in rather than worried about the differences. The only outsider to enter this realm was my thesis adviser, Marie, a strikingly tall, raven-haired young French philosophy scholar on loan from the Sorbonne, who was a model bohemian and the perfect companion for the tenderfoot intellectual in her charge. Under her influence, I learned to work like a French student, to analyze a text in the exhaustive French method, to read meaning in the tense of verbs, to understand how Camus's insistent morality differed from Sartre's "existentialism." Studying Camus's work chronologically, I shadowed his life, moving side by side with him from a recognition of the "absurdity" of the world—the limits imposed on man's deepest desires by the realities of the human condition—to a belief in resistance and absolute revolt within those limits. I confronted the issue of capital punishment. I became an ardent humanist, championing moral responsibility and preaching Camus's doctrine in late-night sessions in the dorm smoker with a new set of offbeat friends. Alone in my carrel behind a mountain of books, I thought about Camus's importance to the twentieth century with a sense of personal triumph. I felt privileged in my allegiance to Camus, almost smug.

I have retrieved two photographs from this era. From my Lagarde and Michard illustrated survey of twentieth-century French literature, there is a full-length profile of Camus directing a play rehearsal in the courtyard of the château in Angers. He is wearing a trench coat, as usual, the collar up, the armbands tightly cinched. His right hand is draped over the seat in front of him; his left is holding a microphone into which he appears to speak very intently, his mouth serious, his eyes slightly narrowed. He could be a captain at sea, directing an invasion. He looks comfortable, authoritative, and unusually handsome, a cross between Gérard Philipe and Humprey Bogart. (On the reverse side of the page is a reproduction of a painting of Saint-Germain-des-Prés by Bernard Buffet, show-ing the twelfth-century church and a corner of the Café Deux Magots, one of Camus's haunts. The caption reads: "At the crossroads of existen-tialism.") From the cover of a work of criticism I discovered in college, *La Mer et Les Prisons* (*Sea and Prisons*) by Roger Quilliot, there is a picture of Camus in the same trench coat, lighting a cigarette, his eyes almost shut, closed in on himself, cheeks sucked in, hands cupped protectively around the match, conveying in the tenderness of the gesture the romance of smoking.

Even before I had mastered the language, speaking French gave me a new personality and brought me closer to Camus. Inexplicably, I spoke French an octave higher than English, a lilting soprano emerging from my very ordinary second alto voice. I took pleasure in odd epithets and formal phrases I would never have indulged in in my native tongue. I reveled in sounds—the crescendo of sentences in French, the nasals, the floating *voilà*. It was the small stuff that seemed crucial. I spent many hours learning to deliver *je ne sais pas* like a native (in a very rapid elision and exhalation), imagining myself in ardent conversation at a café. I learned to say *oui* once on an intake of breath, or three times in quick succession, to punctuate my thoughts with *alors, dis donc,* and *eh bien*. Gradually, I developed a palpable sense of the language and could begin to inhabit it physically. When I listened to myself on a headset in the language lab, I sounded like somebody else—perhaps not yet Simone de Beauvoir or Simone Signoret, but not the familiar and diffident me, either.

I had never heard Beauvoir's voice, but from reading *Le Deuxième Sexe* (*The Second Sex*) I had a distinct idea of how it might sound: rich, assertive, and throaty, with the enviably pure Parisian accent. Her book and her femi-nine existentialism had made a deep impression on me—I still have my original copy of the book, in which key passages are underlined and dozens of pages dog-eared. After *The Second Sex,* I moved on quickly to Beauvoir's novel *Les Mandarins,* which had won the Prix Goncourt in 1954. Beauvoir had been a good friend of Camus's for a while, and with Sartre and an as-sortment of other friends had socialized with him in Paris during the occu-pation. Their madcap, orgiastic evenings—the drinking, dancing, and seductions; the impromptu "fiestas" that often lasted until dawn—were a way of surviving the war. They also inform *The Mandarins,* which I learned later was a roman à clef and a thinly disguised autobiography of sorts. Everyone in Paris recognized the characters. Camus—Henri Perron in the book—is a journalist, the acclaimed author of "the" occupation novel, a relentless chaser of women, handsome, restless, and melancholy. Without any broader knowledge of these lives, I read *The Mandarins* only as a lively story about intellectual Paris. I wanted to be there and began to apply for fellowships.

From the beginning, the path to Camus has been anything but straight, but its myriad detours and distractions all have the potential to be enlightening and, in the long run, relevant. Beauvoir, for example, was a somewhat coincidental reference on my part, but she shared some significant private moments with Camus, and judging from a remark she made to him about the gap between his public and private lives, she perceived his deepest dilemma. Also, her life almost always intimated Sartre, her chosen "absolute" love—and Sartre was Camus's *frère-ennemi,* partly responsible for Camus's warm reception in Paris in the 1940s (he gave *The Stranger* a glowing review in *Les Cahiers du Sud*), and also for his downfall (after the publication of *The Rebel,* Sartre wrote a scathing personal attack on Camus himself). This was one of the reasons that Camus wrote *The Fall,* about the vicissitudes of judgment. I mentioned Edith Piaf, because I loved, and still love, her songs, but perhaps she, too, knew Camus, for they both lived in Paris in the 1940s and 1950s, and both expressed the same postwar angst in their art; also, Camus frequented music halls. Moreover, she had an intense affair with Marcel Cerdan, a world champion boxer, and Camus did some middleweight boxing when he lived in Oran. Jean-Louis Barrault cropped up in a reference to Camus's social life, not only because he was an important figure in contemporary French theater and would direct Camus's play *L'État de Siège (State of Siege)* but because I have always loved Barrault's performance as the lovesick mime in *Les Enfants du Paradis (Children of Paradise),* in which Maria Casarès played the forsaken wife. I saw Barrault and his wife Madeleine Renaud on the New York stage in the late 1960s. Perhaps most coincidentally of all, I had recently learned that a close friend's father, who is Spanish and happened to be visiting New York, had known Maria Casarès's father, Santiago Casarès Quiroga, who was the last prime minister of Republican Spain. So perhaps my friend, too, could provide incidental information that would enrich my understanding of Camus, who had a twenty-year love affair with Casarès Quiroga's daughter, was active in the cause of Republican exiles, and identified deeply with his Spanish ancestors.

This sort of coincidental input has been so frequent that I sometimes feel I have a cosmic connection with Camus. It is also a lesson in biography, probably the first lesson, which teaches you that your subject is only one piece in the enormously intricate web of other people's lives, and that you, as the student and scribe, have predilections, arbitrary instincts, incidental encounters, and personal experiences that alternately cloud and clarify your perspective. At many points in my research, every new detail seemed to be equally weighted and equally promising. Camus had a dog. Aha! What kind? Was it a briard, like my dog? He had an old Mercedes; I once had one, too. He admired Faulkner, had a fistfight with Arthur Koestler, exchanged letters with Pasternak. Each piece of information seemed to be linked to an ever-expanding series of larger pieces of information. And there were always loose threads, incomplete evidence, and uncooperative facts. I wanted to freeze Camus, isolate him, make him stand still in a given place for a definitive portrait. Although I wasn't writing a formal biography, I was encountering all the problems and paradoxes that biographers face. My quest was stranger. I already loved Camus, and yet I needed to know who he was. After decades of devotion, I wanted to understand why I cared so passionately about him. Somehow I still imagined that we could meet.

Young in Algeria

The book that catapulted me into Camus's early years was an auto-biographical work undertaken at the very end of his life, and this timing made its eloquence doubly affecting. In intense, streaming prose, *The First Man* begins the story of a child born in poverty, who caught the attention of a primary school teacher who introduced him to books, proposed a scholarship to the local lycée, and watched him flourish. The setting is the working-class neighborhood of Belcourt in Algiers, where Camus lived with his older brother Lucien and a bachelor uncle, Étienne, in a household dominated by women: a tyrannical grandmother who ruled the roost, and a submissive, sweet-natured mother who was illiterate, partially deaf, and nearly mute. His father, a *caviste* who managed the wine harvest for several local domaines, had served in the *Zouave*[1] regiment fighting for France in World War I and died in the Battle of the Marne when Camus was an infant. Mainly conscripts from the French settlers of Algeria, the Zouaves, dressed in colorful red-and-blue Arab garb that made them look like battle flags, were shock troops and died in great numbers. The shell fragment removed from his father's head sent home by the French government was kept in an old biscuit tin in the kitchen of the three-room apartment, his Croix de Guerre in a gilt frame in the dining room. Albert and Lucien shared a bed in a room with their mother. There was no bathroom, electricity, or running water. The toilet was in the hall. The kitchen had no oven, so every few days Albert or his brother took a platter of food to a nearby butcher to be cooked. These details are recounted in *The First*

Man without any particular drama or intimation of deprivation, for in Belcourt there was nothing unusual about them. From the house, a small balcony opened onto the larger world of the busy rue de Lyon below, with its shops, cafés, and crowded markets. The street was filled with the sounds of many languages—French, Arabic, Italian, Spanish—and of tambourines and castenets, braying donkeys, and the clacking of the tramway. It smelled of saffron, garlic, anise, fish, overripe fruit, honeysuckle, and jasmine. The sun was hot. The sea was at the edge of the neighborhood.

Under the wing of Louis Germain, his elementary school teacher and first surrogate father, Camus was a model student, serious, reserved, but responsive—*d'une sagesse exemplaire,* Germain would say. He liked school-work and school life and rose quickly to the top of the class. This achievement helped Germain to persuade his mother that he should move on to the lycée rather than go to work for the local *tonnelier,* or cooper, where his uncle made barrels. Outside school, Camus led a life like that of any other young boy in the quartier, except for the way it registered on him and how he internalized its every detail. He loved sports as well as books. With a gang of friends, he played games in the street with apricot pits or stones or a wooden club; climbed trees in the park; shared minted cara-mels, the dried lupine seeds called *tramousses,* and an occasional cornet of fried potatoes; swam (and bathed) in the harbor, shouting, diving, reign-ing over life and the sea "like nobles certain that their riches were limit-less."[2] Even boredom was "a game, a delight, a kind of excitement," he writes in *The First Man*.[3] Camus recalled the most humdrum facts of his early existence with equanimity and a warm heart: the single pair of pants pressed nightly; the nails fixed on his shoes to prevent him from playing soccer and preserve the soles; the obligatory siestas with his grandmother, and the odor of her elderly flesh. (As an adult, he admitted that he hated those naps, and that thereafter he could never bring himself to sleep in the afternoon until he was gravely ill.) He was sustained by these memo-ries in later years, when he was disenchanted with Paris and felt like an alien in a forest of concrete and steel. His nostalgia was expressed in his most lyric prose. Each time he returned to Algeria, Camus says, he felt blessed relief and release. "He could breathe, on the giant back of the sea he was breathing in waves, rocked by the great sun, at last he could sleep and he could come back to the childhood from which he never recovered, to the secret of the light, of the warm poverty which enabled him to survive and overcome everything."[4]

It was at the lycée, which was located in bustling, cosmopolitan central Algiers and drew a more diverse body of students from more affluent sections of the city, that Camus first became self-conscious about his background, feeling "singular" rather than unconsciously universal. Before that, he thought all the world was like him, he said. At the lycée, he learned to make comparisons. He was a scholarship student known as a "pupil of the nation," a category open not only to the sons of deceased soldiers but also to sons of military and civil functionaries and officials of the French colony, who had better clothes and bigger houses up in the hills. On his application for the lycée, Camus had to describe his mother as a *domestique,* or cleaning woman; this suddenly filled him with shame, and then "the shame of feeling shame." But the challenges to his mother's stature, like his grandmother's overriding authority or his own growing awareness of her helpless ignorance, provoked in him a greater respect for her gentle endurance and an ever fiercer compensatory love. He would remember with anger and sadness her one brief attempt at a romance, which had given her a new gaiety and glamour, but was rudely quashed by her mother and her brother Étienne. All his life, he would be consumed with protecting and honoring the silent figure whose illiteracy and deafness isolated her from the world outside, who couldn't read newspapers or hear the radio, who had no idea what history and geography might be, who had no expectations or discernible desires, who "did not dare to desire."[5]

Camus's own life could be understood as a response to his mother's— his ambitions as a reaction to her docility and his tireless activism as engendered by her passivity—for it was in almost every way an antithesis. Camus knew this. He dedicated *The First Man,* the first of the books he intended to write about love, to the widow Camus, "to you who will never be able to read this book." In a note to himself, he wrote of "the story of two people joined by the same blood and every kind of difference. She similar to the best this world has, and he quietly abominable. He thrown into all the follies of our time; she passing through the same history as if it were that of any time. She silent most of the time, with only a few words at her disposal to express herself; he constantly talking and unable to find in thousands of words what she could say with a single one of her silences. Mother and son."[6]

The stories about the first decade of Camus's life are very moving, because they are suffused with a sense of innocence and primary love. Few writers have described poverty in the third world with the clarity, eloquence, and total recall that he brought to the subject, and although he describes this world as bleak, "naked as death," "closed in on itself like an island in society," "a fortress without drawbridges," in his memory it is also oddly rich and alluring. Indeed so caught up was I in the minutiae of these early days—the kerosene lamp and the dark stairs, the drama of a lost sou, the occasional pleasure of a hunting trip to the mountains with his uncle or an American western at the dusty movie house down the street (Tom Mix, Douglas Fairbanks)—that I was reluctant to have Camus grow up, and I dreaded the moment when I would lose the direct sound of his voice, when somewhere during the lycée years *The First Man* would abruptly end.

Camus, however, "his youthful blood boiling," was impatient to grow, to inhabit all the places he had read about in school. School was his joy, the drawbridge out of the fortress, an escape from family life to somewhere else. His memory of filling inkwells, the delicious taste of the strap of his bookbag, the smell of a varnished ruler, its sting as a tool of discipline, was as acute as that of the urine and floating orange blossoms in the town fountain. He read the stories, in the textbooks sent from France, about snowfalls and children in wooden shoes as myths about a Garden of Eden. He relived Louis Germain's firsthand accounts of World War I with occasional outbursts of emotion. It was all part of the powerful poetry of school. Germain shared his own life with his students, talked about his favorite books and his philosophy, and set an example that influenced Camus's later desire to teach. In Germain's class, students felt for the first time that they existed and were objects of the highest regard, he remembered; they were judged worthy to discover the world.

When the personal testimony of *The First Man* ends, Camus is fourteen or fifteen years old, an adolescent in the *cinquième* class, which is roughly the equivalent of the eighth grade. A photograph from this time shows him in short pants, posing with his soccer team and grinning to reveal two mischievous dimples. He has a newsboy's cap on his head and a scarf draped around his neck, and although he looks very young and quite small—he was late to grow and was called *moustique,* or mosquito, by his teammates—he already has a seductive and glowing presence. The child has died, he notes, recalling that he had summarily refused his grandmother's whipping (generally a punishment for tardiness or ruining his shoes) and had caught an inadvertent glimpse up a woman's skirt. He had also earned money at a summer job, kissed a girl, and been made the first-string goalie on the lycée team.

Soccer was a passion as consuming as books, and on the playing field Camus made himself respected and liked by the tough guys in school. The lessons were enduring—"What I know most surely about morality and the duty of man I owe to sport," he wrote later in his journal[7]—and the camaraderie was an antidote to his growing awareness of the cultural differences that set him apart from his classmates, whose parents could pass on traditions, a system of values, and a clear sense of right and wrong: a heritage, as he elaborated. In *The First Man,* Camus describes suffering from a sense of otherness, his "ecstasy of joy punctuated by the sudden counterpunches inflicted by a world unknown to him," but he also reports that he was quick to recover, avidly trying to understand and assimilate a world he did not know.[8] Certain of a future, toughened by his childhood, he was ready to find his place almost anywhere. If he felt separate, he never felt inferior. He was learning to fashion something that resembled a style of behavior and to create a heritage on his own, he said. He was "from somewhere else, that was all."[9]

Camus, at center, in short pants at his uncle's workshop, 1920.

As someone with a mission, I read *The First Man* with joy at its truthfulness and its explicit information. Even if his book wasn't meant to be confessional, Camus was explaining himself, revealing in his recollections of childhood the important underpinnings of his character—independence, passion, courage, and (just as important to me) a deep sense of vulnerability. A sort of underdog quality, when paired with strength of character, can be crucial in a hero. Even while knowing humiliation, Camus did not have the slightest desire to have a different family or a different station in life. "How can it be made clear that a poor child can sometimes be ashamed without ever being envious?" he writes.[10] The fact that in order to survive he would camouflage his vulnerability as irony, charm, and sometimes arrogance made him all the more sympathetic, because I identified with his behavior. At the same time, I was glad that Camus dropped a few hints about a dark and rebellious side, because that, too, seemed normal. Without much explanation, he mentions his "violent temper," the "hard and nasty arrogance" that enabled him to cope with guilt, and a dread of death, darkness, and the unknown (particularly intense in the evening as he made his way home from school). About school life, he says, in direct contrast to Germain's earlier report on his calmness and good manners, that he was too rambunctious and liked to show off. Jean Grenier, his professor and mentor in his last year at the lycée, and later at the University of Algiers, noticed the naturally undisciplined air of his pupil and placed him in the front row to keep him in sight.

The most significant event in Camus's years at the lycée was the onset of pulmonary tuberculosis when he was seventeen, midway through his final year of *première supérieure,* which he had to resume the following fall. The incidence of TB and of death from the illness—in eighteen to twenty-four months if it is untreated—was disproportionally high among the underprivileged and undernourished. So dramatic were the first signs of the disease—fainting spells, exhaustion, handkerchiefs drenched in blood—that Camus assumed he would die. He became a regular patient at the predominately Muslim Mustapha Hospital in Algiers, where the standard procedure was periodic artificial pneumothorax, injections of air to collapse the affected lung and allow it to heal. Until he had gained enough strength to resume his studies, he moved into the more comfortable household of his uncle Gustave Acault, a prosperous butcher who could fill the standard prescription of complete rest and large quantities of red meat. The company of his colorful and cultured uncle, a popular fixture in Algiers café life, well known for his love of politics, books, and fine clothes, took the edge off the new isolation and deprivation Camus felt watching his old friends carry on with their lives. Acault had great expectations for his nephew (he thought Camus might become a butcher, since this work would give him plentiful time to write) and treated him as the son he never had, engaging him in long discussions about literature and current affairs (Acault believed firmly in the equality of *les indigènes*) and offering him a generous allowance and weekend motor excursions to the country. In these long months of enforced rest, Camus found compensatory pleasures in Acault's extensive library, where he chose books at random, discovered authors like Paul Valéry and André Gide, and began "to really read." If many things were beginning to pull him away from the child he had been, as he notes in *The First Man,* his illness and his awareness of the inevitability of a foreshortened life pushed him dramatically into adult sensibilities and manhood.[11]

Camus never published any direct recollections of the impact of what in later years he would often refer to as "the flu," although he intended to write about it in *The First Man*—he outlines "school to the illness" in his notes. But in essays written two years after the first appearance of tuberculosis, originally intended for inclusion in his first book, *The Wrong Side and the Right Side,* but later withheld, he described the hospital scene at Mustapha—the hollow laughter, the incessant coughing, the bones without flesh, the brittle aura of resignation. "*Le mal vient vite, mais pour repartir il lui faut du temps,*" "The illness comes on quickly, but for it to go away again takes time," he notes. He also described his mother's quiet response to his crisis.[12] At the time of the first symptoms and the abundant spitting of blood, she had been no more worried than a person of normal sensitivity might be about a family member's headache, he remembers. But if he was initially disconcerted by his mother's "surprising indifference" to the gravity of his condition, he also knew that in his seventeen years he, too, had learned indifference, which was both a cover-up for suffering and a commitment to getting on with life. To a latter-day eye, the very titles of the essays in *The Wrong Side and the Right Side* reveal the state of mind into which Camus was plunged by his illness and his growing, even enforced, intellectuality: "Irony," "Death in the Soul," "Love of Life," "Between Yes and No," "The Wrong Side and the Right Side."

For the official portrait of the *première sypérieure* or so-called *hypokhagne classe* of 1932, which was devoted to preparation for the rigorous exam to qualify for the *agrégation* degree, necessary for teaching in the French university system, Camus has dressed in a three-piece suit and slicked back his hair. He looks like a young man, still tender-faced but also skeptical and slightly aloof. He stands out in the group of fourteen students and assorted professors, in part because of the outrageously wide, shiny lapels of his suit jacket, and also because he has chosen not to wear the ceremonial floppy bow and decorous soldier's hat that the others have donned for graduation day. At nineteen, he was coming into his own. On the streets, he sported a felt Borsalino hat, a white suit, and—a direct sign of his uncle's influence—white socks. He had a new band of intellectual friends, who would become poets, editors, architects, and sculptors, and with whom he passed many hours in cafés and on long walks, weekends with girls at the beach, and Saturday nights in dance halls. His ardor for life had returned, intensified by his confrontation with death, which he described as an "apprenticeship" and a learning experience.

There seemed to be few outward signs of the TB entrenched in Camus's right lung, apart from his pallor and dark-circled eyes, and the fact that he was merely a spectator at soccer games. The illness had hypersensitized him, he said, like André Gide, who had himself contracted TB on a trip to Algeria and subsequently described feeling "porous" to sensations and very introspective. Under the wing of Jean Grenier, the thirty-one-year-old professor who had been born in Paris but whose feeling for Mediterranean culture had elicited a new sense of himself as "a child of the sun," Camus had discovered literature as a resource for his reflections. He was reading Gide with new avidity, as well as almost all the authors later deemed to be his major influences, about whom he would publish essays or whom he would cite in interviews and his journal—the Greek philosophers, Nietzsche, Dostoyevsky, Tolstoy, Gide, André Malraux, and Grenier as well.

Grenier's small book *Les Îles* (*Islands*), which Camus first read at twenty, came as a shock and a revelation to him, as he later described in loving detail in a preface to a new edition. Although it exalted the virtues of Mediterranean culture with an eloquence that moved Camus, the young hedonist, for whom the truth of the world lay only in its beauty and delights, it also warned of the essential limits of that truth, its *fugacité,* and brought Camus face to face with the question of the *oui* and *non* of the universe. As Camus so clearly remembered, the book initiated him into disenchantment, made him more sober, more imbued with the gravity of life; provided the grounds for philosophical inquiry; and, most importantly for posterity, confirmed his determination to write.

As a *premier* at the lycée, Camus had written his first pieces for publication for a small literary review called *Sud,* one of many periodicals that Grenier received from abroad and that his students pored over. These pieces included several literary studies and a handful of personal essays in which he was admittedly searching for the meaning of life. In these essays, written by a fervent, soulful young student, I was both astonished and gratified to find identifying—though still adolescent—marks of Camus's famous literary personality, with all the contradictions and uncertainties that would nourish his later work. Although Camus didn't name it, the notion of the absurd was in place. Camus had also expressed the idea of revolt: "Accept the human condition? I think to the contrary that revolt is part of human nature. To accept or to revolt is to face life."[13] And, "To live, isn't that a sufficient revolt?"[14] As a new writer, he had discovered the poetic essay as a way of expressing his own search for truth. Taking another lesson from Grenier, he had determined that he would write from life, would speak only of "simple and familiar experience in an apparently unadorned language."[15]

After Camus's death, Grenier published his own recollections of these days, trying to minimize his influence on his favorite student. In regard to the impact of *Islands,* he noted that much of post–World War I literature was preoccupied with the same themes of solitude, death, and despair. Nonetheless, Camus always referred to Grenier as his master, and Grenier always played that part. Camus's preface to *Islands,* which appeared a few months after his death, contains a tribute of such fervent gratitude and precise, eloquent recollection that it leaves no question about his perceived debt. Twenty years later, *Islands* continued to live inside him, he said, speaking of his profound personal identification with Grenier's words and ideas. "I admire only my good luck," he said, "I who more than anyone needed this inclination, that I found a master at the moment when he was needed and have been able to continue to love and admire him through the years and the work."[16] Camus dedicated his first book and later *The Rebel* to Grenier. He always sent his manuscripts to his old teacher for a critique, and he remained a faithful and confiding correspondent.

In those formative years, Camus had other heroes who contributed to his growing awareness of why and how he wanted to write, but Grenier was the one to whom he owed almost everything and from whom he still had almost everything to learn. As Camus suggested, what distinguishes a mentor from a mere hero may be the timing, the propitious encounter in a moment of need. "The great revelations that a man receives in his life are few," he wrote. "But, like good fortune, they transfigure us."[17] In his description of his relationship to Grenier, Camus caught the experience of mentorship such as I first knew it with him—the "enthusiastic submission," the gratitude and the respect, the sense of identification that never ends. He noted that the dialogue between mentor and subject, which often overwhelms a life, cannot be extinguished once it has begun.

The First Man leaves indelible impressions of Camus's youth, which help to explain his transition from street kid to university student and young intellectual. In a way that already seems typical of Camus's life, there were opposing forces at work—the rich and boisterous life of the street compensating for the bare and forlorn aspect of his apartment; the exalted feelings about school tempering the weight of the silence at home; Camus turning difficult moments into lessons, into a happy sort of obduracy. He had a capacity for joy, and he had a generous nature. From Germain, whose affection and admiration were obvious to him and who, like a father, had helped him to grow up, he knew that he was someone special, with "a capacity to triumph." But Camus's pain also showed through these years, as the child was irrevocably separated from his childhood. He would never to be able to convey what he learned at school to his ignorant family, he writes, and the silence between them could only grow. Along with pride and wonder, he had experienced heartache at the thought of leaving Germain and entering the lycée, "as if he knew in advance that this success had just uprooted him from the warm and innocent world of the poor, . . . to be hurtled into a strange world, no longer his . . . and from now on he would have to . . . become a man . . . alone, and it would be at the highest cost."[18] The clarity of his memory of these days is startling, a sure measure of how deeply and permanently it always resided within him.

2

Moving On

W hen I was finally able to read the first of Camus's personal journals, published in late 1963, three and a half years after his death and more than a year after I had completed my thesis, I expected to find myself at last in his full presence. Camus had begun to record his private thoughts and ideas in small exercise books when he was twenty-two and in his second year at the University of Algiers, a time potentially conducive to volubility and truth telling. The very first entry was promising—it referred to his nostalgia for "lost poverty" and states "the strange feeling which the son has for his mother which constitutes his whole sensibility."[1] The second was a citation from Grenier, which indicated his loneliness and self-sufficiency. But as I moved through the following pages and the sequence of provocative, often epigrammatic passages, looking for further connections, I realized that they shed virtually no light on the particulars of Camus's life during these years, or on the impact of outside events on his psyche. There was no mention of his studies, financed by a student loan; his money troubles; his marriage, a year and a half earlier, to a beautiful, troubled free spirit named Simone Hié; his deepening involvement in the intellectual and political life of Algiers; or all the other events that in fact were part of his twenties. There was no mention of the signing of the Franco-Soviet Pact, the advance of fascism in Europe, or the increasing disorder in Spain. In the opening pages—which begin in May 1935 and cover a time when he earned the final *certificat* for his degree, joined the local Communist Party, visited Spain with his wife on his first trip outside Algeria, and suffered a recurrence of TB—Camus recorded thoughts about his childhood, poverty, unhappiness, a patch of blue in a stormy sky that was "a torture for the eyes and for the soul, because beauty is unbearable, drives us to despair, offering us for a minute the glimpse of an eternity that we should like to stretch out over the whole of time."[2] Camus sounded like himself, but not like the popular and engaged young university student who was approximately the age I was then.

I have gone back to read Camus's journals now to try to match up the entries with what I have learned of his life. This is a somewhat risky endeavor, for one of the qualities that made Camus Camus was his deep-seated *pudeur,* a protective reserve and modesty, which is a quality that I share. (The word *pudeur,* which almost everyone agrees is impossible to translate satisfactorily, also has important connotations of decency, prudence, secrecy, and scruples.) I wonder if my curiosity could become invasive; if discretion is the better part of valor; whether Camus's own discretion should not be honored rather than challenged. As a famous literary figure, Camus was, in fact, all the more romantic and charismatic for his innate reserve and fierce sense of privacy. He was, as a Parisian friend suggested to me, perhaps the last private man in France. Moreover—as is the true nature of diaries—Camus's journals were documents of solitude and, at least in the early years, meant for his eyes alone. His intentions were literary, connected to that most interior, most serious, and most ambitious part of himself, which had determined to be a writer. "I must bear witness," he repeats several times in the early pages. "I must write as I must swim, because my body demands it."[3] And then he says, like a statement of purpose, "A guilty conscience needs to confess. A work of art is a confession and I must bear witness. When I see things clearly, I have only one thing to say. It is in this life of poverty, among these vain or humble people, that I have certainly touched what I feel is the true meaning of life."[4] Six months later, he further defines his intentions: "People can think only in images. If you want to be a philosopher, write novels,"[5]—and then outlines a patently autobiographical novel that will become *La Mort Heureuse* (*A Happy Death*), an early version of *The Stranger* that was published only after his death.

Despite the determinedly detached nature of Camus's journals—critics believe that in 1952, when Camus, by then famous, typed up his notebooks, he edited out any details that he thought might be construed as autobiographical—they are intensely personal from his point of view. They record story ideas, conversations, observations, reflections, passages from important readings, paragraphs of narrative and description, and the writer's resolutions. Each entry is a provocative fragment, recorded in the personal "I" or "we" or the third person ("he"), without a context or a continuum beyond the monitoring of a consciousness that is drawing from somewhere deeper than quotidian or worldly affairs. "When I was young, I expected people to give more than they could—continuous friendship, permanent emotion. Now I have learned to expect less of them than they can give—silent companionship."[6] "Seek contact. All contacts. If I want to write about men, should I stop talking about the countryside?"[7] As a writer, Camus was finding himself, seeking truth in nature, in the art of others, and in his own travails, as he describes, charging himself to be simple, to be truthful, and to accept and commit himself. "I sometimes need to write things which I cannot completely control but which therefore prove that what is in me is stronger than I am," he observes.[8] Here Camus is who he was to himself, a perceiving, struggling, utterly solitary being. He needed his solitude to confront "this intense emotion which frees me from my surroundings," to impose order on his disordered life, to restore an all-powerful awareness.[9] "I do not know what I could wish for rather than this continued presence of self with self."[10] But he also needed the world and the company of men and women. He suffered from what he called "a Spanish solitude": "Strange: Inability to be alone, inability to not be. One accepts them both. Both profit."[11]

Camus led many lives while he was a student at the University of Algiers, which sat at the center of the city near his old lycée, in the picture-postcard Alger La Blanche, sun-drenched and open, just above the rue Michelet with its bars, cafés, and lively streetscape. (In photographs, the lineup of neoclassical buildings, which housed the faculties behind the stands of tall palm trees, brings Nice or Cannes to mind. People in Belcourt spoke of going to this sophisticated *quartier* as "going to Algiers.") Camus had his academic career—following Grenier's example, he was preparing to be a philosophy professor until the seriousness of his TB disqualified him from the *agrégation* degree and the French system—and he had his circle of young intellectuals outside the university with whom he wandered the city and whiled away afternoons in conversation, drinking anisette in their favored cafés; he also had his new wife, S. (as her friends called her), with whom he shared a house up in the hills; and he had his writing, which included articles for the *Revue Marxiste,* newly founded in Paris, and the student newspaper as well as his work on his personal essays and projected novel. In the final year of study devoted to his dissertation on Christianity and Neoplatonism, which focused on Plotinus and Saint Augustine, he organized a group of his friends into a politically minded theater group called the Théâtre de Travail, or Workers' Theater, and joined a local cell of the Communist Party. His responsibilities there included recruiting young Muslims and directing an adult education program for workers called the Collège de Travail. To all appearances, Camus was a confident young man, energetic, self-sufficient, and slightly formal (preferring *vous* as a form of address to the familiar *tu,* even with his wife). Friends of the time speak of his easy but somewhat studied elegance (well-cut suits and bow ties), his reserve (which nonetheless allowed cordiality and warmth), and a typically grave look that often lit up with a gleam of amusement. "The man was seductive. He was an intellectual, of course, but of an unusual quality."[12] Most of Camus's friends had no idea that he had grown up in nearby working-class Belcourt; nor did they meet his mother, who he had suggested was living in Oran.

If in public Camus seemed to be getting on single-mindedly with an ambitious life, in private, in his journals and his essays, he was self-conscious about his success and preoccupied with putting his past and his present into perspective. In the very first entry of the journals, identifying his guilty conscience, he acknowledged that he had moved into a different class, but said that his childhood was "a glue that has stuck to the soul."[13] Even while he was denying the presence of his mother in his life (he never would do this again), he was contemplating a book about her "symbolic value." In essays, he was writing about his life on the rue de Lyon with more control and circumspection than he had been able to effect in earlier efforts. In the reading notes he took in 1933, which amounted to a first informal journal, he had written: "I must learn to tame my sensibility, too ready to overflow. For hiding it under irony and coolness, I thought I was the master. Now I must sing a different tune."[14] He also said that he had persuaded himself that "one cannot speak of people one loves too much."

Camus's first wife, S., is not mentioned anywhere in his work, except for an allusion in *A Happy Death*, which, in light of these expressed intentions, may reflect the love he felt for her and the hurt she inflicted. Beyond the fact that she was beautiful and unconventional, a seductive mix of flower child and vamp, and was addicted to heroin as the result of an early dose of morphine for menstrual cramps, she is as elusive to biographers as she may have been to Camus. What is known is that they married when she was nineteen and he twenty, and that she was the daughter of a prominent physician. (Camus needed his mother's permission to marry; at his request her wedding present was white socks.) His uncle and most of his friends quietly disapproved of or did not understand the union. He felt tenderness and protectiveness toward S. that can be read in the fairy tales he wrote for her and in his attempts to rescue her from heroin. (In his stories, Camus names his fairy simply "Elle" and describes her as "a child": "She doesn't think of the future or of meals. She lives in her moment and laughs with her flowers."[15]) S. floated (or slept) through her days; met few of Camus's friends, for she was "a creature of the night"; and underwent numerous cures in clinics. Camus separated from her after their second trip abroad—a tour of eastern Europe with a friend in the summer of 1936—after learning that she had sold her body to a doctor for drugs—and recorded the anguish and hollowness of his subsequent days alone in Prague in a story called "*La Mort dans l'Âme*" ("Death in the Soul"). Although it contains no reference to a woman or an event, this story, which was included in *The Wrong Side and the Right Side* the following spring, has the ring of inexorable truth, so clear are the details of disaffection and the sense of entrapment and isolation that Camus describes in the first person as he wanders, an "*être hagarde et lâche*" ("a weary and cowardly creature"), "unable to stomach my own company any longer," through the streets of an alien city. When he returns to Algeria through tropical Italy, his sorrow eases, and he regains his equilibrium.

There are also entries in Camus's journals that may or may not be references to S. and may or may not illuminate his feelings of this time, for they are not tied to any certain context. There is a mention of the desire and the strange joy he finds "in this body which I keep close to my own." There are many remarks about happiness and despair, loneliness and a "longing for tears," but most of them are embedded in a more general concern about the psyche he is constantly examining. ("An intellectual?" he asks himself. "Yes. And never deny it. An intellectual is someone whose mind watches itself. I like this, because I am happy to be both halves, the watcher and the watched."[16]) Nonetheless, during the time of his breakup, Camus inscribed thoughts that might relate directly to this event. He jotted down a story idea about sexual jealousy that gives rise to a feeling of exile and ends with a "return to life." In the final entry of his first notebook, dated September 15, 1937, a year after his final separation, he offers a long and very personal reappraisal of his state of mind, in which he speaks of feeling free from his sense of loss and determined to carry on, even at the price of an almost unbearable loneliness. He was about to turn twenty-four. During the previous year he had learned a lot about himself, in public and political relationships as well as private ones. He had recovered from a period of poor health and exhaustion. He had passed "a turning point," he said, and felt more clearheaded and more confident about his future. "It is as if I were beginning the game all over again, neither happier nor unhappier than before. But aware now of where my strength lies, scornful of my own vanities, and filled with that lucid fervor which impels me forward toward my fate."[17]

Camus sounds like Sisyphus here. That tormented figure was already in his mind, for earlier that year he had noted, "The path up there is so steep that it is a conquest every time you climb it."[18] If he suffered from his defeats, he was also determined to accept adversity as conscious experience. "*Il n'y a pas d'amour de vivre sans désespoir de vivre,*" "There is no love of life without despair of life," he wrote in *The Wrong Side and the Right Side*.[19] "There is much more strength in a man who reveals himself only when it is necessary," he inscribed in his journal. "To go right to the end implies knowing how to keep one's secret."[20] In the future, beyond expressing an occasional sensual thought, Camus never talked about his love life, and he rarely supplied direct personal information. Constantly exercising authority over his feelings of insecurity, he kept his secret. If he was beginning to intellectualize it now, he had learned this modus operandi in Belcourt, as he explains. The poor did not speak of their troubles or intimate matters, nor did they complain about their fate. Dignity resided in forbearance, in a certain elemental morality—one didn't steal, didn't hit a man when he was down, didn't fail to protect one's mother—in self-respect and quiet endurance.

If Camus's life with S. was a private matter, so was his public life, at least to a reader of the journals. This may be what he meant when he said that to think clearly he had to free himself from his surroundings, to strip himself bare of everything."[21] Nonetheless, as I follow Camus's burgeoning life in Algiers, I find it hard to believe that he could have been such an active participant in his times and appear so disengaged in private. I am surprised that, at the very least, his activities in the theater and the Communist Party did not merit mention in his literary journal, and I wonder if he might have later edited out some sensitive material. Camus's first endeavor for the Théâtre de Travail, for example, was an adaptation of an antifascist novel, *Le Temps du Mépris* (*Days of Wrath*), by André Malraux, whom he admired greatly. Camus gave the play an inspired but shoestring production—he staged it in an old ballroom on the beach at Bab-el-Oued, using the surf as backdrop and friends as the cast and crew (even the wife of his doctor had a role). For many reasons, including the communal experience, the ingenuity involved, the message, its timeliness, and its popular success, this production was immensely satisfying to him, as his enduring memories of the time would confirm. It also drew praise from the newspaper critics. Camus's next effort, a collaboration with friends called *Révolte dans les Asturies,* which was based on a recent incident among miners in the Asturias province of Spain, was one of the first public expressions of his deep allegiance to that country. When the mayor banned the play, judging it incendiary, Camus wrote public letters of protest and enjoyed even more celebrity (and hostility from the conservative local government). His friend Edmond Charlot, who had just acquired a printing press, immediately published the play in a quasi-clandestine edition.

Camus's work with the Collège de Travail also led him into political waters. In addition to organizing adult education classes, he and his friends had helped to found a Maison de la Culture, a local chapter of the cultural centers the Communist Party had been sponsoring throughout France. One of his goals was "to make Algiers the intellectual capital that it has the right and the duty to be in the Mediterranean world," as his manifesto read.[22]

Exuberant with the energy and idealism of youth, fanned by the spirit of Leon Blum's Popular Front, the group planned an ambitious series of lectures, debates, concerts, art festivals, films, and new theatrical productions. The theater events included Gorky, Aeschylus, Pushkin, and, defiantly, an extract from *Révolte dans les Asturies*. Many of the programs were political or at least provocative, as suited the twenty-two-year-old in charge. The young organizers were eager to confront controversial issues and, as Camus had said in an early lecture, to help a nation to express itself.[23] They made an effort to showcase "indigenous" art and music. They seized the opportunity to sponsor events in support of the Blum-Viollette bill, which proposed to expand Muslim suffrage in the colony and was about to come up for a vote in the French legislature. Camus wrote and lectured on the importance of the bill, for it represented a first step toward assimilation. But in the spring of 1937, the Communist Party decided to abandon its support of Muslim nationalism and tone down its long-standing anticolonialist policies, a move explained as necessary to fight fascism (and also to support and appease the French government). When Camus refused to change his own position, he was officially tried and then purged from the party.

Camus the young communist has always been a figure of great interest, partly because the idea of Camus as any sort of ideologue is so unlikely, partly because of his very public anticommunism during his later years. It is almost amusing to think of Camus as an agent provocateur *trotskiste,* as he was described in the official report to party headquarters in Paris and Moscow. He was also accused of "developing a systematic campaign of slander" against party leaders and their policies. The information that was unearthed after the end of the cold war in the Komintern archives in Moscow described Camus's cell, which was located in Belcourt, as "the intellectuals' cell," consisting almost entirely of young student types like himself. Party dossiers indicated that his membership lasted about twenty-three months, giving Camus's experience the cast of another phase of his maturation. Virtually all of Camus's friends were communists for a while, for in Algiers then, to be communist was not to be fascist. In the fall of 1937, with the changes in both party and national politics, most of these friends also resigned. Although they described Camus as the most focused among them, and by then Camus had more prestige, they were organizers and teachers, ran printing presses, dispensed culture, and believed in Muslim equality. It was a beautiful time for creative young people, they recalled many years later, evoking an interlude when they believed that together they could change the world. In the climate of the day, communism was an intellectual adventure that had far less to do with pure Marxism than with the idealism of the Popular Front. Camus used the word *expérience* ("experiment") when he talked about his communism to Grenier. "If you do philosophy, you must do politics," Grenier had said to him. It was easy, avuncular advice, but Grenier later confessed that he also had thought that with all his talents, Camus might have been destined to play an important role in politics.[24]

About the time that he joined the party (exactly when this happened remains a question that continues to nag scholars), Camus wrote a long, earnest letter to Grenier explaining his thinking. It was sent from Tipasa, up the coast from Algiers, where amid the ancient ruins and wild, windswept vegetation he always found a sense of inner quiet and connection to the truth. It is clear from this letter that his decision to join the party had come after a difficult period of weighing and reflecting. (Thirty years later, Grenier, rereading the letter in the course of working on his memoir, was still worried that he had unduly influenced the decision.) Camus was concerned about communism's lack of a spiritual or human dimension —"I will always refuse to put a volume of *Das Kapital* between life and mankind," he says—but he was also motivated by his deep identification with the working class: "I . . . subscribe sincerely to ideas that take me back to my roots, to my childhood friends, to everything that constitutes my sensitivity." Your advice was right, Camus says reassuringly to Grenier, explaining that he wants to confront his reservations about the system firsthand, hoping that they are only misunderstandings. "Communism sometimes differs from the Communists," he notes. "But also, perhaps, Communism can be seen as a foundation . . . that will prepare the ground for more spiritual concerns . . . in which man can rediscover the meaning of his eternity."[25] He signs off like a devoted son: "Tell me what you think about this. You understand what my doubts and hopes might be. I have such a strong desire to see diminished the sum of unhappiness and bitterness that poisons mankind."[26]

Despite the confusion, disillusion, and anger that accompanied Camus's time as a communist—by 1937, the Arab militants whom Camus was once meant to bring into the ranks were being jailed, with the party's approval—it does not register as a negative experience. Looking back, knowing how the rest of Camus's life will progress, I see instead how useful it was, how many important interests and associations date from these two years, how rapidly essential elements were dropping into place. Under the umbrella of the party, Camus discovered acting, directing, and theater as a forum for political ideas. He came into contact with Muslim leaders such as Amar Ouzegane, Messali Hadj, and Ferhat Abbas, who had significant roles in the nationalist movement in Algeria; and he showed himself to be a strong and early advocate not only for Muslim rights but for Muslim culture. He began to speak publicly. He also began to establish a public persona—"one of the most fervent and most remarkably talented organizers of the House of Culture," as the local papers described him. He had charisma and natural authority, and young people talked about him.

If these were heady times for Camus—and it is hard to believe that they weren't—he did not admit it to his journal. Only when he expresses dismay at "giving way" to vanity, at thinking and living "in order to show off," does it seem possible that he has recently been in the public eye.[27] Only a passing reference to "a year of unrestrained and overstrained life" or to "nervous exhaustion" indicates the frenzy and stress of recent events. Otherwise, the Camus of the journals is simply a serious young romantic in search of a noble life. He sees himself as alone and often lonely. He has been seriously ill, he admits in a rare and very affecting passage written on his way to the Alps in August 1937. "This fever beating in my temples. The strange and sudden withdrawal from the world and from men. The struggle with one's body. Sitting in the wind, emptied and hollowed out inside."[28] That month, traveling homeward through Provence, Pisa, and Florence, he enters notes about the light, human faces, a cloister, sun among the flowers. He has a passion for life that is anchored in the sensual. This is sometimes heart-wrenching, with its suggestion of the ephemeral and the tragic. Camus speaks of happiness and unhappiness many times in this first journal, and of despair even more frequently. Despair is often coupled with strength, as if they were collusive. "Smiling despair," he writes down one day—a singular and unforgettable phrase. "I have noted a disparity between Camus and his acts," a friend from this period has observed. "Camus continues to think despair. Even to write it, but he lives hope."[29]

Camus, A Romance

It is particularly affecting to enter the solitude of a man as social and socially conscious as Camus, not only because he is so vulnerable and so needy, but because shorn of his friends, his achievements and engagements he is simply a human being, a young Algerian of humble origins, full of ambition and doubt, struggling to reconcile his enormous appetite for happiness with his commensurate capacity for unhappiness. He is not a man of action but a man of feelings, and it was the man of feelings to whom readers like me responded so readily in the novels and essays. In this way, reading the journals may put me in the presence of the essential Camus, the true working model of the modern man of his prose.

Nonetheless, I feel dissatisfied, even disgruntled. Camus may be gradually disclosing his identity as a writer and thinker but, despite his extraordinary powers of description and his noble thoughts, he remains ageless, faceless, out of reach even in his self-doubting and pathos. I realize that I am annoyed with my subject because he is not willing to grant himself even a modicum of self-satisfaction or a sense of accomplishment, and because he cannot divulge even an occasional concrete detail from his everyday life—even the name of a favorite café or a bit of local news, anything that would allow me to ground him in familiar reality. Perhaps that is why I always return to the photographs for their specificity, their ordinariness, their candid facts. With the photographs, I am somehow included in Camus's life by the very act of seeing him with my own eyes. Even though the frames are still, I can picture him in motion.

In a photograph from 1937, Camus is surrounded by a trio of pretty women on the beach in Tipasa. This is an illustration from a recent biography and must have been chosen for its iconic as well as its documentary value, for Camus always seemed to be surrounded by pretty women and was well aware of his charm and his power of seduction. In the photo, he is wearing a tight bathing suit and stands tall and looks straight ahead, as if holding a pose for the camera. Although he is lean, his chest slightly hollowed, his legs are muscular; he might be a dancer. The sea, breaking in small waves, is directly behind him. The women are laughing, playful. Two of them—Marguerite Dobrenn and Jeanne Sicaud—were college friends, colleagues in political and cultural activities, *copines;* the third, Christiane Galindo, was a new lover. For a year, they all shared a small hilltop house they called La Maison Devant le Monde ("The House on

Top of the World"). Camus worked at a small wooden table facing the sea. There, he began a draft of a play called *Caligula* and finished his first attempt at a novel called *A Happy Death*. The novel evokes a faithful record of the carefree communal life in what he calls the "house of happiness": the breakfasts of salted tomatoes, potato salad, and honey; the dog; the cats, who were named Cali and Gula; toast-colored Christiane sunbathing nude. "Sometimes he was amazed by this universe they had created around him," Camus records. "Friendship and trust, sun and white houses, scarcely heeded nuances, here felicities were born intact, and he could measure their precise resonance."[30]

In the fall, Camus brought a young woman named Francine Faure to the house before she returned to her studies in mathematics and music in Paris. She was different from Camus's string of *petites amies*—in addition to Christiane, there were Blanche, Lucette, and Yvonne—not in her beauty, which was striking (she had large, dark, vulnerable eyes; high cheekbones; elegant legs; and a dazzling smile), but in her presence, which was reserved, unassuming, and gentle, and in what Camus called her *coeur droit,* or "honest heart."[31] Like Camus, Francine had lost her father in World War I. She had a strong mother and two devoted sisters in Oran, a deep identity as an Algerian, and a passion for the piano and for Bach. Camus dressed up as Prince Charming to amuse her, talked about her to all his friends (even former girlfriends), and undertook a proper formal courtship, in part to win over her family. (They questioned her choice of a divorced, penniless writer who was afflicted with TB and enjoyed his freedom. They also thought that he looked like a monkey.) Although he was reluctant to give up his freedom and his free-ranging passions—his desire to *aimer sans mesure*—Camus trusted Francine, had confidence in her, and confided in her about his work, his self-doubts, and his resolutions—"I wanted to be honest and clear" with you,[32] he writes to her in Paris—and felt serene and happy in her company. In *Nuptuals* he had written, "It isn't always easy to be a man, and even less to be a pure man."[33] Meanwhile, working on a chapter on Don Juan for *The Myth of Sisyphus,* he was describing the side of himself that would have to be tamed in marriage.

★ ★ ★

In another photo from 1937, Camus, in eighteenth-century dress (doublet, blouson, wig, and skullcap), poses with the traveling theatrical troupe of Radio Alger, with whom he had taken a job to make some money. During his first postgraduate years, he also worked as a meteorologist, checking weather stations, a civil servant in the prefecture of Algiers, and continued to tutor. (He adds "selling motorcar parts" to this list in his journal.) Camus looks like a young Spaniard in this picture, which must have pleased him because he liked to identify with his mother's ancestors, who had come to Algeria from the Balearic Islands in the nineteenth century. During most of this year, Camus thought he might want to be an actor. Acting was a way to communicate his feelings, and a form of participation that involved him physically as well as intellectually, as soccer once had. "The matches on Sunday in a stadium full to the breaking point and the theatre which I have loved with an unequaled passion are the only places in the world where I feel innocent," he would write twenty years later, in the voice of Clamence in *The Fall*. In *The Myth of Sisyphus*, he describes the actor as the perfect model of the absurd man, "mime of the perishable," the ephemeral hero. (In his journal, he noted that a man who was something of an actor was always happy with women because women were an appreciative audience.)[34]

Camus loved to perform and was always tempted by acting assignments —Sartre offered him both the leading role and the position of director in an early production of *Huis Clos* (*No Exit*) in 1942; Visconti, the role of Meursault in a movie of *The Stranger* that was planned for 1948; Sidney Lumet, the lead in a production of *Caligula* that he was hoping to mount in New York in 1962; Peter Brook, the lead in his film *Moderato Cantabile*. Camus had a strong stage presence, his colleagues always said. Offstage he was a natural raconteur, a compelling comic, and a ready mimic, who liked to try out accents. It was clear that he loved the spoken language almost as much as the written word. But as he was learning in his work with the Théâtre de Travail (which became the apolitical Théâtre de l'Équipe, or Team Theater, after his break with the Communist Party), his greater talent seemed to lie in staging dramas and leading a cast. Like the famous example of Molière, who had spent many years as a comedian and a director before becoming a playwright, Camus was undergoing a

practical apprenticeship in theater that would convince him of its importance as a public forum for his own ideas. Over the next two decades,
Camus wrote four major plays and half a dozen adaptations. He did not
agree with those who thought that this was the minor part of his oeuvre.
Theater was a metaphor for life as he saw it, and thus perhaps his natural
medium. Some people surmise that without the early and phenomenal
success of *The Stranger,* Camus might have chosen theater as a career. In
his last years, discouraged by literature and Parisian literati, he returned
passionately to a world in which he had always felt productive and safe.
He had hopes for his own repertory theater. At the time of his death,
André Malraux, by then the minister of cultural affairs for de Gaulle, had
arranged to grant him a theater in Paris, but Camus did not live to receive the telegram bearing this news.

From 1939: a group portrait of the crew of the *Alger Républicain,* a liberal,
iconoclastic newspaper founded in the spirit of the Popular Front. Camus,
in his first commitment to a breadwinning career, had joined the staff as
an editor and city news reporter. In this photo, he stands in the foreground,
serious, elegantly dressed (light-colored suit and tie, dark shirt, casually
draped scarf), and distinctly glamorous (although for the first time I notice that his left ear sticks out rather comically). The other men wear fe-
doras, casques, and buttoned-up jackets and coats, and hold up copies of
the paper as if they were showing it off. An easy camaraderie is evident in
the picture, perhaps because the paper was so new, perhaps because it
was under pressure and concerned about closing. The editor, Pascal Pia,
a seasoned mainland journalist and writer, formerly the editor of the
communist paper *Ce Soir* in Paris and the author of several fine biographies and numerous esoteric literary works, squats at center. Until a
mysterious falling-out in 1947, Pia will be Camus's close friend and new
mentor. They seem to fascinate each other, although they are careful to
maintain a certain distance. Pia, who is ten years Camus's elder, was
originally named Pierre Durand and took his pseudonym as a teenager
when he published a book of poetry. After the outbreak of World War II
shuts down the paper, Pia will find Camus a newspaper job in Paris on
the tabloid *Paris-Soir;* send his manuscript of *The Stranger* to influential

friends and hence to Gallimard, Paris's leading publisher; introduce him into the Resistance movement; and make him coeditor of the Resistance newspaper *Combat*. Like Louis Germain, Pia will change Camus's life. Pia and Camus share a background as war orphans in poor circumstances, a love of art and literature, and a dislike of politicians, and each has an independent spirit.

During the publication of the *Alger Républicain* and the afternoon edition *Soir Républicain* that briefly replaced it, Camus distinguished himself as a frank, fearless, compassionate reporter. He was surprised to be so taken with journalism, for he was committed to a very different kind of writing, and he would not have accepted the job if he hadn't failed the medical exam that was a prerequisite for the *agrégation* degree and a teaching career. Camus's way of thinking, academic and philosophical, and his natural expression, subjective and lyric, were not well suited to reports on municipal budgets and electoral politics. Yet he had learned how to stage a story for popular consumption in the theater. He had an eye for significant detail and he had always been committed to seeking out the meaning behind the facts. In his own words, his artistic imperative was to bear witness, a reporter's task. Not incidentally, the paper's chosen constituency was the Muslim population and the working class; its implicit concern, the Arab cause and eventual assimilation. Not surprisingly, Camus quickly found a voice.

Of the estimated 150 pieces that Camus wrote for the two dailies in their fourteen months of existence, several have particular significance because they were early treatments of subjects now thought of as belonging to Camus. Others have less significance: they are anecdotal or ironic, insinuating and suggesting the later and larger life. A few of Camus's fifty-odd literary and cultural pieces fall into this latter category—his reviews of the French translation of *Bread and Wine* by Ignazio Silone, for example; and of first *La Nausée* (*Nausea*) and then *Le Mur* (*The Wall*) by the new writer Jean-Paul Sartre, "a spirit (from whom) one can expect everything," he said.[35] Camus's critique reveals a natural affinity between the three writers—and in the case of Camus and Sartre, the potential snags—many years before they met and became friends. This sort of thing makes a reader very happy, creating an illusion of privileged information, suggesting an inside position in Camus's life.

In his role on the city desk, Camus wrote about a wide spectrum of Algerian life, from the sort of incidental news he referred to as stories about *chiens écrasés,* "run-over dogs," or tabloid news, to investigative reports on social and judiciary matters. It was in this latter category that he began to make a name for himself, first with his court reporting on three misbegotten criminal cases, and then with his eleven-part series on social and economic conditions in the Berber territory of Kabylia. These assignments now seem to have been tailor-made for a budding young moralist with a particular interest in justice. At the time, they were of course simply assignments—good ones, which his friend Pia directed his way.

Camus had been reluctant to relinquish his novel in progress to the dictates of daily events and the "baser" rewards of journalism. But once committed, he took the profession seriously. The work of reporting gave a new structure to his life and thoughts. He was comfortable at the paper; he was learning the trade—writing, editing, proofreading, makeup, typesetting —the way one does at a small hometown newspaper; and he liked hanging around the typesetting plate known as the stone. "I am not constrained and all that I do seems lively to me," he had written to Grenier a month or so into the job. The *Alger Républicain* was a morning paper, so Camus generally wrote his copy in the late afternoon and was on the premises until whatever hour the paper was put to bed. To cover his big stories, he spent much of the spring on the road. Somehow he also managed to keep his many other lives in motion: the novel, the productions at the Théâtre de l'Équipe, social life, his courtship of Francine Faure, literary work for a short-lived magazine called *Rivages,* editing for Charlot, and, during a brief period when Charlot had to stop operations of his press, an attempt to start a publishing house with Claude de Freminville (the press was named Cafre, after their names). His second book, *Noces,* or *Nuptials,* came out in May.

Nuptials, with its eloquent, sensual essays about Algeria and the lessons Camus had learned from living in a geography of sun, sea, and desert, had a printing of 120 copies from Éditions Charlot and was not much noticed in Algiers that spring, although the novelist Henri de Monterland sent a fan letter from Paris. Camus's journalism, which by now carried his byline, had greater impact. Beginning with his stories about a Muslim public agency worker named Hodent, who had been imprisoned for stealing wheat, he effectively issued an indictment of the colonial system of justice. In Hodent's case, which he thought a frame-up, he created something of a cause célèbre for the paper by questioning judicial procedure and calling for humanity and human rights even before the trial was under way. In two subsequent cases, which also involved Muslims and had political overtones, Camus again suspected frame-ups and again took an active role in establishing the innocence of the accused and exposing judicial corruption and bias. A year after leaving the Communist Party, he had found another way to work to improve the lot of Muslims and to express his allegiance to the working class. Unintentionally, during these six months of hanging out around courtrooms, he was also gathering material that would inform the trial setting in *The Stranger*. At Christmas, Camus had mentioned to Christiane Galindo that he had begun to work on *"L'Absurde."* By that time, he had already committed to his journal the now famous opening lines: "Today Maman died. Or it might have been yesterday. I don't know."[36] And nine pages later, "There is only one case in which despair is pure: that of a man sentenced to death."[37] In fact, looking closely at entries about funerals, undertakers, and conscious death, I can see that Camus's journal of late 1938 was brimming with this theme.

There was something fierce about Camus as a young reporter, something unusually confident, something of the avenging angel. He was disarmingly direct. His first piece on the Hodent affair was an open letter to the governor-general that was as clearly a form of protest as the open letter he had written to the mayor who had banned his second play. He also did not hesitate to settle certain accounts, pointing out again and again in his municipal coverage the failings of his former bête noire, the mayor. He reported on the basis of information, but he also took aggressive personal positions. In the series entitled *"Misère de la Kabylie"* ("Poverty in Kabylia"), he effectively entered combat. It must have been a significant *oui et non* situation for him, because as he was gathering his ugly facts, Kabylia was in its most beautiful season, its olive and fig trees in flower along the roads and sweetening the air. Writing in the first person, as he had done in all his news stories, Camus gave vent to his deepening distress at the disparity between the lives of French Algerians and unprivileged indigenous Muslims. Every day for eleven days, he provided a searing eyewitness account, grounded in statistics and social studies, of the abject poverty of a forgotten population, victims of the colonial system. He used his powers of description to evoke and provoke and his sense of personal indignation to condemn the "general disdain" of the *colons* for the *colonistes*. Camus was intimate with urban poverty, but he had never before seen the humiliation he encountered in the workers earning less than subsistence salaries, the beggars and hungry children, the villages without medicine or sanitation. "I would not like to melodramatize. But I am forced to say here that the working system in Kabylia is a system of slavery,"[38] he wrote. "If colonial conquest can ever be justified," he lectured his readers, "it will be insofar as it helps conquered people keep their own personality, and we owe it to this land to let a proud and humane populations stay faithful to themselves and their destiny."[39]

If Camus had long believed in equality for all Algerians and the need to bring the French and Arab communities together, he was also disillusioned by his recent experiences with the Communist Party and with the Blum-Viollette bill, which was stagnating (and would soon die) in the French legislature. Referring to these and other matters, he had confided two remarks to his journal in 1937. "Every time I hear a political speech or read those of one of our leaders, I am horrified at having, for years, heard nothing that sounded human."[40] One month later, even more emphatically, he wrote, "Politics and the fate of mankind are shaped by men without ideals and without greatness. Men who have greatness within them don't go in for politics."[41]

In his reports on Kabylia, Camus wrote as a French-Algerian and testified to his own *"mauvaise conscience,"* but he also was stepping outside the boundaries of traditional journalism to assert moral authority, to judge his countrymen, and to act. The boldness of his position further alienated the government officials who already regarded him as a renegade, if not a revolutionary. At the same time, it made him ever more visibly a champion of democracy and Muslim interests to the leaders of that community. Of particular note to both sides must have been the pieces Camus wrote in support of the Parti Populaire Algérien (PPA), the most radical of the nationalist movements, led by Messali Hadj, which had just been banned. "Each time the PPA has been attacked, its prestige has grown a little more," he observed. "And I can say without paradox that the immense and deep favor the party enjoys today among the masses is completely the work of the high officials of this country," adding, "the only way to defuse nationalism is to get rid of the injustice of which it was born."[42] Camus was always proud of these early pieces on Algeria and proud that his voice had been one of the first to expose the economic plight of his country. In the heat of the Algerian war twenty years later, when he was accused of being silent on the issues, Camus cited "*Misère de la Kabylie*" as evidence of his long and active commitment to the democratic future of his country. He reprinted most of its text in the collection of political essays called *Actuelles III,* which was published in 1958 and amounted to his position paper on Algeria.

France went to war in September 1939, although there was a lag in Algeria, where café life continued as usual and the sun still shone on a sparkling blue sea, even as men were being mobilized and newspapers were suffering from censorship and paper shortages. That month in his journal, Camus wrote of current events: "The war has broken out. But where is it? Where does this absurd event show itself, except in the new bulletins we have to believe and the notices we have to read . . . ?"[43] In the following months, he described scenes of leave-takings and of recruitment exams, including his own. He was sickened by the gathering force of war, but also upset by his own rejection by the army on medical grounds. His older brother Lucien was an artillery officer and had left for mobilization. His mother, heavy with dread, had fallen even more silent. To clarify his own moral position, Camus composed a long "Letter to a Man in Despair," which was in fact a letter to himself—an early version of the form he would use later, during the war, in his *Lettres à un Ami Allemand* (*Letters to a German Friend*). It began, "You write that you are overwhelmed by the war, that you would agree to die, but that what you cannot bear is this universal stupidity, this bloodthirsty cowardice and this criminal simplemindedness which still believes that human problems can be solved by the shedding of blood."[44]

In mid-September, Pia had made Camus editor in chief of the new *Le Soir Républicain,* which coexisted with *Alger Républicain* for a month until the shortage of newsprint and manpower closed the morning paper down. *Soir* was a distinctive but peripheral publication, only two pages long—the back and front of a single sheaf—emphatically left-wing, and, given the paucity of news from the front, essentially a journal of opinion. Here Camus could openly express his despair at the reality of a war that he had thought could be avoided. He wrote as a partisan of peace, arguing for total disarmament, a new international world, and a solution more enlightened than violence.[45] He denounced the conditions of the Treaty of Versailles. After its attack on Poland, he pronounced the Soviet Union an imperialist nation of the first rank. Rather than supporting the war, he analyzed its causes and searched for perspective. Camus wrote in the first person, occasionally using the plural *nous* for emphasis or to indicate Pia's collaboration. He often wrote under a pseudonym—Jean Mersault, Suetone, César Borgia, or Nero—for protection and for effect. His were opposition positions in a country beginning to burn with patriotism and nationalism. Conservatives were not alone in regarding Camus, Pia, and *Le Soir Républicain* as seditious and anarchistic; certain of Camus's friends were angered by his inflexible stance. As Camus expressed ever bolder and more independent views, the military censors often reduced the paper to little more than a patchwork of empty spaces. In response, Camus and Pia baited the authorities by inserting quotations from venerable, uncensorable authors like Pascal and Voltaire, or cryptic slogans of their own invention. In those last days of the paper, this literary cat-and-mouse game was a form of entertainment for both readers and writers. The gallows humor, courageous and ironical, was typical of Camus. The war was the ultimate example of the absurd.

The government finally shut down the paper and the renegade editorial voices of Camus and Pia in January 1940. One of the last editorials, although unsigned, sounded like a farewell from Camus: "Man's only greatness lies in struggling against that which is beyond him. It's not happiness that one must wish for today, but even more this sort of desperate greatness."[46] Camus found himself again reduced to tutoring for a living. At least for the present, he had no hope of another position in journalism in Algeria, for he was officially banned from this line of work. The army had rejected him. The government was keeping tabs on him. He had three books in print—*The Wrong Side and the Right Side, Nuptials,* and his collaborative play *Révolte dans les Asturies*—and he was hard at work on *The Stranger, Caligula,* and *The Myth of Sisyphus* simultaneously, the "three absurds" that he saw as one entity and had begun to refer to as the first part of his oeuvre. Already he had determined to give his body of work a well-defined structure, and to write in what he called cycles or trilogies, which would consist of a novel, a play, and a long essay, each component a different way to illustrate a large concept such as the absurd or revolt. But Camus also was full of doubts about his writing, quite desperate doubts about his ability to deliver what was in his head. He was not writing with his whole being, he confided to Francine. "The truth is that I no longer know how to write."[47] He was also concerned about committing himself to Francine when he was still actively attracted to several other women.

Camus missed Pia, his kindred spirit, who had already returned to Paris to look for work. "*Je n'ai plus un sou,*" he wrote to Pia, bemoaning his penury and his need for a job. By March, Camus, too, was in Paris, living in a hotel in Montmartre near the cemetery and, thanks again to Pia, working with him at the popular daily *Paris-Soir*. Two months later, when Germany invaded and occupied Paris, he decamped with the paper to temporary headquarters, first in Clermont-Ferrand and then in Lyon. At the end of the year, however, when the paper was forced to reduce its staff and expenses, he had to be discharged. By mid-January he was back in Algeria, tutoring and teaching in Oran, almost as if his European interlude had never occurred.

By now I am intimate with the chronology of Camus's life. So I know that the eighteen months Camus will now spend in Oran with Francine, whom he has married (exchanging brass rings in a civil ceremony in Lyon in early December of 1940, with Pia as the witness and a celebration with *Paris-Soir* staffers in a local bistro), are a sort of downtime, a treading of water before all the elements that have been put in motion take hold and his famous life begins to happen. I know what Camus, of course, couldn't know—that a serious recurrence of TB in the spring of 1942 will force him to leave Algeria for a rest cure in the mountains of France and land him near the thick of the Resistance movement; that his political conscience raising, his work as a journalist, and his experience with censorship will serve him well when he moves to Paris a year later and becomes the editor of the underground newspaper *Combat;* that his moral leadership in *Combat* will make him a public hero even before the impact of *The Stranger.* Most poignantly, perhaps, I know that, once settled in France, Camus will return to his homeland only for visits. In my mind, then, these are his last days in Algeria, and I feel the weight of this inevitability.

Although I have always thought of Camus as an Algerian, distinct from a Frenchman, this identity did not always register as deeply as it does now, when I contemplate his expatriation. The entries in Camus's journal— street descriptions, local anecdotes, snippets of conversation, random expressions of appreciation ("This morning full of sunlight. The streets warm and full of women. Flowers on sale at every street corner. And the smiling faces of these young girls")[48]—take on a potential melancholy. In the eight years that Camus has kept a journal, he has recorded more words on his Algeria than the sum total of his other concerns. Many of these isolated fragments will find their way into his work; others may have been intended for that purpose. (An item noted from a local newspaper provided the inspiration for his play *The Misunderstanding,* which is about a son robbed and murdered by his mother and sister in a case of mistaken identity. A murderous sun, a night full of stars, and countless other recorded details reappear in *The Stranger.*) I read Camus's words now not just as useful notations, but as a reminder of his constant involvement with the physical surroundings and the everyday people of his place of birth. I flip pages and choose selections at random: "In September, the carob trees breathe a scent of love over all Algiers, and it is as if the whole earth were resting after having given itself to the sun, its belly still moist with almond-flavored seed."[49] "The heat on the quays—it crushes you with its enormous weight and takes away your breath. The thick and heavy smell of tar rasping in your throat. . . . It is this which is the real climate of tragedy and not, as people usually consider, the night."[50] "In the evening, the gentleness of the world on the bay. There are days when the world lies, days when it tells the truth. It is telling the truth this evening—with what sad and insistent beauty."[51] As I read, I note the dozens of small human anecdotes that attracted his interest: a docker with a broken leg, an ugly husband and wife on a train, tears over the death of a dog, an old people's home. Camus had a good nose for stories that caught the element of the absurd in ordinary lives, and he loved the odd detail. He was never more observant or more openly feeling than when he was writing about Algeria. His lyricism was sometimes almost painful. He wrote tenderly and sensually, as if he were writing about a woman—and also fiercely and darkly, as if he were writing about death.

Camus's Algeria was essentially Algiers: the sun and the sea; the working-class neighborhood of Belcourt in the western section of the city; the social and intellectual hubbub around the central artery of the rue Michelet, with the university, the restaurants and bars and elegant shops. Edmond Charlot's bookshop Les Vraies Richesses was a meeting place for writers. There was the lively Mediterranean port, with its quays and beaches, and, down the coast, the Roman ruins of Tipasa with their austere beauty and their lessons in history and transcendence. More than simply *algérien,* Camus considered himself *algérois,* of his particular coastal province. He loved his city with its terraces and changing perspectives, built around its bay like an immense amphitheater. He was always walking through it, visiting and revisiting his favorite places—the casbah with its labyrinthine alleyways and simple white Arab houses; the nearby Cemetery of the Princesses with a huge twisted fig tree presiding over the tombstones like a weeping woman; the Padovani bathhouses on stilts on the beach where the young crowd from Bab-el-Oued danced all night (and where he had staged his first play); the heights of the city, Bouzaréah and Hydra, where he expected to live someday. He loved the cypress trees, the "fugitive" Algiers evenings, even the hot sirocco that dusted the city with red sand from the desert. He was actively engaged with this landscape—he hiked; he camped out in the hills; he took to the sea like a fish, rediscovering himself in the water, he said.

Camus was rooted on the coastline, a true *"homme des rivages,"* as one of his friends pronounced. Although he had traveled to the interior of Algeria as an actor with Radio-Alger and as a journalist, he did not seem to be sensitive to these other environments, for he recorded only perfunctory impressions of the towns he visited there. When he was given a substitute teaching post in the charmless inland town Sidi Bel Abbès, (an outpost for Foreign Legion troops, it turned out), he lasted only a day. He made a point of detesting Oran, Algiers's rival city, where he spent most of those last months after his marriage, tutoring, teaching in private schools to keep afloat, living with Francine's family in their double apartment. He was idling uncomfortably, and he found Oran ugly and boring, berating it for turning its back on the sea. As artistic revenge on the city, he painted its distinctly unflattering portrait in the essay *"Le Minotaur"* and then in *The Plague,* which provoked a storm of threatening letters from the *oranais.*

Given Camus's deep engagement with Algeria and Algiers, I can't help wondering how his life and the fate of Algeria might have been altered if he had stayed in his homeland. He would have written his books, which, except for *The Fall* and the short story collection *Exile and the Kingdom,* were already *cycles* in his head; directed his theater, for which he had planned numerous productions; continued to agitate for equality for the Muslim population; founded a publishing house or a magazine or pursued one of his other entrepreneurial ideas. Yet my question is academic, for in late August 1942 Camus had to leave the humid climate of the Algerian coast to recover from a life-threatening new episode of TB and heal his now completely diseased lungs. The government was eager and happy to have him gone.[52] Once in France, Camus was caught up by a war that changed his life and life in Algeria. In the spring of 1945, when he returned to Algeria to write a series of articles on his country for *Combat,* he just missed the tragic events known as the Repression, when the French massacred thousands of Muslims in response to the riots over their exiling of Messali Hadj. It was the beginning of the end of the country as he had known it. The seeds of the revolution had been germinating for several decades. Had Camus still been living in Algiers, would he have had any impact on these events? Would his thinking about independence have been altered? Months later, Camus was asked to join a government task force on the Algerian problem. Although amenable, he suggested then that he was not a politician but a writer.

Perhaps the unexpected sadness I feel now on the eve of Camus's departure for a mountain retreat in central France is only my belated appreciation of the enviable life he led in Algiers during his so-called Camelot years. Perhaps it is the knowledge that his leaving home will mark the definitive end of his youth. Or perhaps it is simply my anticipation of a change of climate. Following Camus around like a shadow, I, too, have become familiar with the sultry heat, the fragrant trees, the breath of the desert at my back, and I have felt the power of the rude country that so nourished him and yet was so full of contradictions. I can imagine how in contrast to Algeria, any other landscape would inevitably pale, how the sounds and smells of Algeria would ineradicably inhabit the soul. In Algeria, I picture Camus working at his small desk at the hilltop house called Maison Devant le Monde or in some other panoramic place, watching the ships move about the bay below. In Paris, I picture him in a makeshift study in a cramped apartment, besieged by his new worldly obligations and family responsibilities. (Paris, he had just written in the voice of Meursault in *The Stranger,* "is dirty. Lots of pigeons and black couryards. Everybody's pale."[53] Meursault has rejected the idea of taking a job there.) I think, too, of the friends Camus is leaving—his band of promising young writers, artists, and academics, the "tender company of women" who had been his housemates in the hills. They would all remain lifelong friends. "I could not live among strangers, far from friends. I need you all," Camus had confessed to his friend Charles Poncet in a rare moment of openness. In their various memoirs, these friends, many of whom remained in Algeria, would recall the boisterous bonhomie of their young adulthood, the walks and the midnight swims, the frequent dinners with Camus, ever the natural host, singing songs and telling stories in the local dialect. After the war, Camus regularly staged Algerian evenings for his visiting friends in Saint-Germain, or took them to one of his favorite couscous places in the North African neighborhoods around Belleville in the 20th arrondissement.

I read *The Stranger* now as the purely Algerian novel that it was, a product of Camus's twenty-eight years in Algiers. Its setting is familiar to me, because it is from Camus's life: the beach at Sidi-Ferruch where Camus often swam and where Meursault strolls idly with Raymond and Masson until the *bagarre* with two Arabs (the pivotal story of the murder of an Arab after an incidental fracas on a beach came from a similar but less deadly episode experienced by his friend Pierre Galindo, Christiane's brother); the cinema on the rue de Lyon, near Camus's home, where Meursault and his girl-friend Marie watch a comic film; the courtroom where Camus covered cases for the *Alger Républicain* and Meursault stands trial. Suggestively, or at least playfully, Camus wrote himself into the courtroom scene. Noting a very young journalist dressed in gray flannel and a blue tie among the press, Meursault says, "All I could see in his slightly lopsided face were his two very bright eyes, which were examining me closely without betraying any definable emotion. And I had the odd impression of being watched by myself."[54] Meursault was not Camus, who had a distinctly lopsided face, but he was in significant part Camus, as Camus himself verified.

It is one of the quirks of publishing and of history that *The Stranger,* written in prewar Algeria under the influence of a blazing sun, arrived in Paris during the black hours of the occupation and "the bitter spring of the coal shortage," as Sartre pointed out in his review of the book. Camus, who was then still living in Oran and again very ill, read the reviews months later. The book was received abroad as both an exotic story from south of the equator and an unconventional but timely lesson on the value of the individual. "Amidst the literary productions of its time, this novel was, it-self, a stranger," Sartre said in the long, thorough, seemingly fascinated appraisal that appeared in *Cahiers du Sud,* which had remained uncontestedly independent of Nazi control. (Jean Grenier had a shorter review in the same issue.) He suggested that the book might be called "a moralist's short novel," explaining that it was very close to the tales of Voltaire."[55] Given the paper shortage and the complicated process of distribution in wartime France, *The Stranger* became a best seller only after liberation, by which time Camus was residing in Paris. By the end of Camus's life—and at the time of my first encounter with him—it was a best seller in twenty-one languages.

3

To France

I dreamed about Camus for the first time in our very long relationship. He was sitting as close to me as if we were in conversation, although we didn't speak or even make eye contact. I was simply there watching him, in slight profile, while he talked with someone else. The scene was in black-and-white, perhaps because I cannot imagine Camus in color. Here, however, the blacks—of his hair and his beard line—were blacker than usual, and distinctive. Camus's presence was very strong, and I was very happy and secure within it. This may have been the equivalent of my first dream in French, which signaled to me that by dogged effort and some uncontrollable natural process, I was beginning to infiltrate the language.

During my postgraduate year in France, I wasn't very far from Le Chambon-sur-Lignon, where Camus spent some fifteen months in 1942–1943 on a mountain farm trying to regain his health, although I could not have known it then. I remember noticing the town from the train down from Paris as I traveled farther south to Annecy, in the Haute-Savoie, to begin my fellowship. I remember, too, that no one met me at the station and that a frail, elderly porter hoisted my steamer trunk on his back for the walk to my lodgings half a mile away. "*Le voilà*," he said simply when he deposited the trunk in my room. I lived on the top floor of a stone house with a mansard roof and tall windows on the rue Eugène

Sue, named for the famous nineteenth-century author of long heart-wrenching novels, in a neighborhood that accommodated many other foreign students. My room had a lumpy double bed tucked under the eaves, at center a table where I studied, along one wall a counter that held a hot plate and sink, and in a corner a bidet. The WC and shower were down the hall. There was nothing romantic about my new place, although it was cozy when the heat was working, and there was a small window from which I could see the distant peaks of the Alps, which I came to know by their names—Les Dents de Lanfon, Le Parmelan, La Tournette—and, judging by their surrounding mist or new snowfall, to count on as a dependable barometer of the weather. Because the room was a garret, it seemed respectably French to me. My landlord, Monsieur Henri, who watched my comings and goings from behind a lace curtain, seemed like the prototypical concierge.

Initially, I had been disappointed to have been sent to the provinces—the terms of my fellowship included duties as the English assistant at the girls' lycée in Annecy as well as courses in literature at the University of Grenoble, half an hour away—for I was light-years away from Café Flore and Camus country. Moreover, in an unfortunate misunderstanding, Roger Quilliot—the author of the most important work on Camus that I had encountered in college, and the professor whom I had expected to supervise my study in Grenoble—turned out to be teaching nearly 190 miles to the north. I had read Quilliot's book *La Mer et Les Prisons* as an act of passion, so intensely engaged was his analysis of Camus's work, so deep his sympathy for Camus's metaphysical issues and instinct for life. He had written his book years before Camus's Nobel Prize and dramatic death, so I understood it as sincere devotion, although it was strange to read of Camus's life as still open-ended. Unquestionably, Quilliot had shaped my thinking about Camus, for I sensed that he understood the artist as a human being. I thought of him as a secondary mentor, a sort of halfway house to Camus, and I felt a kinship with him.

Because of Quilliot's absence, I more or less abandoned serious studies that year and succumbed to the social life of a French *universitaire*. As a source of enlightenment, the café was as promising and Camusian as the lecture hall. My crowd during my first months in France was one of those peculiar assemblies of happenstance friends that are typical when one is a newcomer—an assortment of English, Italian, Jamaican, and German students; a Moroccan painter named Mohammed, or Mo; two young Indian engineers from Madras; and a few French students with international inclinations. Together we haunted the cinema, hiked in the mountains, prepared fondue or *boeuf bourguignon* on Saturday nights, and generally bided our time until the onset of ski season.

Paris as a destination receded in my mind as France herself took me over. Every detail of the French scene was a revelation—the mottled bark of the plane trees that lined every boulevard, the early-morning ritual of washing down the sidewalks, the blue smocks of the working class, old women in black, old men playing *boules,* the ubiquitous gray Citroën Deux Chevaux, and the corrugated-back *camionettes.* The streets had new sounds —cars with short soprano city horns, police vans with a two-tone warning that brought wartime to mind, the buzz of the Vespas and *motos* that rose like an invasion of insects during the lunch hour and at the end of the workday. The streets smelled of herbs, pungent cheeses, Gauloise cigarettes, wine, diesel fuel—something new and indescribable. I felt like a child, drawn to the small and incidental, seeing only what was different. Women walked arm in arm; men wore strange shoes. Bread came in many shapes, milk cartons were triangular, everyone carried a *panier* or else a string bag. In everything that was different—square-lined school notebooks, steel-rimmed eyeglasses, handshakes at greeting and parting, 367 kinds of cheese—I found the essence of the French identity.

Even when I was homesick, I was happy to be in France, in part because I liked who I was in France. My hair grew longer, my clothes more stylish, my thinking more complicated, my manner bolder. As I promenaded through town with my friends in the late afternoon, I felt pretty and distinctly feminine. As I settled into French as an everyday language, adding all the argot I could master, I realized that outside the confines of my native tongue I could be entertaining, perhaps original. My experiences then were standard fare for the foreign student—the wide eyes, the imitation of manners, the rejection of one's original culture, the discovery of a new, more sensitive, and more liberated self, which is, in fact, the one that has been lurking in the wings all along. I knew this as I watched my English friend John, the epitome of baggy tweeds and heavy sweaters, undergoing the same transformation. I hitchhiked with John until

I took to hitching on my own, and together we learned to decode license plates so that we could flag down cars headed for our destination. We ceremoniously crossed all the *cols*—mountain passes—in the Alps and then moved on to explore Provence. We met truck drivers who talked with familiarity about philosophers such as Pierre Teilhard de Chardin and Henri Bergson, confirming my notion that the French were by nature more intellectual than Americans; others filled us in on the farmers' artichoke wars or offered their assessment of the Fifth Republic and de Gaulle, *le grand Charlot.* One day when I was hitching alone across the border to Geneva, the driver asked me what I thought about *le blocus,* a word I didn't know. It turned out to mean Kennedy's blockade of the Havana harbor during the Cuban missile crisis, which I had missed. This happened again with the riots in Birmingham and the first Freedom March on Washington. Triumphantly, but sometimes sadly, I was far away.

I now know that simply by living in France that year, I was closing in on Camus, and never as intimately as when I fell sick with bronchitis and then pleurisy, which led to the collapse of my right lung. Then, in a small, temporary way, I found myself inhabiting a world in which he was a perpetual resident. It was a world not so much of physical pain, although the constriction of a collapsed lung causes considerable discomfort—I remember the sensation of being tied up from within—as of lethargy, exhaustion, dullness, and occasionally an odd exhilaration. As a beneficiary of the French system of socialized medicine, I was dispatched to a sort of sanitarium-hotel high in the mountains, similar to situations Camus had known, where I was subjected to an almost enviable routine of long walks, good food, and regular naps. I was given no medication, but I was instructed to drink several glasses of red wine in the evening. In the morning, like Hans Castorp in *The Magic Mountain,* I lay out in a reclining chair wrapped in a blanket, breathing in the cold pure air, too tired to read or think, but quite content simply taking in the long meadows of snow, the bleached-out sky, and the passing cloud formations. At dinner, I sat by myself at my regular table and tried to imagine the lives the other patients might lead outside this strangely peaceful place where we all existed in a state of suspended animation. In the peacefulness, there was acceptance and also denial. I was aware of an unspoken camaraderie and also of a solitude so complete that it felt like a form of strength.

Camus, A Romance

Camus read *The Magic Mountain,* which was published in France several years before the onset of his TB, and it remained one of his favorite books, because it captured not only the essence of the world of the unwell, but also the postwar crisis in western culture. Eerily, in rereading it now, I feel a new connection to Camus that, had I been more informed about his life, I might have experienced thirty-five years ago at my first reading. In the story of Hans Castorp, I can see Camus's disease in motion. I welcome Mann's other characters as further illumination. When I encounter Hermine Kleefeld, the young woman who is the pride of the Half-Lung Club, I wonder if Camus's pneumothorax whistled as hers did, if he had scars on his chest from the incisions. From Dr. Behrens's ministrations, I am reminded of the primitive state of medical care for respiratory disease earlier in the century. Apart from the mechanical procedures, the pneumothoraxes and the pleural inflations, there are very few details available on the care of Camus's disease, a very private matter. Camus's close friends speak only of his symptoms—the pallor, the exhaustion, the sweating—and his periodic disappearances and the fact that he was always haunted by the specter of death. His relatives mention "almost losing him" several times. It is generally accepted that even without the fatal accident, he would not have lived into old age.

In the 1960s, however, no biographies of Camus had yet been written, so I did not know when, either literally or figuratively, I was following in his footsteps in France. And although the presence of Camus may have been hovering over me that year—he was my sponsor, after all—I was too involved with my own adventures to think very often about his life. Yet in my travels to Clermont-Ferrand, Lyon, Provence, and other places, I unwittingly crossed my subject's earlier path. In Angers I sat in the courtyard of the feudal castle where he staged a summer theater festival; in Avignon, I passed through the station where he put his wife and children on the train to Paris that he too was meant to take in January 1960, before a last-minute decision to drive in his friend Michel Gallimard's Facel Vega. My memories of these places, long forgotten, now resurface across a span of more than three decades.

When I examine the letters I wrote home that year, dutifully saved by my mother, I again encounter the mysterious ways of memory. Where I expected to find an independent-minded young intellectual as narrator,

I find only a breathless girl who annotated her prose with "wows" and smiley faces. To my dismay, I am still hopelessly young and guileless, devoid of the self-awareness and consciousness I was certain that I had acquired in France. Even in my private journal, I find no mention of the things I remember most vividly now, the confusing emotions of a first love affair, the exhilaration of being on the road and at large in the world, the countless small details in which the true meaning of France seemed to reside. It is only in my last letter that I proffered more than a cheerful résumé of days, meals, and places, but its introspection was part of the closure.

When I wrote this letter, I was at last in Paris, which was effectively shuttered for the August national vacation, and I was three months short of my twenty-third birthday. I didn't mind the emptiness of the city, because it seemed to reflect my own desolation at the thought of my leave-taking. I was with a German foreign student I had befriended, who was equally morose at her own pending departure, and we were bound together in the joy of discovery and the despair of imminent loss. We were seeing everything for the first time and possibly the last, and our every move had urgency and a dramatic sweetness. The last days we sat in parks and cafés, especially the Flore, where I thought a lot about Camus. The Flore was the same place it had been only a few years earlier when he was still around, with the same lace half-curtains and tricolor wicker chairs, the same fluorescent lighting and blue cigarette haze. A waiter told me that Sartre and Beauvoir still came in some mornings and still sat upstairs or in the back. When I asked him if he ever saw Madame Camus, he gave me one of those haughty French looks that indicated I had asked a foolish American question.

I didn't try to track Camus in Paris beyond the Flore and the Deux Magots a few doors away, although I wondered where he had lived, where he and Sartre's crowd had partied. In fact, many of his favorite hangouts were just around the corner—bistros and bars such as Les Assassins and the all-night Tabou and, a few blocks away, the Pont Royal bar, where Gallimard's staff and the writers at *Nouvelle Revue Française* gathered after work. Perhaps if I had visited these places then, they would still have been redolent of the 1940s and 1950s and would still have conveyed some of the intensity of the Left Bank intellectual life of the recent past.

CAMUS, A ROMANCE

Yet the Paris of 1963 was not the Paris where Camus had lived. Even as a newcomer I sensed the changes. No one discussed existentialist issues anymore—or Camus or Sartre, either. Cafés were filled with a new invasion of foreign tourists. Everything seemed to be "new": *nouvelle vague* films (*Breathless* with Jean Seberg selling the *Herald Tribune,* Brigitte Bardot appearing nude in *Le Repos du Guerrier*), *nouvelle vague* literature, the *nouveau franc,* the newly founded magazine *Le Nouvel Observateur.* The new late-night hot spot was Le Drugstore, at the top of the Champs-Élysées, a complete replica of an American drugstore. Paris itself was being renewed: *le blanchissage,* or facade washing, of historic monuments had begun, initiated by Camus's old friend André Malraux, whom de Gaulle had named to the new post of minister of cultural affairs. The French had feared that their sense of history would be washed away with the dirt, but they were pleased with the results. As I walked around the Place de la Concorde and the courts of the Louvre, I was dazzled by the statues that were as fresh as if it were the sixteenth or eighteenth century. But I was disconcerted to see Paris so young and so pale. I felt cheated by the clean lines and the bright gilt, which seemed to be an official statement of closure on the postwar era.

It was only in seeing the political graffiti that were still fresh on public walls—*Algérie Française,* OAS *Assassins,* FLN, *Paix*—that I began to connect to a Paris of the recent past. No one talked about the Algerian war, which had ended the previous summer, for after almost two decades of bloodshed, the French were trying to put that chapter of their history behind them. But in the angry scrawls I could sense the emotions and the turmoil of the last two years, when *bombes plastiques* were exploding daily in metro stations and apartment houses, when the insurrection of four retired French generals threatened the safety of the city and the stability of the Fourth Republic, and tanks guarded the National Assembly. Standing on those hot, lazy, peaceful streets of August, I remembered de Gaulle's emotional call, "*Aidez-moi, françaises et français,*" and I remembered a newspaper photograph of Algiers behind a tall wall of barbed wire.

Camus had not been alive during the last and most desperate phase of the war, when France had half a million men in arms in Algeria and thousands of Muslims were being murdered on the streets of Algiers and Oran; when a new, more militant band of leaders ruled the Front de Libération

National, independence seemed inevitable, and the Algerian-born European settlers, or *pieds noirs,* were beginning their mass exodus to Marseille. He did not know Ben Bella. Although he had refused to take sides with either the French patriots or the FLN rebels, and continued to believe in the possibility of a federation of Europeans and Arabs in Algeria, Camus must have known in his heart that it was too late for reason. He had consistently denounced terrorism, but he also understood Arab terrorism, which he explained was born of solitude, of the idea that no recourse existed, that the walls were too thick and had to be blown up.[1] Even while he did not support Algerian independence, he had warned, as early as 1945, "*L'Algérie n'est pas la France.*"

Late in the year that Camus died, his friend Jules Roy, who was also a third-generation *pied noir,* published a book on the war that had a great impact on the French, in part because it brought Camus back into mind. The book was Roy's first-person account of his trip back to Algeria that summer, undertaken partly in memory of Camus. As he described his anger and grief at all he saw when he crossed the ruined countryside of his youth, his painful conversations with Arabs and army *ultras,* and his conclusions that simple "social injustice" had opened the road to the Algerian rebellion, that the only way to stop the war was to negotiate—"on the condition that each of the adversaries abandon part of his pretensions"—Camus's voice, too, seemed to rise from the pages. Roy dedicated his book to Camus and ended it with a tender invocation of his friend: "You could have saved me all this by returning by train on January 5th, as you wrote to me you would, instead of leaving by car a day earlier."[2]

In 1996, at the age of eighty, Roy published another memoir, *Adieu Ma Mère, Adieu Mon Coeur,* which I read as an epilogue to his history with Algeria and with Camus. It tells of his sentimental voyage back to his homeland that year to decorate the grave of his mother, and of his encounter with contemporary Algeria. The countryside he finds is dangerous; the farm where he grew up no longer exists; the cemetery, which is overgrown and surrounded by barbed wire, is "the only place on the plain where one can meet the French." He is escorted everywhere by Arab soldiers with AK22s. In the front of his book, Roy quotes the Algerian writer Kareb Yacine: "We are not a nation, not yet, know that:

we are only decimated tribes." He also quotes from Camus, speaking in 1955: "Algeria is not France, she is not even Algeria, she is that unknown land, lost in the distance . . . the absent one, the memory and the abandon of whom wrench the heart of some people, and of whom others wish to speak well on the condition that she herself remain silent."[3]

By the time of Roy's visit, the memorials to Camus that had been erected after his death had been either renamed or removed. The rue Albert Camus, running through the center of Montovi, his birthplace, is the rue Feddaoui-Messaoud, Martyr Combatant; Montovi itself has become Drean. The ancient stone placed in Camus's memory at Tipasa by friends has been desecrated, although the inscription from *Summer*, carved by his sculptor friend Louis Benisti, endures: "*Je comprends ici ce qu'on appelle gloire, le droit d'aimer sans mesure*" ("Here I understand what one calls glory, the right to love without measure"). Camus's mother, who died nine months after her son, was buried in Algiers, officially El Djazaïr. Camus lies in the cemetery at Lourmarin in Provence, down the hill from the country house he purchased with his Nobel Prize money.

Camus did not reach Paris to begin the famous years of his life, to become part of the new cultural leadership and the voice of the future France, until the fall of 1943, more than a year after his arrival in France. During those first fifteen months he was convalescing in the hamlet of Le Panelier on a farm and *pension* high on a plateau in the Haute-Loire that belonged to a relative of Francine's and where she had spent childhood summers. His life here was rustic and quiet, for there were few guests, and, after the summer months, when Francine returned to her teaching post in Algeria, solitary. The journals speak of deprivation, celibacy, torpor, and a commitment to work. Looking back on this time, I can also see that coincidental events and encounters were setting a stage for Camus: the Allied landing in North Africa on November 13 that cut him off from his wife and his homeland until the end of the war; the biweekly trips for treatment in nearby Saint-Étienne, which was a center of Resistance activity; a weekend excursion to Paris in the spring of 1943, when he met Jean-Paul Sartre and Simone de Beauvoir at the opening performance of

Le Panelier

Sartre's play *Les Mouches* (*The Flies*). (Camus had given Sartre's first two novels good reviews in the *Alger Républicain,* and Sartre had written twenty pages of praise for *The Stranger,* recognizing Camus as an exceptional artist and a kindred spirit, so the conditions for friendship were favorable.) During that first meeting, according to Beauvoir, they talked about books.

I can also see how Camus's particular circumstances nourished his work, how his feelings of separation and deprivation were transferred to the pages of *The Plague*—"Caught like rats!" was his first journal entry on the day of the Allied landing—and how in the many hours of reading possible during his recuperation (he was again immersed in philosophy) he began to develop the thinking laid out in *The Rebel*. Indeed, with its asceticism and lack of distraction, the solitude proved very productive, for during this time Camus finished his play *The Misunderstanding,* wrote the first *Letter to a German Friend,* began a second draft of *The Plague,* and laid out the framework for *The Rebel*—a considerable output. In the future, he would always turn to a monastic existence when he needed to gather the force necessary to work. The pattern of alternating social engagement and lonely withdrawal was his personality, two elements in constant opposition, the *solidaire* and the *solitaire,* essential to the making of Camus the artist.

For Camus, however, this year as he lived it appears to have had no particular shape or significance and certainly no association with his future. Camus, in fact, had little thought of remaining in France then, for he had booked his return passage to Algeria for November 21 and Francine was looking for a house for them to rent in the hills of Bouzaréah. ("I wouldn't mind Paris, but considering my precious health, I'd die there," he wrote to a friend).[4] In France, Camus, far from his accustomed friends, family, resources, and weather, was an outsider. It was wartime, and he was subject to the occupying Germans, who had moved into what had been the unoccupied southern half of France. Recovering from a life-threatening bout with TB, he was also a patient, passively biding his time until his forces returned and his illness lifted. "Keep quiet, lung! Fill yourself with this icy pure air that feeds you. Keep silent," he recorded in his journal. "Illness is a cross, but perhaps also a guardrail. . . . Let it be the retreat that makes one stronger *at the proper moment*. And if one has to pay up in suffering and renunciation, let's pay up."[5]

In other words, 1942–1943 presents an opportunity to see Camus utterly on his own, without props, plans, or a country, caught betwixt and between. He might be pictured in a pretty, nearly empty *pension,* pallid and thin, with chickens, ducks, and goats for his sole company, or riding the train to Saint-Étienne, absorbing the misery of the countryside in wartime. I take a certain pleasure in this situation, because I feel as if I am catching Camus in the wings of his life, where few people have paid him any attention and where I may be the keenest observer. I look over Camus's shoulder at his reading—the journals mention Kierkegaard, Spinoza, the Bible, Proust, Nietzsche, and a wide variety of others: Milton, Gide, Flaubert. Together with his citations and notes, all this indicates that he is working out some large moral and philosophical questions. I look to small events for evidence of his character. For example, he sometimes rode his bike over the tortuous mountain road to the village of Le Chambon-sur-Lignon, despite his shortness of breath and weakened condition. He turned to the serenity of the woods and to mushroom hunting as a respite from the grimness of wartime. He adopted three dogs to keep him company. (His cat, Cigarette, had died at the end of the summer.) I can identify with all this behavior, and I like this Camus, ambitious in his reading, physically irrepressible, resourceful, softhearted with animals, happy in nature, honest, taking life as it comes. He evinces his usual stoicism: "Sometimes I think of health as a great land full of sun and cicadas which I have lost through no fault of my own. And when I have too much desire for this country and the joy it brings me, I go back to my work."[6] Only occasionally is it tempered by a touch of melodrama. "When a man has learned—and not on paper—how to remain alone with his suffering, how to overcome his longing to flee, . . . then he has little left to learn."[7]

Despite his solitude, Camus doesn't seem as solitary to me here as he does in later life and in fame. He seems resilient, determined not to center his life on either his illness or his expatriation, which presumably was only temporary. As if to counteract his current situation, he wrote many letters, sustaining old friendships with his company of women, with Grenier, and with his former coeditor Pascal Pia, who in a fatherly way was watching over him from Lyon, sending him books and foodstuffs, arranging for a monthly stipend from Gallimard for temporary support, wondering if the Maritime Alps or the Riviera might not be a better climate for recovery. Camus was at ease in these letters, serious, soul-searching, confiding, and also playful and witty. Occasionally, particularly with women, he was even forthcoming about his state of health.

Through correspondence, Camus developed important new friendships with several writers and kept in touch with some of the people he met on excursions to Saint-Étienne or Lyon—a Dominican priest, Father Bruckburger; the journalist René Leynaud and his wife, Marianne; a couple named Fayol, whom he first encountered at Le Panelier. Camus knew that many of his new acquaintances were active in the Resistance—he listened for messages on the BBC with the Fayols and was very close to Leynaud, but he did not know the extent to which small, isolated Le Chambon-sur-Lignon was committed to fighting the Nazis. Nor did he know the townspeople—the two Protestant pastors, the schoolteacher, and the mayor—who had quietly orchestrated the sheltering of some 5,000 Jews. There is no record that Camus himself joined the movement; we know only that he supported friends in their own various roles, the way he had done those last months in Oran, when he helped fugitive resisters escape the country and tutored Jewish children who had been banned from state schools. (He taught in the classes organized by his friend André Benichou, a high school teacher who was himself a Jew, as well as in a private school in Oran.) Nonetheless, he was acquiring connections to new circles, and he was thinking deeply. Even in wartime he was also acquiring a public. Gallimard had published *The Myth of Sisyphus* in October (edited to exclude the chapter on Kafka, who was a Jew, though Camus published it independently in the fall of 1943)[8] and issued a second printing of 4,000 copies of *The Stranger* in November. As Camus discovered during his two visits to Paris, the literary world was eager to meet its exotic new writer.

Most of all, to fend off his sense of isolation, Camus worked. Even more than usual his journal was devoted to this work, his reading, his ambitions, and his uncertainties. He was always planning, beginning, doubting, and then beginning again—"That's how it always is with me: I must start things over again if I want to do them really well."[9] He laid out thoughts and projected paragraphs for *The Misunderstanding,* which was then called *Budejovice* to reflect its Czechoslovak setting; set down some rather untrackable ideas for an essay on revolt, which was the germ of *The Rebel*—"Introduce theme of oscillation," one note reads[10]—and, most copiously, entered notes and text for *The Plague*. Inevitably perhaps, because stress and unhappiness always find outlets, everything Camus was experiencing that year seems to have found direct expression in this work. The real-life Camus appears everywhere in *The Plague,* which is set in Oran and tells the story of the town's struggle to control a typhus epidemic. He is in the description of Oran as a "thoroughly negative place." He is in the situation of confinement, in the search for appropriate action, and in the character of the committed and quietly courageous Dr. Rieux, who is separated from his wife by the quarantine and whose mother sits quietly at her window in the evenings, as Madame Camus did. He is also in the character of the nonviolent Tarrou, who keeps a plague journal, and in the newspaperman Rambert, who at first wants to flee—"he was not one of them, he didn't belong there"—and in the end chooses to stay to fight. The nature of Camus's daily life is annotated in countless details—the curfews, blackouts, and food shortages; the feelings of claustrophobia and suffocation; the slow, relentless pace of the days; the increasingly mechanical letters to loved ones; the abstraction of passion. ("Everything will be better when you come back," Rieux writes to his wife. "We will begin again.")

The Plague is an allegorical novel. The plague is Nazism and evil; the brown rats are the brown-shirted Nazis; the citizens of Oran caught in the quarantine are the French under German occupation; the townspeople who fight the epidemic, each in his own way, are *résistants;* their actions are forms of revolt. The book also presents a portrait of the author in transition. I can see the younger Camus of the sun in *The Stranger,* a maturing and more resolute Camus in *The Plague.* He has suffered from his illness and from separation. He has been changed and radicalized by exile and wartime, has moved beyond his earlier pacifism to engagement, moved from a mere recognition of the absurd to a demand for an active response. Camus knew that his thinking had been evolving. *The Stranger* and *The Myth of Sisyphus* describe "point zero" or "the nakedness of man facing the absurd," he explains in his journal; *The Plague* progresses from there to propose a response. Camus already had a plan in mind for a new trilogy of books on revolt; the novel *The Plague* was the first of them. But there were still two years of war and Resistance to figure into its final draft.

Knowing the heavily autobiographical nature of *The Plague,* I can't help looking to the book for further revelations. I read every line carefully, with expectation, finding scores of distracting but illuminating details that ultimately personalize the novel. Like Camus, the priest Paneloux has a particular interest in Saint Augustine; Rambert plays soccer; and, as Camus tries to complete a third draft of this book, his pathetic M. Grand is struggling to progress beyond the first sentence of a novel. Dr. Rieux often makes statements that sound exactly like Camus: "Heroism and sanctity don't really appeal to me, I imagine. What interests me is being a man."[11] The tenderness between Dr. Rieux and his mother brings Camus's own maternal relationship poignantly to mind. "Something always changed in his mother's face when he came in. The silent resignation that a laborious life had given it seemed to light up with a sudden glow."[12] And, "Looking at his mother, he felt an uprush of a half-forgotten emotion, the love of his boyhood, at the sight of her soft brown gaze intent on him."[13] As I comb through *The Plague,* I feel a sense of complicity and intimacy.

The Plague was a very difficult book for Camus to write. The notes in his journal that suggest its course—the extended research, the various outlines and statements of intention—are revealing, ambitious, and exhausting merely to read. From a writer's point of view, they are also fascinating. The most detailed and extensive of them begin soon after he has been cut off from Algeria and has no choice but to focus on his work. In order to ground his work in realism, Camus read medical and epidemiological histories and literary accounts of great scourges. He thought about including an official report on the plague in Oran in the book, as well as other forms of "objective narration." The idea of a symbolic novel on the problem of evil came from *Moby-Dick,* which had appeared in a new translation the previous spring. Sartre also admired this book— Melville was a new favorite among the French. Camus, who thought that the great novelists were the philosophical novelists, put Melville in that category along with Stendhal, Balzac, Dostoyevsky, and Proust.

Seven years passed between the time Camus recorded his first thoughts for *The Plague* in his journal and the completion of his third and final draft. When he fixed on his central idea—inspired by a typhus epidemic outside Oran in which the wife of his friend Emmanuel Roblès was stricken— he was still living in Algeria and the war was young. While he was working on his second draft of the book in Le Chambon, he was newly exiled and still only marginally involved in the Resistance. By the time he finished the book in 1947, he had moved to Paris, lived through the war and its aftermath, and completed his time as the editor of the Resistance newspaper *Combat.* During these years, as the war was evolving it was also affecting the contents, characters, and meaning of his novel. Camus corrected and revised accordingly (for example, adding to his fiction real scenes from the day Paris was liberated, and transposing emotions he was feeling). He was subject to his story at the same time that he was trying to dominate it, and this was an unwieldy situation. "Plague. Impossible to get away from it. Too many elements of 'chance' this time in the composition," he writes in the journal in late 1942.[14] Also inscribed about that time: "What is touching in Joyce is not the work but the fact of having undertaken it. Need for distinguishing thus the emotional aspect of the undertaking (which has nothing to do with art) and the artistic emotion proper."[15]

The Plague, which is written in a calm, measured style and in the voice of an impartial, disembodied narrator, is radically different from *The*

Stranger. It is long, dark, and orderly whereas *The Stranger* is short, sun-struck, and errant. It is a formal morality tale whereas *The Stranger* is an existential slice of life. Camus always said that he wanted to write his novels in different styles, and as it turned out he did. In *The Plague* he found a style that particularly suited him, that delivered big truths in a voice that didn't judge or preach. With its "indirectness," as Camus refers to it in his journal, and its slow, almost classical cadence, *The Plague* has a distinctly mythic quality. Camus was drawn to mythology; his journals are full of references not only to Sisyphus and Don Juan, but also to Orpheus and Eurydice, Prometheus, Odysseus, and Nemesis. He often alluded to his affinity for the Greeks. As he explained in an interview, he did not fit the usual definition of novelist. He was an artist who created myths according to his passion and anguish, he said. In *The Plague,* the anguish was separation. It was the great theme of the novel and the theme of the whole war era, as Camus had said. In one way or another, separation was a theme of all his fiction. Separation, he said in explaining *The Plague,* was a distraction that could keep one from thinking that he was going to die.

I have been rereading *The Plague* in the country, where I come to sim-plify life, to work without interruption, and to be near the ocean. We have a beach house that is quiet and isolated—at least it is a long way down a dirt road and there is nothing in our view except the sand plain with its grasses and scrubby vegetation, a twenty-foot-tall platform on which ospreys nest each spring, and in the distance the dunes. We hear only the sea and other natural sounds and an occasional tractor or air-plane. In the morning as a regular routine I fall out of bed and jog to the beach and back. Yesterday at 8 a.m. I encountered a dead rat in my path, his mouth frozen open in an awful snarl. This morning I noticed another rat and a dead mouse by the side of the road. Later I discovered that rats had eaten through the packets of seeds meant for my vegetable garden. Under normal circumstances I would not have thought too much about the sudden confluence of rodents in my life, for in the country these things happen. Given my reading, however, it seemed momentous. This may be only a sign of how deeply *The Plague* has affected me.

Camus, a Romance

It is easy to feel a special connection to Camus in a place where the sea is omnipresent and the sun so obviously rules. The landscape around me in fact reminds me of Africa. The few trees, twisted by the wind into gnarled and lopsided shapes, could be thornbushes. The wind, which blows hard and humid off the sea, wails plaintively through the house like a sirocco. When I swim I occasionally think about Camus and how free he felt in the water. He described swimming almost like a sexual act, the water slipping along his arms and closing in tightly on his legs. He always rediscovered himself in the water, he said. Sometimes I imagine him swimming at night in the harbor in Algeria, as Rieux and Tarrou do in *The Plague,* with the moon on the sea and the town rising behind. I like to swim at night in late summer when the moon catches the phosphorescence in the Atlantic and seems to light up the waves from within. I often wonder how I ever survived growing up so far from the sea, the taste of salt, and the sensation of buoyancy and floating. It occurs to me only now that when Camus was in Paris, among other things, he must have felt painfully inland.

4

Paris 1943

It is hard to think of Camus as an exile during the next years in Paris, when he occupied center stage. It is hard to remember even his dark and lonely time in the provinces when, after only a few months in the city, he seemed to be in medias res. I am looking at a famous photograph taken by Brassaï to commemorate an evening in March 1944 when Camus, less than six months after his arrival, directed a reading of Picasso's play *Le Désir Attrapé par la Queue* (*Desire Caught by the Tail*) in the apartment of his friends Louise and Michel Leiris. The play, a surrealist farce about love, one of Picasso's literary experiments of the time, provided the excuse for the first of the events baptized as fiestas, which usually lasted all night. A grinning Camus, Sartre, Beauvoir, an assortment of the literary friends who were in the cast, and also Brassaï himself are in the picture. Georges Braque, Dora Maar, Jean-Louis Barrault, and the twenty-year-old actress Maria Casarès, who had recently made a spectacular debut in Synge's *Deirdre of the Sorrows,* were in the audience.

I am entering this chapter in Camus's life with excitement, for I have arrived at the beginning of an era that is the most dramatic in twentieth-century French history. Camus himself seemed to enter this next chapter nonchalantly, as if he were simply following a natural course. In early November, he boarded a train to Paris and on arrival found a room in a small hotel in the heart of Saint-Germain that was run by an elderly woman who befriended Resistance workers. Several weeks later, he ran into Sartre and Beauvoir at the Café Flore, charmed them, and was—immediately, it seems in the retelling—welcomed into their social circle. (In her memoirs, Beauvoir recounts that Camus's interest in Sartre's new play broke the ice—"Camus was crazy about the theater"—and Camus's youth and independence created a bond between them. "He relished success and fame . . . but he didn't seem to take himself overseriously," she further notes, very helpfully. "He was a simple, cheerful soul. . . . His great charm, the product of nonchalance and enthusiasm in just the right proportions, ensured him against any risk of vulgarity."[1]

By day, Camus worked as a reader at Gallimard, a position arranged by the ever-supportive Pia. At night he worked on his novel, and sometime in mid-winter he began to engage in certain "*travaux de journalisme*" for the monthly underground newspaper of the Resistance movement, *Combat*. He took the code name Bauchard and was given false identity papers as Albert Mathé. By March he had assumed Pia's place as the editor of *Combat*. (Pia, code name Renoir, who by now had other, larger responsibilities in the Resistance, remained as its director.) By then Camus had also written his first column (warning against lack of involvement in the war) and was busy planning the first postliberation issues. He did the makeup for these issues in his apartment; like a variety of other tasks, this was very dangerous. In August 1944, when Paris was liberated, *Combat* became a public daily, dedicated to charting a new course for the nation—"From Resistance to Revolution," in the words of the triumphant motto that Camus had selected. Camus's editorials ran on the front page left. Within a few months they were the talk of the town, and *Combat* had a national readership.

There are many other significant things to record from Camus's first twelve months in Paris beyond his work at Gallimard and *Combat*. During this period, for example, around the time he joined the Resistance,[2] Camus wrote a second essay, "Letter to a German Friend," which expressed his thoughts on the war and was published clandestinely. He became active in an underground writers' group, the Comité National des Écrivains (CNE), but he resigned after the war when it became apparent that it was a Communist Party front. He wrote an essay, "*Remarque sur la Révolte*" ("A Remark on Revolt"), that read like a précis of *The Plague*. He moved into the studio wing of a larger apartment on the very respectable rue Vaneau that belonged to André Gide, who was spending the last war years in Algeria and did not take up residence across the hall from Camus until 1945. (Six years later, in an homage to Gide, his boyhood master, Camus recalled listening to news of the armistice with Gide, but otherwise maintaining a friendly and cordial distance.)[3] In the spring of 1944, Camus made his debut as a playwright, first with Gallimard's publication of *Caligula* and *The Misunderstanding* in a single volume, and then with a production of *The Misunderstanding* at the popular Théâtre Mathurins, starring Maria Casarès, with whom he had fallen in love. Its opening was a big, stormy event in Paris, which despite mixed reviews made him a quasi-celebrity. *Caligula,* written first, opened a year later. During the summer, when the Germans tightened their surveillance of the underground movement, Camus often had to hide out for safety, eventually decamping by bicycle with a trio of friends to a refuge fifty-five miles east of Paris. With news of the Allied advance, he returned to the city for the final days of the occupation. In September, he received a visit from André Malraux in the *Combat* offices. (A photograph shows a very thin Camus looking intently at an equally intent Malraux in beret and fatigues.) In October, Francine rejoined him in Paris and he broke off his affair with Maria. In November, he celebrated his thirty-first birthday.

Following the sequence of changes in Camus's life, I am breathless. I am struck by the ease with which Camus adapted to his new situation in Paris, particularly given his illness, and impressed by the range of his war activities. I am amazed at the fullness of his days, dazzled at the speed with which he ascended to celebrity. In November 1943, from a cold room in the Hotel de la Minerve, Camus had written to a friend, "I feel curiously sterile, full of doubts and sad."[4] By November 1944 he had effectively entered history. Although few Americans other than intellectuals and wartime correspondents knew of the impact of *Combat,* the French would not forget the voice that was sounded at their darkest hour. After fifty months of occupation, it was a voice of courage and commitment that the disheartened needed to hear, a voice of a younger generation that had hope, a new perspective, and concrete plans for the future.

Rereading *Combat*'s editorials even now, in a lazy summer far removed from August 1944, I can sense the impact the first ones had on battle-weary Frenchmen. The prose is heroic, often lyrical but also hard-biting; the message is patriotic and idealistic. In the headlines alone—"They Will

Not Escape," "The Blood of Liberty," "The Night of Truth"—the drama of the time resurfaces. Against a background of the Resistance's "Song of Partisans," Camus had read the first editorial, "From Resistance to Revolution," on Radio Liberté and spelled out the paper's political platform for a free, uncorrupted France. "In the present state of affairs, such a program goes by the name 'Revolution,'" he said.[5] For emphasis, this broadcast was repeated the following day. On August 23, as the Allied forces were approaching the city, Camus urged *Combat*'s readers to set up barricades in the street and fight the Germans. "A people that wants to live does not wait for its freedom to be delivered to it. It takes its own," he wrote.[6] On August 24, as Paris was being liberated, he expressed the exhilaration: "As freedom's bullets continue to whistle through city streets, the cannons of liberation are passing through the gates of Paris amid shouts and flowers. On this sultriest and most beautiful of August nights, the permanent stars in the skies above the city mingle with the tracer rounds, smoke from burning buildings, and variegated rockets proclaiming the people's joy."[7] In the next days, while happy mayhem continued in the streets, Camus and *Combat* began to delineate the new political and moral order. "Politics is no longer dissociated from individuals," he wrote on September 1, charging his following with responsibility for their future. "It is addressed directly by man to other men. It is a way of speaking."[8]

The peacetime *Combat* was not all gravity, for as Camus added other young professionals to his staff, theater and cinema criticism, sports items, foreign correspondence, and literary notes were included in its pages; significant writers such as Sartre, Malraux, Gide, Raymond Aron, and André Breton contributed special reports. Camus did not write all the editorials, which were usually unsigned or signed with a pseudonym and, as he explained, expressed the common thought of the *Combat* team.[9] Nor was he exclusively responsible for their content, which also came from Pia and several other editors. But from the language and the message, it is obvious that in the early days it was Camus who was speaking. The lyrical tone is Camus's, the idealism and the honesty are Camus's, and the high moral purpose is unmistakably his own. If this voice was also the voice of the *résistant* with whom everyone wanted to identify, the participant in the Free France movement who wanted the years of struggle to count for something, who was ashamed of the occupation and the collaboration and all that made it possible, and who still believed that "revolution" or change for the better was possible, that was because for this moment in time these two voices were in complete and uncomplicated accord. That was the inspiration and the irony. It seemed as if the times and the newspaper had been created for Camus, and Camus created for them.

It strikes me now that this may have been Camus's purest moment of glory. Never again would the truth as he saw it be so clear, so patently patriotic, so uncomplicated by power or politics or his own standing, so utterly indivisible. Never again could he simply react to events, bear witness, write honestly without self-consciousness or nasty consequences. It is another irony that later on Camus would say that he didn't like journalism, because it allowed him no time to rewrite or to lay out his full thinking and because it inevitably created enemies. But then, in late 1944, Camus was writing under very favorable circumstances. He had a podium at a financially independent paper. He had a glorious cause. He had the authority and the prestige granted him by his several hundred thousand dedicated readers, who counted on him for their daily word, as a friend

put it. He was also part of a team that, much as in the theater, offered camaraderie and put him at ease. He liked the milieu of a newspaper, the noise of the presses, the smell of hot lead and ink, the jargon, the sense of community. He was particularly comfortable around the typographers, linotypists, and proofreaders—and the men of the "marble," as the printing stone is called in France. He thought that in publishing the workers and the writers should be on closer terms and equal footing because they had a common goal. After his death, some of his former coworkers at *Paris-Soir* and *Combat* put together a small volume of reminiscence and tribute whose honesty and simplicity would have touched Camus deeply. They liked Camus enormously, because he put them at ease. He was easy to know, sympathetic, a *copain,* a *chic type* or super guy, they said. He was *vrai,* which means both true and real.

Camus had lofty ambitions for the paper, as he explained in an early series of articles in which he critiqued France's dailies. He wanted the postwar press to be different from the prewar press, which he described as ruled by an appetite for money and by indifference to noble things. Unwittingly, his experiences with first *Paris-Soir* and what he called "its shopgirl sensibility," and then with the censored *Alger Républicain,* had served him well. Working with Pia, who was fiercely independent, had helped to set his thinking. Camus was determined to have an honest press with a high quality of writing, to remain above politics and sensation, and to be free to criticize both the left and the right. Pioneering American journalists of the time, such as Dwight Macdonald, and A. J. Liebling, remembered him for the example that was set at *Combat.* In the late 1940s Macdonald introduced the readers of his journal *Politics* to Camus and *Combat* with an excerpt from Camus's essay on revolutionary violence. Liebling, who had encountered *Combat* and other Resistance newspapers, such as *Franc-Tireur* and *Défense de la France,* while he was covering the war in France for *The New Yorker,* considered Camus one of the finest journalists of the twentieth century. Nonetheless, *Combat* did have a point of view, which was decidedly liberal, and it had a distinctly moral tone, which for better or for worse was associated with Camus: for better, because it established Camus as a principled and charismatic young leader; for worse, because it created expectations, pressures, and public responsibilities that would come to plague him and cause enormous personal pain.

Camus's celebrity came so quickly that it had to affect him. Friends suggest that for a while he acted rather starlike, "*un peu vedette.*" At the very least, Camus was aware of his growing influence, for he was increasingly asked to lecture and write articles and he received thousands of letters a month. Some critics thought that his editorials, with the use of the majestic "we" and the grave moral imprecations, seemed to speak from on high. In person, too, Camus could project a certain hauteur, although his friends explained that this was his Spanish side, his way of covering up his uncertainties, just as they attributed other surprising manners to his "African temperament." Sartre and Beauvoir thought that Camus was very pleased with himself, but that he hid it well. Beauvoir also suggested that to be blasé about his new status would have been unnatural. These two famous people were not the most reliable of reporters, because a certain competitiveness colored their feelings toward Camus. Beauvoir herself admits that she was jealous of Camus. She also admits that she had always wanted to protect Sartre's reputation. To this end, she had a tendency to slight Camus in her memoirs, to revise reality, and occasionally to turn mean. For his part, Camus commits two remarks to his journal that indicate a full recognition of his new standing. "What is a famous man? It is a man whose given name doesn't matter,"[10] he writes to himself in October 1946, using a touch of irony to convey nonchalance. More directly: "At the age of 30, almost overnight, I knew fame. I don't regret that. . . . Now I know what it is. It's not much." ("*C'est peu de choses.*")[11]

I have been searching Camus's journals for remarks illuminating his term at *Combat,* although I don't expect to find much of substance here, given that his days were long and demanding and *Combat* itself was then the primary workshop for his ideas. In his essays in *Combat,* I can follow important issues in postwar France—the new government, the punishment of collaborationists and war criminals, the hopes for a new Socialist Party, Charles de Gaulle's brief ascension to power—and I can also follow Camus's responses. As the months go by and he speaks out on the need for a new press or the disappointments in de Gaulle's provisional government or the *épuration* (purge), I can see him articulating principles, formulating public positions, and also learning about politics and about himself. He tries to be painstakingly honest in print, providing careful explanations for his thinking, even, presumably in response to public criticism, offering a "self-critique." "We aren't sure that we have always avoided the danger of implying that we can see the future more clearly than others and never make mistakes. Of course we don't believe anything of the sort."[12] As the country begins to return to prewar patterns and the spirit of the Resistance dims, I can feel impatience and sadness beneath Camus's words. As the high court begins its summary executions of collaborationists, I can sense his growing malaise. I can also sense that his role as editor is changing from confident spokesman to troubled critic.

By the fall of 1945, a few months before he took an extended leave of absence from *Combat,* Camus sounds like a different person, compared with what he was a year earlier. He is less likely to perorate, and less absolutist, than he was when he had faith in an imminent "revolution." He is sobered, remorseful, and weary. The issue of the purges has been central to this change. In the first months after liberation, Camus had supported the "swift and harsh" punishment of the guilty, as faithful to the spirit of the Resistance and necessary to a fresh moral start for France—as he said, "necessary to save its soul." From that position, he had engaged in a long public debate with François Mauriac of *Le Figaro,* an older, conservative Catholic writer who had himself been very active in the Resistance but who argued for forgiveness and clemency. Despite his growing concern about the possibility of justice and his deep-seated distaste for the death penalty, Camus had maintained a firm position. His editorial of January 5, "The Purge Gone Awry," was almost tremulous with rue and distress at the dissolute proceedings, but it nonetheless accepted "the order of things." A country that forgoes self-purgation had to be prepared to lose its rebirth, he insisted. Later in January, however, when the young journalist Robert Brasillach was sentenced to death for his pro-Nazi and anti-Semitic remarks in the collaborationist press, Camus added his signature to a petition for a stay of execution. He was taking a stand against the death penalty, not for the individual, "whom I detest with all my forces," he wrote in his letter of support, alluding to friends who had been tortured or shot as a result of Brasillach's work. The writers Paul Valéry, Jean Cocteau, Colette, Paul Claudel, and Jean Anouilh as well as Mauriac were among the fifty-nine signers, who did not succeed in saving Brasillach's life. Sartre and Beauvoir did not sign. By summer, Camus had also condemned the purges in print. "The word 'purge' itself was already rather distressing. The actual thing became odious," he wrote on the front page of *Combat*.[13] The following fall, he published "*Ni Victimes Ni Bourreaux*" ("Neither Victims nor Executioners"), a series of eight articles in which he spelled out his new convictions. "After the experiences of the past two years, I could no longer hold to any truth that might oblige me, directly or indirectly, to condemn a man to death," he said.[14] "I shall never again be among those who, for whatever reasons, accommodate themselves to murder."

What is surprising in all this is not Camus's change of mind—for the world knows him now as a passionate opponent of revolutionary violence and capital punishment—but the intensity and the wording of his initial position. In the first months after liberation, Camus seemed to be writing in a fever. He was emotional about the brutality and the sorrows of war, "the other death sentences that struck innocent men . . . beloved faces lying in the dust . . . hands we longed to hold."[15] He was convinced that a moral revolution was the country's last hope for greatness. He was so committed to justice that he was willing to sacrifice lives and accept the executions as "the black chores of justice." "France bears within herself, like a foreign body, a small minority of men who were the cause of her recent woes and continue to be the cause of her woes. They are guilty of treason and injustice," he had concluded in Ocober, pointing out that the very existence of these men raised the problem of justice and the question was one of destroying them.[16]

Two days later, after learning that the Nazis had executed the journalist and *résistant* René Leynaud, who had become a close friend in Le Chambon, he wrote lyrically of the "dreadful irreparable sorrow" and said that such losses should not go unheeded. In January, addressing Mauriac, he invoked his friend again, saying that he would pardon collaborationists only when Leynaud's wife permitted him to.[17] Most of the left felt as Camus did about the purges, and Camus himself was painfully aware of the awful contradictions of his position—"Is this hard, impossible, and inhumane? We know well that it is. But things are as they are, which is why we are right not to take them lightly."[18] This does not make it any less distressing now to see Camus even briefly on the side of expediency, sounding disturbingly like a witch hunter. Yet the fact is that Camus changed his mind, in public, and as it became clear that justice was not being effected the way he thought it could be, and that old-style politics, self-interest, and cynicism ruled the *épuration,* he had faced his own moral dilemma. The rest of his work is so firmly grounded in what he learned in these days that a firsthand lesson in realpolitik seems fortuitous. Camus himself seems all the more human for his mistakes and disillusion.

Very few remarks in Camus's journal reflect directly on the events that were so crucial to his development as a moralist that year. He doesn't mention Leynaud's death, which devastated him. About his decision to sign the petition to save Brasillach's life, he enters only a line recording the fact, although according to his friends and family he paced the floor all that night. But I am becoming more skilled at reading between the lines, and I can sense in even the elliptical entries of late 1944 and 1945 that questions of justice were very much on his mind, and that he was still having doubts about his position on the purges. In July, a month before he publicly condemned the purges, he writes in the declarative first person: "Revolt. Finally, I choose liberty. For even if justice is not realized, liberty maintains the power of protest against injustice and keeps communication open."[19]

Later that month, in what would be the final entry of his fourth journal, Camus paused to take stock, as he usually seemed to do when he was confronting the last page of a notebook. Once again, it is a surprise to find him speaking so openly, even confessionally, although presumably in private. "At the age of thirty a man ought to have control over himself, know the exact reckoning of his faults and virtues, recognize his limits, foresee his weakness—be what he is," he reflects, charging himself to be natural, "but with a mask."[20] Camus sounds stalwart but slightly tragic now, determined to stand up for his principles but also self-protective and wary, and above all painfully honest and self-critical. I read the line "I have known enough things to be able to surrender almost everything" as a reference to the lessons of illness and poverty. I ponder the line "There remains an amazing effort, daily, insistent" and wonder what Camus is really after, what will ever put him at ease. "The man I should be if I had not been the child I was," he had written on the preceding page of the journal. I feel a rush of sympathy and caring, the old intimacy returning. For a brief moment, Camus seems so vulnerable as to be transparent. Oddly, I worry for him, as if I didn't know about all the events of the rest of his life—the other books, the Nobel Prize, the international reputation. Knowing about the rest of his life, I think of him as trapped, but this is, in part, biographical hindsight. It is also what Camus was writing about—entrapment, courage, and carrying on.

On a recent trip to Paris, I decided to track Camus in the mid-1940s, to put myself in his various physical situations in the hope that I might somehow slip through the cracks and be on the scene. I had mental pictures of what the occupied city and then the newly liberated city had been like—Beauvoir's descriptions in her memoirs are meticulous—and I had made a list of all the places where Camus had lived and spent time. As it happened, I was staying at the Hotel Lutétia on boulevard Raspail, which, like the Meurice and the Crillon, had been taken over for Nazi headquarters during the war.

My room looked out over the Bon Marché and a landscape of eighteenth-century and nineteenth-century rooftops, which provided a view that was essentially unchanged from Camus's days, and the staff was friendly and solicitous. Nonetheless, it was disconcerting to be ensconced in onetime enemy territory, and I often felt the presence of ghosts. I remembered the photographs of tanks on Raspail, traffic signs in German, flags flying the swastika from rooftops. In the end, this was useful. It has taken the French several generations to be able to look at the Lutétia as the place it is and not the place it was.

On the night of my arrival, suffering from jet lag but determined to last through dinner, I went down to the hotel brasserie, which I knew was popular with the literary crowd, including Camus's most recent biographer, the French journalist and novelist Olivier Todd. Since the house specialty was *fruits de mer,* I ordered a dozen oysters and a glass of Sancerre. I was seated at a table for one, wedged in between two other singles: a loud, jolly older man and a sweet-faced middle-aged Englishwoman. Both of them were also eating oysters and drinking wine; that and being elbow to elbow led to conversation and to *le monsieur*'s ordering more oysters and wine all around. It seemed that he lived in the Luberon, came to Paris to eat oysters as often as possible, and was a retired army colonel who had served in Algeria and the Sahara during the 1950s. He said that Algiers was still very beautiful then, but he made a few racist references to the Muslims. He also mentioned that Lourmarin, the village in the Luberon where Camus found his country house, was now full of English tourists. The woman, Caroline—by then we had exchanged names—was an academic who was writing a book about the influence of *La Princesse de Clèves* on French literature, and we chatted about Camus's high regard for that early novel. I felt rather buoyed by these easy connections, however incidental they were, although I was not surprised, because with Camus I have come to expect them.

The Lutétia proved to be a very convenient address for my explorations. It was only blocks away from Camus's first hotels, Gide's apartment, Gallimard's offices, and most of the restaurants, bars, and cafés where Camus was a regular, all located in the heart of Saint-Germain. I set off to view his apartment first, because I thought I had spotted the street around the corner, a quiet single block running off Raspail, although I failed to find number 1 bis, the address of the studio. I took photographs of number 1 anyway and was studying the small six-story structure, waiting to feel something special, when a woman in an adjacent antiques store stuck her head out of the door and asked if I was looking for something. She had no idea where Camus had lived but said that there was a plaque marking Gide's residence several blocks away in the rue Vaneau. As I made my way to the correct address on a rather somber street in a more stately residential *quartier,* I wondered what difference the viewing of an architectural pile made to my understanding. The place where Camus really lived turned out to be more ornate than the simple *immeuble* I had been ready to accept as his—it had a curved cornice line and decorative iron terraces—and there was a plaque attesting to Gide's presence from 1926 until his death in 1951. But I was not able to summon forth any more of the life that had gone on in that small studio than I had sitting at my desk in Manhattan. I tried to imagine the trapeze that hung from the ceiling (which every friend of Camus's who entered the apartment felt obliged to try out, and Camus in response grew to hate) and the lively postwar parties that simply happened there, despite the cramped quarters. By all reports, the place was a natural social center, with friends passing in and out as a matter of course and Camus ever the congenial host. I thought about the old crowd from Algiers paying visits, Francine playing Bach on the piano, Camus trying to eke out a few more pages of *The Plague* after work. It all seemed very far away—small cold stories.

I had the same experience when I visited other places that I thought might provoke a strong visceral reaction: the office building on the commercial rue Réaumur that the collaborationist press had taken over during the occupation and where *Combat* was subsequently published, or Marguerite Duras's apartment in an old house on the rue Saint-Benoît, which was a central meeting place for members of the Resistance (who had to be particularly careful, because collaborationists and high-ranking Germans frequently gathered at a literary salon two floors above). In the restaurant Petit-Benoît across the street, however, I felt something different. Perhaps it was because I went inside the establishment instead of just viewing its facade, and because the place was old, simple, and timelessly functional, and I was eating the *poireaux vinaigrette* and *hachis parmentier* that Camus, Sartre, Arthur Koestler, Giacometti, and Hemingway may well have eaten at the same table fifty years before, but in any case I felt a sense of continuity and potential excitement—as if but for an accident of birth, I might have been part of the scene. It did not seem so long ago that would-be saboteurs had sat at neighboring tables or that papers and messages were exchanged in the very rudimentary WC just as they were in back rooms of eating establishments all over the Left Bank. At the Café Flore, too, despite the bill rendered in euros, and the fact that the place is now part of Flo's chain of restaurants, it was not difficult to imagine blackout curtains at the windows, acetylene lamps, ersatz beer and coffee, and the other details of wartime. Outside the café, bicycles would have been stacked up against the lamppost or the newsstand, for with the shortage of gasoline everyone traveled by bicycle. Without cars, the street would have been quiet except for the frequent sounding of sirens, particularly at night. Patrols stood at the corner near the eleventh-century church from which the area had taken its name (across the street from the new Emporio Armani that has now taken the place of Le Drugstore). Sartre, Beauvoir, Camus, and most of the intellectual world came to the Flore for its light, heat, and comfort. "It was our own special resort. We felt at home here; it sheltered us from the outside world," Beauvoir remembered. The Germans didn't come in, she reported, because they knew that the crowd was all anti-Nazi.[21]

Beauvoir offers many other evocative details about Paris in wartime that give the scene an everyday reality. Far more important than the food shortages, make-do fashion, and other efforts to carry on that she describes is the sense of camaraderie, which I now realize propelled the existentialist movement forward. She speaks of the bond between her set of friends as that of "a secret fraternity." It came in part from the ideological like-mindedness of the group and in part from the experience of sharing a disaster. Beauvoir explains how the fiestas with the heavy drinking, dancing, casual sex, and desperate fun—Dora Marr used to mime a bullfighting act; Sartre conducted an orchestra from the bottom of a cupboard; Camus played military marches on saucepan lids or danced a *paso doble*—were acts of defiance against the war. They made it seem that victory was just around the corner. She describes how the communal nature of the day-to-day activities—attending Resistance meetings, listening to BBC broadcasts together, talking out hopes and fears—generated energy and a sense of shared strength that, when the war ended, were directed to shaping the future. "We were to provide the postwar era with its ideology. We had a detailed plan ready," she says, mentioning specifically a manifesto that Camus was working on and the magazine that Sartre was determined to found, under the direction of the group. "We had come through the night, and dawn was breaking; we stood shoulder to shoulder, ready for a new start."[22]

Little more than a year after Beauvoir made this forecast, existentialism was in full flower. It was as surprising to Sartre and Beauvoir as it was to the rest of the world that a certain way of thinking was suddenly transformed into a movement and its chief exponents were elevated to public heroes. In 1944, although intellectuals were aware of Heidegger's "existentialist thinking," the word *existentialism* had only recently been coined. Although the publication of Beauvoir's first novel, *She Came to Stay,* had established her as a writer of particular interest—it was read as a thinly disguised version of her private life with Sartre—the appearance of Sartre's *Being and Nothingness,* soon to be the bible of existentialism, had attracted little notice. But then the fall of 1945 brought a rash of events that turned into *l'offensive existentialiste,* as Beauvoir put it. In that first literary season since the restoration of peace, everything seemed to carry a sweet scent of newness and rebirth. In addition, there was a wealth of new newspapers and magazines—thirty-four new dailies in 1945—to report on post-war life. In September, Beauvoir published her Resistance novel *The Blood of Others,* and Camus's *Caligula* reached the stage, with the twenty-three-year-old conservatory student Gérard Philipe in the role of the young tyrant. In October, Sartre published the first two novels in his trilogy *Roads to Freedom* and launched the monthly magazine *Les Temps Modernes,* which would serve as his mouthpiece and showpiece for many decades. The name, with a nod to Charlie Chaplin, was meant to signal a new age of "committed literature" and intellectual change. The writer had to take hold of his era, Sartre said in his twenty-page *"Présentation."* "Our intention is to work together to produce certain changes in the Society that surrounds us" and in "the social condition of man and the conception he has of himself."[23] The editorial board included most of the *famille*—Raymond Aron, the *Combat* associate Albert Ollivier, Michel Leiris, Jean Paulhan, Beauvoir, and Maurice Merleau-Ponty, writers now recognizable as distinguished representatives of postwar thought. A notable exception was Camus, who was too busy with *Combat* to serve.

All these events captured the public's attention. But it was a scholarly lecture by Sartre—"Is Existentialism a Humanism?"—that registered in history as the cultural milepost of the year, and was probably most responsible for the mythic aura that would henceforth surround both Sartre and the existentialist movement. The substance of the evening was generally deemed too academic for popular consumption, but newspapers nevertheless reported its drama in vivid detail—the suffocating heat, the overflow crowd ("a mob rather than an audience"), the fifteen fainting spells, the thirty broken chairs, and the "victory" of the lecturer.[24] From that day on, Sartre became a powerful public figure, and he and his literary friends made widespread news. Of course, a combination of factors set off the explosion of interest in existentialism as a philosophy, not least the needs and feelings that had been simmering deep in the war-ravaged French soul. Beauvoir said that she thought the new ideology, with its claim to reconcile history and morality, helped people to "face horror and absurdity while retaining their human dignity, to preserve their individuality."[25] Others spoke simply of a hunger for new ideas, new formulas, and new heroes or antiheroes. In fact, although everyone was talking about existentialism, few people knew what it really was. Two months earlier, before the tidal wave of fame reached him, Sartre himself had said, "Existentialism? I don't know what that is. My philosophy is a philosophy of existence."[26] To add to the confusion, tabloids like *France Dimanche* and *Samedi Soir* ran features on the lifestyle of the existentialists, identifying their favorite cafés, nightclubs, and seedy hotels, playing up the negativism and depravity of the movement, giving it a seductive notoriety.

Many of the social haunts made famous in the flood of publicity had been on my list of places to seek out—jazz clubs like Le Tabou or the Rose Rouge, where the writer and composer Boris Vian played the trombone and Juliette Greco performed songs I had listened to in college; the Mephisto; the Bar Vert; the Cave Saint-Germain. Most of them were only a few blocks away from the Hotel Louisiane, where Sartre and Beavoir then lived. In the first postwar years, Sartre's crowd frequented these and other places, moving from café to bistro to club and back in a night, picking up friends like Arthur Koestler and his girlfriend Mamaine Paget in their travels. Their stories now pass for cultural history. The most trivial details have been reported—Camus liked vodka and champagne, Sartre drank a lot and left big tips, Sartre gave Greco her famous song "La Rue des Blancs-Manteaux," which he had first written for *No Exit*. Perhaps because of this popularizing of existentialism, I soon stopped looking for old nightclubs. I didn't want to feel like just another tourist. Most of the establishments in question had changed names and hands anyway, although I noted that Les Assassins on the rue Jacob was still blaring music into the night. One afternoon I walked over to the Louisiane, which still sat modestly, almost anonymously, behind the noisy stalls of the market on the rue de Buci. I had spent a night there many years ago, specifically because of its history. I had a very cheap, shabby room under the eaves, and the bed was lumpy. In the morning, the smell of cheese and fish rose up with the sun. The concierge, unasked, left a bowl of coffee and a fresh croissant outside my door.

Whereas I used to take pleasure in imagining Camus in this famous existential scene, I now find myself pondering his place there. That he had a regular social life with Sartre's crowd for a few years seemed clear—Beauvoir mentions a variety of sorties in 1945 and 1946, including a few evenings *à deux* with him, when Sartre was in the United States on a cultural tour, and plans for a skiing trip together. (It seems obvious in

Beauvoir's narrative that she was drawn to Camus, although her criticism of him is often harsh. It was rumored that she wanted to sleep with him, and also that he thought she talked too much.) That Camus was a glamorous social figure who attracted attention is also indisputable, according to friends and official sources. With the success of *The Stranger* and *The Myth of Sisyphus,* the stage productions of *The Misunderstanding* and *Caligula,* and his leadership of *Combat,* he was often recognized walking down the street. Although I can't find a photograph for documentation, Camus and Sartre must have made an odd and appealing couple when they were together: Camus with his casual good looks, taller, leaner, younger; Sartre with his short bulldog body, thick glasses, and distinctive froglike face.

But the scene in Saint-Germain was really Sartre's. He was the one who was besieged for photographs, autographs, and lectures and was profiled and defiled in the tabloids; he was called the pope of existentialism. Camus was a sidekick—a "country cousin"—a charismatic young author and journalist and a very different phenomenon. He was not really a member of the Sartre *famille* beyond the convivial socializing. He was not part of the intellectual club at *Les Temps Modernes.* Whereas most of the Sartreans came from a comfortable bourgeois background and had been nurtured at the elite École Normale Supérieure, as Sartre had, Camus had a different upbringing, a different education, and a different ethos. He also had his own family, which in September 1945 had grown to include the twins Catherine and Jean. (It seems that we had a boy and a girl at the same time, he wrote to a friend.) He had his Algerian friends, such as Pierre Galindo and Edmond Charlot, who had come to live in Paris after the war, and many others, including Francine's mother and two sisters, who frequently came to visit. In spite of all this, Camus was always linked with Sartre, often to his own annoyance. In an interview late in the fall of 1945, he stated emphatically that he was not an existentialist and then went on to say, "Sartre and I are always astonished to see our names associated. We are even thinking of publishing a little advertisement in which the undersigned affirm they have nothing in common and refuse to answer for the debts of the other."[27] (He also wrote to a friend that he was forced to give up the casual phrase "It's absurd," because it attracted too much attention.)

It seems important to separate Camus from Sartre and existential lore, in part to grant him his own personality and his own success. But I may be particularly keen to do this now because I know the terrible effect their falling-out over *The Rebel* in 1952 will have on Camus's reputation and his self-esteem. From the beginning, Camus and Sartre were very different types of thinkers: Camus a moralist taking his lessons from experience, Sartre a philosopher proposing a system; Camus rejecting history as a rationale, Sartre embracing it. ("Why am I an artist and not a philosopher?" Camus asks himself in his journal the same month that Sartre gave his famous lecture. "Because I think according to words and not according to ideas."[28]) Many people considered Camus an existentialist because of the tone and message of *The Stranger,* and despite his very real objections —he said he had written *The Myth against* existentialist philosophies and also said he disagreed with the existentialists' conclusions—he may well have been one in effect. But in his work on *The Plague,* Camus had already moved beyond existential doctrine. A companion book on revolt was beginning to take shape in his mind. "To accept the absurdity of everything around us is a step, a necessary experience: It must not become an impasse. It provokes a revolt, which can become productive. An analysis of the notion of revolt can help to discover notions capable of restoring a reliable meaning to existence," he had explained in an interview in late 1945 to clarify his own position on existentialism, and this statement also sums up the message of *The Rebel.*[29] The *Combat* series called *"Ni Victimes Ni Bourreaux,"* "Neither Victims nor Executioners," in which he focused a critical eye on the postwar world and spoke out on violence, war, and dangerous ideologies, was part of the buildup to *The Rebel,* and far from existential doctrine, too.

Many of Camus's thoughts had crystalized that winter during long conversations with Sartre and particularly Arthur Koestler, who had arrived in Paris in late October, bringing firsthand news of the crimes of Stalinism.[30] Koestler, who had been imprisoned during both the Spanish civil war and World War II, had recently published *Darkness at Noon* in France and, later that year, *Yogi and the Commissar*—both novels about the evils of totalitarianism. He and Mamaine were in town for the staging of one of his plays, and they spent time almost daily with Sartre and Camus, often drinking late into the night. Koestler felt a natural kinship with Camus, grounded as they were in an anti-Stalinism that Sartre and Beauvoir did not share. Camus could now discuss with new immediacy the place of Marxism in the world or the "reign of terror" in the Soviet Union.

Even before meeting Koestler, however, Camus had been increasingly consumed by what he would later call the "human crisis." In September 1945, he had taken a long leave from *Combat* and Gallimard to finish *The Plague,* but he also needed to resolve the moral uncertainties that had been clouding his thinking. He filled many pages of his journals with his own questions about Christianity and historical materialism and the consequences of accepting the doctrines of either. As early as November 1945, he had indicated that as a writer he felt a responsibility to speak out. "What to do between the two?" he writes, referring to the standoff between East and West. "Something in me tells me, convinces me that I cannot detach myself from my era without cowardice, without accepting slavery, without denying my mother and my truth." And in the same paragraph he says, "That is the question: can I be merely a witness? In other words: have I the right to be merely an artist? I cannot believe so."[31]

Camus's journal entries are unusually dark during November, the month of his thirty-second birthday. After a year of public politics, he appears to be disheartened and morally depleted, a reflection of the "staggering testimonies" of war and his own fatigue and low self-esteem. Again I am perplexed by Camus, seemingly oblivious of all that has happened outside his journal, discontent with his very nature. There is no hint of the committed, self-assured young man who has several jobs, a national voice, a successful play on the stage, and a fair share of fame and glamour. There is only an acknowledgment of pressure, a fear of failure, an implication of a struggle with illness. The mention of illness, so rare with Camus, so unguarded of him, suggests his ragged state of mind. A letter to Pia that month reporting a bad case of the flu corroborates his poor state of health. In one of the next entries, Camus also speaks of himself as a family man and a father. It is the only reference of this sort to be found anywhere in the journals, and it is startling to have, even so briefly, a sight line into such intimate quarters. In a curious way, it dignifies Camus to find him in a common albeit high-minded quandary. He questions his right "as an artist attached to liberty" to accept the advantages of money and privilege. He speaks of poverty as his anchor and then worries about refusing his children "even the very modest comfort I am preparing for them" and worries further about his decision to have children, even the right to have children when one doesn't believe in God. He concludes with admonitions to himself. "How easy it would be if I yielded to the horror and disgust that this world gives me, if I could still believe that man's task is to create happiness! Keep silent at least, keep silent, keep silent, until I feel I have the right. . . ."[32] The ellipsis trails off into the painful unknown.

Exactly a year later, "Neither Victims nor Executioners" filled in the ellipsis and expressed what Camus felt he could not yet say and had not said. It was the first piece he had published in *Combat* in more than a year, and it turned out to be his swan song at the magazine, from which he resigned the following June. He wrote barely a handful of other pieces before a farewell letter to his readers. Camus's departure meant closure on the brief utopian postwar period when he and his colleagues had hopes for a new society and a certain faith in politics as an instrument of change. With the friendships and ambitions that bound its ranks, *Combat* had been an extraordinary time for all the staff. But by 1947, even this paper had not been able to maintain its nonpartisan voice and revolutionary zeal in the increasingly divisive political climate after liberation in France. Its readership was falling, its deficit was growing, its voice was moving to the right. The editors disagreed about how to save the paper. Pia, who wanted to close immediately in order to be able to pay all the staff, withdrew in the fall, precipitating Camus's return. However disaffected by the discord at the paper and by French politics, Camus still believed in *Combat,* or at least in its ideals, and nourished a faint hope that his series might provide new energy and focus. During those two years of operation they had maintained a paper of absolute independence and honor, he would sum up later. "Journalism is one of the most beautiful professions that I know," he says with rather uncharacteristic exuberance, explaining that "it forces you to judge yourself."[33] Coworkers said that during Camus's long absences the paper had suffered from the lack of a real boss, but the changes may have been inevitable in a changing France. In his last editorial, Camus passed the torch to a fellow *résistant,* Claude Bourdet, and ceded the paper to "new directions," saying simply that only newspapers with a huge circulation could break even. "I leave it to the reader's imagination to decide what this simple rule of economics means for freedom of the press."[34] The paper was turned over to Bourdet and a Tunisian businessman with socialist leanings, and it continued to operate, under various editors, until 1974.

That winter Camus's friendship with Pia also abruptly ended. The cause is still a matter of conjecture among their old colleagues. Some sources blame Pia's ego and his resentment of Camus's receiving the accolades for a newspaper that was really his. But Pia had always chosen to remain behind the scenes, and he was too much of a bohemian and a loner to care about fame. Others say simply that Pia was a nihilist and Camus an optimist and that it was a parting of two complex personalities who had shared a goal and a profession but ultimately had their differences. These sources say that dozens of small things finally produced the rupture, that it was "a slow cooling" and "a thousand little griefs."[35] But they also say that Pia felt a true and unusual tenderness for Camus and that Pia was one of the most important people in Camus's life.

In the forty-odd letters that have survived from their eight years of friendship, it is clear that "the two men respected each other with passion," as the editor of a new volume of these letters has put it. (During the Resistance, Pia destroyed the bulk of his correspondence with Camus, as well as with Malraux, for reasons of security, whereas Camus, living in safer places, saved his. This gesture was also typical of Pia, who had a need for anonymity and at an earlier point had burned all his poetry.) In the letters, they are fellow travelers, Pia leading the way, Camus reporting back; both of them serious and focused; Pia tireless in his efforts to help Camus in every conceivable way; Camus occasionally playful, as he was with comfortable friends. Pia's letters are suffused with concern, Camus's with gratitude. As the problems of war and illness intensify, the sense of complicity on which the friendship was constructed grows deeper, and the underlying affection and admiration shine forth more clearly. In a letter of November 1945, which is, in fact, a letter in which he criticizes Pia's recent direction of *Combat* and asks to take leave of the paper, Camus has begun to *tutoyer* Pia and addresses him as Pascal. "There. I've told you what I have in my heart . . . perhaps without enough caution . . . because of my true confidence in you," he ends.[36]

Those who knew Camus at the time of his departure from *Combat* sensed that he was bitterly disappointed that the lessons of the war and the occupation had gone unheeded and that his work at the paper had been in vain. "This press that we wanted to be worthy and proud is today the shame of this unhappy country," he wrote to a colleague the following summer.[37] Camus tried to see Pia that summer, and their friends attempted to arrange lunches, but Pia always declined. The break was definite. "I am not a person of intermittent friendships," Pia explained later. "From the moment I broke with Camus, my attitude towards him was all indifference and abstention."[38] After 1947, Pia returned to literature and wrote essays for magazines such as the right-wing weekly *Carrefour*. He wrote harsh reviews of both the *The Plague* and *The Fall* and disparaged the choice of Camus for the Nobel Prize. At the few other times when he referred to Camus in print, he spoke as if Camus were a distant acquaintance. Pia never called himself a critic, just as he never called himself a poet or a writer, although he produced several thousand pages of critical prose and had a considerable following. His work has now been collected in two fat volumes in France, although he said he didn't wish to be remembered or reprinted after his death.

Camus never expressed, even indirectly in his journal or his fiction, his own feelings about the break with Pia, who for almost a decade had been a caretaker, mentor, and kindred spirit. Perhaps the matter was too private to discuss, or beyond his understanding. A small firsthand report comes from Roger Grenier, Camus's friend and colleague at *Combat* and Gallimard, who remembers an afternoon after the estrangement when Camus came upon a coworker carefully separating his books from Pia's on her bookshelf. "You can put them back together," Camus said softly, Grenier reports.[39] Grenier, who has written memoirs of both Camus and Pia, has other small, incontestably real stories to tell. He tells of General de Gaulle saying of *Combat* to Malraux, "Too bad your friends are such do-gooders, they are the only honest ones around," and then offering to grant the paper an unconditional million francs to keep it in existence. He recalls how late one night after the paper had been put to bed, Pia pulled several staffers into his office to read them Camus's editorial for the next morning. He also says that in the end the break between Camus and Pia was more surprising and more important than the quarrel with Sartre. In 1978, when Herbert Lottman published his biography, he described Pia as Camus's "best friend and then worst enemy," a description that prompted corrections from Pia. "It would be truly inconceivable that Camus did not have among his childhood friends some closer friends than I, who was ten or twelve years his senior and about whom he knew almost nothing," he said, rather haughtily and perhaps protesting too much.[40] Pia sent copies of his remarks to Francine Camus, to which she responded with a poignant ferocity. "I think that you are wrong," she wrote, addressing Pia as *cher ancien ami,* "dear bygone friend." "The admiration and friendship that Albert carried for you (indeed without knowing much about you, or perhaps because he did not know much about you) could not compare to the fraternity he felt for a countryman and to a companionship . . . whose convictions he did not share." As for the rest, she said in closing, "we will all die with our enigmas and our secrets and our nostalgia."[41] Pia, tired and depressed in those last years, died eight months later.

The letters between Camus and Pia are stunning to encounter, because amid a sea of secondary supposition and explanation they are fresh and breathing. Even the smallest, most incidental bit of information is a potential revelation. Camus sends Pia three pounds of wild mushrooms from his mountain retreat at Le Panelier. An editor at Gallimard thinks *The Myth* was strongly influenced by Malraux. Pia suggests that Camus consider

a job as a forest agent in the countryside, in large part for the fresh air and good food. (He suspects that Camus will object to wearing a kepi, the pointed hat that is part of the uniform.) There is so much to learn in this inner sanctum that there is a tendency to hang on every word. It all sounds like real life. Casually, bigger new facts surface. Camus, still in Algiers after the closing down of the *Alger Républicain* and accused of having written "insane" articles harmful to the national cause, has lost his case in court and has been deprived of most of the salary still due him. In 1941 Pia and Camus are hatching ambitious plans to start a literary magazine called *Promenthée* in the free zone to supplant the now censored *Nouvelle Revue Française*, published by Gallimard. Pia supports Camus's refusal to censor the chapter on Kafka in *Sisyphe*. (Nonetheless, it is cut and appears thereafter in the literary magazine *L'Arbalète*.) As if I were panning for gold, I gather up bits and pieces with mounting expectation and excitement. Many such nuggets are bright with suggestion. From Oran in early 1940, Camus writes to Pia, "*Je m'ennuie comme un rat mort*," "I am as bored as a dead rat," and it occurs to me that even though this is a common expression in French, it, too, like the short reference to a rat in his journal, may be an inadvertent sign that *The Plague* is taking form. Even the paper on which certain letters has been written may have significance. Camus's letters appear variously on a page pulled from a ruled notebook or stationery from the Brasserie de la Renaissance in Algiers (the so-called Maison de la Bière, or House of Beer, where his uncle Gustave is a regular).

Considering such seductive material and the crop of new insights, I am distressed to realize that all this represents only a partial truth. For one thing, the correspondence between Camus and Pia is lopsided, because three-quarters of the letters come from Pia, skewing one's perceptions from the start. The correspondence also has gaping holes, because few of the letters are sequential—there are four from Camus, followed by a bundle from Pia, and then a few more from Camus at the end. In addition, several of Camus's letters—rather typically—are not dated. Often, to make sense of some bit of news, it is necessary to resort to sleuthing and supposing. (Camus must be writing from Lyon in the fall, because he sounds forlorn and makes a reference to *Paris-Soir*, but then why is he talking about Francine as a roommate?—because, according to all known facts, she is still supposed to be teaching in Oran.) Yet in the slippery venture of trying to understand the inner workings of another life, gaps and lapses may have as much veracity as solid facts, for full disclosure is not possible, even among friends. In the end, despite the discrepancies, there is in the letters a sense of continuity that comes from the intensity of feeling and the mutual involvement of the correspondents. There is also a story here, with a beginning, middle, and end. In the penultimate letter, dated November 1945, in which Camus expresses his disaffection with *Combat* and his need to take his leave, he is also asserting his independence and paying tribute to Pia's nurturing by relinquishing it. "We have done together what we had to do," he says. "All the same, each time that you and I find something else to do, you will find me there again."[42]

Looking back as an outsider over the last several years and taking account of the pressure building around Camus, I can find many reasons to explain why he was frayed. That he was even living in Paris was in itself remarkable, given how sick he was at Le Panelier, and the fact that, according to his doctors, he should not have ended his cure so soon. Little more than a month before leaving the farm for Paris, Camus had reported in a letter: "I don't have all my resources. I am very tired. It's more than a year that I have been doing combat with the angel." To dispel the gloom, he added, in his usual way, "It's necessary to know how to make friends with your rock."[43] Two years later, Camus was again depleted. The hardships of wartime and the effort to maintain several jobs, finish *The Plague*, and provide for his new family had taken their toll on his body and spirit. The disturbing state of the world sat ever more heavily on his mind. Camus was the only editorial journalist in France to express his unequivocal horror when the A-bomb was dropped on Hiroshima and to warn of the dangers of a cold war before it had even begun. He declared it indecent to celebrate the scientific achievement of the bomb, which he referred to as an instrument of "organized murder." Civilization has just reached the last stage of savagery, he wrote in his editorial of August 8.[44] After more than a year at *Combat,* Camus was also suffering from the stress of being a political and ideological spokesperson when he was struggling with his own political and ideological issues. The letter of withdrawal from the paper that he sent to Pia in November expressed his quandary: "Among the reasons I had for quitting the paper [a leave of several months the previous January], the first was certainly the disgust that came to me from all forms of public expression. I wanted to be silent. Practically speaking, I continue to speak every day, but I don't speak with my voice, every day I say things that two days out of five I don't approve. It's a terrible way to address the problems of coherence and responsibility as I intended."[45]

Camus had also written about Algeria in 1945. Prompted by his concern for his country in the aftermath of war as well as his desire to return home after an absence of almost three years, he had assigned himself a series of articles for *Combat* in the spring. In order to be able to report with authority, he had visited extremities and recesses that he had never seen, including the Saharan territories. He covered some 4,000 miles over the course of three weeks and gathered information from a cross section of the population. As in his prewar investigation of Kabylia, his purpose was to open eyes. In this case, it was also to diminish the abysmal ignorance in France about North Africa, he wrote, and "to remind people in France of the fact that Algeria exists . . . that the Arab people also exist . . . [that] these people are not inferior except in regard to the conditions in which they must live."[46] But by May 13, when the first of his six articles appeared, he was reporting not only on the poverty, the crop failures, and the continuing famine, but also on a grave political crisis.[47] Camus had still been in Algeria in late April when the French, in response to a mounting series of incidents involving Arabs against *colons,* sent the nationalist leader Messali Hadj into exile. But Camus was not on hand for the subsequent demonstrations for independence that began on May 8 in the small Muslim towns of Sétif and Guelma, near Constantine, touching off five days of spreading violence and bloodshed that took an estimated 150 European lives. Nor did he witness the gruesome reality of the so-called Repression—the bombardments, summary executions, and mass killings by which the French army and its aircraft restored order. The bloodbath was played down in metropolitan France, which during that week of May 8 was celebrating the end of the war in Europe. The communist paper *L'Humanité* counted only 100 or so rebel casualties, whereas military sources estimated Arab deaths at 6,000 to 8,000.

Camus's true feelings about "the events" are not on record, nor are his feelings about not having been present for what historians regard as the first shots of a war that officially erupted nine years later. His pieces in *Combat* are his only testimony, and they are determinedly measured and prudent—presented to readers as the important findings of a recent investigation. (Camus, writing as usual in the first person, did not identify himself as a homegrown Algerian. When letters to the editor questioned his authority and allegiance, *Combat* ran a note about his special credentials.) In these pieces, Camus describes the political discontent in the country as far deeper than a famine, noting that the world has been changing and that it is now too late for a policy of assimilation. He carefully explains the new coalition political party called Amis du Manifeste de la Liberté (referring to its manifesto of 1943 seeking an autonomous republic in a new anticolonial French federation) and its leader Ferhat Abbas, whom he trusts. He scolds the French press for inaccurate and irresponsible reporting, and for blaming the crisis on professional agitators. In conclusion, he speaks urgently of a need for resolution, persistence, and above all justice. Well before the beginning of the war, Camus is painfully aware of the increasing alienation of the Arab population is Algeria. "It is the infinite force of justice, and justice alone, that must help us to reconquer Algeria and its people," he writes.[48]

There is great urgency in Camus's words, and there is a sense of confrontation in his thinking, but the alarm and anguish that must have consumed him are held in check. Camus uses the words *hostility, fear, hate, indignation,* and *defiance* to describe the atmosphere in Algeria, but he mentions massacre and repression only once or twice. In the end, when he refers to the situation as serious rather than tragic, it is almost as if he were trying to reassure himself, as if he wanted to believe that the Repression hadn't happened. Camus had missed the political changes that had come in the war years when France's attention had been concentrated on fighting Nazi Germany and he had been more engaged in the Resistance than in monitoring the growth of Arab nationalism. He also did not have the ready information on the events at Constantine that he would have had if he were still living in Algiers. But clearly Camus was also playing the diplomatic role that he always would choose—taking the long view, struggling to keep a cool head whatever his private fears. As he said, he was trying not to add to the rancor and the hatred.[49] And clearly these events fed into the thoughts about violence and imperialism that he expressed in "Neither Victims nor Executioners" and then later into his plays about revolutionary violence. They also must have added to his sense of isolation. Few people in France showed any concern for the situation in Algeria, which seemed very distant. Most simply turned their heads. In the jubilation of V-E Day and liberation, the Parisian press gave the colonial crisis very little coverage, and what coverage it gave distorted the facts. As Beauvoir said in her memoir *La Force des Circonstances* (*The Force of Circumstance*), it was only later that they would learn of the enormity of the lies.

The pressures that Camus was experiencing in the mid-1940s were a small preview of what was to come in the 1950s. In his thinking, Camus was veering away from Sartre. As early as 1946, friends had detected cracks in the relationship, caused by Camus's anticommunism as well as his moralism. According to Sartre and Beauvoir, who, sounding like pure Marxists, described moralism as "the last bastion of bourgeois idealism," Camus was too concerned with moral issues at the expense of political ones. They said that for this reason they didn't think much of "Neither Victims nor Executioners," although, as Camus was openly criticizing Stalinist communism in these articles, that was only part of the truth. Camus "had no taste for the deliberations and the risk entailed in political thought," Beauvoir commented; "he had to be sure of his ideas so that he could be sure of himself."[50] He always kept himself covered, she continued; "he had an idea of himself which no task, no revelation, would have made him give up."

Beauvoir was quite smart about Camus, although she seems to have known little or nothing about his background or his illness, and she herself notes that they never talked about each other's books. But she was also quick to criticize him, particularly for not being what she wanted him to be, and for not being more like Sartre. She identified two Camuses: the funny, cynical, impulsive young lover of life and pleasure; and the serious, guarded, righteous writer. "Pen in hand, he became a rigid moralist who seemed to have nothing in common with our happy nocturnal companion," she complained. "He was aware that his public image utterly failed to coincide with the truth of his private self, and this occasionally embarrassed him."[51] Needless to say, Beauvoir preferred the fun-loving Camus, who, as she describes, would sit down on the sidewalk in the snow at 2 a.m. and meditate pathetically on love. She hoped that he would be able to rid himself of "yesterday's values" as she and Sartre had done, to throw some of his ballast overboard, as she put it. At this time, she still thought that nothing separated Camus from them ideologically "except a few nuances of terminology."[52]

Beauvoir's remarks struck me as self-serving and harsh when I first read them, but I liked her story about Camus sitting in the snow. It was charming, and it also offered a view from the outside world, a candid snapshot. I had not been able to identify with the public, social Camus as easily as with the private Camus, with whom I had a growing relationship. Sometimes I had to remind myself that while Camus was anguishing internally about this or that, he was also leading a relatively normal, even glamorous daily life, except during bouts of extreme illness. While I was concerned about his depression and stress, he was still writing and working productively at two jobs (at Gallimard, he was made the editor of his own series of books, which he called *Espoir* [*Hope*], and he published, most notably, the works of Simone Weil), as well as lecturing, keeping up a wide correspondence, encouraging other writers, flirting with attractive women, driving his old Citroën DS around Saint-Germain, and generally carrying on. He moved with Francine to a borrowed house in the outskirts of Paris for the birth of the twins and then back to Saint-Germain to a larger apartment on the rue Séguier. He was developing a close familial relationship with Gaston Gallimard's nephew Michel and Michel's wife, Janine, with whom he and Francine lived while they were waiting for the new apartment. He shouldered the role of new father; he worried about his babies in the cold winters and continuing food shortages; he grew impatient with their crying, which interfered with his work. (There are the typical album photos of him cradling the twins or holding them aloft.) He traveled again to Algeria to see his mother, to the United States for a long cultural tour, and to the provinces for vacations and rest cures.

In a way, the story about sitting in the snow was also sobering. I envied Beauvoir that moment with Camus—particularly its spontaneity. I sensed that I was developing an understanding of Camus. I had come to know and even anticipate his moods, the rises and inevitable falls. I was becoming more sensitive to different sides of his nature. His physical presence was growing on me too, the long face, the challenging eyes, the comical ear, the cigarette between his fingers or hanging from his lip. Sometimes I felt that he was about to enter the room. That spring in Paris, I half expected to see him on the street. Yet whatever the perceived intimacy, I was clearly the most distant of observers, a secondhand witness, a third party. I might have gathered many facts, read certain letters, seen certain photographs, always responding with the utmost sympathy and sensitivity, but in the end I was only a reader like the millions of others. Perhaps I was more assiduous, perhaps more caring. But the Camus I claimed to know existed only in my head. I was like an author who has fallen in love with one of his own characters.

It was beginning to dawn on me that if Camus was ever going to be more than an extension of my imagination, or a glorified research project, I needed some real-life contact with him—as a friend put it, some DNA. That is, I needed to find someone to talk to who had actually known Camus. Since almost everyone I encountered seemed to have some remote connection to him, I assumed that this was still possible. Recently at the theater I had encountered a man who worked at *Esquire* and had edited a short story of Camus's in the 1950s. He had never met Camus or even heard his voice, but this still seemed to be a positive sign. Given that Camus would have been in his late eighties then, there were not many surviving colleagues or friends. But I knew that Roger Quilliot was alive—he was the mayor of Clermont-Ferrand and by repute a crusty old socialist. There were Camus's children, Catherine and Jean, who were about my age, and to whom I could readily relate. Furthermore, after her mother's death in 1979, Catherine had assumed the role of literary executor, so I hoped that she would feel a professional responsibility to see me. I dispatched letters, which took me several days to compose, given the importance of my request. I described myself as an American writer who had been deeply influenced by Camus, and I signed off with an expression of my utmost respect, as is the formal custom in France. When several months passed and I had no responses, I decided to focus on sources closer at hand, specifically in New York, my home turf, where in my chronology Camus was about to land. In a way, it was a relief to leave Europe for a while. Knowing New York as well as I did, I wouldn't have to work as hard to imagine Camus's every move. In New York, too, the degrees of separation narrowed to one or two.

5

New York 1946

I n March 1946 Camus, too, was relieved to leave Europe. He had worked for three years without a day of rest. The long winter without heat or household staples had taken its toll, and the political scene as it was evolving deeply distressed him. "I am nauseated by the stupid and terrorized life that is made for us here," he wrote to Grenier in Egypt. "Like many French people, I am both immensely tired and indignant to no avail."[1] Life in Paris wears down your nerves and dries up your heart, he explained to his other faithful correspondent and former teacher Louis Germain.[2] To his friend Nicola Chiaromonte, an Italian author whom he had met as a fugitive from the Nazis in Oran and who was now writing for *The New Republic* in New York, he noted that he had devoted the time it would take to write *La Comédie Humaine* to trying to keep his babies warm. He was only mildly attracted to America, he added, and he longed for the sun, the light, and a sense of physical well-being. None-theless, the three-month tour on behalf of the foreign ministry came at the right time for Camus. Both Sartre and Malraux had preceded him to America. The tour was an honor, and it offered a much-needed respite. Camus wanted to talk with American students and writers, he told the committee. At sea on a slow freighter amid a few amiable new acquaintances, he seemed to find some ease.

To follow Camus around New York is also to visit the city in the year after the war, seven months after Eisenstaedt caught the joy of V-J Day with an image of a sailor kissing a girl in a tumultuous Times Square.

On the corner of Forty-sixth Street, there was still a GI exhaling puffs of a Camel on a high billboard. ("Real smoke," Camus noted in his journal on the night his ship docked.) Many of the men Camus met, like the Columbia University professor Justin O'Brien and the theatrical director Harold Bromley, were just out of the military. The devastation abroad hung heavy in the public mind. Columbia University dedicated the proceeds of Camus's lecture there to the children of France. Magazines like *Vogue,* which featured a Cecil Beaton portait of Camus in its June issue, carried essays about the precariousness of life in Paris and full-page ads for an emergency food drive. Before he left America, Camus would send home a 176-pound crate containing sugar, coffee, powdered eggs, flour, chocolate, soap, and baby food.

New York in the spring of 1946 looked much as it had a decade earlier, before the war, although change was in the air. The Empire State Building, which had broken into the skyline during the Depression, was still a wonder. The Bowery was still lined with bridal shops and flophouses for twenty cents a night. The El was running on Third Avenue and West Fifty-second Street was the place for jazz. I extracted these details from Camus's journal, which also records his visits to Harlem, Chinatown, Coney Island, Sammy's Bowery Follies, department stores, nightclubs, a roller ("rolley") skating rink, the Metropolitan Museum of Art, the Museum of Natural History, Reuben's for lunch, and the Plaza Hotel. In this log, Camus sounds like the stranger he was. America was a shock to him, and he found its way of life "curious" or contradictory. On debarkation, he had been detained by Immigration without any explanation —the result of the FBI's concerns about his work for a newspaper with the motto "From Resistance to Revolution." This made him feel all the more *dépaysé.* But all that he entered in his journal about the incident was, "Mysterious. This after five years of Occupation!" At first, Camus saw a lot of fellow Frenchmen—friends from the ship, friends of friends. He noticed the small things a foreigner would notice—the old-fashioned military costumes of doormen; the fleets of taxicabs "like scarabs" in red, blue, and yellow; the atrocious taste in men's ties. He liked ice cream, the zoo, and the way the skyscrapers always seemed to be revolving overhead. The city smelled like iron and cement, he said, *"un parfum de fer et de ciment."* The traffic on the West Side Highway sounded like the sea.

The orgy of light on Broadway and the magnificent stores full of food overwhelmed him. "I am just coming out of five years of night," he notes that first day.[3]

The timing of Camus's visit to New York was dramatic, even more so in hindsight. The nearness of the war, his role in the Resistance, the recent advent of the existentialist movement, and his new celebrity in Paris all make him an unusually compelling figure to imagine on the American scene. Only a month earlier Hannah Arendt had issued a first American report on existentialism to the readers of *The Nation,* naming Sartre and Camus as its chief exponents. (Books on philosophical problems were selling like detective novels in Paris. Plays of ideas were running for months. Philosophers were becoming newspapermen, playwrights, novelists. They were not members of faculties but "bohemians" who stayed in hotels and lived in the café, and for the moment their arguments appeared to be more important than the talk of politicians, she wrote, as if describing life on another planet. J. Edgar Hoover and others in the FBI had read her piece carefully.[4]) That Camus was also in New York for the publication of the English translation of *The Stranger* in April adds excitement to his arrival, for while still unknown to the world, he was on the verge of international recognition.

But Camus was at least a year away from the worldwide fame that would come with *The Plague,* and even among intellectuals he was probably best known as a courageous young journalist. The first mention in the United States of Camus's literary works had appeared in the *Herald Tribune* on the Sunday that his ship entered New York harbor. In a long, adulatory piece Justin O'Brien, who had been stationed in Paris during the war, pronounced Camus "the boldest writer in France today," mentioned *The Stranger* and *The Myth of Sisyphus,* and indicated that word about Camus was beginning to spread to America.[5] "Sartre has paved the way for him," O'Brien wrote, probably referring to Sartre's frequent mention of his friend's work during his visit, most famously in a lecture at Harvard, "Vercors has praised his young friend in New York, Chicago and San Francisco; our little reviews are beginning to mention his name with something like reverence. Genêt made some swash comments in *The New Yorker* on his popular play now running in Paris." By little reviews O'Brien meant magazines like the *Partisan Review,* which devoted a special spring issue to new French writing that year—"a gala presentation of what looked like a French Renascence in letters," the magazine's editor, William Phillips, described it.[6] Vercors was the celebrated Resistance author Jean Bruler, who had written the novel *Le Silence de la Mer* (*The Silence of the Sea*) and had also run an important clandestine magazine, *Éditions de Minuit*. Genêt was Janet Flanner, whose "Letter from Paris" was the best source of French cultural news in the country.

O'Brien also predicted that Camus's arrival would be one of the cultural events of the season, a forecast that was fulfilled four days later when more than 1,200 people attended Camus's lecture at Columbia (300 was the norm for such an evening). As the McMillin Theater had only 688 seats, it was packed to overflowing. This was the first such academic event since before the war, and the audience was primed by a new awareness of Europe and a new interest in the intellectual life that had been closed down since 1940. Camus shared the stage with two older writers from the Resistance (one of them was Vercors), but according to O'Brien, Camus "clearly dominated the evening." In his journal, Camus himself notes that after a few moments of stage fright, he was able to engage his public immediately.[7]

Camus's lecture was called "The Human Crisis" or, as delivered, "*La Crise de l'Homme*"—not surprisingly, he had chosen this subject over a survey of contemporary French literature and theater. The original text has been lost—an English translation published in a small American magazine serves as the historical record—but a copy of a similar lecture can be read in French in the Camus archive in Aix-en-Provence, and it suggests some of what Camus must have said that night. "*J'ai pour ma part toujours pensé qu'il y avait dans l'homme plus de choses à admirer que de choses à mépriser. C'est pourquoi il faut toujours commencer par la sympathie.*"—"For my part, I have always thought that there was more to admire in a man than to despise. That is why it is always necessary to begin with kindness." In addition to lines like this, which immediately conjure up an earnest Camus, the mere handling of this manuscript—a carbon copy typed without accents on pale blue tissue paper, and therefore probably typed in America—has some of the same grounding effect as reading the French text.[8]

In both these lectures, Camus sounded like a writer for *Combat*—as he had been and would be again, briefly, the following winter. He was direct, clear, and full of purpose and principle. He wanted to speak about the spiritual experience of the men of his generation, he said, men who were born on the eve of the Great War, experienced the Depression during adolescence, and were twenty years old when Hitler took power. "To complete their education, they were then provided with the war in Spain, Munich, the war of 1939, the defeat and four years of occupation and secret struggle," he continued. "I suppose this is what one calls an interesting generation." Camus described the human crisis by telling four stories that illustrated indifference toward and disregard for human life. He blamed the ills of society on "the cult of efficiency and abstraction," condemning Hegel's "detestable principle" that "Man is made for History and not that History is made for Man." He told his audience that as people of the twentieth century, they were all responsible for the war and its horrors, including torture and the death camps.

Camus had spent all day that Thursday writing and rehearsing his lecture. The previous afternoon, he had met with O'Brien and the other speakers in his hotel room to plan the evening. O'Brien always spoke of this first encounter with Camus in a shabby hotel on Upper Broadway as defining. He was struck by Camus's youth, he said, mentioning, too, how appreciatively Camus had eyed an attractive young woman on the elevator. He was charmed by Camus's ease and informality—during the meeting Camus was sprawled on the bed amid odd bits of notes—and by his disarming smile, that of a gamin, or street urchin, in O'Brien's description. It was clear that Camus took his role as a cultural ambassador seriously, at least with students. With the war still close and its effects still unfolding, he seemed to feel personally responsible for communicating its lessons. As a European and particularly as a Frenchman, Camus had experienced a war very different from that of the Americans. The contrast between the Paris he had just left—tired, dilapidated, devoid of traffic—and the exuberant, victorious New York he was encountering made this point concisely. While Paris was still caught in the miserable aftermath of the war, New York was all confidence, bubble, and new Buicks.[9] Camus found many things to admire in Americans—their energy, generosity, cordiality, and endless hospitality—but he worried about their compulsive optimism and lack of a sense of the tragic. While he wished that Europe could borrow some of America's energy, he thought Europe offered America a useful sense of disquiet.

Camus's schedule during that long spring included a dozen other lectures—at the New School, which was new then; at Brooklyn College, the French Institute, and the Associated Press in New York; and then on the road to a number of the top eastern schools: Vassar, Bryn Mawr, Harvard, Wellesley. At some of these stops, he spoke about theater or literature—he was often asked if he had been influenced by American novels, and he acknowledged that he was, mentioning Melville, Faulkner, and Hemingway. At other stops, he dug deeper into his original subject, warning of the dangers of inertia and the need for engagement, speaking forcefully, waxing ever more eloquent. Many of the lines he delivered now sound like classic Camus. "There is no liberty without dialogue, no dialogue without contradiction." "Our task . . . is to render justice imaginable in a world so evidently unjust. Naturally that is a superhuman task, but we call superhuman the tasks that men take a long time to accomplish."[10] Some of the language in the lectures can be found in Camus's future work. "There is in France and in Europe today a generation that takes the view that whoever puts his trust in the human condition is a madman, while whoever despairs of events is a coward," Camus told an audience of students. Seven months later, in "Neither Victims nor Executioners," he wrote: "I have always believed that if people who placed their hope in the human condition were mad, those who despaired of events were cowards."[11]

Camus has little to say in his journal about his lectures or the sessions with students, which he welcomed. (Nor does he write about being booed at the New School when he said that the Russian Revolution had taken too many lives.) Of his two days at Vassar, he writes, "An army of starlets who recline on the lawns with their long legs crossed. What they do for young people here is worth remembering."[12] But then neither does he mention the publication of *The Stranger* or his gala book party on the roof of the grand Astor Hotel on Times Square. He offers only a random account of his social life, which appears to have been very full, given his wide assortment of activities with old and new friends; his intense romance with a bright, pretty nineteen-year-old American student, Patricia Blake, whom he met at his lecture at the French Institute; and his general reluctance to be alone. ("He seemed to need constant companionship," one of these friends has recollected.) In addition to all the walking, sight-seeing, and dinners in cheap restaurants and cafeterias, there were nights at dance halls, jazz clubs, and bars, parties in Greenwich Village, and excursions to New Jersey, Washington, Cape Cod, and the Adirondacks. In the company of Patricia Blake, there were evenings at the theater and the opera, sorties to Chinatown, and visits to funeral parlors and cemeteries, which fascinated him. There were long talks and downtime with Nicola Chiaromonte, an intellectual soul mate and fellow activist, who also introduced him to his most interesting friends. His home base was a small duplex in the art deco Century Apartments on Central Park West, a loan from a generous fan, which was convenient for frequent strolls in the park and some twenty visits to the zoo.[13]

The spare impersonality of Camus's journal in America, which is more pronounced than it is in other journals, may in this case be revealing. Camus's visit lasted ninety-three days, almost the entire spring, which was the longest trip outside France of his life; but by his own admission, Camus didn't quite get America, and something uneasy and occasionally agitated rides behind his notes. While his entries are never dull, they are quite dispassionate, like routine attempts to keep a meaningful record of his travels. Despite keen observations and some animated description that brings a whiff of the1940s, eloquence comes only toward the end, after he has said that he is ready to go home. "I have suddenly ceased to be curious about this country," he announces sometime in May, with almost a month of his stay remaining. "And I see clearly the thousand reasons one could have for being interested in this place . . . but my heart has simply ceased speaking and. . . ."[14] The "and" and the final ellipsis are Camus's, as if to suggest the fruitlessness of further discussion.

In his last remarks about New York, Camus writes of rainy days, sepulchral skyscrapers rising from the gray fog, and his feeling of entrapment and abandonment in a landscape of "cement prisons." His prose has touches of poetry, but it is heavy and sad. Even on the long sea voyage home, when he is back in his element and comforted by the calm immensity of the Atlantic, sadness is there. But by then, it has become the familiar sadness of disappointment and discontent. He misses youth, with its impetuousness and passion, longs for "the impatient heart that I had at 20," and looks to the sea to restore his equilibrium. "Sad still to feel so vulnerable," he writes. "In 25 years I'll be 57. 25 years then to create a body of work and to find what I'm looking for. After that old age and death." He knows what is most important and yet he still finds ways to waste time. "I've mastered two or three things in myself. But how far I am from the kind of superiority that I so badly need," he concludes.[15] Camus, in his seriousness, has the ability to sound both young and stubborn and old and weary at the same time.

While he was in New York, Camus suffered from a recurrence of TB that could be at least partially responsible for his halfhearted response to the city toward the end of his stay. In his journal he speaks openly of fever and flu and, here and there, of a day in bed. ("Tired. My flu comes back. And it's on shaky legs that I get the first impact of New York," comes from the day of his arrival. "Wake up with a fever. Incapable of going out before noon," is from the next day.)[16] Casually, he put himself under the care of a doctor, Pierre Rubé, who had been one of his cabinmates on the *Oregon*. Rubé had trained as a psychiatrist and served bravely in the war, and Camus liked to socialize with him. Some of Camus's friends noticed his thinness, pallor, and sweaty brow—telltale symptoms of his disease—although newer acquaintances such as Lionel Abel and William Phillips, who knew only the fact of his TB, spoke mainly of his youth, good looks, and elegance. Patricia Blake, the most intimate of the observers, has said she thought Camus's condition that spring was grave. She became familiar with the hidden side of Camus: the daily fevers, the frequent exhaustion, and the four or five episodes of breathlessness and spitting of blood, when he felt so sick that he had to ask her to leave him. She knew all about his interest in deathbed stories, undertakers' journals, and the American death industry, which she attributed to a painful awareness of impending mortality.[17] She thought that he didn't expect to live a very long life.

Friends describe Camus's North American trip as a time apart, indicating that the experience was peripheral to the rest of his life. This tour and a similar trip to South America in 1948 were Camus's only ventures outside western Europe and Algeria. (His journals from these two trips were published together as *American Journals* after his death.) Camus used his South American material in an essay and a short story he wrote in the 1950s.[18] However, nothing about the United States ever cropped up in his future work, except in a magazine essay in France called "*Pluies de*

New York" ("Rain in New York"), which he wrote the following year as a form of closure.[19] This essay is melodic, dramatic, insightful, sometimes funny, and a reminder of how well Camus wrote. It is also a glimpse into how he wrote. All the raw material from the journal is there—the notes and comments about mournful skyscrapers, the sound of traffic, love of animals, and old floozies on the Bowery—but it has been refined and refigured into long, rolling, seductive sentences that build into a sophisticated and provocative portrait of a city that has ultimately eluded him. "After so many months, I still know nothing about New York," he writes: "whether one moves about among madmen here or among the most reasonable people in the world; if life is as easy as all America says, or if it is as empty as it often seems . . . whether New Yorkers are liberals or conformists, modest souls or dead ones; whether it is admirable or unimportant that the garbage men wear well-fitting gloves to do their work."[20] As Camus proceeds to pose his questions and enumerate the alternately endearing and infuriating aspects of a city that he finds alternately "delicious and unbearable," it becomes clear that he did get New York, and that his unwillingness to draw conclusions was a wise response to a restless, heterogeneous, multifarious city. It turns out that Camus liked things that devoted New Yorkers like—the morning and the nighttime skies (it was possible that New York was nothing without its sky, he said); the vertiginousness of tall buildings; the cry of a tugboat in the middle of the night; the sense of solitude and abandon. He liked its basic aspects of humanity—the bums, the eccentrics, the ethnic neighborhoods like Chinatown and Harlem. He enters notes about black kids playing ball in the upper reaches of Central Park and about the Negro population in general —"impression that only the Negroes give life, passion, and nostalgia to this country which, in their own way, they colonized."[21] At the end of the essay, Camus says that he loved New York, but then he qualifies his passion: "Sometimes one needs exile."[22]

My first interviews in New York made only the tiniest incursions into Camus's life, but that didn't matter at the time, when the mere fact of the interview process had its drama, and there was immense gratification in the live connections. Looking back now, I find that the sessions with

William Phillips and Lionel Abel, who appear directly or indirectly in Camus's journal, had an agreeable sameness. This is not to say that each one wasn't informative in an unpredictable sort of way and provided an impressive overview of Camus. What I mean is that what I was seeking from them was not ambitious, just a description, a firsthand report that would validate all the material I had been gathering. I wanted something personal.

The recollections of two members of the intellectual crowd that Camus came to know had seemed like an appropriate beginning. Phillips and Abel were writers, critics, and prominent, internationally connected voices at the left-wing monthly *Partisan Review* (*PR*). Phillips was its editor then, and he held spontaneous parties in his town house on East 12th Street, so he had known the social Camus as well as Camus the subject and author of pieces in his magazine. (*PR* reviewed *The Stranger* that spring and, later in the year, long before its American edition, published several chapters of *The Myth of Sisyphus* in a series called "New French Writing.") When he met Camus, Phillips was in his mid-thirties, a feisty young intellectual who a decade earlier had, together with Philip Rahv and F. W. Dupee, revived or, as it was said, "liberated" *PR,* which had begun as an organ of the Communist Party's John Reed Clubs. Although he was six decades older when I interviewed him in his apartment in a high-rise on the Upper West Side, he was still recognizable as a onetime firebrand, and he still enjoyed expressing his opinions—he thought *The Myth of Sisyphus* was too metaphoric and said that *The Stranger* had "aroused a surprising amount of attention"—and he was happy to recall the old days, if somewhat foggily. Arriving in the company of Nicola Chiaromonte, Camus had encountered Hannah Arendt, Mary McCarthy, Dwight Macdonald, Sidney Hook, and an assortment of other unnamed writers and radicals at his house, Phillips recollected. He didn't talk a lot—"only when he had something to say, which was refreshing"—and he spoke very little English, so there was constant translation. Phillips left it to me to imagine the intense, smoky atmosphere of those evenings and the connections Camus may have made among this company.

Decades after meeting Camus, Phillips published *A Partisan View,* a memoir that records a more deeply considered view of Camus than he offered me. Camus was "almost the opposite of Sartre," who was "short, odd-looking, one eye out of focus, tense, nervous" and endowed with "rhetorical flashiness" and "theoretical sweep," he describes in these pages. Camus, on the other hand, was "reserved . . . inordinately handsome, with a combination of sensitiveness and ruggedness, and a suggestion of bold-ness and adventurousness that must have been most attractive to many women. He was not an ideological talker . . . [but] talked about people and events in a rather personal and casual way, and though he indicated his disagreements, he was not nasty or malicious or self-promoting. One had the feeling that his vanity, which appeared to be enormous, was in his work and in his idea of himself—that is, at the core of his being, not in any aggressive behavior."[23] Wishing to be more expansive about Camus, Phillips had referred me to this book, and I was grateful for his portrait, which is unusually precise and something of a rave. In a practical way, however, I was much more affected by his remarks to me in person. "All I can tell you is that Camus was the most attractive man I have ever met," he had said in a rush at the very beginning of our interview. "Not just physically, in every way an attractive personality. He reminded me of Humphrey Bogart. I told him that. He had the same getup—he wore a tan raincoat—and he had the same jaunty appearance."[24]

Camus's resemblance to Bogart also came up immediately when I interviewed Lionel Abel. The startling thing was not the perceived likeness—*Vogue,* too, in its June feature, compared Camus to "the young Bogart"—but the fact that another radical intellectual from *PR* was choos-ing to comment on Camus's particular handsomeness before mentioning his work or his ideas and politics. Camus had elegance, Abel said several times, trying to recapture his aura. He had sophisticated Parisian manners and an incisive wit but also seemed to be a provincial. Camus was very French, and Abel specified that by this he meant French in a nationalist sense, too. "We were all thrilled with him," he said happily. Camus, for his part, was delighted by the comparison to Bogart and spoke of it fre-quently. He marked the tribute with exclamations points in one of his long letters to Michel and Janine Gallimard, adding, "You know, I can get a film contract whenever I want."[25]

Abel saw Camus four or five times in New York, and later they social-ized in Paris during the years when Abel was publishing a small magazine, *Instead,* with the surrealist painter Matta. In New York, he remembered a Sunday outing to Staten Island and Chinatown and a cocktail party at the home of Dorothy Norman, a columnist at the *New York Post* and a patron of the arts. She had arranged for Camus to meet the best-selling black novelist Richard Wright, who was about to become an expatriate in Paris. In Paris, there were lunches and dinners that included Francine, whom Abel found very attractive. Abel was offhand and chatty in giving his recollections, and ready to supply unexpected annotations—Albert and Francine looked like brother and sister; Edmund Wilson had doubts about *The Stranger*. This information had value then, because it was new and, like gossip, suddenly put me in the know. Abel mentioned that the writer Dwight Macdonald also happened by the Chiaromonte's that first afternoon, for example, and that he and Camus liked each other immediately— a very small piece of information, but it connected me to the fact that Macdonald later published several of Camus's essays in his magazine *Politics*. About Dorothy Norman's gathering (where there was a black pianist who had been invited in order to make Wright comfortable), he remembered that Camus talked to Wright about the status of Negroes in America and urged him to enjoy himself in Paris but to return to his country to fight for civil rights. Camus was instrumental in the publication of *Native Son* and *Black Boy* at Gallimard, and he saw Wright for an occasional dinner or in connection with a left-wing cause in Paris, but Wright of course never returned to America.

About Camus's life in Paris, Abel had very few substantial anecdotes to share, but he had an insider's view, and the fact that for a few years he had touched Camus's world and had known some of its principal players, added weight to a comment, a piece of gossip, or even an attitude. Abel, who had a keen memory and seemed to like to make pronouncements, spoke with confidence when he said that Camus didn't like New York, that everyone knew Camus was seeing other women, and that Sartre had remarked at a *PR* luncheon that Camus was a very good writer but not a genius. In describing Camus, Abel referred to Sartre frequently, perhaps because they had met during Sartre's own visit to New York a year earlier, or because, as Abel said, he had a particular affinity for the older, tougher, bleaker writer—he translated several of Sartre's plays for him for Knopf—or simply because the coupling and the comparisons had become automatic. Abel expressed deep disappointment that his own friendship with Sartre had reached an impasse over Sartre's unflinching support of

Stalin. He liked Sartre and Sartre liked him, he said. He also said that he was very sad when Sartre and Camus had their dispute in the pages of *Les Temps Modernes*. He liked both of them. Abel was still in Paris in 1952 when the controversy over *The Rebel* began. It was a time that was far more interesting than the present one, he concluded.

Fifty-two of the people Camus encountered in New York are mentioned by name in the biographies. Phillips and Abel are among them. So are two people with whom I spoke by telephone: the French writer and play-wright Michael Vinaver, who was a college student and an aspiring au-thor in 1946 when he contrived to meet Camus in the latter's hotel lobby; and Patricia Blake, who declined to talk about Camus because she was still hoping to write her own memoir about their long relationship. ("We were younger then than we would be now," is all that she would say.) Principal characters such as O'Brien, Chiaromonte, and A. J. Liebling all died in the 1960s, but there were others who might have been inter-viewed—I made a list that I still consult from time to time, consider ac-tivating, and then put aside. I got as far as looking in the telephone book for Marthe Eidelberg, the young French wife of a prominent Viennese psychoanalyst who had given a small dinner party for Camus. I went to the public library to check out Waldo Frank, a prominent journalist and cultural critic whom Camus met and liked, now relatively forgotten and long deceased. Frank, who wrote for the serious magazines of his day— he reviewed *The Stranger* for *The New Republic*—and also was the author of several lyric novels, was a radical, an idealist, and in later life some-thing of a mystic, I learned. "W. Frank. One of the few superior men I've met here" was Camus's journal notation. I considered the possibility of contacting Eleanor Clark, who was a Trotskyite, wrote for *PR,* and had reportedly sent Camus a bouquet of flowers. Her late husband, Rob-ert Penn Warren, was the author of *All the King's Men,* which had been a best seller while Camus was in town. But then I came upon Clark's obituary in the *Times*.

There were a few other interesting local characters that I either tried to or intended to contact before death or a serious illness intervened. The great-est loss may have been a nearly legendary professor of French literature,

Germaine Brée, with whom I had once planned to study for a PhD, and with whom Camus had stayed when he lectured at Bryn Mawr. Brée had established herself as an early and eloquent authority on Camus, but what I didn't know was that she had also been a childhood friend of Francine's family in Oran and had met Camus as a young man, and that she had known—specifically and profoundly—what she was talking about when she spoke of the power of the African landscape or of Camus as typically Algerian.

There are other lists that I have made, somewhat obsessively. For example, Camus might have met then some noteworthy people who aren't on record. Elizabeth Hardwick? Edmund Wilson? James Baldwin? Fiorello La Guardia? Georgia O'Keeffe? According to his journal he met O'Keeffe's husband, Alfred Stieglitz, whom he referred to as "the American Socrates," in their famous apartment on lower Fifth Avenue. Stieglitz died two months later. More provocatively, whom did I know later who had met Camus earlier and with whom I might have exchanged thoughts had I known then what I know now? This list is unsettling, because it includes major figures such as Dwight Macdonald, A. J. Liebling, and Janet Flanner, all people I encountered at *The New Yorker,* where I went to work on my return from France in October 1963. Macdonald, a big, stoop-shouldered man with a goatee and fierce opinions, was someone I saw, at least in passing, every day when he was around. Flanner, equally daunting in her own way—she had a heavy footfall, a whiskey voice, and a disarmingly direct manner—was only occasionally on hand, usually in the vicinity of the Teletype. In fact, I had numerous conversations with Liebling that autumn, because his office sat directly across the hall from the receptionist's desk, where during my first three months at the magazine I did the relief shift at lunchtime. Liebling died in late December, so those few months were his last. We talked about French food, horse racing, and John F. Kennedy. I brought him the afternoon newspapers, and he gave me his book about Earl Long to read. But neither he nor I ever brought up the subject of Albert Camus. I had no idea how deeply Liebling cared about Camus. It never even occurred to me that they might have been friends.

As a connection to Camus, even a belated one, Liebling is a prize. Liebling loved Camus. That is poignantly clear in the last piece Liebling wrote for

The New Yorker, a review of the first volume of Camus's notebooks that reads more like a final homage.[26] In a way, it was the second installment of the obituary that he had written for the magazine four years earlier, enriched by perspective and personalized almost to the point of intimacy. Liebling had first encountered Camus's work in 1943, when a friend in the Free French brought an issue of *Combat* to his hotel room in London, he wrote by way of introduction. When they met in New York, Camus looked "like a grave precocious boy" dressed in a weird, outdated 1920s-style suit, or as he described in his piece for "Talk of the Town," like a character in the comic strip *Harold Teen.* Liebling summed up Camus's career with pride and ironic understanding. He spoke of the impact of his early books and sudden fame—"Liberation found him internationally famous before he had been translated . . . which gave him the false aura (and one he did not need) of a prodigy." He explained Camus's diminishing status in Paris during the 1950s—Camus "commenced to disappear" and then was "buried for good"—as a consequence of his "reservations about the significance of Stalinism" and his refusal to take sides during the war with Algeria. With an almost audible cheer, Liebling noted Camus's renewed popularity since his death ("he is read, never so much read"). Liebling had a deep sense of what made Camus distinctive and different, and like any avid reader he was happy to have the private notebooks in hand for corroboration. The notebooks proved Camus's case all over again, he said. "He was not only a great writer but a great man, almost before he ceased being a boy." He was also the foremost North African writer in a western language since Saint Augustine, Liebling added for good measure, along with the fact that both men had been born in the region of Bône.[27]

Behind the frosted door of his office, Liebling must have been laboring over the review of Camus's first notebooks during the months of our short acquaintance. It is easy now to picture a dog-eared proof of the book lying amid the helter-skelter of newspapers and racing forms in the room, and a sheet of the mustard-colored copy paper that *The New Yorker* writers used then rolled up in his fat old Underwood manual typewriter. But Liebling was also very ill that fall and struggling to find his old eloquence and clarity. He had been carrying Camus's book around with him for months, it seems, worrying his thoughts and worrying his prose, trying to break through fatigue and depression to pay proper tribute to Camus. When Liebling died, Camus was still foremost in his mind; according to Jean Stafford, Liebling's wife, in the last delirious days he spoke only in French and addressed himself to his old hero.[28]

That whole year was a terrible one for Liebling, Stafford recalled. To combat his melancholy and his writer's block and perhaps to jump-start his review, Liebling had returned to North Africa in the spring, revisiting a place that he loved and from which he had reported in earlier decades. His experience in Algeria—"that strange country that was distinctly not a province of France," he called it knowingly in his text—had begun with his months in Oran and Algiers as a war correspondent after the Allied invasion, the very months when Camus was first sealed off from home. In November 1942, Liebling was following the shifting line of the First Infantry Division, but he was also "getting the feel of North Africa," as he put it, and by his second dispatch he was able to write perceptively about corrupt politicians, rich *colon* landowners, and the disenfranchised *indigènes*. ("They talk like Mississippians," he said of the landowners.[29]) Fourteen years later, he was covering the war of independence and telling the story of a French friend near Algiers whose farm and orchards had just been destroyed by rebel terrorists.[30] Referring to guerrilla activity in the countryside and bombs exploding in popular cafés in the city around the rue Michelet, his tone was ominous. As he described the sticky heat and patrols of soldiers with tommy guns weaving among the tables, Liebling referred to Camus, saying that the people in town had the agitated air of the crowds in *The Plague* when the epidemic is first rumored. That trip Liebling stayed at the Saint-George Hotel, high on a hill above Algiers, which had been Allied headquarters during his first tour. He was given Eisenhower's old room. The Saint-George was also where Camus stayed when he came back to visit his mother.

Camus would have liked Liebling's pieces on Algeria. It is possible that he read them. He also would have liked Liebling's pieces on Izzy Yereshevsky's I & Y all-night cigar store or Colonel Stingo and the various other con men and low-life characters he memorialized in the pages of *The New Yorker,* and of course he would have applauded the press criticism that Liebling wrote from 1945 on. In fact, Camus and the high quality of *Combat* were the factors more or less responsible for Liebling's decision to revive *The New Yorker*'s "Wayward Press" column, once Robert Benchley's turf, and to keep a sharp eye trained on the state of the American newspaper, in his opinion sadly diminished from its glory days in the nineteenth century. Liebling's deeply fraternal feelings for Camus were founded on their shared ideals in journalism—in the second sentence of that first "Talk of the Town" piece, he mentioned Camus's idea for a newspaper whose chief concern would be to evaluate the probable element of truth in other papers' main stories. At the time they met, Liebling was completing a volume called *La République du Silence,* a sampling from the thousands of pieces of Resistance writing he had compiled to tell his own version of the heroic daily struggle under the occupation. And there were a dozen other areas of common interest to link the two men: Stendhal, Gide, prizefighters (among the sources, Liebling is the only one to mention that Camus was a middleweight boxer before his TB was diagnosed), undertakers, language, and racism or any other form of injustice. Liebling was an instinctive, wide-ranging reporter, and an immense variety of people and things activated his wry, compassionate prose. He wrote like a storyteller and he loved to write, but he was also disappointed in himself because he had never written a novel, and this disappointment added to his admiration for Camus.

Rereading Liebling, it is easy to see how he and Camus could be friends. (Camus told a friend that it was love at first sight.) Rereading Liebling is also the only way to interview him about Camus now. Because I trust his instinct for choosing the right people as objects of his affections and his prose, his friendship with Camus is affecting in ways that go far beyond the fact of it, or the frequency of the encounters, or even the intensity of the feelings. Liebling was a master at spotting phonies, and he immediately recognized Camus as authentic. I don't know how many times the two men met—three or four times in New York, it seems; more than that in Paris. In his magazine pieces, Liebling mentions only an evening of "pubcrawling" on the Bowery, and the fact that in 1948, Camus arrived at his hotel in Paris on a motorcycle. During the evening on the Bowery (the most sinister quarter in the city, Camus said), the two had a rather rowdy time together, moving from a tour of the fancy bridal salons in Little Italy to a string of neighborhood bars, drinking a lot (particularly Liebling), ending up in a seedy café listening to old actresses sing about wasted lives and lost love. Liebling was flattered to be hanging out with a heroic and companionable young Frenchman who also seemed to be very interested in him, and Camus loved seeing the underside of the city with such a wry and seasoned guide. They also found a lot to talk about.

I have not located any letters between Camus and Liebling, despite the fact that letters seem like a very likely extension of their relationship. Letters might provide more details about their social life over the decades. But, in the end, none of this matters very much, because the simple truth is that who Liebling was points up who Camus was. It's not that they both liked sports, women, and bonhomie and were devoted to their mothers. It is not even that Liebling seemed to be unusually perceptive about the private Camus. "He felt the world as close as water then and never grew the scales appropriate to a Big Fish. He was without insulation—the antithesis of the detached Stranger," Liebling wrote at the end of his obituary on Camus.[31] The fact is that when I reread Liebling and see the qualities that made him such a singular reporter, I relate him to Camus, his mentor and in many ways his hero. There is a reflected image, refracted light.

I am sorry that there isn't a photograph of Camus and Liebling on record, for they would have made a curious contrast: Camus the gazelle, Liebling the walrus. I am sorry, too, that I have not found a photograph of Camus and Blanche Knopf in New York, because it might suggest some of the chemistry between them—this smart, difficult woman with red nails and heavy gold jewelry and the handsome young North African in the oddly cut suit. Blanche, who had cofounded the Knopf publishing house with her husband, Alfred, in 1915, was of *un certain âge* when she met Camus at the Ritz Hotel in Paris just after liberation, the year that Alfred put her in charge of Knopf's European list. ("Better buy Camus," he had cabled his European representative in March, just before he sent Blanche abroad on what would become her regular spring and autumn rounds.) She had a particular genius for making connections and attracting the right people, and during these early postwar years, she and Knopf were pioneers in publishing modern European literature in English. (In 1949, the French government duly made her a *chevalier* in the Légion d'Honneur for her support of French literature.) In a stable that grew to include Sartre,

Beauvoir, and Genet in addition to earlier members such as Jules Romains and André Gide, Camus always held a special place. As Blanche recorded in a long, loving memoir published the year after Camus died, "within that changing transient Paris, there was established between us a trust and an honesty I have rarely felt with anyone else."[32]

There was more to their relationship from Blanche's point of view. Her memoir conveys intellectual interest, understanding, and ease between the two of them that ran deeper than the usual sense of camaraderie and cooperation that accompanies an author-editor relationship. "I had the feeling of being with a close and intimate friend. I believe this was true. Camus said very often it was so," Blanche writes. Her portrait of Camus may have been self-serving, as memoirs about famous people often are, and there is very little beyond some correspondence to document Camus's own view. The memoir is effusive almost to the point of girlishness or silliness, devoting considerable space to Camus's physical description as well as his brilliance. "In spite of his youth and the small amount of his produce, his outlook on the world we were in then (three weeks after the end of the European war) was enough to show me his greatness as a philosopher and as a humanist." But Blanche's portrait is also rich in personal details, and so infused with feeling that however romanticized it may be it is also quite convincing.

At least twice a year for the next fifteen years, author and editor met for a few morning hours at the Ritz Hotel in Paris, always occupying a quiet corridor that in the afternoon filled with *grandes dames* taking tea. They drank coffee, bourbon, or Badois (a sparkling water), smoked incessantly, and talked—about Camus's work, his future, his past, young writers in France (for Blanche's benefit), American writers, "everything except politics." As a matter of course, Blanche came to know about aspects of Camus's life outside his books: his bouts of poor health, his involvement with young intellectuals during the Hungarian revolution, his long hours of work in the theater, his deep depression after winning the Nobel Prize, his search for a house in the country, even his devotion to his mother: "his most beloved lady," as Blanche describes her. Blanche purchased a much-coveted American raincoat for Camus at Brooks Brothers—the one he wore in Cartier-Bresson's photo on the dust jacket of *The Fall*. (When he announced that "it fit him like a glove," she wrote

back that to know that the raincoat fit like a glove frightened her.) Together with Alfred, she was present at the Nobel Prize ceremonies in
Stockholm, where "he delivered one of the great speeches of our time"
and "chacha-ed all night." (It was the first time she had made the trip,
although ten of Knopf's authors had been winners.) Primarily, she was
his editor and played a role in the development of his career. "Thank you
for your constant kindness . . ." he wrote in 1955. "I know I'm very lucky
. . . and my gratitude to you is always there."[33] The last communication
between Blanche and Camus was an exchange of letters in December 1959
about *The First Man,* on which Camus was finally hard at work. He wrote,
"I am working for you because I know how passionately you feel about
this book in which I am so deeply engaged."[34] He had promised Blanche
that he would come back to New York for its publication and that they
would be photographed with the book between them. Blanche wrote
back, "You are *un amour* to tell me that you are writing for me—yes, and
for you and for the world. This you well know. Bless and all my best."[35]

Blanche, of course, was a secondary editor for Camus, responsible for
bringing his work to an American audience, often in tandem with Hamish
Hamilton, who published Camus in England. Nonetheless, she still seems
to have had considerable impact on the course of his work simply by encouraging him and prodding him at crucial moments. She came to know
how slowly and fastidiously he wrote, and she worried about bridging the
long gaps between books—urging him to publish *The Fall* as an independent novella instead of as part of a later collection of stories called *The Exile
and the Kingdom,* and pushing him on with *The First Man.* Knopf issued
Camus's works for Americans in a different order from Gallimard's publications for the French. Camus's first two novels were published long before
The Myth of Sisyphus, for example—even Camus thought it best to hold
back the philosophy until Americans were acquainted with his other work—
and his plays did not appear until in the late 1950s, and then in a collection.
This meant that Camus's work in English did not have whatever added
impact came from publishing a play, a novel, and an essay together in a trilogy or themed cycle, as he had so carefully conceived. As for Camus the
public figure and public speaker, Americans were not exposed to his journalism and political commentary until after his death and after the fact, when
a catch-up collection, *Resistance, Rebellion and Death,* was published in 1961.

Apart from the memoir that was published in *The Atlantic Monthly* after his death, Blanche's correspondence with Camus provides the only source material for their relationship. About fifty of their letters are stored in the Knopf archives at the Ransom Center at the University of Texas in Austin, filed together with Blanche's letters to translators and agents, copies of radiograms of congratulations, and various in-house memorandums. They are not as rich or as riveting as some literary correspondence, because they address almost exclusively the practical questions of royalties, text cuts, and press reviews that were their raison d'être. Yet however prosaic, the small matters of publishing a book manage to take on seductive meaning when they involve Camus's royalties, jacket photos, or inclusion on the best-seller list, and when they are couched in the ever-warming prose of two characters of considerable interest.

After the success of *The Plague* in America, for example, Camus writes to ask if he has enough money to buy a motorbike. After the death of Dylan Thomas, he asks that fifty dollars be taken out of his account and contributed to the poet's memorial fund. Camus's interest in his sales figures is interesting, as are the sales figures themselves. Three thousand copies of *The Plague* were sold during the first week after publication, for example, which was spectacular even for Knopf. (During the previous month, in what must have been a historic compaign for the publicity department, Knopf had released at three-day intervals a series of cards with the figure of Death and this message, in sequence: "THE PLAGUE is coming! It has already struck Europe! More than 100,000 in France have been swallowed up by it! It will sweep America! ALBERT CAMUS is responsible for it!")[36] Six years later, expectations for *The Rebel* are so modest that only 1,500 copies are printed at first. *The Fall* makes number seven on the *Times* best-seller list for two consecutive weeks. Walter Wanger options it for a movie in which he hopes Spencer Tracy will star. Blanche keeps an eagle eye on the marketplace. She proposes "two smash ads in the dailies as quickly as possible" to advertise *The Plague*. Wondering if existentialism isn't passé, she questions the publication of *The Myth of Sisyphus* (which eventually appears in 1955). Ever hopeful, she sends complimentary copies of *The Rebel* to Arthur Schlesinger, Lionel Trilling, Allen Dulles, Eric Severeid, Edward R. Murrow, and others. The years roll by, and the salutations between editor and author shift from "Dear Albert

Camus" and "*Chère* Madame Knopf" to "*Cher ami*" and "*Chère amie*" and even "*Cher* Albert" and "*Chère* Blanche." It is like a series of small dance steps, with an occasional unexpected flip (in the case of a contractual misunderstanding, there was a sudden reversion to "Mr. Camus" signed "Mrs Alfred A. Knopf") and an occasional warm embrace (from Camus: "*Et je pense à vous, comme toujours, de tout coeur,*" "I think of you, as always, with all my heart."). Blanche's letter of December 29, 1959, her last, closes with "Now a very, very Bonne Année—and that Bonne Année means a great deal to me where you are concerned."

For an eager reader of the letters, there is rewarding peripheral material too, which provides its own historical enlightenment. In 1948, there is a bill for $17.43 for cartons of cigarettes to be shipped to agents and publishers across Europe. Embroidered men's handkerchiefs are also dispatched abroad. As a reminder of Blanche's many close literary relationships, a small sampling of her letters to other clients—V. S. Pritchett, Madame Prunier (of the famous restaurant), Eric Ambler, Elizabeth Bowen, Angela Thirkell—is found in the Camus files. ("Darling Angela, You are as wonderful as ever.") Blanche also conducts a steady correspondence with her longtime friend Jenny Bradley, who with her late husband, William, had founded an influential international literary agency in Paris in the 1920s and handled Americans such as Edith Wharton, John Dos Passos, and Henry Miller. (On June 16, 1949, Blanche notifies Jenny that she has rejected the first volume of Simone de Beauvoir's *The Other Sex*." It seems to me that a great big two-volume Kinseyan report is pretty much out of line today, particularly with the Kinsey report on women coming through, and I believe you can let this go elsewhere." Several months later, however, Beauvoir's *The Second Sex* appears on Knopf's list, so Blanche has apparently changed her mind, perhaps on Jenny's advice.)

In her letters Blanche shows herself to have been tough, clever, and astute. When another publisher, New Directions, is interested in bringing out *The Myth of Sisyphus,* she squelches the competition. Where other readers waver, she is quick to grasp the metaphoric nature of *The Plague* and the full meaning of *The Fall*. Despite obstacles (including a poor translation that eventually must be redone), she thinks that it is important to publish *The Rebel*. Because Camus's Nobel Prize acceptance speech has dazzled her personally, she sends it out as a brochure. Not surprisingly,

Blanche cares about clothes, maintains relationships with French couturiers, and for the Nobel ceremonies engages Dior and Balenciaga to make her dresses. "You have my measurements, can't spend too much but it must be elegant," she writes to Dior, who offers a silk dress in a "ravishing green faille" that is, conveniently, on sale.

All these small details are strangely satisfying. At first, because they are newly unearthed, they seem to bear almost as much weight as the larger facts of Blanche's life. This is also true of the small revelations about Camus, which surface unexpectedly. There is a mention of a little notebook in which he was always writing, which I imagine full of snippets of street conversation. There is his resistance to requests for biographical material for book jackets, which provides new evidence of his innate modesty. His desire to help a Brazilian couple he has met on his South American tour find work in France confirms his irrepressible generosity. Camus turns down Blanche's request to write a preface to a book called *The Tunnel,* explaining, "I detest prefaces. I'm not old enough for that."[37] He declines to read a book called *A Long Day's Dying*—ironically—because he is *"toujours malade."* When Camus actually refers to his illness or his inability to write, or in late 1949 when his secretary, Suzanne Labiche, writes to say he is *souffrant* and indisposed and working a maximum of two hours a day, the gravity of his condition takes on a new reality.

Even if the letters ultimately provide only brief glimpses of Camus, they have an effect. Sometimes they are out of sequence or misdated or contain puzzling information—in the mid-1950s Blanche refers to Camus's working on a novel about the Hungarian revolution; this novel must be *The First Man* but, as it exists, that work has nothing to do with Hungary. Sometimes the letters are simply humdrum and thin on information, but they still register as genuine handwritten or hand-typed artifacts, and in some mysterious way they affect the psyche. Suddenly 1946 doesn't seem so distant, and the thought that *The Stranger* is about to make its appearance in America produces a jolt of excitement. Suddenly Blanche materializes as the force that she was in American letters. It took courage to introduce a new foreign writer then, Justin O'Brien said of her, adding that it was not necessarily the moment for America to prize pessimism and lucidity. Suddenly, Camus has come a step closer too. His voice—his everyday voice, relaxed as it was only in letters and with friends—is almost audible. He is there the way he is in the photographs, caught in a freeze-frame and 100 percent authentic.

In Austin there was another moment of connection, and it had nothing to do with Camus's presence, or at least not with his voice, his thoughts, or his image. This came on day three of my research, when the librarian at the Ransom Center brought in its copy of the first American edition of *The Stranger* and set it down on the desk before me. It was a small book, perhaps five by seven inches, presented without the heavy-duty protective wrapping and white gloves that usually accompany an old and rare book, so I was unprepared for the emotional response it elicited. I don't know what I had expected the dust jacket to look like—I think I had imagined only a straightforward rendering of the title. This jacket, in sophisticated sepia-and-white, showed the face of a dark-haired young man with his eyes obscured by the word *Stranger,* and it evoked such loneliness, defiance, and sadness that it was searing. The copy on the front jacket flap described the book as "an indelible picture of a helpless human being." "*The Stranger* is a short novel about an ordinary little man living quietly in Algiers. Slowly but inexorably life begins to stalk him. The pace quickens until the little man commits a useless murder and reaches its climax after its trial," it said. As I held the book, I found myself on the verge of tears. It was a relic, still warm with its origins. For a moment, I could feel the pulse of 1946. Camus was new then. He was a European, and to many readers his thinking was foreign. In *The New Republic* that spring, Nicola Chiaromonte praised *The Stranger* as "a tragedy of integrity such as modern man can sense it."[38] Meursault, he said, was "everyman, with a vengeance." In *Time,* the reviewer labeled Meursault "Trigger Man" and dismissed *The Stranger* as "philosophical doodlings." "Existential pessimism underlines every cold gross irrational detail of the story," he said with palpable anger. Like a measure of Camus's infancy, the biographical material on the back flap of *The Stranger,* although it identified him as one of the leading writers of the Resistance, was only a sentence long. By the time *The Plague* appeared, he merited a photograph at his desk (he was wearing a suit) and a résumé that mentioned his early jobs in the weather bureau and at a shipping company. "Camus enjoys sea-bathing, bright sunlight, human emotions, the simpler pleasures and—on the intellectual side—thinking clearly," the copywriter, who sounds a lot like

Blanche, said. "He has been described as the precursor of a new French classicism, a literature of clarity, logic, and mental independence."

I was in Austin for almost a week that summer, which was the summer before George W. Bush was elected president. From 9 a.m. to 5 p.m. I was researching Camus in the Knopf archives, working against the clock to read the files that were retrieved for me each day from a vault deep beneath the library. After hours, I was exploring the city in a half-hearted way that resembled killing time. The school year had ended, so the campus was quiet and lazy; the fraternity houses around its periphery were being cleaned and spilled broken furniture and empty beer kegs onto the front lawns; the coffee houses and taco joints on the main drag were virtually empty. I wandered farther afield and found the governor's mansion in the center of town, where small bronze Texas stars are embedded in the pavement. I ate ribs and cheese grits at the original Stubb's. On my last night, I drove my rented car down to a park by Town Lake where a hundred thousand bats take to the sky at sunset. As I waited for their appearance, it struck me as comical that I was spending my days in close quarters with Camus and Blanche and my nights touring the capital of Texas. Yet I was as much a tourist in Camus's past as I was in the coincidental present in Austin. I was also getting accustomed to ironic situations. The sort of double displacement I was feeling was in the nature of research.

When I decided to move from being a reader and researcher to being a part-time investigative reporter, I was moving from a quiet armchair into a busy street, a livelier but riskier situation. The street was not as busy as it might have been ten or twenty years earlier, when more of Camus's friends were alive, but it was still full of promising characters with connections. Over the next several years, I interviewed eighteen people who knew Camus. They were an odd and unpredictable lot—Chiaromonte's widow Miriam, the son of Camus's good friend Urbain Polge from Provence, Camus's theatrical agent, and an exceedingly modest Algerian friend were among the first—but they were generous with the truth, in small and sometimes in surprisingly large ways. I came to think of them as live wires that ran through Camus's life to mine and charged all that I knew with new energy. From their memories, I began to put together a tentative portrait of Camus—one that was by nature more like a series of working sketches. To fill in gaps, I interviewed an assortment of people who knew a lot about Camus—his biographers, a TB specialist, and several prominent critics—and I talked with some of my friends who had important experiences reading Camus and who felt, as I did, that he had influenced their lives, or, as William Styron put it, "radically set the tone for my own view of life and history."[39] To this living matter, I added numerous extended sessions in the Camus archives in France and a few briefer ones in the Beinecke Library at Yale, where the Chiaromonte papers, and in particular the Camus-Chiaromonte letters, are kept. I watched tapes of many of the talk shows and documentaries on French television that had followed the release of *The First Man*. I continued to read and reread, often finding that I either had forgotten or was revising earlier impressions. The vintage copies of Camus's notebooks that I had acquired in college began to separate and shred in all this latter-day hyperactivity.

Rather typically, the two people I wanted most to see, my original designated targets, were the most difficult to corner. Roger Quilliot, secondary mentor and *frère semblable,* responded to my letter after six months of silence (and wrong addresses). By the time I heard from Catherine Camus, I had become somewhat desperate about my inability to reach her, for it was becoming increasingly clear not only that she was the most significant living relative, but that, as literary executor, she held the keys to the kingdom. Without her explicit permission, I had no ability to see any relevant artifacts or papers at the Bibliothèque Nationale or the literary archive called the Institut Mémoire de l'Édition Contemporaine (IMEC) or even at the University of Texas. It was only at the Beinecke Library at Yale, to which Miriam Chiaromonte had strongly recommended me, with what I perceived to be a spirit of complicity, that I was able to pass under the screen, as it were, and enter without a note from the family. It was also at Yale that I felt, at least for an afternoon, that I had entered a rare state of intimacy with Camus.

6

Back to Europe

Nicola Chiaromonte, it turned out, was a charismatic figure in his own right. This is clear in the recollections of the intellectual crowd in New York, into which, by my timetable, he had recently introduced Camus. Exiled from Italy as an antifascist; a member of the air squadron André Malraux organized for the war in Spain (he was the model for the character Scali in Malraux's novel *Man's Hope*); stocky, dark, and intense, Chiaromonte had seductive credentials as a man of action. With a distrust of ideologies and a belief in the power of the individual to pioneer change, he had made a name for himself in America with his articles in *The New Republic, Politics,* and *The Nation.* Mary McCarthy pronounced Chiaromonte "the friendship of her life," in large part because he had changed the way she saw the world. Chiaromonte was interested not in practical politics but in ideas for their own sake. He talked about the classics and had a passion for Tolstoy and Plato. His friend Niccolò Tucci, the novelist, said Chiaromonte was like a Benedictine monk, "both brilliant and truly good."[1] (William Phillips, in pointed contrariness, said to me that he considered Chiaromonte a rigid moralist and an anarchist.)

Most of these attributes also bring Chiaromonte's close friend Camus to mind. Camus had first appeared in Chiaromonte's life in Algiers in 1941, when Chiaromonte was being chased out of Europe as an antifascist and an anti-Nazi and Camus gave him shelter at Maison Fichu until he found safe passage to Casablanca and subsequently New York. In Chiaromonte's memory, Camus was then a very seductive young man to encounter. At twenty-eight, he was famous locally as the leader of a convivial group of young journalists, aspiring writers, students, friends of the Arabs, and enemies of the local bourgeoisie and Pétain. He loved theater and put on plays—at that moment he was directing himself as Hamlet with his new wife, Francine, as Ophelia. Evoking the desperate gaiety of the last days before the immediacy of the war hit North Africa, Chiaromonte recalled how Camus and his *copains* "lived together, passed the days on the seashore or hillside, and the evening playing records and dancing, hoping for the victory of England and giving vent to their disgust with what had happened in France and to Europe."[2] Solitary and sick of the war, he liked being in their company, he said; he liked the warmth and the youth. Older and already dangerously engaged, he, in turn, awakened Camus and Camus's friends to the possibility of doing something to fight the Germans.

Chiaromonte described his friendship with Camus as instinctive—their way of being together. At its core was something unspoken, something that shows up in the trust and openness that lie at the heart of the letters they exchanged over the years, and something that by 1946 had been revealed as a shared system of values. "We are so few, Chiaromonte, so few," Camus had written to his friend in November 1945, speaking of their desperate concern about the state of the world. "I don't know what I would give to speak to you one day with an open heart."[3] In the months leading up to his departure for New York in March—Chiaromonte was there on the pier to meet his ship—Camus had already begun to address issues, as if laying the ground for their reunion. "Justice is the concern of everyone, freedom of only a few. That is what must change," he writes in January, adding that they will examine this issue fully at a more opportune time. (He has a cold, he explains, and a shot in his arm has made it difficult for him to write legibly.)

The revelations in Camus's letters are unpredictable and abbreviated, but tantalizing nonetheless, shorthand notes from a real life. Mixed in with everyday chatter ("Devoured by money troubles" or "We're without a government . . . but the French, naturally, don't care"), local news ("what a funny Bible," he says of Beauvoir's *The Second Sex,* which has just been published), and general updates, there are relatively few references to the political matters of conscience that are so fundamental to their relationship. Camus speaks of an important common undertaking, a keen inter-est in having John Hersey's *Hiroshima* translated, the publication of cer-tain *Combat* pieces in America, a passing encounter with Koestler, a falling-out with Sartre and the staff at *Les Temps Modernes* over his criti-cism of an essay on the Moscow show trials by the philosopher Maurice Merleau-Ponty. ("I'm not in great shape with the team at *TM,* having told them a little crudely, I fear, what I think of the magazine and the articles of M. Ponty. It's idiotic, but there are some moments when one is not in control anymore."[4]) There are a few comments about *The Plague;* he has finished it, but wonders whether it merits publication. There are more comments about his fatigue, his sickness, and his family. (To the twins, who have just begun to talk, he has given a first lesson. To the question "who is the plague" Jean responds *c'est Cathie.* To "who is chol-era," Catherine responds Jean. To "who is the victim," the two of them say, *c'est papa.*) Most constantly, there is the expression of his affection for Chiaromonte and his wife, Miriam (or "Myriam"), and of his belief in the importance of loyalty and friendship. None of this material is very substantial, but that doesn't matter. The steady stream of small facts and private references over the undercurrent of trust and emotion provides another take on Camus.

Reading the Camus-Chiaromonte correspondence was my first ex-perience using original material, which gave the contents a flush of moment that has become inseparable from their significance. I was not prepared for the immediate sense of intimacy that came with handling these letters, which were handwritten and, even when presented in card-board boxes and manila folders, had the special aura of love letters. Nor had it occurred to me that once the letters were in my possession, I would be unable to read them because of Camus's notoriously difficult hand-writing. Trying to read Camus's script, which at a casual glance looked quite elegant, if rather small, was like trying to see a tiny object in a very dark closet. Struggling to decipher the meaning of the remote islands of tight little letters, I thought of the foreword to *The First Man,* in which Catherine Camus tells of the many years it took her to translate her father's manuscript from his original hand into a typescript. For the better part of an hour, in and out from behind the magnifying glass that I had initially disdained, I would study configurations of letters that I knew to be the key to something important, but without even a wisp of a clue as to their intent or their identity. Was it a *r* or *t*, *vous* or *nous* or maybe *voir* or *voix*? *Témoignage* or *voisinage* or Voltaire? Was there another word or letter that resembled the one in question that I could discern from its context and use to crack the code? Again and again I would read a sentence, backing up to begin it again in an effort either to jump-start or jump over a recalcitrant passage, only to find myself still stuck. I photocopied Camus's most important letters so that I could continue my decoding at home. But my transcriptions from the Beinecke holdings still contain passages that read something like: "The least—now knows that we are dying in the—of borders (or limits?) and that it is necessary to make it break out, blow it up? ring out?)." ("*Le moindre—sait maintenant que nous crevons dans le—des frontières et qu'il faut le faire éclater.*")

Eventually, when I figured out that Camus's *d*'s were shaped like backward 6s, that his *r*'s looked like *v*'s and his *c*'s and his *c'est*'s began aloft like breaking waves, and when I came to recognize that a tiny, cramped, often jagged hand was a sign of sickness or stress, I knew that I had logged some significant time with him. Far more than a lesson in cryptography, it had been a personal confrontation, a wrestling match, a game of cat and mouse, he and I. In the process, I knew that I had entered into a different relationship. That first morning of research something happened that impressed upon me the power and the poignancy of my new situation. Absorbed in Camus's letter of August 27, 1946, which turned out to be relatively mundane—"try Lobster Newburg," he wrote to Chiaromonte, who was en route to Cape Cod, and "haven't seen Sartre since my return."—I rested my thumb on a corner of the page so heavily that I blurred one of Camus's words. I was incredulous, looking at that smudge of blue ink, at first with horror at my carelessness in handling a rare manuscript, and then with amazement that in a very real way I had just interacted with Albert Camus. I felt giddy and a little spooked. But the smudge was actually there, physical evidence of my connection and of the fact that sometimes the passage of time doesn't matter.

It was helpful to encounter the Camus-Chiaromonte correspondence when I did, because even as shorthand the letters evoke the Europe to which Camus had returned in late June of 1946 and provide a window on his conscience. In France, life was beginning to return to normal—the metro had reopened in May, theaters were booming (theatergoers' taste was for unreality), and in August there had been the first big exodus since 1937 for the national *vacances*. (Camus, Francine, and the twins spent the month at Michel Gallimard's mother's vast, ancient house near the sea in Brittany, where Camus worked long hours on *The Plague*.) Joyful at first to be home, Camus had found Paris "more beautiful than ever" but was more aware of the Americanization of Europe and also of a serious malaise. "Europe is waiting for a new gospel and there isn't a gospel," he noted. "Thus it will be the atom bomb."[5] After the Paris peace conference ended, and the Soviet Union and the United States emerged as the big bosses, Europe seemed to be slowly entering a new ice age, Janet Flanner wrote in her "Letter from Paris" to describe the dawning reality of a cold war.[6] During the fall, Camus wrote to Chiaromonte that "the general cowardliness was confounding,"[7] and more fiercely to Jean Grenier, "Everyone is afraid, remains silent and hides."[8] His explicit thoughts on the state of the world began to appear in *Combat* in November.

Camus must have discussed most of the material brought to the public in the essays called "Neither Victims nor Executioners" with Chiaromonte in New York. Although Chiaromonte was eight years older, the two friends had been born and bred in the same historical era and they had reached the same conclusions about ideologies, revolutionary violence, the death penalty, and internationalism—issues that Camus was raising in print. (Miriam Chiaromonte had sent me a letter her husband had written to a friend about a dinner in New York at which Camus dominated a conversation regarding "the problems of 'the city state' and 'what to do,' " referring to him as one of the few of those speaking out in public to take the problems of the day truly seriously.[9]) Like the long talks with Chiaromonte, the three months in America had intensified Camus's thoughts about the need for an intermediary group to sponsor a movement toward peace. Several weeks before his articles began to appear in *Combat*, Camus had met with Sartre, Koestler, and Manès Sperber at Malraux's house to think about undertaking a joint initiative. Around the world, other intellectuals were beginning to have similar reactions to what Camus called "the vast conspiracy of silence" about the cold war. Individually,

Camus was planning to write the articles in *Combat* out a sense of moral obligation. He had been turning the issues over and over in his head for months, he told Grenier; given the alarming tension in the world, he had to clarify his position, however difficult that might prove to be. The pressure he was feeling made him edgy and ill-tempered. A week earlier, he had broken with Sartre's philosopher friend Maurice Merleau-Ponty, who had attacked Koestler in print. Recounting his situation to Grenier, Camus described himself as in a state of madness. "Never before has this dilemma been given an image more distressed and insistent than today."[10]

As Camus intended, however apprehensively, "Neither Victims nor Executioners" read like a major political statement. Its impact was heightened by his long absence from the pages of *Combat*. Over the course of a week and a half, he spoke out in his pieces against totalitarianism, revolutionary violence, the death penalty, and "legitimized murder" of any kind. He issued a plea for dialogue, for politics of moderation and mediation, and for a "third way." He warned against any thinking in which the end justified the means; he discussed the new meaning of revolution and the new global world.[11] "We know today that there are no more islands and that borders are meaningless," he writes, pointing out that there was not a single instance of suffering or torture in the world that did not reverberate in daily lives.[12] Full of purpose, writing in the first person, Camus sometimes sounded like a hardworking professor, which was a measure of his need to convey his message. When he warns that the clash of empires was becoming secondary to the clash of civilizations and that colonial voices everywhere were demanding to be heard, I think first of Algeria.

Given the nature of his message and his oratorical tone, it should not be surprising that Camus provoked criticism from the progressive establishment. He may have anticipated it, even though he always seemed to be taken aback when it came. Sartre and Beauvoir thought him self-important and dismissed his series in an offhand manner. Others attacked him in print. After the work was reprinted in Jean Daniel's new magazine *Caliban* in late 1947 (with a preface by Daniel emphasizing its value), Camus was roundly derided by the editor of the communist-supported daily *Libération,* who thought Camus naive, unrealistic, and poorly versed in Marxism, a "lay saint," as he put it, whose desire to "save bodies" was only creating further problems.[13] Camus, in a rare personal reference, retorted that he had learned about freedom not from Marxism but from *la misère,* destitution: "But most of you don't know what this word really means." His role, he explained, was to transform not the world or man, but the values without which the world would not be worth inhabiting and a man would not be worthy of respect.[14] In drama and tone—Camus against the elite, arrogant establishment; Camus skewered because, as it was said, "You flee politics, and take refuge in morality"—this affair brings to mind the coming feud with Sartre. I shiver with apprehension, partly because I am beginning to understand Camus's irrepressible conscience.

In content, too, the essays foreshadowed what was to come. They were the first explicit evidence of the evolution in Camus's thinking. I can see now that in one way or another, almost everything Camus wrote from 1946 to 1951 was a conduit for his thoughts on ideologies, war, and revolt. Everything had a direct relation to the terrifying events in Europe: Franco in Spain, communist guerrillas in Greece, the Soviet boot advancing on Prague and Berlin, the excommunication of Tito. These last three events happened in 1948, the most dangerous of the early cold war years, when another world war already seemed imminent. Camus's play *State of Siege* opened that October, and a second play, *The Just Assassins,* a year later, each of them sounding its timely warning. *State of Siege* was set in Spain under a tyrant named *"la Peste"*; *The Just Assassins* was about two young revolutionaries in czarist Russia. These works were "art as a final perspective on the content of rebellion," as he put it in *The Rebel.*[15] Camus published an early version of a chapter of *The Rebel* early that year, too.

After he finished his long tour of duty at *Combat* in the spring of 1947, Camus had intended to withdraw from politics and public life in order to concentrate on finishing his cycle on revolt and to regain some sense of balance. He was increasingly uncomfortable taking public positions, and it was increasingly clear that he was not well suited by temperament to the combative sort of politics practiced by *Libération,* Sartre, and most of the progressive intellectual left in Paris. According to his letters and journal, he often felt isolated in the intellectual community in which he was still a leader. It was not just that he had changed his ideas about revolution, or had come out firmly against communism while others continued to turn a blind eye toward Stalinist methods, but, more basically, that he was too deeply nonpartisan in his convictions to function well in such a hyperpoliticized climate. As time went by, he also did not have the psychological armor to withstand the continual ideological conflict and criticism. Despite his talent for polemics, he was not really political.[16] His thinking was bigger and more conceptual than party allegiance. He was concerned about liberty, justice, and measure.

In ways that seemed to belie his need to withdraw from the fray, Camus nonetheless continued to be a conspicuous activist. From the fall of 1948 to the summer of 1949, when he left on a two-month South American tour, he seems to have given himself over completely to the needs and pressures of the increasingly fractured national and international scene. Keeping track of his steady output of magazine and newspaper articles, the various forms of support he offered to peace organizations, his founding of the Groupes de Liaisons Internationales (GLI), designed to aid European intellectuals endangered by totalitarian regimes,[17] and his continuing allegiance to the cause of Republican Spain and its exiles, anyone might forget about the demands of his other lives—the five weeks of full-day rehearsals for *State of Siege,* the research for *The Rebel,* the founding of a new magazine, the family life and love life (including his reunion with Maria Casarès), the sickness and travel, not to mention all the new obligations and pressures that came with the *succès fou* of *The Plague.* However reluctant a joiner he may have been at heart, Camus was not reluctant in fact. His sense of responsibility, like his conscience, was unflagging. That was admirable but also worrrisome, as he knew. In May 1949, he explained his public commitment by saying that, modern man was obliged to be concerned with politics. "I am concerned with it, in spite of myself and because, through my defects rather than through my virtues, I have never been able to refuse any of the obligations I encountered."[18] On the next page (which could or could not be the same day, given his disregard for dates), Camus digresses slightly, apparently mulling over yet another public criticism. "Mounier advises me in *Esprit* to give up politics since I have no head for it (this indeed is obvious) and to be satisfied with the quite noble role, which would be charmingly appropriate to me, of sounding the alarm," he writes, waxing cynical. A noble role would require a spotless conscience, he explains, and his only vocation was telling consciences why they are not spotless.[19]

Given what Camus was writing then, it is easy to see how morally inconsistent it would have been for him to drop out. "We do what we can," he explained as chief spokesman at one of the large, noisy rallies in late 1948 in support of the American former bomber pilot Gary Davis, who had torn up his passport and taken refuge at the UN's temporary headquarters in the Palais de Chaillot to promote world citizenship. Davis's actions were ridiculed, as were Camus's, but Camus was sympathetic to Davis, who he thought had made a courageous, solitary effort to clarify the problem of nationalism. "I believe we must still try to save Europe and our country from a vast catastrophe," Camus wrote in a long letter of defense to his own critics, including the ever antagonistic François Mauriac—"the Nonbeliever," Camus called him. Like Camus, Davis "didn't pretend to bring truth to the world," but "had only raised a cry of alarm."

A few weeks later, Camus was onstage again, this time at the vast Salle Pleyel with Sartre, Richard Wright, André Breton, the Italian antifascist Carlo Levi, and intellectuals from all over Europe, to take part in a panel sponsored by Rassemblement Démocratique Révolutionnaire (RDR), a political group dedicated to forging a European force between the cold war powers. Although he had not joined RDR, which had been co-founded by Sartre and was short-lived, Camus still held out hope for European socialism, and he still thought of himself as a member of the progressive left. His speech, "Le Témoin de la Liberté" ("Witness to Freedom"), addressed not only a world gone wrong but also the artist's response. "Today it's not that Cain killed Abel . . . but that Cain killed Abel in the name of logic and then demanded the Legion of Honor," he said, describing the general *malheur*. Artists were asked to do something to change the world, he continued, yet by their very function, they were witnesses to freedom and champions of life. Paying tribute to all his colleagues gathered in the hall, Camus noted that despite their differences and irrespective of national borders, they were working together on a single artistic creation that would rise up to challenge totalitarianism.

This speech was obviously important to Camus, because after it appeared in the RDR house paper, *La Gauche,* he reprinted it a month later in the premiere issue of a magazine called *Empèdocle,* which he had founded with the poet René Char, and then a year after that in a volume called *Actuelles.* The question of the artist's responsibility to his time weighed heavily on him, and he revisited it frequently in essays and interviews, most famously in his Nobel Prize acceptance speech. It was integral to the question of conscience—having one and, in his case, for better or worse, being one. He believed in the veracity of experience—"*vivre c'est vérifier,*" he enters in his journal.[20] That was why he felt compelled to speak out; that was why he was so personally present in his essays; and that was the raison d'être of *Actuelles,* a collection of pieces he called *témoinages* ("personal accounts"), which amounted to a reliable record of his thinking on important contemporary matters. Over the course of his life, he published three volumes of *Actuelles.* In the preface to the first volume (1950), which covered the years 1944–1948 and included his pieces advocating purges, Camus said that he wasn't able to reread some of the old pieces without feeling sadness or discomfort, and yet he could not in honesty omit them.

In the confines of Camus's journal, the issue of honesty had surfaced in an earlier draft of this same preface, written in early 1949. Ever watchful of his own thinking, Camus had chided himself for his lack of forthrightness on the subject of Stalinism and for his misguided effort to be equitable in assessing capitalism and communism. "One of my regrets is having sacrificed too much to objectivity," he writes. "Objectivity at times is a self-indulgence. Today things are clear and what belongs to the concentration camp, even socialism, must be called a concentration camp. In a sense, I shall never again be polite."[21] Camus was apprehensive, too, about his work on *The Rebel,* expressing to Grenier his uneasiness about morality.[22] Still more than two years away from the completion of his new book, still gathering material on the forms, theories, and faces of revolution throughout history—reading scores of philosophers and their critics; keeping track of terrorists and assassins in nineteenth-century Russia—Camus was still trying to formulate his own position on the subject.

During the busy winter of 1948, Camus had made friends with three seasoned revolutionaries he encountered at GLI meetings. From Nicholas Lazarévitch and Alfred Rosmer, who had the authenticity and drama of historical figures, he received uncommon lessons in the pragmatics of revolution, which had a direct impact on his work. Lazarévitch, an anarchist and onetime electrician, construction worker, and proofreader, who dressed in the leather and velvet of a nineteenth-century Cossack and had known Simone Weil, was the history of the workers' movement incarnate. He "bowled Camus over."[23] Rosmer, a onetime bureau chief for the communist newspaper *Humanité* in Moscow and an executor of Trotsky's will, was the embodiment of revolutionary hope. Both were men of deep conviction, in Camus's eyes pure revolutionaries who were still hopeful, honorable, and true. Together with an anti-Bolshevik "syndicalist-communist," Pierre Monatte, they were Camus's tutors, providing the first-hand experience he saw as truth, and passing on information about the state of Soviet society.[24]

But the most immediate of Camus's lessons in revolution came from Spain, where as a young man he had first encountered "injustice triumphant in history." Beginning with a wartime piece in *Combat,* expressing France's "secret shame" at having effectively abandoned its neighbor, Camus had kept the Spanish civil war as a point of reference and Spain as a personal cause, consistently writing articles against Spanish tyranny, drafting appeals for political prisoners, and seeking aid for political refugees. In 1948, he publicly opposed the admission of Spain into the new UN. In the fall, he registered a sweeping moral protest against the regime in Spain in *State of Siege,* which had a star-studded production at the Théâtre Maligny. The play was invested with his passion, he said, and to those who noticed, it also gave life on the stage to his new thinking about revolution. The same passion burned hot in an essay in *Combat*—"Why Spain?"—which Camus wrote in response to a charge that it had been cowardly of him not to set his play in eastern Europe. "Why Spain? . . . Why Guernica . . . ?" he retorted to his critic, speaking of the shame of France's collaboration with Franco ("It was Vichy of course, it wasn't us."), the odious role of the Spanish Catholic church, and a new lot of political prisoners condemned to death. "It is this, deservedly, that I cannot forgive in our contemporary political society: that it is a machine to drive men to despair," he writes in concluding. A few lines later he says, "The world in which I live repulses me, but I feel connected to the men who suffer there."[25] In this last statement, he uses the adjective *solidaire.*

Replaying Camus's political activities in the late 1940s is a reminder of the strong sense of community that existed among intellectuals across

Europe, and also across the Atlantic, at a time when letters and word of mouth were the principal means of communication. "One way or another we kept in touch," William Phillips had said with pride. It is also oddly gratifying to know that Camus, George Orwell, and Pablo Casals worked together for Spanish relief and that Camus, Richard Wright, Carlo Levi, and Ignazio Silone were part of the same panel discussion on peace. It makes a small and intimate world of these scattered, celebrated, necessarily solitary artists.

"Small fact," Camus wrote in his journal in early 1948; "people often think 'they have met me somewhere.'"[26] His observation came about a year after the publication of *The Plague* in France and not long before the appearance of a dozen foreign translations—first in Austria, the Netherlands, Scandinavia, England, and the United States, followed by Japan and Yugoslavia, then Israel and Turkey in 1955, and Spain, beginning to ease up, a few years later.[27] (Even *State of Siege,* considered a flawed, failed play, was published within a year of its Paris production in Argentina and Japan—and elsewhere after Camus won the Nobel Prize.) Camus's comment was comically offhand, because his new fame was undeniable and dramatic, even by comparison with his earlier success. In a matter of days, he had been swept out of the *Combat* era and onto the world stage. He had resigned from the newspaper on June 3, 1947, had published *The Plague*

With the cast of *State of Siege;* Marla Casarès at center,
Barrault, corner left, next to Honegger, Balthus, top right.

on June 10, and two weeks later had won the prestigious Prix des Critiques. By fall, 100,000 copies of *The Plague* had been sold in France, where buying books was still a luxury, as Chiaromonte pointed out in his review in *PR,* concluding that "the general public have apparently found in it an answer to their yearning for ordinary humanness and good sense."[28] In America the following summer, *The Plague* won critical acclaim, and its sales were a record high for Knopf, prompting Camus to ask Blanche if his royalties would permit the purchase of a *motocyclette.* To her news that several reviewers had praised but completely misunderstood the novel, Camus reminded her that the story was, in effect, a parable. With attentive reading, one might perhaps be able to perceive distant echoes of the great Melville, he added.

After the years of hardship, Camus was pleased with the first rewards of his new success, which offered the prospect of relieving his financial pressures. He had a larger than usual percentage of the royalties from Gallimard on this book, and he kept up with his sales figures with a certain wonder. In the aftermath of publication, Camus had a few months of relative leisure *en famille* with Francine and the twins back in Le Panelier, and then in August with Jean Grenier on a road trip around Grenier's native Brittany. In Brittany, Louis Gilloux, an old friend from Algeria whose writings Camus had published in *Espoir,* took him to find the military cemetery where his father was buried, a trip that affected him deeply. But his distress about the failure of *Combat* lingered on. And although, perhaps even more than most authors, he needed success for reassurance, he also had come to understand the mechanics of success, and he seemed to know that the early fame of *The Stranger* had taken its toll on *The Plague* in the self-doubt and apprehension that troubled its years of gestation. From the notebooks on June 25, the day when the Prix des Critiques was announced: "Melancholy of success. Opposition is essential. If everything were harder for me, as it was before, I should have much more right to say what I am saying. The fact remains that I can help many people—in the meantime."[29] A month later, winding down time at Le Panelier, he worries about losing his grounding sensibilities. Rereading his notebooks, beginning with the first, he has noticed that little by little landscapes have been disappearing. He ponders the weight of a good reputation: "one has to prove oneself always up to it and any lapse is looked upon as a crime. With bad reputations, a lapse is to your credit."[30] Camus's clarity may be impressive, but the fact that he had already learned a lot about fame did not mean that he was properly armored against its aggressive ways. Grenier always insisted that Camus never let success go to his head, but friends closer at hand suggest that he had his moments of arrogance, however fleeting. In either case, his fame had to be recognized as a factor in his existence, a lens through which his contemporaries viewed him, and extra baggage that could be as heavy as notoriety.

Uncannily, in terms of anticipating what the public wanted to read, a full seven years after he had conceived the idea for *The Plague,* Camus was the man of the hour in the late 1940s. (Flanner mentions that although the reviews were mixed, the first edition sold out the first day.) With heightened visibility, of course, came criticism, to which he always seemed particularly vulnerable. It came not only from contentious intellectuals in France, raising objections to his *Combat* series, his position on Gary Davis, or his choice of a setting for a play—these were to be expected—but from distant sources such as the Soviet newspaper *Novy Mir,* which, in August 1947, lambasted him as a "propagandist of decadent individualism." "Albert Camus attracted the attention of European and American critics by the perseverance with which he repeats impassively, like a functionary, that existence is absurd. Camus made his entry into European literature in parodying the sinister croaking of Poe's allegorical raven. He fears that men will prefer heroic struggle and action to the ivory tower and vegetal life."[31] Camus's earnestness as well as his fame made him an easy target.

With *State of Siege,* Camus and his own celebrity seemed to work at cross-purposes. The play was honored with a big production and a historic, dazzling all-star company—Jean-Louis Barrault and Maria Casarès in the leading roles, supported by Madeleine Renaud, Pierre Brasseur, and Marcel Marceau; sets and costumes by the painter Balthus; music by Arthur Honegger; direction by Barrault himself—and it quickly entered the public buzz. But it also drew the sort of savage reviews reserved for newsworthy works and artists that have raised great expectations. "On the opening night, the 'Parisians' found it hard to hide their joy at the idea that we had failed. I felt a physical pain the scars of which I continue to bear," Barrault, for whom this was his first bad press, recalled a few years later.[32] Few plays have benefited from so complete a panning, Camus wrote in his ironic, defensive way in the preface to its American publication, which he found sad because he had always considered *State of Siege* to be the piece of writing that resembled him the most. Barrault and Camus had different artistic styles, and their failure was generally thought to be the result of an ill-conceived collaboration. They never worked together in the theater again—Barrault feared that Camus would forsake theater altogether after the experience—but Barrault always said that he retained an extraordinary fondness for this production, which ran for only seventeen performances. Camus spoke often of reworking the play and staging it in an outdoor amphitheater, but he had suffered a deep and lasting hurt.

As a matter of course, the fame that came with *The Plague* brought the sort of attention to Camus that further complicated his life and challenged his innate sense of *pudeur*. Even the cursory recounting of the requests for interviews, articles, lectures, speeches, sponsorships, and assorted other public appearances that can be pasted together from the sources makes this clear. "I've been offered eight minutes to speak [on the radio] on 'What Is Truth,'" he notes sarcastically to Grenier (for whom he had just broadcast a tribute of greater length). There were new Gallimard editions of earlier works on the agenda—*Nuptials; Letter to a German Friend; The Myth of Sisyphus* with the addition of the Kafka chapter—new productions of *Caligula* in London and Los Angeles, discussions of a movie version of *The Plague* (with Camus in a featured role), and untold smaller new obligations. This was when Camus hired Suzanne Labiche as his full-time secretary—he called her "*La Biche*," "the doe," or in slang "my sweet"—who managed the onslaught of correspondence and callers and in general ran interference for him. Camus had once taken a pledge with his Algerian friend, Jean de Maisonseul, to answer all fan mail, should it ever arrive. It came from all directions, as the model letters of refusal that Labiche kept in her desk drawer for reference describe. "I have established a rule never to accept any honorary title and not to collaborate with undertakings in which I cannot participate personally," one model read. More adamantly: "Not being able to keep up with the abundance of my tasks, I have established the principle of no longer replying to any survey or interview and in general to refuse all new activities." This was the late 1940s, when Camus was again dangerously ill, so there was a letter, similar to the one I picked up in the Knopf files, that says simply and formally (and awkwardly in the existing translation): "Problems of health now place Mr. Albert Camus in the obligation, on his doctors' orders, of reducing his activity considerably."[33]

As a corollary to success, there would always be intrusions and distractions, curiosity seekers, challengers, and fans good and bad. A year earlier, a new nursemaid for his children had been unmasked as an undercover reporter seeking material for the tabloids. Several months after hiring Labiche, Camus had to confiscate (and burn) a private journal she had been keeping of their relationship. Responding to admirers and aspiring writers meant that letters from old friends piled up unanswered. In early 1948, Camus writes to Grenier that he has accomplished very little in the last months. A year later, he apologizes for having become a "pretty bad correspondent."[34] The prying and pulling by outside forces were eroding any interior calm and control he had acquired and also made focus all the more difficult. Domestic life in a small apartment with toddlers and, all too often, a disapproving mother-in-l[aw] own form of entrapment. By the end of 1948 Camu[s] ing to work at home and holed up after hours in h[is] door locked, telephone off the hook. "The fight [between] my children and me ended to the former's advantage. occupy all the conquered territory and behave like cally," he wrote to Grenier, attempting humor, evi[ncing] slight sourness after an admittedly "heavy trimester' ended with the failure of his play. "Naturally I prefer that my plays be successful. But I also find a number of subtle satisfactions in a failure. Example: I have fewer appointments."[35]

As Camus's life became ever more public, concerns that usually found expression only in his journal and personal letters began to spill over into his work, which was a measure of his fame. "To make a name in literature, it's no longer indispensable to write books. It's enough to be thought of as having written one which the evening papers have mentioned and which one can fall back on for the rest of one's life," he writes in 1950 in the essay called "*L'Énigme*." "An artist must resign himself good humoredly and allow what he knows is an undeserved image of himself to lie about in dentists' waiting rooms and at the hairdresser's," he continues, describing his own "reputation for austerity." "I actually have so weighty a reputation [that it is] a source of great amusement to my friends (as far as I'm concerned, it rather makes me blush, since I know how little I deserve it)."[36]

Seizing the opportunity to correct his reputation, Camus takes sharper aim at those who read too much into his work. He also takes issue with his seemingly unalterable image as a prophet of the absurd and a purveyor of literature of despair. "Yet what else have I done except reason about an idea I discovered in the streets of my time?" he asks, and then explains his intentions with perceptible impatience. It is astonishing to find Camus speaking so freely in public about his writing and his career, for this would once have been unimaginable. Even more urgently than a defense or clarification of his work, "Enigma" is a humble plea for understanding. "No man can say what he is. But it happens that he can say what he is not," he writes, evincing a new uncertainty. "I don't know what I am looking for, cautiously I give it a name, I withdraw what I said, I repeat myself, I go backward and forward," he elaborates, speaking to his need for change and the growing disarray in his working life.[37]

In Camus's journal, for corroboration, there are increasingly dark hints of a spiritual crisis. "At the height of happiness—and night comes to meet me." "I no longer believe in my star." Most specifically, and in the end helpfully, in the summer of 1952 there is a mention of the short story "Jonas or the Artist at Work," which has begun to take form. "Jonas," which was finished several years later and drew on material from the drama surrounding the publication of *The Rebel,* was Camus's own tale of the tragedy of glory, projected onto the person of Gilbert Jonas, a painter who is gradually undone by success.[38] Its scene is painfully familiar—the dutiful, loving wife, the two children, the cramped apartment in Paris, the fans, camp followers, and critics who take over Jonas's life—and the rendering of his helpless decline is all the more devastating for its transparency and likely truth. In the end, when the painter finally produces a last work, it is a large blank canvas inscribed with a tiny indecipherable word that could be either *solitaire* or *solidaire.*

Camus dedicated "Enigma" to the poet René Char, with whom he had struck up an instant friendship in 1946. ("Here's my brother—you'll like him," is how Camus introduced Char to his mother the following summer.)[39] Char also appears in a principal role in "Jonas" as the

ELIZABETH HAWES

supportive friend Rateau—a reference to the enduring salvation of the
real-life friendship. The year after they met, Camus found a house to rent
for the summer near Char in the village of L'Isle-sur-la-Sorgue in the
Luberon. The following year, they created the monthly literary magazine *Empèdocle* together. They shared a love of the Greeks, a susceptibil-
ity to romantic affairs (*rateau* means "rake" in French), a distaste for Parisian
literary life, and a number of other significant principles, passions, and
adventures. In the tales recounted about Char, Camus jumps to life—in
their trips together in Camus's aging black Citroën down from Paris, where
Char kept a small apartment; in their hours sitting over pastis at Char's
kitchen table. Camus felt like himself in this friendship, which was important at a time when his fame was beginning to work against him. "But
the only people who can help the artist in his obstinate quest are those
who love him," Camus writes in closing "Enigma."[40]

The Luberon was as close an approximation to Algeria as Camus ever
found—the house he purchased in Lourmarin in 1958 was only twenty
miles from L'Isle-sur-la-Sorgue—and he was beginning to sound serious
about his intent "to leave Paris for good (at least!!)," which also meant
leave the impinging world of Paris.[41] "It was hard to paint the world and
men and, at the same time, to live with them," he writes in "Jonas." In
the aftermath of *The Plague,* Camus had been thinking first about buying
a house in Algiers, in the heights of Bouzaréah or in outlying Tipasa, and
had enlisted his old friends to look for one, although prices were prohibi-
tive and the growing tension between the Arabs and the French was troubling. With each of his trips home—the regular visits to his mother; the
emergency trips for his uncle's funeral or his aunt's appendectomy; and
in the fall of 1948 several leisurely months with Francine in pursuit of old
and romantic pleasures—he noticed the passage of time and felt the same
melancholy at the leave-taking. "Algiers after ten years. The faces which
I recognize, after a hesitation, and which have aged. It's the gathering at
the Guermantes house. But on the scale of a city in which I get lost. There's
no going backwards."[42]

For several years, in the sanctuary of his journals, Camus has been expressing a need to be less guarded and speak his heart and mind, "to say all
that I feel," "what is deepest in me"; to be "in accord" with himself and
the world; to be able to speak in his own name. "Begin again anew—(but

without sacrificing *the truth, the reality* of the prior experiences. . . . Reject nothing)," he writes in late winter of 1950 as he focuses on finishing *The Rebel*. [43] That spring, Camus is in unusually bright spirits. "Radiant light," he begins. "It seems to me that I am emerging from a ten-year sleep—still entangled in wrappings of misfortune and of false ethics—but again naked and attracted toward the sun. Strength brilliant and measured—and intelligence frugal, sharpened. I am being reborn as a body too."[44]

What I could not know until I checked on his whereabouts is that Camus was entering these last thoughts from Cabris, a small hill town high above the Riviera in the Alpes-Maritime, and that he was referring to his remarkable physical recovery as well as the new energy in his work. The previous fall, exhausted and spent after his two-month tour in South America, he had learned that his TB had advanced to an aggressive phase, and his doctors had ordered immediate rest at high altitude and a year's leave of absence from Gallimard. By January he was convalescing in a rustic inn, the Chèvre d'Or (a name I recognized from the stationery on which he wrote to Blanche Knopf at the time), and a month later had moved to a more comfortable situation in a house that belonged to a neighbor from the rue de Varennes. By the time of his declaration of "mastery on every plane," he had recovered enough strength to be proceeding well with *The Rebel* and traveling back and forth to Paris.

It is surely a measure of its impact on his work that Camus included some explicit information about his medical crisis in his journal. The details are all the more alarming because they are there in cold print. Beginning in September, there is a trail of entries that register like points on a fever chart, so clearly are they addressing the encroaching illness and the ensuing loss of control. "The sole effort of my life: to live the life of a normal man. I didn't want to be a man of the abyss. The tremendous effort did no good." In late October: "After such a long certainty of being cured, this backsliding ought to crush me. It does indeed crush me. But following on an unbroken succession of crushings, it rather makes me laugh. In the end, I am liberated. Madness too is a liberation." Camus jots down a quote about Keats, who died of TB at the age of twenty-six—"So sensitive that he could have touched pain with his hands"—and from Keats—"I am glad there is such a thing as the grave." He lapses into mournful observations and descriptions. "Beauty, which helps in living, helps likewise in dying." "Those moments when one yields to anguish as one does to physical pain: lying down, motionless, devoid of will and of future, listening only to the long stabs of pain." In early November, he writes down "Strepto and P.A.S.," referring to the miracle antibiotics that had just become available, and lists his exact dosage.[45] After two decades of living with his disease, Camus still did not have "the vocation for sickness," as he put it. "I have a use for it, but not a good one, I think," he wrote to Grenier in mid-February. "And I'm biding my time."[46] By then he had gained weight and had all the appearance of health, including his old defiant spirit. "The fact is, I usually lead an exhausting life, in so many ways, and I only need to get some rest to miraculously blossom again."

For more than a year Camus bounced back and forth between sickness and health, and between Cabris, Le Panelier, and Paris, his spirits being calibrated accordingly. He was wretched before the rounds of medication began: breathless, feverish, and too exhausted even to read. "I've come to a standstill and can't write a word about anything," he confessed to Blanche in October, meaning, pointedly, that he couldn't work on *The Rebel*. Camus worried about the flight of time, especially when he was sick and uncertain of the future. He had turned thirty-six in November. Thinking not only of his unfinished essay but also of an ambitious novel that was beginning to claim space in his head, he entered a note about Tolstoy: "He was born in 1828. He wrote *War and Peace* between 1863 and 1869. Between the ages of 35 and 41."[47] However diminished, Camus didn't shut down completely that first winter, managing to attend to assorted revisions, proofs, and prefaces (and still trying to help the couple he had met in Brazil). He was in bed when the dress rehearsal of his play *The Just Assassins* took place, but was there on opening night, looking very tired, Beauvoir commented, "but the warmth of his greeting brought back the best days of our friendship."[48] The play, which Beauvoir and Sartre pronounced "academic," received unanimous praise only for the passionate performance by Maria Casarès in the role of the young revolutionary Dora. Nonetheless, it was still running in the spring when Camus returned to Paris.

The convalescence in Cabris was imbued with loneliness and fear, but it also brought the relief of a pastoral life, far from the pressures of a cramped apartment, marriage, and *la vie parisienne.* Apart from "the disgust of being in bed" and "some black moods," Camus expressed little discontent with his situation.[49] His first notes about the landscape of Provence are nostalgic and tender and describe the sun and light flooding his room; a blue, veiled sky; sounds of children in the village that remind him of long-ago days in Algiers. As soon as he could work, he set down an ambitious agenda for the next few months, which included finishing three volumes of essays and a first draft of *The Rebel,* all to be accomplished under a new discipline: "Rise early. Shower before breakfast. No cigarettes before noon." He welcomed a rugged routine, and he ordered his days accordingly, waking at 8 a.m. to breakfast and writing until 11 a.m., then correspondence, a walk, lunch, rest, and work again from 4 to 7 p.m. (There is also a more detailed version of this schedule on record: "Wake at 9 o'clock, reading of Hegel and notes until 11 o'clock. Promenade until 12:30. Lunch. Nap from 1:30 to 2:30. Mail or filing nails until 4. Revolt from 4 to 8 and 9 to 10:30. Bed. Read Montaigne. Sleep."[50])

Camus thought frequently and wistfully of his mother, whom he had not seen since the fall—and he worried about his memory slipping, resolving to keep a diary. He had visitors—Francine for several weeks; his brother Lucien, who was recuperating from an operation; devoted friends like the Gallimards and the Bloch-Michels—and he had a few outings to the nearby home of the writer Roger Martin du Gard, whom he admired. Camus had formidable energy, his old friends always said, recalling swims far out into the Bay of Algiers or tireless days in the theater. They were really describing his *ardeur de vivre,* which in adversity became the will to survive. In late March, when the doctors ordered an additional three months of rest, he was devastated but stoic. Only in noting a friend's suicide did he suggest the depth of his despair. "Completely upset because I liked him greatly, to be sure, but also because I suddenly realized that I had a longing to do as he did."[51] A year later, again back at Cabris and finally nearing the completion of *The Rebel,* he wrote to Francine about the pain of his earlier struggle to work. "I am not happy and I have never ever felt as black, but at least I've finished with those dishonorable days when I hung around ashamed of doing nothing, incapable of either dealing with my shame or doing what was needed to end it." He was at his worktable ten hours a day and hoped to finish his book by mid-March, he wrote to Char a month later in brighter spirits. "But the birth is long, difficult, and it seems to me that the baby is really ugly. This effort is exhausting."[52]

Following Camus's illness is entering forbidden territory with him, and it brings a great sense of intimacy. In illness, Camus is again alone—dramatically so in 1949–1950, when, according to family members, he again thought he was going to die. To be present to observe his physical and mental duress now is a strange sort of privilege; to be alone in his company is a welcome relief after the recent social turmoil. Almost like an evening at home à deux, it offers a moment to sort things out. Solitude simplifies and clarifies, and in Camus's case this effect was reaffirming. His first journal entry from Cabris, dated January 10, 1950, reveals most directly his anguish about working, but it also raises the deeper subject of who he is. "There is in me an anarchy, a frightful disorder. Creating costs me a thousand deaths, for it involves an order and my whole being rebels against order," he reports, but only after having confessed, "I have never seen very clearly into myself in the final analysis. But I have always instinctively followed an invisible star."[53] The same invisible star appears in the first sentence of the story "Jonas": "Gilbert Jonas, the painter, believed in his star. . . . But his serenity, attributed by some to smugness, resulted, on the contrary, from a trusting modesty. Jonas credited everything to his star rather than to his own merits."[54]

Camus's star was also his sun. In even the substitute Algerian landscape of Cabris, Camus found a touchstone, the faint evocations of Algeria pulling him back into an earlier life and self. He had already begun to write the essay "*La Mer au Plus Près*" ("The Sea Close By"), which he explained as a conscious effort to reclaim the more lyrical and subjective style of his youth. It was a meditation on his sea voyages to North America and South America and, it might seem, on his whole life. "I grew up with the sea and poverty for me was sumptuous," he opens; "then I lost the sea, and found all luxuries gray and poverty unbearable. Since then, I have been waiting."[55] As Camus moves toward completion of *The Rebel*, his journal, too, catches a palpable energy, even exhilaration, as he looks forward to writing "*all that I feel,* little things at random," "writing pell-mell, everything that goes through my head," and pledging himself to "free creation." In the pages from Cabris, there are ever stronger intimations of the desire to write in a freer and more autobiographical spirit. Most suggestive of all are the many notes for a new novel about love: thoughts about suffering, descriptions that appear to reflect his own complicated love life, a list of people to draw upon as characters—Grenier, Pia, Lazarévitch, Algerian *copines* like Christiane Galindo and Blanche Balain, a dozen others including Patricia Blake and Mamaine. In March, in Cabris, Camus writes in the journal: "It is only too late that one has the courage of one's knowledge."[56]

Illness registers as the most daunting element in Camus's life during these last years before the publication of *The Rebel*. But fame had been almost as disruptive a force as his perilous state of health, and it is easy to see them both as agents of change, pushing him along in his search for what he called "his truth." For the moment, therre is a sense of a lull in Camus's life as he focuses on finishing the book that has hung over his head like the sword of Damocles. The longer the days, the more morally obligated he seemed to feel to deliver this message to the world, to speak his piece, or peace. On March 7, 1951, he declared in private that the end was near: "Finished the first writing of *The Rebel*. With this book the first two cycles come to an end. Thirty-seven years old. And now, can creation be free?"[57]

7

Camus in the country with Michel Gallimard.

TB

Albert Camus rarely shows up in the familiar roundup of artists and writers who suffered from tuberculosis—Keats, Shelley, the Brontës, Robert and Elizabeth Browning, Chopin, Chekhov, Katherine Mansfield, Robert Louis Stevenson. (And Cicero, Paganini, Rousseau, Goethe, Locke, Poe, Kafka, Washington Irving, D. H. Lawrence, Ralph Waldo Emerson, George Orwell, Stephen Crane, Laurence Sterne, Simone Weil, André Gide—almost compulsively I now keep track of the afflicted.) This indicates that Camus succeeded in keeping the nature of his condition from the public, or that it was effectively eclipsed by the drama of the car crash that actually killed him. That Camus had a serious and irremediable case of TB is indisputable. That it had a radical impact on his life and thought is undeniable. More than any of the other hardships he endured—the poverty, the silent mother, the expatriation—each its own kind of separation or exile, his illness altered him. As he confided to his friend Michel Gallimard about the trauma of its onset when he was seventeen, "The horror explains a lot about the man that I have become, but finally, these are not the noblest things."[1]

There will never be a full account of Camus's struggle with TB. Illness is too intimate a matter and Camus's *pudeur* too strong a force for that. There will always be questions and issues, not only about the gravity of his condition and the specifics of his suffering, but also about the possibility of contagion, particularly in view of his many relationships with women. Tuberculosis is an airborne disease that generally infects about

5 percent of those exposed to it, so the risk with Camus is assumed to have been small, but then numerous factors that might have affected the degree of his infectivity can never be known. Camus's friends bring their own understanding and perspectives to his case. According to one, Camus was very sick only during the occupation; according to another, in the early 1950s "we almost lost him." Emmanuel Roblès remembers their student days, when it was known that Camus had contracted tuberculosis, even though he rarely spoke of it but simply dropped out of sight periodically and then resurfaced, always with the same pallor. Jean Grenier, who for thirty of Camus's forty-six years enjoyed the privileged position of adviser and mentor, discusses the impact of illness on Camus's character, how it might explain Camus the *camarade de combat* and Camus the *grand homme solitaire*. Neither Camus's daughter nor his son ever saw him sick, because he didn't want them to see him sick. With Michel Gallimard and Mamaine, Koestler's girlfriend, who also suffered from TB, he was entirely forthcoming.[2]

Beyond the account of frequent pneumothoraxes, sundry alternative therapies, and treatments by perhaps a dozen doctors over the course of three decades, the medical record is also rather patchy. Nonetheless, by dribs and drabs, with sleuthing, deducing, and some forays into the history of TB, Camus's life with the disease becomes clearer. Surprisingly, when various sources are assembled into a story, Camus's own contribution turns out to be substantial. In his journal, he may not be the emotional resource that Katherine Mansfield was in her many notebooks, but he describes the humiliation of rejection by the army, the torment of not being able to swim, and, very infrequently, physical duress or pain. "The concentrated effort of walking uphill, the air burning lungs like red-hot iron or cutting into them like a sharpened razor," he writes in his early twenties.[3] (He also quotes from Mansfield, which in itself is a helpful cross-reference.) In letters to trusted friends, he is matter-of-fact about "*les misères de santé*" and his vulnerable condition, his need for rest, the distress of relapses, his distaste for being in bed. To Pia, he writes of the struggle to live with a diminished body. In a very moving letter from Le Panelier in 1944 to a tubercular friend, he despairs of ever being cured.

It is not surprising that Camus is at his most revealing in his first published works, composed in his early twenties, only a few years after his initial attack and the diagnosis that dramatically transformed his view of life. Read closely, both *The Wrong Side and the Right Side* and *Nuptials*, which appeared in Algiers in 1937 and 1939, respectively, seem almost confessional, as if thoughts and feelings were spilling over into print. Except in his unedited last work, *The First Man,* Camus is rarely as specific as he is in these early works when he speaks directly about his *"crise"* and reconstructs moments of trauma. There is a passage in *Nuptials* in which he recalls the agony of confronting his imminent mortality. "What does eternity mean to me," he asks. "You can be lying in bed one day and hear someone say: 'You are strong and I owe it to you to be honest; I can tell you that you are going to die;' there you are with your whole life in your hands, fear in your bowels, looking the fool. What else matters: waves of blood come throbbing to my temples and I feel I could smash everything around me."[4] Camus's slightly disjointed prose and his sudden, seemingly inadvertent, slip into the first person make his candor very convincing. In another passage, a fragment from a draft of the essay *"Entre Oui et Non,"* the fulcrum piece in *The Wrong Side and the Right Side,* also written in a youthful, sometimes awkward, transparent prose, Camus addresses the complicated feelings of a son for his mother, who has shown a surprising lack of concern about his life-threatening illness. "And yet he knew her to be extremely emotional; he also knew that she had great feeling for him," he writes. "People told him that they had seen her cry. But . . . to him the tears seemed only mildly convincing."[5] The fact that Camus ultimately decided not to include this fragment in the finished essay gives it the edge of censored material.

The pain in these passages also weighs heavily in the metaphysical climate of the essays. These are Camus's very personal meditations on his young life, and they draw upon all of the people and places in his "circle of experience," as he called it, family: Belcourt, Algiers, Tipasa, Djémila, and the desert, in all their metaphoric meaning and soul. In addition, the essays are his first efforts at expressing a credo, and his thoughts as captured on the page are so full of feeling that it is as if they were still tethered to raw experience. The most powerful feeling is about death, a presence that figures in even the sensual and celebratory essays of *Nuptials,* so closely linked is it, for Camus, to the rhythms of nature. Sickness is ubiquitous, too—a sick old woman; a cat who has to eat one of her young; the words *malade* and *maladie* cropping up with suspicious regularity.

Of course, my awareness that Camus has been—and is still—gravely ill adds a surge of new meaning to these works and a personal charge to the prose. Phrases such as "my secret anguish" and "the lost paradise" are troubling. A line like "Great courage is keeping your eyes open to light as well as to death" has a brave new edge. When Camus begins to explain himself in "*Amour de Vivre*"—"There lay all my love of life: a silent passion for what would perhaps escape me, bitterness under a flame"—it is almost impossible not to insinuate TB into the picture.[6] Camus's own comments seem to corroborate such a reading. In a letter sent to his friend Jean de Maisonseuil just after the publication of this first book, he explains that he has allowed himself "to say everything with all my passion—to go the very end," and that he has worked with an openness, "*une manie de nudité*," that has drained him. The reviewers who have found his work bitter or pessimistic distress him. "If I haven't communicated all the taste that I have for life, all the desire I have to bite fully into its flesh, if I haven't said that even death and sorrow only exasperate my ambition to live, then I haven't said anything."[7] In closing, Camus confides to Maisonseuil that his attitude toward his illness has changed, because he has found that he has something to say, "I'm working a lot. I want to live for that and it is the essential thing. Isn't it admirable, Jean, that life is a thing so passionate and so sorrowful?"[8]

Camus isn't either ironic or metaphoric in this letter, and so his youthful earnestness is doubly affecting. In the last line, there is a gentle echo of something found in his first notebook. "Bring together secret despair and love of life," he instructs himself, and that is what he did in the essays, finding a stance between life and death, *oui et non, l'envers et l'endroit*. In that early entry, he also wrote down the words "*Absurde. Absurde.*" Suddenly it registers in a more immediate way than ever before how deeply illness affected Camus, how crucial it was to the measure of the man, to his thought, and to the writer he became. If poverty and sunlight were his sources, as he said twenty years later in a new preface to *The Wrong Side and the Right Side,* illness was his despair and his challenge, part nemesis, part catalyst, a practical model of the absurd. Whatever strength, indifference, or self-sufficiency he learned in childhood was fortified by his struggle with TB, although at considerable cost. For a while, a grave illness took away the life force that transformed everything for him, Camus admits, while explaining how in the end it promoted a freedom of heart, a slight aloofness from human affairs that protected him from any sort of resentment. Everywhere in the essays, there are lines that seem to reflect a response to illness as well as to the puzzle of existence. "I was in need of greatness," he writes after weeks of solitude and sickness in Prague. "I achieved it in confronting my deep despair and the secret indifference of one of the most beautiful landscapes in the world."[9]

In *Nuptials*, which is like a sequel to *The Wrong Side and the Right Side,* Camus is more explicit, while giving himself over to full-blown, highly metaphoric lyricism. The first shock of his diagnosis and the period of spiritual turmoil have resolved into a commitment to lucidity and a rededication to earthly pleasures, and in response, Camus's prose has a startling new power. Writing from Djémila, a mountain village near the coast that he loved for its savage winds and arid splendor, he sums up his thinking and faces his future. "But men die in spite of themselves, in spite of their surroundings. They are told: 'When you get well . . . ,' and they die. I want none of that. . . . I have no wish to lie or to be lied to. I want to keep my lucidity to the last and gaze upon my death with all the fullness of my . . . [feelings]."[10]

In many ways, Camus's life in the mid-1930s, when he was writing these essays, belied his illness. There was so much going on every day that it might be assumed that his TB was in remission, were it not for the stories of interrupted travels, enforced rest, chest pain, and, in Prague, another incident of coughing up blood. In 1935, when Camus was writing the first of the essays, he was in his third year of philosophical studies at the University of Algiers, deep into Saint Augustine, his countryman from Bône, writing a dissertation for the *diplome d'Études Supérieures,* holding a variety of part-time jobs, involved in a complicated new marriage, a full round of political and cultural activities for the Communist Party, and an expanding circle of intellectual friends and interests. He was a young man-about-town in Algiers, very engaged and very engaging, a bit of a dandy and the leader of his pack. In the spring of that year, he began to keep a writer's journal. In the next year, he began to write *The*

Happy Death, his first novel; in the next, *Caligula* and *The Myth of Sisyphus;* then *The Stranger.*

Behind all this activity, however, illness was there with its heavy hand, effecting a chain of events that became an inevitability, keeping Camus out of active combat in World War II, upending his plans for the *agrégation* and a career in teaching in the state system, and eventually forcing him to leave Algeria. Roger Quilliot gives illness a strange role in the love between Camus and Simone, too, suggesting that their respective handicaps—his TB, her drug addiction—bound them together in a mutual support system that was like a secret society and a form of redemption. Long after their breakup, Camus continued to send Simone books on cures and detoxification, Quilliot notes, always without any message, because he didn't want to see her again. "I had the impression that the failure of this marriage mattered more to his life than he wished to believe," he concludes.[11]

It is very tempting to think that Camus's vision can be traced back to his first brush with death at the age of seventeen, when he effectively left the circle of the living, never to fully return. But malady was only one of the ingredients thrown into the mix of experience and aspirations that shaped his morality. And the absurd as such was in the very fabric of his times—that was his point. Camus and his generation grew up in a climate of negation and disillusion that raised serious existential questions and provoked malaise and metaphysical angst. Modern literature is one of the products. Nonetheless, the fact stands that Camus's spiritual turmoil was grounded in a very real, firsthand fear, the kind of fear that "shatters some sort of interior setting," as he described it. His belief that death is the essential discovery and the beginning of lucidity had its origins as a personal tool of survival. From *Nuptials:* "Illness is a remedy against death—it prepares us for it. It creates an apprenticeship whose first stage is feeling sorry for yourself."[12] Camus's philosophical studies—during that final year, a seminar on existential precursors such as Heidegger and Kierkegaard and his dissertation on Plotinus and Saint Augustine—plunged him into the same metaphysical territory as had illness, and helped him to organize his thinking. "Camus perhaps learned more about himself in writing this dissertation than about Greek and Christian thought," Quilliot comments rather puckishly in his annotation for the Pléiade at this time. His subjects "simply helped him to name his problems."[13]

CAMUS, A ROMANCE

★ ★ ★

It is a factor of my new focus that fellow sufferers seem to show up in every corner of Camus's life—friends, lovers, favorite authors, and passing encounters include André Gide, Michel Gallimard, Suzanne Labiche Agnely, and Mamaine in the foreground, with Maria Casarès's father, Orwell, Kafka, Dostoyevsky, and Simone Weil as a backdrop. But it also produces a potential statistic, a straw poll measuring the high incidence of TB in a population that until after World War II had no recourse to antibiotics and no other reliable cure. With TB came a sense of communal doom.

Had Camus been born a decade or two later and treated with, for instance, streptomycin earlier in his life, his disease might have taken a different course. But in 1930, when he was stricken, the treatment of TB was almost as primitive and uncertain as it had been in the days of Chekhov or Keats, when the disease was the most common cause of death in the western world. Since 1882, when it was discovered to be a bacterial infection, little had improved beyond hygiene and sanitation to affect the mortality rate very much or to alter the assumption that contracting TB meant an early death. Like a token of its intractability, the Old Testament name of consumption lingered on in common usage until the twentieth century. Many of Camus's therapies—supplements of herbs and chicken embryos or, later, oligo-mineral supplements—were only variations on proposed cures from the past: goat's milk or lobster and wine, near-starvation (the single anchovy and morsel of bread fed to Keats), or twelve eggs a day. By the time Camus had access to the first antibiotics in 1949, he had lived with TB for almost twenty years and his lungs were irreparably damaged. Whether or not he was dosed three years later with the new miracle drug isoniazid, which offered the first promise of a cure and rendered obsolete the pneumothoraxes, special diets, and bed rest that he had endured, is not on record. But this is ultimately irrelevant, because Camus had effectively lived too long in an earlier era. As a medical study, he was necessarily an old-fashioned case.

As Susan Sontag writes in "Illness as a Metaphor," her famous essay that deconstructs the popular mythology surrounding TB, it is highly desirable for a specific dreaded disease to come to seem ordinary.[14] But for most of Camus's life, TB was not perceived as either ordinary or curable, and this may be why the mythology still seems to pertain to him, at least as an oddly compelling narrative. The old idea that consumption afflicted the sensitive, sensual, and intellectually gifted and the idea that it nourished genius, fostered individuality, and increased sexual desire do not seem outrageous so much as intriguing. Camus himself includes an anecdote in an early essay about a local hospital that describes a tubercular man who makes love to his wife two or three times a day, every day. "The disease made him that way," he notes.[15] As with myths, there is a germ of truth in such fantastical thinking. A fever can indeed sharpen perception, speed up intellectual processes, and make someone more "porous" to sensations, as Camus and Gide described. In its nature, TB is a disease of contrasts: aggression and remission, hyperactivity followed by languor, "odd exhilaration" alternating with melancholy and depression. In this way, it seems to have a relation to Byron's bipolarity and Keats's delicate nature, and it matches the rhythms of a writing life and, to some extent, Camus's nature.

Camus's notebooks, populated in his years of crisis with the specters of Keats, Mansfield, Dostoyevsky, Kafka, and Nietzsche—the last not tubercular himself but an intimate of illness—evoke a sense of kinship with his historical peers. But if Camus took comfort or solace in this intellectual company or in its shared climate of morbidity, he did not allow himself to give in to the disease after the shocking beginning, and the alleged passivity of the tubercular patient is rarely in evidence. More typical in the first years was a reckless defiance—"I burned everything I could burn," he writes to the author Guy Dumur, advising Dumur, who also had TB, to be more prudent than he had been.[16] As the years go by, Camus's letters express frustration, disbelief, and helplessness about "the most frightful poverty I have ever seen"[17]; impatience with the constraints on his activity; moments of fear; but never defeat. With his old circle of female friends in Algiers, as with the other women in his life, he could nonetheless be heartbreaking, yearning for normalcy and health and attempting stoicism. From his convalescence at Le Panelier in the fall of 1942: "I needed silence. Now, I don't detest anyone anymore. If only I could be cured and live like before (since I've been ill, I haven't gone running once), I think I would once again be capable of happiness, but naturally, it would be better to try to arrange what exists rather than wish for improbable things."[18]

CAMUS, A ROMANCE

Camus turns different faces and moods to different friends. With women he is gentle, wistful, confessional, waxing lyrical, dramatic, even sentimental and ever so slightly self-pitying in illness. With Grenier, he is thoughtful, inclusive, and manly, somehow addressing issues of character even as he is discussing a dangerous pause in the pneumothorax treatments or a new infection in his right lung. At the very beginning, when Camus dropped out of school, Grenier was there, the new philosophy professor from mainland France who came to visit his student at home, overwhelming him. Grenier begins his memoir with a recollection of that day and of the new invalid, young Camus, who responded with monosyllables to questions about his health and seemed wary and distant. "That distance was a measure of the time for reflection," he explained. "Albert Camus didn't take anything lightly."[19]

With Michel Gallimard, his best friend and fellow inmate, Camus demonstrates most clearly how he has coped with TB. He had sixteen years of experience with the disease by the time Michel's own infection was discovered, and he writes as both a sidekick and an elder statesman, teasing and mocking Michel out of a gathering gloom, turning grave when confiding important thoughts on survival. He wields his ready gallows humor, which is useful as a distraction and a defense mechanism, particularly between friends who are bound together in a sense of fun. "Minor fainting spell in the airplane because of claustrophobia. But I landed, fresh as a daisy," he reports of his Algerian trip to "great saint Michel," who is confined to eight months of bed rest in a sanatorium in Leysin, Switzerland.[20] That winter Camus was in retreat at Briançon, but he still monitored Michel's treatment and spent three weeks visiting the sanatorium. Several years later, Janine and Michel duly visited Camus in Cabris. Both men were good at friendship—fraternal, generous, loyal. They loved to laugh. They joked about displaying their caskets side by side in the front room at Gallimard.

Little could be more binding than sharing the suspense of a life-threatening disease—Nietzsche described this mental anguish as the suffering that came from thinking about the illness, which could surpass the suffering of the illness itself.[21] Camus, who by 1947 had long overcome the initial horror of being tubercular and had formulated a metaphysical response, passed on his hard-earned lessons to Michel by word and by example. In his letters to Michel at Leysin, he talks of Dostoyevsky's "new man," to whom dying will become indifferent. He relates the experience of illness to a religious experience: "Even if you don't believe in religion, even if God is dead (assassinated from behind, as one of my friends says), there is still something true in religious experience, just as there is in simply experience: it's that *personal* life has only the most distant rapport with happiness."[22] He promotes the Greek idea of equilibrium as the answer to the problem they both face. Ever the *copain,* he ends, "Of course, love of life is the contrary of wife swapping and boogie-woogie or driving at 150 kilometers an hour. When one has quality, and although I'm not extravagant in praising you, one must admit that you do, one ends up benefiting from every experience."

The photographs as well as the correspondence attest to the zone of comfort that Michel and his wife Janine, trusted friends, adopted family members, and preferred playmates, provided for Camus and also for Francine. In the official Pléiade album, there are snapshots of Janine and Camus in prewar days as colleagues at *Paris-Soir,* where they first met, and later of the two couples at small moments and in easy bonhomie—lounging on a lawn or a park bench; walking the dogs—although there are also some solemn images from Camus's visit to the sanatorium in Leysin. When he was sick or needed peace and quiet, Camus sometimes stayed with Janine and Michel in Paris. He talked about his problems—his marriage as well as his health. After 1951, when the Gallimards purchased an ancient *auberge* in a sleepy village in the Eure, Camus and his family spent frequent weekends there in happy retreat. The two TB patients practiced "cautious living" as Camus had been advised to do: reading, fishing in the river, playing Ping-Pong and family games.

There was very little time in his adult life when Camus was not under treatment for TB. The early years were ruled by the regimens of fortnightly pneumothoraxes, weekly radiology, and special diets to hasten his return to health. In later years, when the new drugs appeared to have arrested the advance of the disease, Camus's state of health was precarious in a different way, for by then his respiratory capacity was severely diminished—the result of damage from the pneumothorax injections and incessant smoking as well as the tubercle bacilli. The consequences included difficulty breathing, oxygen deprivation, and what one of his doctors described in 1957 as a condition of half-asphixiation. Judging from his own notes and reflections, Camus suffered his worst episodes with TB in the aftermath of his long lecture tour in South America during the summer of 1949. At its start, he was already sick and depressed, writing from Brazil that he had lost his hard-won equilibrium and was having a full psychological breakdown.[23] (Nonetheless he was able to comment: "If my hosts here knew the effort I was making just to seem normal, they would at least make an effort to smile from time to time.") Having believed that after enduring four years of lung collapse therapy he might have conquered the disease, Camus was distraught to find himself again, twenty years after the first indelible crisis, in a life-or-death situation, facing "the abyss." "To overcome? But anguish is just that, the thing to which one is never superior," he writes before his first course of antibiotics.[24] As usual, he turns to literary mentors for corroboration: "One must love life before loving its meaning, Dostoyevsky says. Yes, and when the love of life disappears, no meaning consoles us."[25] On the road to recovery in Cabris the following spring, he relates to Nietzsche: great style is feeling as much master of one's happiness as of one's unhappiness. A month later, Camus is better and puts the crisis behind him but cautiously, between parentheses, like a tentative sigh of relief: "(Be able to say: it was hard. I didn't succeed the first time and I struggled at great length. But in the end I won out. And such great exhaustion makes the success more lucid, more humble, but also more determined.)"[26]

Within several weeks of this last entry, Camus finished the first draft of *The Rebel,* which is a reminder that much of this book, like *The Plague,* was written when he was in a state of serious illness and in the throes of a physical struggle. Illness had its effect on the course of the book, which took Camus seven years to complete, and the course of the book undoubtedly had its effect on the illness. Issues of work, fame, and conscience intensified the drama of illness, adding weight to the feeling of powerlessness and entrapment. Later in the 1950s, when Camus's life seemed to be falling apart, the psychological effects of the disease seemed to be almost inseparable from the physical ones. Tuberculosis was less like an assault than an impossible stricture then, closing in on him as the world seemed to be.

It is difficult to deconstruct the anguish of these later days, for it sprang from so many interacting sources: the war in Algeria, the hostility of the

Parisian intellectual establishment, writer's block, bad lungs, and even the honor of the Nobel Prize. It was as if an Olympian force were working against him. Camus, who was suffering from depression, panic atttacks, and severe claustrophobia—he stopped riding the metro—and enduring moments of near-suffocation and a *"déséquilibre"* that was a sort of madness, expressed feelings of helplessness and was often close to tears. His notebooks from this time are scattered and spare, offering only a string of staccato notes—"new panic attack," "interminable anguish," "anxiety redoubled"—and a long passage promoting positive thinking to convey his state of mind.[27] Rather valiantly, he described his condition in early 1958, several months after the events in Stockholm, as simply "diminished." To Roger Quilliot, he was more precise: "I've just passed through a long and terrible period of depression, complicated by respiratory troubles, in which there was nothing for me to do. Just recently, I have caught my breath, as the expression goes."[28] Quilliot found Camus's survival a miracle.[29]

People close to Camus said that he didn't seem to be himself, or "cured," until mid-1959, when he was fully engaged in his novel *The First Man*. But he moved doggedly forward in new directions: successful productions of his adaptations of Faulkner's *Requiem for a Nun* and Dostoyevsky's *The Possessed;* negotiations for his own repertory theater; happy new alliances with an English actress named Catherine Sellars and a young Danish art student named Mi. Once again, he seemed relieved and renewed to be granted another uncertain reprieve, to be back on the fringes of normalcy. If Camus was vulnerable, he was also full of drive and dreams. "I always choose tasks that are beyond my powers, and that's what makes me live in continual effort, and what exhausts me," he had written to Francine after completing *The Rebel*.[30] With Mi, Camus put his illness in the past tense, and, despite their intimacy, she never suspected more than depression. Even now, it seems incredible to her that he had still been sick when they were together. "He was too dynamic," she said to me, looking back, and then, "He carried it well, but alone."[31]

Camus's long episodes of illness are imbued with a terrible sense of loneliness, which he came belatedly to accept. "Around the middle of my life, I had to learn all over again painfully how to live alone," he wrote in his notebooks on the way back to Cabris in early 1951.[32] To be stoic, like his mother, was to be silent and uncomplaining. Friends say that Camus expected to be touched more and more by illness and aging, and this expectation made him very melancholy. It is sobering to see him refer to himself in his last journal as a man of maturity, *un homme mur,* and express fears about growing old. Yet even when he was young, he had worried about aging. *"Ma jeunesse me fuit, C'est ça être malade,"* he had written from Le Panelier at twenty-nine.[33] He always marked his birthdays, obsessively taking stock, and he was always measuring his accomplishments against those of mentors like Tolstoy and Melville. This, too, reflected his illness and the inexorable ticking of its clock.

In the published photographs, it is impossible to discern Camus's state of health. Sometimes he is noticeably thin. Sometimes when he has admitted illness, as when Cartier-Bresson took his portrait for the book jacket of *The Fall,* he merely looks tired. In a home movie I saw, taken at the Gallimards' country place in the 1950s, he is playing the matador for his friends, dipping and twirling about with a woman's scarf, the picture of grace and fun. In many photographs Camus is smoking, even in Michel's room at the sanatorium in Leysin and during rehearsals for *The Possessed* in 1958, when, medically, he was in trouble. From time to time he cut down—no cigarettes before breakfast, he resolved in Cabris, and in the 1950s he reportedly managed a month of abstinence—but as much as a habit, cigarettes may have been another form of defiance, a way to appear normal, to carry on. In any case, they remain part of his lasting image.

Recently, I happened upon a little-known photograph of Camus and Michel Gallimard, which is so evocative of their friendship that it also registers as a comment on the saga of illness. It was a friend of mine who, in fact, happened upon the image, or rather the magazine supplement that had the image on its cover, at a garage sale outside Tours. "Could be from an old *Nouvel Obs* or *Match,"* she scribbled on a Post-it before sending it on to me. The dates are uncertain, but the setting and general ambience suggest one of the Mediterranean excursions the friends made in 1958: to Cannes and sailing in the Greek Islands. Whatever its provenance, the photograph is arresting, because it is large and in full color, and because it captures something special about the relationship between the two men. They are having lunch at an outdoor café and have paused to pose for this photo. Camus, in casual khaki with rolled-up sleeves, and unshaven, has thrown his arm over Michel's shoulder and leans into him, smiling so deeply that his dimples show. Michel, under Camus's wing, looks directly into the camera and wears the beginning of a puckish grin. Both men are tanned and look healthy and rather macho. They project an air of confidence and insouciance and a sense of togetherness that is almost a challenge. Above their heads the magazine has imposed a banner in red block letters that reads "*Camus Le Fraternel,*" which is only a suggestion of all that can be read in the image.

8

L'Homme Révolté

After exchanging a handful of letters about the possibility of an interview, Catherine Camus finally agreed to see me in Lourmarin, but she was not specific about dates, saying only, "It's better that you call me when you're in Paris." In her words, there was only the lightest implication of the frenzied life that comes with being the executrix of a literary estate including works that have been translated into several dozen languages. The return address on her envelopes, written in a hand that was a larger and more graceful version of her father's, was rue Albert Camus, which had a make-believe quality to it that was oddly disturbing.

The responses from Roger Quilliot bore the official logo of the *sénat*, where he represented the *département* of Puy-de-Dome, although at about that time he had stepped down as the local mayor, apparently for reasons of health. As a result of his acknowledged *mauvaise santé*, Quilliot had postponed our meeting twice, always with the most gracious of regrets, but sounding a new note of urgency. As I combed through the fine print in the Pléiade volumes, I could see through Quilliot's running commentary, which is both scholarly and intimately biographical, to the nature of his access to Camus—the long sessions with a complicated body of manuscripts, papers, and letters; the interplay with Camus's close friends and family; the memory of conversations with Camus—and I was struck again by his passion and compassion for his subject. In 1954, when he was twenty-nine and embarking on his book *La Mer et les Prisons* (*Sea and Prisons*), Quilliot was the first person for whom Camus opened up his "dossiers" (packing up a full valise of disorderly drafts and documents for him and putting himself *"à votre disposition"*). He was the first person to undertake a full study of Camus's work. At the time, Camus was both flattered and reassured by the project, for he recognized a "soundness" and a "sympathy without complacency" in Quilliot's thinking that touched him. The "ensemble" had always interested him, he wrote to Quilliot in a tender letter of gratitude, referring to his concern with having a unified body of work, and expressing his admiration for the work. In parentheses, as if in confidence, he expressed his extreme pleasure at being the subject of such a sympathetic study.[1]

In 1954, Camus's expression of gratitude for the sympathy that Quilliot had shown toward his work was touching in itself because, as Quilliot came to understand many years later, it was a quiet way of admitting how deeply he had been hurt by the rush of criticism that greeted the publication of *The Rebel*. Camus always asserted that *The Rebel* was his most important book and the book most like himself; this statement was a measure of his personal investment, commitment, and courage. Morally, it represented a brave concerted effort to speak to his times and to say what had been on his mind for years—as he put it to himself, for the good of everyone and without his habitual attempt at objectivity or *politesse*. After that, as his notebooks confirm, he felt he would be able to write more freely—he was, in fact, already commiting to paper long passages for future novels. *"La création en liberté,"* Camus promises himself going forward.

In a drama that has since become famous, Camus was undone by the hostile response to *The Rebel* in Paris, which even now seems like an ambush. Beginning even before the official publication of the book in October 1951, there were voices on both the right and the left challenging its content, but ultimately it was the attack from Sartre, his onetime friend and the self-acknowledged pope of letters, that gave the intellectual quarrel its power and fateful resonance. Camus may have been anxious about the reception of his new book, and worried about the tone of the first wave of criticism—"I am waiting patiently for a catastrophe that is slow to come," he wrote in his journal in December. But he could not have anticipated the full frontal assault on his work and character that came in *Les Temps Modernes* (*TM*), first at the hands of Francis Jeanson, the ambitious young disciple whom Sartre had selected to review the book, and then, in response to Camus's subsequent "Letter to *Monsieur le Directeur*," from *le directeur* himself. With this last exchange, the friendship between Camus and Sartre came to an end. Over the course of Camus's lifetime, they never spoke to each other or of each other again. Within months, the distance separating Camus from the intellectual establishment in Paris had widened to an unbridgeable chasm.

It is tempting to see the publication of *The Rebel* as the fulcrum event in Camus's life, one that divides his life into distinct parts: a before and an after, a rise to celebrity and a fall from grace. By the time the turmoil over the book, the letters back and forth with his critics, the explanations and *explications,* the anger and hurt, and the inevitable self-examination had begun to abate, Camus was caught in a downward spiral of other troubles—Francine's nervous breakdown, the Algerian war, and, in no small part as a product of all the foregoing, a long episode of writer's block. It seemed as if the direction of his life had abruptly shifted, that he had been thrown off course. In even his bleakest moments, however, Camus never wavered in his commitment to *The Rebel*. He didn't like to have enemies any more than anyone else did, he said, but he would write the book again if he had to.

In Paris, the press, which had reviewed *The Rebel* extensively, and in general very positively, covered the "polemic" or "literary quarrel" that erupted between the two celebrated thinkers like a major news event. As the August issue of *TM* that carried the exchange of letters had sold out, been reprinted, and sold out again, *Le Monde, L'Observateur,* and Camus's former newspaper *Combat* included lengthy extracts from the original texts in their coverage. (Camus was distressed that *Combat* had even entered the fray.) The weeklies played up the rupture in their way—"The Sartre-Camus Break Is Consummated" the tabloid *Samedi-Soir* announced in a three-column banner over a feature on the ten-year friendship. In the close-knit network of cafés and publishing houses in Saint-Germain, everyone knew the specifics of the controversy, judged the performances, and took sides. Few people besides Camus were surprised at the split, which—given the nature of the personalities and their respective positions on communism, and in particular Stalinism—had been long in the making. But no one could have predicted that it would assume such historic magnitude, or that the two protagonists would come to represent the forces of right and wrong in the twentieth century. The standoff between Camus and Sartre and their respective camps continued for another four decades, until the cold war had ended. At the moment, the reputations of the two men have been reversed, and probably will be again, but no rapprochement is in sight. There are still Camusians and Sartreans, and intellectuals who still choose to take sides between Camus and Sartre. New books attempt to shed nonpartisan light on the friendship. In Paris, an annual colloquium continues to try to effect a reconciliation.

It seems important to remember that Camus was a famous author when he wrote *The Rebel,* because his considerable fame figured in the mission of the book and also its reception. As his detractors charged, Camus was writing from a podium, for he knew that his name meant something, as he did when he used his signature to protest against the situation in Spain, Greece, or Hungary, and he wanted to exert an influence on contemporary thinking. Although he had avoided politics since 1948, he felt pressured by his own conscience to deliver his personal diagnosis of the current situation in Europe, his "attempt to understand the times," as letters and the journal show. In speaking out on the need for revolt, he was speaking of his own experience, he explained to an early critic, and he duly recognized the intrinsic dangers and limits of such an undertaking. He wanted to be both truthful and useful, he had said to Char, with whom he forged so much of the thinking in the book—"our work," he called it when he presented the rough copy of his manuscript, with scratch-outs and typos, to his friend. It never would have been a book of hope without you, he noted in his inscription.

For Camus the book was *une somme,* a sum total of all that he had learned since the Resistance, all that he had written since *The Myth of Sisyphus,* all his culture, he said, a mixed bag of reading, reflection, and experience, including material drawn from the real-life stories of revolutionaries like his new friends Rosmer and Lazarévitch, or Ivan Kaliayev, the Russian poet and terrorist who assassinated Grand Duke Sergei

Romanov in 1905 and who was, for Camus, the embodiment of a moral dilemma. (Kaliayev aborts his first attempt at assassination to avoid also killing the grand duke's wife and nephews, who are in his carriage.) It was also the last, grand installment of his cycle on revolt, an explicit theoretical illustration of *The Plague* and a companion piece to *The Just Assassins* (in which Kaliayev is the protagonist), a full-blown analysis of man's instinct for revolution, and of how revolutions create their own tyranny. Camus had searched philosophy, history, and art for his material, reaching back to the Greeks and the early Christians, moving forward through romanticism, dandyism, surrealism, Hegel, Marx, Nietzsche, the Nazis, and the Bolsheviks, including *Wuthering Heights* and *The Brothers Karamazov* in his view, and in the end finding answers in the Mediterranean commitment to moderation and measure. No one else could have written such a work, Char said, referring to the combination of ambition, idealism, and courage that Camus had brought to the book.

It was perhaps naive or arrogant to take on the subject of revolt and revolution (including the French Revolution) in so unorthodox a manner, for it almost invited criticism, particularly from the watchful Sartrean circle. Camus expected *The Rebel* to be denounced by the communist left, and he seemed to sense that the work might also be unpopular in other quarters. Grenier had warned him that he was going to make enemies, and he found himself wondering about the "solidarity" of some of his friends. "In a few days, there won't be many people any more who will extend me their hand," he commented darkly. During the first round of criticism, Camus had tried to keep his distance because, as he confided knowingly, he could never take things lightly. He reined in his combative instincts, at least for a while. "Never attack anyone, especially not in writing," he admonishes himself in his journal, "totally eliminating criticism and polemics." "The worst of fortunes is a bad temperament."[2] Months before the onslaught in *TM,* he was already exhausted and depressed —*vidé,* he described himself to Char, hollowed out. In response to the early commercial success of the book—it sold 60,000 copies in four months—he wondered if people were actually reading it, indeed if much of the criticism might not be secondhand. He seemed almost primed for bad news, or at least vulnerable. He had his recurrent dream of being executed. When he ran into a fellow *résistant* whom he had not seen since the tumultuous days of liberation, he was almost tearful with nostalgia for his comrades.

Camus's friends had some questions about *The Rebel,* but mostly they kept their thoughts to themselves. Grenier, whose intimacy with Camus's thinking went back to his years as Camus's philosophy professor at both the lycée and the university and who had done a fastidious critique of the manuscript—the book was duly dedicated to him—thought it worthy of praise, but lacking in organization and subtlety. He also questioned its "tone," which could sound reactionary to certain ears. Char, like others, had reservations about the disparaging pages on the Marquis de Sade and the Comte de Lautréamont, writers who had been important to him in his surrealist youth, although he thought the work as a whole admirable and courageous. ("Ah, dear Albert, reading this rejuvenated, refreshed, strengthened, expanded me, thank you.)"[3] Char's response was note-worthy because it was Camus's critical treatment of the mystical poet Lautréamont, revered by surrealists as their founding light, that inflamed André Breton, leader of the movement, and effectively set the stage for the wars to come.[4] Breton, keeper of the flame, responded accordingly. "One cannot protest enough when writers who enjoy public favor oc-cupy themselves by attacking what is a thousand times greater than they."[5] So began the "year of polemics" that Camus later described as "*le procès de ma personne,*" "the indictment of my person."

In the course of his sweeping inquiry into the nature of revolt, Camus dealt harshly with others in the pantheon of French letters. He also de-bunked the official version of the French Revolution, denouncing its bloodiness and drawing comparisons between Jacobinism and Bolshevism, between 1789 and 1917. He was making points about different theories and forms of revolt, describing the perversions, illusions, and bad faith that could turn the instinct for freedom into a justification of murder and servitude in the name of history, describing how revolutions always cre-ate their own tyranny. It was daring to be so candid and confrontational, but it was also provocative if not heretical to execute so many local heroes. "Every French schoolboy, if his family wasn't of the extreme right, has an admitted or secret respect for Robespierre and St. Just," Olivier Todd explains.[6] "In the lycées of France and Algeria, one accepts the axiom that the execution of Louis XVI was perhaps precipitous, but necessary."

Camus's friend Robert Gallimard says simply, "*The Rebel* had a moral that went against everything one thought then."[7]

At the heart of *The Rebel* was the question of communism. Here Camus was the most confrontational of all, although he never mentioned the name of Stalin. "We are living in an era of premeditation and the perfect crime," he declares three sentences into the book. "One might think that a period which, in the space of fifty years, uproots, enslaves, or kills seventy million human beings should be condemned out of hand. But its culpability must still be understood." How does it happen that man, in the name of revolt, can rationally accept mass death, concentration camps under the banner of freedom, and "massacres justified by philanthropy or by a taste for the superhuman?" he asks.[8] "In an age of negation, it was helpful to examine one's position on the problem of suicide," he recalls, referring to his focus in *The Myth of Sisyphus*. In the age of ideologies, we must examine our position on murder.

In Paris during the winter of 1951–1952 and in the world where *The Rebel* surfaced, the time was ripe for a showdown on communism and ready for a figure (or a controversy) to point up the stakes. Many intellectuals who identified with the party (Sartre's philosopher friend Maurice Merleau-Ponty, as a prime example) were finding it difficult to sustain their belief in the Soviet Union's system. Independent leftists who had hoped to develop a "third force" had become skeptical about the possibility of meaningful action. Meanwhile, as the Korean conflict widened— China began its offensive in April 1951—the cold war seemed more immediately threatening to Europe than ever. A year earlier, after North Korea invaded South Korea and American troops began to move north, there had been talk in France of an imminent invasion by the Soviet Union. From these weeks, Beauvoir recounts a conversation in a café between Camus and Sartre about the scent of danger in the air. "'Have you thought about what will happen to you when the Russians get here?' [Camus] asked Sartre and then added with a great deal of emotion: 'You mustn't stay!' 'And do you expect to leave?' asked Sartre. 'Oh, I'll do what I did during the German occupation.'"[9] Camus still thought of Sartre as a fellow traveler on the noncommunist left, but Beauvoir confides that merely thinking about an invasion from the Soviet Union had spurred the "rethinking of Marxism and man" that transformed Sartre into a political realist and pro-communist. In other words, the lines had already been drawn.

By now an assortment of books have been devoted to sorting out the Camus-Sartre "affair"—a term that seems just right given the fact that it involved, as almost everyone agrees, an undeniable component of love. This effort has meant tracing the rift back to many possible origins.[10] The end of the cold war and the possibility of a more balanced view have aided the process. Perhaps because Camus and Sartre are still seductive characters (or because no one has shown up to take their places), or perhaps simply because their lives abound in provocative parallels and contrasts, their falling-out now makes an even bigger and better story than it did as a political *mano à mano* more than half a century ago. Their seemingly small contretemps of the postwar years fit into the narrative. Camus's attack on Merleau-Ponty's position on the Moscow trials takes on new weight when we know the course that Sartre, who supported Merleau-Ponty that evening, will follow. ("Camus, shattered, left, slamming the door behind him . . . [and] refused to come back," according to Beauvoir's eyewitness account.)[11] In the 1950s, ironically, Sartre and Merleau-Ponty will have their own differences over Sartre's "ultrabolshevism." All the issues of conscience on which Camus took an independent stand—the editorials on the A-bomb and the purges; the series "Neither Victims nor Executioners" in which even in 1946 he was equating communism with murder—mark the steadily diverging paths. Sartre's major works do too. Most pointedly, his play *Le Diable et le Bon Dieu* (*The Devil and the Good Lord*), which opened just a year after *The Just Assassins* finished its run, seemed to issue a direct warning to Camus, for its hero, caught in a different revolution and torn between the forces of good and evil, embraces violence as the necessary engine of change, whereas Camus's hero Kaliayev, even after his crime, had rejected it. The play, according to Beauvoir, was the mirror of Sartre's entire ideological evolution. As a follow-up, in much the same way that Camus had just published *The Rebel* to elaborate on the thinking in *The Just Assassins,* Sartre made his message unequivocal in a 300-page doctrine, "The Communists and Peace." Like a final challenge to the relationship, the first of three installments ran in the July 1952 issue of *TM* and established Sartre as the leading independent pro-communist in France.[12]

Most accounts of the public exchange that appeared the following month in *TM* mention the number of pages it consumed in the magazine —seventeen by Camus, twenty for Sartre's reply, and then an additional thirty for a second text from the original reviewer, Francis Jeanson—as if the editors were trying to quantify its intensity. Of the three voices, Sartre's is the unforgettable one. "My dear Camus: Our friendship was not easy, but I shall miss it. If you end it today, that doubtless means that it had to end." The first sly sentences of his text still make one squirm in anticipation of the attack to follow, one of the most vitriolic of Sartre's life. The length was pounding and the content was punishing, all the more so because the tone was so confident and knowing. Clearly, the words were intended to wound, and of course this intention was part of the public entertainment. Certain phrases like "the portable pedestal" caught on and stuck to Camus all his life; these taunts became as facile as slogans. "You do us the honor of contributing to this issue of *Les Temps Modernes,* but you bring a portable pedestal with you," Sartre says, winding up, denigrating the references Camus had made in his own letter to his poverty and the Resistance, carrying Jeanson's earlier jabs about Camus's "*l'âme révolté,*" or "soul in revolt" (in French, close in sound to his book title) or his "Red Cross morality" a step farther.

Sartre had been put on the defensive by Camus's letter, which made him relentless and cruel. Jeanson was ironic and condescending and disagreed aggressively with Camus's ideas about revolution as expressed in his book, but Sartre, addressing himself only to Camus's letter, slashes directly at the man and his character. In showing outrage, hurt, and self-righteousness in his own letter, Camus may have brought out the bully in Sartre, a bully who becomes ever meaner because of the guilt of knowing the pain he is inflicting. "Your combination of dreary conceit and vulnerability always discouraged people from telling you unvarnished truths," Sartre explains, saying that for the first time since their acquaintance began, he will speak unsparingly. "The result is that you have become the victim of a dismal self-importance, which hides your inner problems, and which you, I believe, call Mediterranean moderation. Sooner or later, someone would have told you: let it be me."

Having thus introduced his remarks, Sartre proceeds with a virtual flogging, chastising Camus for his moralism, his sanctimoniousness, his philosophical incompetence, and his style—"its pomposity, which is natural to you," its calculated ease and expedient rage—ridiculing his poor grasp of the issues, lecturing him like a wayward student. There is almost always a nasty edge. About Camus's letter: "Tell me, Camus, for what mysterious reasons may your works not be discussed without taking away humanity's reasons for living?" About his identification with *la misère*: "Perhaps you were poor once, but you aren't any longer; you are a bourgeois like Jeanson and me."[13] About his book: "And suppose you did not reason very well? And suppose your thinking was muddled and banal?" Somehow, the subject in contention between the two men, their respective attitudes toward communism, never seems as urgent as that of comportment or manner.

Whether from a release of pent-up anger or from sheer pride at his own performance, which everyone would say was brilliant, Sartre on the offensive seems positively gleeful. In concluding (over fourteen pages in the reprint), he speaks to Camus about what he once meant to him and what had changed—a parting send-off that says much about himself, too. Ironically, the lines that are so frequently cited to describe Camus (and are discernible in the Nobel commendation) have their source here: "You had been for us—you could again be tomorrow—the admirable conjunction of a person, an action, and a work. That was in 1945. We discovered Camus, the Resistant, as we discovered Camus, the author of *The Stranger* . . . and the editor of the clandestine *Combat* . . . : Then you were not far from being exemplary. For in you were resumed the contraditions of our times, and you transcended them through the ardor with which you lived them."[14] Tracking Camus through the postwar years, Sartre reduces him to a has-been. "You should have changed if you had wanted to remain yourself, but you were afraid to change," he concludes, referring to Camus's position on communism and "against history." "Your personality, which was real and vital so long as it was nourished by events, has become a mirage. . . . You are only a half-life among us." In saying farewell, Sartre formally closes the door and takes the last word as his own. He would not reply further to Camus, he said, and hoped that their silence would cause the polemic to be forgotten.

No one has fully explained the viciousness that makes Sartre's letter still so painful to read. That it arose from something personal and amounted to a settling of scores seems to be clear from the content. Even the well-placed snideness betrays an underlying interest and caring, however reconfigured. That Sartre was hurt as well as angered by Camus's letter, which abstracted him into "The Editor," and put him on trial, may explain some of the venom. Camus was talking not to him but about him, he said, transforming him into an object or a dead person, speaking of him like a soup plate or a mandolin. Camus, for all the clumsiness of his letter, had hit some tender spots, too—certainly in pointing up Sartre's lack of engagement and even of manhood during the occupation. "I am beginning to become a little tired of seeing myself—and even more, of seeing former militants who have never refused the struggles of their time—receive endless lessons in effectiveness from critics who have never done anything more than turn their armchair in history's direction," he said, referring to an incident during liberation when he had come upon Sartre asleep in an orchestra seat in the theater of the Comédie-Française.[15] In a very deliberate way, he may have been baiting Sartre. And Sartre, who loved a good scrap, and who for the first time in his life was politically fully engaged, responded to the affront with his own cool version of self-righteousness—in order not to lose face, as he put it—and set off the full blast of his rhetoric.

The pain inflicted in the course of this literary quarrel is part of why it is so mesmerizing and so memorable. ("If you find me cruel," Sartre posits early on, reveling, it seems, in his *mal d'esprit* as much as attempting to recuse himself.) After a few pages, even as I was flinching for Camus, my stomach in knots, I found it impossible to extricate myself from the language of the assault, which is so driving and canny that it had an almost paralytic effect on me. This resulted not only from the skill of Sartre's rhetoric, but also from his palpable rage and from my own sense of anticipation. "Oh, Camus," "Believe me, Camus," "Tell me, Camus"—the dialogue is direct and real, the target ever closer. Knowing Camus's vulnerability brings a shudder at the thought of the damage that could be done, at the mental setback that will be inevitable, and an empathetic stab of hurt. In the end, the saddest part of the story may be that Camus—who counted so explicitly on the loyalty of others—never really seemed to understand the attack or its savagery. Nor did he understand why no one rushed to his defense or how even in the corridors of Gallimard his colleagues were rather amused by the matter and seemed to side with the

Sartreans. His journal records his wounds and anguish. "Every man and woman on me, to destroy me . . . without ever, ever lending a hand, coming to my aid, loving me finally for what I am, so that I may remain as I am." Like a cry in the wilderness: "I am the most deprived and needy of beings."[16] To Grenier, he wrote of being in the midst of an immense mystification. To Francine, he wrote of his solitude and somberness. He was struggling to find equilibrium, "to resist the temptation of despising too much, as well as not despising enough," he said. "Such acrobatics are not easy, but they are my destiny."[17]

Instinctively, Camus seemed to sense that Sartre had prevailed in this public display, as the members of the literary crowd were saying among themselves—certain leftists assigned grades, giving Sartre a superior 18 and Camus a middling 9 or 10. Camus's friend Jean Daniel, who was on the scene in 1952, says simply, "Sartre was wrong but at times more brilliant."[18] Even more troubling for Camus was the suspicion that there was some truth in the accusations, and that the attack might have been justified. Camus did not take criticism lightly—he had his own self-doubt to contend with—and Sartre had played on his fear that success had come too easily, that he had become self-satisfied, self-important, and ponderous. Whereas Sartre could and did pass off the incident as just another intellectual exercise, and another annoying encounter with Camus—"*Il m'enguele,*" "He's in my face," he had said about Camus recently—Camus did not, and could not, get away from all its distortions and implications and his own sense of betrayal. For many months he avoided the public and public places, certainly those cafés and restaurants that Sartre frequented in the 6th and 7th *arrondissements,* seeking comfort and a safe haven with Algerian friends and non-Parisians such as Char. The mail, which was heavy, brought support for him and for his book from ordinary readers and well-known intellectuals alike, and he kept those letters for reassurance. He still wanted to send Sartre a second response, which Char and Grenier encouraged, but he knew that it could be seen only as defensive, an *apologie de soi.* Privately, in an attempt to put the case to rest, he set down his thoughts in a fifteen-page essay, "*Défense de l'Homme Révolté,*" that was never published. He expounded carefully and gravely on how and why he had come to write his book, and how he had developed the reasoning for what was simply his "testimony." He referred only in passing to the "vain uproar" of recent weeks and he closed with an effort at transcendence, speaking of the usefulness even of the hostility, which "one day or another, everyone, ourselves included, will understand."[19]

There were those who thought that Camus was not such an innocent party in this quarrel, that not only had he explicitly provoked Sartre but that indeed he knew, or should have known, what was coming. Sartre's changing politics were evident in the play *The Devil and the Good Lord*—and Camus, who was intimately involved with its star, Maria Casarès, and showed up regularly at rehearsals, was certainly familiar with this play—as well as in the new direction that *TM* was taking. The relationship between the two men had cooled since the early days and was becoming more superficial—what Robert Gallimard has called *une amitié de surface*—since they couldn't really talk anymore about serious issues. Beauvoir cites as evidence the lapse in their weekly lunches, although Camus's illness and his long absences from Paris might also have explained this. Camus wasn't easy, other friends say, pointing out that he had his share of enemies, that he was by nature combative and drawn to *la bagarre,* which, of course, is exactly what was also said about Sartre. Sartre, too, was very complicated, and despite his many close relationships, except for Beauvoir, he was not very constant.

By now, critics have acquired the distance necessary to see the two lives and the two bodies of work in counterpoint and in tandem. They note the men's different backgrounds, different styles and strategies, and different public images—Sartre, the *école normalien* of the cultivated elite, the philosopher and systematic thinker, who had effectively rejected his background; Camus, the scholarship student without a heritage, a moralist in the old French tradition, and, as he described himself, not a *philosophe* but an *artiste,* who was proud to be an Algerian. They point out the professional rivalry between two men, who had the same publisher, who each edited a left-wing periodical, and who wrote novels, plays, essays, journalism, and literary criticism, with similar tones and themes and, in the beginning, a common purpose. Looking back, the critics find the seeds of this confrontation in their first exchanges, when Camus praised *Nausea* in the *Alger Républicain* but found it too theoretical, and Sartre, although praising *The Stranger* extravagantly, felt it was not well thought out. They say that even at their closest Camus and Sartre were on divergent political paths and sooner or later would have parted ways.

There was an element of happenstance in the ultimate showdown, a wild card, as it were, in the person of Jeanson. Sartre, it seems, who had held back for months on running a review of *The Rebel,* and casually warned Camus that the magazine's comments would be "reserved" or "possibly severe," had chosen Jeanson with the expectation that he would produce a discreet, mild critique of a book that Sartre unquestionably disliked but did not plan to trash. Camus, after all, had published two chapters of this work in the magazine and was a highly respected writer as well as a friend. Camus, for his part, had no reason to expect a personal thrashing, particularly from a fledgling critic, and his letter to *le directeur,* which expressed his surprise that such treatment had been permitted, may have also been an ill-conceived plea for Sartre's intervention. When it came, Sartre's response was shocking, in part because it struck him as the explosion of long-suppressed hatred. "It proves that these people were never my friends and that I always offended them by what I believe," he wrote to Francine, his tone conveying a vague hope that somehow he might be proved wrong. There was no other explanation for the extreme vulgarity of these attacks, he said.[20] It seems more than likely that Camus never fully recovered from the blows dealt by Sartre. One measure of his pain and disaffection may be how many years it took him to find a voice and a sense of purpose. That came, at least perceptibly, with the writing of his novel *The Fall,* which was, precisely and spectacularly, a response in kind to Sartre—a biting, ironic replay of his accusations and a brilliant thesis on judgment. In his famous eulogy for Camus, Sartre would refer to *The Fall* as his masterpiece and perhaps the most beautiful and the least understood of his works.

In his Pléiade notes, Quilliot describes the split between Camus and Sartre as a friendship killed by history. Robert Gallimard, who knew the two parties in different ways but equally well (he socialized with Camus and edited Sartre), has referred to the fall-out as "the end of a love affair." Todd calls it "fratricide." Tragedy and loss are part of the story, perhaps because the relationship was distorted by the partisanship and polarization of cold war politics, perhaps because it ended so badly, perhaps because the silence that replaced the years of conversation did not feel like silence. Almost if they were addressing each other, there was still a dialogue in the air, which could be perceived in their respective essays or political editorials, particularly during the Algerian war.[21] "He and I had quarreled," Sartre said in his eulogy, explaining that a quarrel was just another way of living together. "It didn't keep me from thinking of him, from feeling that his eyes were on the book or the newspaper I was reading and wondering: 'What does he think about it? What does he think of it *at this moment?*'"[22] In an interview many years later he referred to Camus his "last good friend."

In the public mind, Camus and Sarrtre are forever linked, sometimes even confused. The events of 1952 are a reminder that Camus stood distinctly apart from the Sartreans and the intellectual elite in Paris. They offer a clarification after the fact, however, for Camus had never been and had never wanted to be part of the *TM* crowd, and he had never been comfortable in the Parisian world of letters, where he somehow felt *coupable*—guilty—as if he were wearing a mask, he said. Intellectually, he had more in common with writers like Koestler, Orwell, and Hannah Arendt, who spoke the same moral language and took up the same causes. They too were exiles and outsiders. After reading *The Rebel,* Arendt, whose book *The Origins of Totalitarianism* had appeared earlier in 1951, went to see Camus. Miriam Chiaromonte ran into Arendt on the street that day and remembers that she was all dressed up for the occasion and wearing a new hat.

Camus suffered for a long time from the quarrel with Sartre, which affected his work—he was thinking about writing but not writing, he reports to his journal a year later—and then the quarrel fed into darker and darker times, so that the whole last decade of Camus's life, irrespective of his achievements, seemed to move along at a heavy, ominous pace. When war broke out in Algeria in late 1954, and Camus's politics and principles again marginalized him and eventually made him what Jean Daniel called the scapegoat of the intellectual left, the Sartre affair came to look like not only a preview of times to come but also a rude introduction.

When I was in college, *The Rebel*—or *The Rebel, An Essay on Man in Revolt,* the full title—provided the grist for my thesis, because it set forth in detail

Camus's thoughts about the limits of reason, particularly in regard to violence and murder, and my thesis was about Camus and his idea of limits. At the time, however, I wasn't wild about this book, which I found rather dull, even didactic, and also hard going, although I couldn't admit it then. For this reason, I was amused to see in the Knopf files that according to the initial report from its expert reader, the book was "difficult in every respect, difficult to evaluate, difficult to understand, and above all, difficult to read."[23]

Beyond the tantalizing assortment of letters between Blanche and Albert, the Knopf files that I saw in Texas amounted to an armload of in-house and transatlantic communiqués that anyone who wasn't primed for new insights might have dismissed as rather thin material. Nonetheless, spottily and in slow motion, in the way of radiograms and old-fashioned long-distance letters, the story of the evolution of *The Rebel* in America emerges month by month, from October 1949, when Blanche writes to Camus, applying discernible pressure—"I imagine that you are getting on with *L'Homme en Révolte*"—to December 1953, when Camus reminds Blanche that Waldo Frank wants to review the book for *The New Republic*. In the interim, there are plans to publish the book in a single volume with *The Myth of Sisyphus,* memos about sharing the cost of the English translation, negotiations over the proposed cutting, and a barrage of ever more negative readers' reports from ever more elevated sources. (The eminent Willard Van Orman Quine of the philosophy department at Harvard wrote: "The book gets distinctly bad at those points, happily infrequent, where the author goes through the motions of demonstrative reasoning. . . . Because of the morass in which he has chosen to plant his morals, not many readers will wade through.")[24] During this time Blanche, who overrides Quine's remarks (and sends him twenty-five dollars), is determined to stand by this book and her favorite author despite the prospect of a poor reception and grim sales, although she is also hard-nosed and pragmatic—"If Camus is unhappy about it, then I would say to h . . . with the whole thing and I will forget about it and let someone else publish it"—and presumably the affair tests her mettle. Even after publication, there is the daunting problem of the translation, which was so full of errors "of such a shocking and disfiguring nature, and in such numbers as to damage the content of the book, if not the reputation of its author," as one of the many letters of criticism warned, that Knopf felt it had no choice but to commission a revision, which appeared a year after the initial publication.[25]

Monitoring the progress of the book, I can feel France, the French, and even the presence of Camus receding. It is a reminder that the American version of *The Rebel* was a new entity, with a new title, a new nature, and a new audience. Transplanted, translated, and cut—the discussion about the surrealists is missing—and released in a country where the collective experience and the political psyche were very different, it had its own life, and Camus as its author his own perceived personality. This was also true of the many other foreign editions of the book. Among the foreign editions, *The Rebel* postdated those in Scandinavia and western Europe by a year or two—a Dutch version and a German version came first—and was followed by the Japanese version a year later. In the 1960s and 1970s, a contraband text of *The Rebel* was circulated underground in the Soviet Union—thermo-faxed page by thermo-faxed page at the University of Moscow, according to a Russian friend who was helping to distribute the text at the time. There were similar stories from young dissidents all over eastern Europe.

In New York in the spring of 1954, an early review of *The Rebel* in *Commentary* magazine seemed to question its relevance, even while finding the book "noble in concept" and Camus something of a hero. "The English or American reader may be rather bewildered by *The Rebel* if he fails to understand that what he has before him is an intensely Parisian book, written for an audience that in the immediate postwar years was the most lively and interesting in the world, but that recently has been showing signs of a growing provincialism," the reviewer wrote in his explanation of the intellectual fireworks in Paris a year and a half earlier.[26] He described *The Rebel* as "an attempt to convince French intellectuals of something that in Britain or the United States no longer requires proof— that the great revolutions of our time have been perverted to ends that are nearly the opposite of those [their] progenitors had in view," a rather haughty reading, I thought. It sent me to the Internet to seek out other opinions. Google retrieved 8,170 sources from the keywords Albert Camus/The Rebel that day, which was the first time that I became aware of the vast network in cyberspace discussing Camus. I was grateful for the exposure but I did not pursue the leads, nor did I join a Camus chat room. I admired the constancy and breadth of his fans, but I was enjoying my own deepening relationship with Camus. "Don't you sometimes wish they'd stop?" one of my most vigilant Parisian friends had scribbled on a note accompanying a review of a memoir of Camus by the actor and singer Sergio Reggiani, who had appeared in several of his plays. Sometimes I suppose I did, but like a good friend I was also pleased by Camus's popularity.

9

Friends

Camus reported in his journal that the uproar over *The Rebel* had consumed at least a year of his life. That was a measure of the time devoted only to polemics, from his early skirmish with André Breton over his attack on surrealism to his long, careful "Defense of The Rebel," which he ultimately kept to himself. In a larger view, the whole affair appears to have been far more invasive. It is not difficult to see Camus's future moves as a reaction to the attack on his persona, as he had put it—his extensive travel in Algeria, his return to the theater, the short stories he wrote, the house he bought in Provence. Yet as he proceeded to distance himself from everyone and everything that had oppressed him in Paris, it was less like a retreat than an attempt to reclaim earlier happiness, to reassert who he was—to get closer to his center, as he described in the new preface to *The Wrong Side and the Right Side,* which was reissued in 1958.

This preface, like almost everything written in the aftermath of the *The Rebel*—the last essays in *Summer;* the stories, such as "Jonas," that were the beginning of *Exile and the Kingdom;* a second volume of *Actuelles;* a piece on Oscar Wilde in prison; and some other efforts that were just work as usual—seems to have stunning relevance when seen as reflecting Camus's frame of mind and as providing a running commentary. In "Return to Tipasa," perhaps the most confessional essay in *Summer,* which dates from the long trip to Algeria in December 1952, Camus issues his now famous testimony of survival—"In the depths of winter, I finally learned that within me lay an invincible summer"—which I had long ago adopted as my own. The preface to *The Wrong Side and the Right Side* effectively says the same thing. "I had not yet been through the years of true despair," Camus explains as he looks back on the work from his twenties. "They came and managed to destroy everything in me, except an uncontrolled appetite to live."[1] The story "Jonas," originally subtitled "The Artist Takes Refuge," is also about retreat and isolation, and it has lines that echo Camus's journal. In *Actuelles II,* the second volume of pieces that "touch on current affairs," Camus included both his response to Breton and his letter to Sartre, as if he was determined to make his case and still trying to prove himself to his critics.

Knowing from the notebooks and biographies that during these months Camus was deep in a *"solitude tragique"*—Francine uses the word *prosterné,* or "prostrated," to describe him to Grenier—makes me ready to read pain and sensitivity into his every word, to sniff out distress or defensiveness in his every action. There are some obvious moves and easy calls. In an interview, Camus denies any allegiance ever with existentialism and the existentialists, while noting in his journal "the total disappearance of compassion in their universe of pushy old men."[2] He openly expresses his disrespect for *TM* and its values, and agrees to write for a new magazine, *Témoin.* The words *la morale* and *un moraliste* crop up more frequently than usual, as if he is consciously or unconsciously mulling over the criticism and feeling the weight of his reputation for virtue and conscience. "Every society, and particularly in literature, aims to shame its members with their extreme virtues," he writes in the journal.[3] With its intimate climate and trenchant thoughts—on censure, pardon, or punishment—the journal can be all too seductive, too leading. But as a sounding board, it can also be unmistakably explicit. "Noble trade where one must, without budging, let oneself be insulted by a lackey of letters or one of the party!" Camus records, with an uncharacteristic exclamation point, in October 1953, apparently still reacting to Sartre and Jeanson a year later. Then, in the next entry, he makes an attempt at closure: "There are people whose religion consists of always forgiving offenses, but who never forget them. For me, I don't have what it takes to forgive the offense, but I always forget it."[4]

Of the documents of this time, the most startling—for its candor, its content, and its full inclusion in the journal—is a letter Camus drafted to his journalist friend Pierre Berger in mid-February 1953. Reprimanded by Berger for breaking a recent appointment and for his "haughty solitude" in general, Camus responds with a searing description of an unhappy, overwrought life in which he has no time to see his friends ("ask Char whom I love like a brother how many times *a month* we see each other") or to write for magazines, "even to take control of an argument with Sartre"—no time, unbelievably, to be sick. Most gravely, he continues, he no longer has the time or peace of mind to write his books; he spends four years writing something that should have taken one or two, and feels enslaved rather than liberated by his work. Far beyond active despair, without a twinge of irony, Camus seems utterly depleted, like Jonas, and also sad. "Some mornings, tired of the noise, discouraged by the interminable work to be done, sick of this crazy world . . . finally sure that I won't be up to it and that I will disappoint everyone, I want only to sit and wait for evening to come."[5] In closing, he notes that Berger's letter, which is only one of the reasons that he has to flee Paris and "the strange existence I lead there," is also the price that he pays for staying. He is writing without bitterness, he says, ending with "Forgive me for having disappointed you."

It may be that this letter, a rare window into Camus's weary soul, is equally valuable as a reminder of the nature of his life, particularly at a point when life was threatening to crush his spirit and will. Camus had missed his rendezvous with Berger because he had been enlisted at the last minute to sign books to benefit refugees; he was always juggling responsibilities and fighting to keep up. "To measure up, today I would need three lives and several hearts," he notes, adding grimly, "But I have only one, one that people can judge and I often judge to be of middling quality."[6] To find a reference to his exchange with Sartre in the middle of a long lineup of other issues is to realize that there are multiple sources of stress behind Camus's current state of despondency and that the cumulative effect of celebrity, illness, and exile, in collusion with the unusual portion of hurt that came from the criticism of *The Rebel,* have worn him thin. "One by one the stars fell into the sea," Camus had written in his journal during the summer of 1952.[7] It is a dramatic and haunting image, and Camus eventually used it in a short story in *Exile and the Kingdom.* Floating alone on the page without a context, it also seems to apply to Camus's life, and it stays in mind like a terrible parable.[8]

After the months of drama and tension, it comes as a relief that Camus took himself off to Algeria for an usually long stay that first December, in flight from "the night of Europe, the winter of faces," seeking out places he has never been. A soggy week in Algiers was eased by his visit to Tipasa, only the second one during his fifteen years of expatriation, and a side trip to the farmland west of the city where his maternal grandparents had settled a century earlier. Both trips are clues to his need for reconnection. Then he was on the road, driving deep into the Sahara and wandering to the oasis towns of Laghouat and Ghaedaïa, breathing more deeply in the silence and solitude, taking in a landscape that helped to pacify and restore him even as it saddened him. He was looking for something to move him, he told a friend, and again his own country—the ancient calm and the mossy gods of Tipasa, the howling wind and the vibrant earth colors of southern Algeria, and everywhere the brilliant light—awoke in him the physical response that was his measure of life. That much is conveyed by what he wrote immediately afterward, in the essay "Return to Tipasa" and the story "The Adulterous Woman," each with its lyrical yearning prose, its scent of the earth, and its moment of connection. But this journey also made it more difficult to resume normal life in Paris and sharpened the feeling of entrapment and persecution that had surfaced in the letter to Berger, which was written only a few weeks after his return.

In a climate of transition or uncertainty, I have learned to open the journal and take a reading on Camus. He is off the cuff and off the record here, perhaps less inclusive than he was before he had a public and visibility, but still, for Camus, who was otherwise a man of many drafts, convincingly spontaneous. I know Camus better now, and even when I find hard information sparse or spotty, there are moods, tones, and impressions to soak up, all of which make him seem more transparent. Nonetheless, I was still making new discoveries about him. The way Camus writes and the medium of a journal create a sense of depth and truth. Sometimes a random notation can be a timely reminder of what Camus was really like. "Socrates learned to dance at an advanced age," he writes. "The white rose of morning has the fragrance of water and pepper." The lone phrase "a courageous tie." After a quote from Ben Jonson, there is a "curious thought" from the same source: "We do not receive letters in our grave."[9] Sometimes, too, I know that the words, however intriguing, are only writing.

Camus added fifty-odd pages to his journal between late 1952, when he was beginning to recover from the Sartre affair, and late summer of 1954, when he ends notebook number VII with a description of having been precipitated into "*malheur muet,*" "misery beyond words." Until this last passage, the entries convey no sense of the darkening aspects in Camus's personal life or their potential effect on his ability to write. In 1953 and early 1954, Camus appears to be carrying on quite appropriately for an author who has just finished a long, major, controversial volume. A new, restless energy percolates through pages filled with copious notes for two new novels, outlines for numerous plays, and musings on theater. A convincing picture emerges of Camus afloat on a sea of ideas, confronting the next cycle of his work, assembling an inventory.

Beginning well before the completion of *The Rebel,* Camus had described the foreseeable future as one of "creation." Now, he explained his intentions more precisely in a letter to a friend. "My future books will not turn away from the problem of the hour. But . . . I dream of a freer creation, with the same contents. . . . Then I will know if I am a true artist."[10] In the notebooks, where he inscribed this excerpt from his letter, Camus focused on the process, nurturing images, closing in on recurrent ideas, giving his mind free rein. He attaches the name *The First Man* to a novel, and funnels into the project personal anecdotes and thoughts about a mother, poverty, and the search for a father. He enters long notes about Nemesis, whom he describes as the goddess of moderation and names as the patron saint of his next cycle of work. If he didn't publish any significant new work for the next several years, he was intent on finishing work already in progress—editing his essays, writing the final piece for *Summer,* organizing his texts on contemporary events for two volumes of *Actuelles.* In other words, he was clearing his desk. It was a way of working, of getting ready to write.

With a prospective novel in mind, Camus had also begun to work on a series of short stories in the more personal, "experimental" mode that he had conceived as the proper preparation for his new work. In his first efforts—"Jonas," his portrait of an artist destroyed by fame, and *"La*

Femme Adultère," a story set in Kabylia—he was already writing more openly and venturing into recognizably autobiographical fiction. Four of the six stories later collected as the volume *Exile and the Kingdom* are set in North Africa. One of them, *"Les Muets"* ("The Mutes"), is set in the working-class world of his uncle Étienne—a first attempt at social realism, he said. Others take place in the sere existential plains of the desert Camus was working on a new preface for *The Wrong Side and the Right Side* at this time, too, and in rereading his early prose, he had recognized its innocent truths and his own dilemma. "Quite simply, the day that an equilibrium can be established between who I am and what I say, this day perhaps . . . I will be able to construct the work I have been dreaming of," he wrote in that preface.[11]

Along with the promise of fiction, Camus's journal also conveys a revival of his strong interest in theater. Ideas for plays pop up on almost every page: "The Return and Truth" "The Pillory," "Bacchus," and an adaptation of Dostoyevsky's *The Possessed,* which he had begun within the year. There is a plan for a work about Don Juan and Faust, in Camus's mind the same person, "Don Faust"—"Don Juan is Faust without the pact," he notes—which is meant to be the theatrical component of his new cycle.[12] Most intriguing, and provocatively timely, he is also thinking about staging a little-known confection of a play, *"L'Impromptu des Philosophes,"* which he had written in 1946 as a comic send-up of both the new existentialist movement and Sartrean philosophy. In this play, a character called Monsieur Néant, "Mr. Nothingness"—surely a reference to Sartre's masterwork *Being and Nothingness*—who is in the provinces peddling an enormous tome that contains the "new Gospel" from Paris, is revealed to have escaped from an insane asylum. Camus had originally signed the play with a pseudonym.

What was presumably behind some of this new show of energy was Camus's agreement to share the directorship of a theater festival in the town of Angers in the Loire valley with his colleague and friend Marcel Herrand, who was ailing. Herrand was the force behind the Théâtre Mathurins, where *The Misunderstanding* had played. During the spring of 1953, Camus translated and adapted two of the five plays to be presented, and when Herrand died two days before the opening in June, he assumed full control of the festival. Its success, and his own, were reflected by the coverage in national newspapers, which was a timely validation of theater as an outlet for his talents, although his sadness at Herrand's death hung over him for many months. The experience of repertory theater was in itself renewing, and the multiplicity of his responsibilities, the bonhomie of the actors—Maria Casarès and Sergio Reggiani, from *The Just Assassins* were among the cast—and the open-air setting in the courtyard of a thirteenth-century château recalled his happy days at the head of the Théâtre de l'Équipe in Algiers. In a photograph taken at a rehearsal, Camus has his old glamour: his collar is up, his hair long and tousled, his mien distinctly commanding and rugged.

Camus, however, had begun to enter new thoughts about theater in his journal soon after the completion of *The Rebel* and before his commitment to Herrand. This was partly a reflection of the way he worked. He was always leaving notes to himself about his masters and mentors—Euripedes, Molière, Shakespeare, Cervantes. Even without the prospect of a summer festival, he seemed to keep in mind a full inventory of plays he hoped to write or adapt. In the past, he had set his cycles in motion with plays, first with *Caligula* and then with *The Misunderstanding*. As he said, the form itself helped him to avoid the abstraction that always threatens writers, to ground his imagination in something as real as a stage set or a prop. But theater also energized him. He delighted in its physical aspect, its long hours and hard work—"it's a *métier* where the body counts"—its communal sense of risk and adventure. He liked directing, having a hand in the costumes and sets, being *le chef,* and he was excited by the idea of a play as something malleable, of the stage as life, a *culture vivant. Caligula* is the best example of how he felt theater should work, because it was a young man's play, a first vision of the absurd, which he continued to revisit and rework all his life. It is also the only play of Camus's that was and still is widely revived and adapted. In the version that I saw in Paris in 2006, directed by and starring the innovative Charles Bering, the decor was "new age," the opening scene was set in a bar with a piano and a rasping band saw, and the five acts were played without intermission.

In 1953, however, the most striking reason for Camus's reengagement with theater was a simple one—it relaxed him and gave him joy. His subsequent adaptations of *Requiem for a Nun* and *The Possessed,*[13] his frequent theatergoing, and his new friends among actors and directors have to be seen in this light. So, too, must his persistent and ambitious efforts to found a theater of his own. In 1959, looking back on a difficult decade, Camus opened up about his feelings on the television show *Gros Plan (Close-Up)* and described how theater offered a way to get away from everything that troubled him in his life as a celebrated writer. When he explained why he preferred the company of theater people to that of his fellow intellectuals, with whom "I always have the impression of having done something wrong . . . of having broken one of the rules of the clan," he was referring to the Sartreans, his *confrères parisiens*, and their recent chastisement. To combat his feelings of isolation he needed the camaraderie of the stage, he said: its sense of solidarity, purpose, and community— "*la chaleur de la collectivité,*" its great collective mass of human warmth.[14]

By the late summer of 1954, when Camus allowed himself to speak about his misery, Francine was beginning to emerge from a year of aggravated and often terrifying depression. It had begun the previous fall with fatigue and retreat, but had become serious to Camus only after a suspected attempt at suicide after Christmas, which was followed several months later by a second fall, or jump, which broke her pelvis. During Francine's slow, uncertain recovery, at clinics in Oran and Paris where she was subjected to a sucession of treatments, Camus was in a new kind of despair. He was isolated from his children, who were only eight and were subsequently sent away—Catherine to live with her grandmother Faure in Oran, Jean to live with the Polges in the Midi—and he was also isolated in a private tragedy of concern and guilt. He blamed himself for not taking Francine's initial symptoms seriously and for ignoring the troubles in his marriage. In retrospect, Francine's family would mention relatives with nervous conditions and say that Francine had always been fragile, but it was clear that they also implicated Camus, his nature, his infidelities, and in particular his liaison with Maria Casarès, in Francine's collapse, which Camus, in fact, did too. He made this clear in his behavior, addressed the issue in letters to friends, and spelled it out in his work—first in "Jonas," in the character of the devoted, overburdened wife, Louise, the "good angel" and good mother, whom Jonas ruefully neglects; and then in *The Fall,* in the person of a drowning woman who calls in vain for help. The book was in its way a confession, a self-accusation, and a form of expiation.

Coming little more than a year after the Sartre affair, Francine's nervous breakdown caught Camus in an already humbled state and inflicted another blow to his psyche and his sense of self-worth. "I don't have the right to talk about her unhappiness or about my pain," he wrote to Mamaine in the spring of the crisis, recognizing his own part in Francine's anguish and taking the blame. Like Clarence in *The Fall,* he had not committed a crime, but he had effectively allowed a crime to happen. He who profoundly respected human life had knowingly inflicted pain on someone he loved. "I have no gift for love, nor for suffering," he said in the same letter. "I wander around without knowing what I am here for."[15] During the summer, when Francine was able to convalesce with her sister in the Midi, Camus vacationed with his children and then returned alone to a hot, vacated Paris. He walked a lot, went to some soccer matches, and, to fill the time, committed to writing a screenplay of *La Princesse de Clèves* for Robert Bresson. His other work, he told the Gallimards, was "vegetating."

Just as theater provided a refuge for Camus after the trauma of *The Rebel,* so did his friends. Constant, sympathetic, nonjudgmental, they were the antidote to Sartre's betrayal—"Sartre, the man and the spirit, <u>disloyal</u>," Camus entered in the notebooks with pointed clarity, his underlining catching the crux of the matter. In a time of turmoil and distress, they were his confessors and his confidants, too. Camus had countless good friends, all of them important to him, which is telling. Only after long, intensive tracking can I begin to give the recurring names identities and sort them into compartments—Gallimard, the writing life, the theater, politics, pleasure, Algeria. Overall, the early Algerian friends—Poncet, Roblès, Guilloux, Jaussard, André Benichou, Margaret Dobrenn, and Jeanne Sicaud, the names that keep surfacing like family members or secret resources—are the most steadfast, turning up in evolving roles as the years go by, almost universally granted permanent places in his heart, and in the end, after his death, producing among them the lion's share of the memoirs and homages. Women, many of them onetime lovers such as Patricia Blake, Mamaine, or later the actresses Catherine Sellers and Mi, fall into a category of their own, for they engendered his natural confidence and trust. So, too, do his working-class friends, with whom his instinctive *pudeur* seemed to lift like so much smoke. Camus behaved differently with each group of friends, and yet he was always himself, as Grenier observed. "To say that he led multiple lives is exact, with the stipulation that each mode of life was not incompatible with the next. In short, he played straight while playing on several levels."[16]

Like reflected interests and refracted images, Camus's friends are a way to see him as he was. With Janine and Michel Gallimard, he is funny and playful, easy and ever so ironic. To read the letters he addressed to them, to Cavaliera and Rusticana or Laura and Petrarch or a dozen other loving sobriquets, is to catch his sense of humor. With Char, he is intellectual and deep, a writer-philosopher communing with a poet-philosopher. With Chiaromonte, he is more political and more restrained, a moral revolutionary working in lonely times. In their respective ways, these friends provide ballast as well as understanding, including self-knowledge. The Gallimards defuse his bad moods; Char and Chiaromonte restore his sense of worth and his mission. In the controversy brought on by *The Rebel,* both Char and Chiaromonte wrote articles in praise and defense of the essay. Over almost a decade, they have all become familiar with Camus's vulnerability and insecurities and the *"infinis faiblesses,"* the "countless weaknesses" he claimed. To different degrees of detail, they know about his disenchantment with Paris; his domestic complaints; his long love affair with Maria Casarès, and the other women; his worsening inability to write. They are also among a small circle of intimates with whom he shares the drama of Francine's illness.

As the 1950s progress, it becomes increasingly difficult to sort out the strands of Camus's *malheur,* but it also seems clear from his own words that he suffered most deeply from Francine's illness. Among the letters he wrote during this time—to Grenier, whom the couple had planned to visit during his posting in Egypt; to the ever-responsive Mamaine, who was herself in failing health by then; to the Gallimards; or to the Polges, his friends in Provence, with whom he was in constant touch—some of the most intimate and the most personally revealing are those that he sent to Chiaromonte, "one of the dozen friends with whom I have always lived, even when apart."[17] If Camus had previously "lacked abandon" with Chiaromonte for want of confidence, as he notes apologetically in the first of these letters, he speaks now with newfound humility and palpable need as he tells his friend all about his pain, his moral distress, and his personal and professional disarray. He even addresses the subject of adultery, a misfortune for all concerned, he admits, but also a "search for an innocence, a love that is newer and truer." His situation is truly hell, he says, discussing the burden of his public image as a moralist, the terrible sense of duplicity and cheating that arose in the contrast with his private life, the unbearable hardship of being judged or of feeling judged. The crucial thing was Francine's recovery—"More than everything in the world, I hope that she is cured and comes back to us," he says fiercely— but after that, there was the question of his *"fatigue à vivre,"* his spiritual exhaustion and almost sickly inertia. As Francine's recovery became more imminent, Camus's despair seemed only slightly mitigated. "Doubtlessly I'm wrong to take all this too much to heart," he wrote the following summer, "but I haven't been able to prevent myself. It's true that I've found a good reason to correct this epic pride of mine. But that isn't everything, and it's the future, and life itself, that appear impossible to me."[18]

The pain in these letters is part of what makes them so valuable, although at times they seem so personal and internal that I am uncomfortable reading them. In his candor with Chiaromonte, Camus is offering a glimpse into the private torment of a good person who isn't always good, of someone who, as he describes, has the pretension of living according to morality but then finds that he is not capable of serving it—someone who, as a famous and also a vigilant person, senses that he is always being watched and judged. Camus is always looking inward and taking his own failings to heart in order to take their human measure, to translate them into literature. But this case seems to be different, because deep down he is at odds with himself, confronting a problem that may be unresolvable, and behavior that can't be changed. "I can no longer work," he admits in February. "I feel as if I have written lies until now and can no longer write without lying."

During 1954, Camus corresponded with Chiaromonte regularly before visiting him in Rome in December; between letters he found sustenance in the endurance of their friendship, "There is not a day when I haven't thought of you with all my affection," he wrote that November, a week after his forty-first birthday, which he had spent alone. As with Char and the other constants, he expressed his feelings and his fidelity frequently and dramatically. "Know that you can rely on my long friendship." "I'm not too good at talking at this moment, but I know how to listen to those I love." In his words there is always an implication of gratitude for the relationship, which, as he explained himself, was gratitude for being loved and respected for who he was. "Only certain privileged beings know enough never to judge," he said.[19]

The concept of judgment had been on Camus's mind since postwar days and the purges, but now it had a complicated new personal dimension that was feeding his thinking. In that autumn of 1954, as he begins to enter notes for *The Fall* in his journal, the source of his material seems all too obvious. "God isn't needed to create guilt or to punish. Human beings suffice. He could, if worse comes to worse, establish innocence," Camus writes in September. "How could he preach justice, he who has not even managed to make it reign over his own life?" In December, when Camus introduces the term *juges-pénitents*, "remorseful judges," the concept that lies at the heart of the story, and uses it to describe the existentialists, there can be little doubt that direct experience is firing his imagination, and that his new work is under way.[20] "When they accuse themselves, one can be sure that it is always to crush others," he parries. Camus wrote this last remark at the close of a long trip to Italy, his first in sixteen years, which he hoped would help him come to terms with the events of the last two years—to regain some *maîtrise* and control of his life. Travel was a way of "working out his problems without really working them out," he said to Chiaromonte, and obviously the three weeks in the sun and light were having their effect.

Camus devoted many journal pages to his time in Italy, which was in itself a sign of restoration and rising spirits. As he writes about his travels, he sounds more like the former effusively descriptive Camus than he has sounded in years: evoking ravishing piazzas, magnificent weather, the greatness of Caravaggio, and the many *journées superbes;* comparing the diffused, silvery, spiritual light of Florence with the round, glimmering, supple light of Rome; evaluating his own state of mind. Struck by "a sort of mysterious joy," he regrets more than ever the "dark and derisory years" he has lived in Paris, years that have cost him so dearly. On the Appian

Way, with his heart swelling, he vows that the current setback will serve as a step forward. "One year I did not work, even though the topics were waiting, which I knew were exceptional and I still couldn't tackle. About a year since and I have not gone insane." His words are entered between parentheses, like a private reminder or a personal accounting. In either case, the forthrightness itself seems to be an act of healing. Toward the end of his tour, when he is feverish and bedridden for several days, he still seems as resolute. "I need my strength. I don't need life to be easy for me, but I want to be able to match myself up to it when it is difficult, being in command of whether I want to go where I am going."[21]

The sense of change in Camus's life is insistent now. Change has been imposed by events and eventualities, but it has also been willed by Camus—"I would like only that people allow me to live as I wish," he wrote to Mamaine, possibly referring to multiple sources of unhappiness—Paris, celebrity, the strictures of morality. But the comment was directed particularly at his home life—"that universe [at home] which for a year has destroyed me cell by cell."[22] Even before Francine's illness, friends had been aware of a tension in Camus's marriage, of her indecisiveness and dependence and his resilient Don Juanism and increasing feeling of entrapment. Camus still loved his wife, they said, sometimes describing her as a sort of perfection, but the two of them were more like siblings; perhaps they never should have married. A surprisingly direct reflection slips into the predominantly literary journal: "For years I have lived cloistered in her love. Never having ceased to love her, today it is necessary that I flee . . . which is difficult," he writes in August, several weeks before Francine's return to rue Madame and after she is out of danger.[23] In letters to their friends, he was also direct. "If she recovers, which I wish with everything in me," he writes to Polge, "I will try to extricate myself, with the help of my energy, and also my pessimism, so useful in certain situations in life."[24]

With Roger Quilliot, who was now fully engaged in his book-length essay on Camus's work and met with his subject three or four times during 1954, Camus spoke about the feeling of entrapment from another point of view. He was tired of his reputation for virtue, and weary of the Manichaeism and moralism that for him had been the logical sequel to the Resistance, he said. He felt like a prisoner of his name, of his work, and even of his vocabulary, even more so because he sensed that he was changing and was, furthermore, determined to change. But Camus was also worried about his long, frightening dry spell, the possible "*tarissement de son oeuvre,*" and about growing old. He feared that fame was working against him, that the world had already written his life story, which was effectively a burial that denied him a future and the right to change. These last words are particularly unsettling, because they have a whiff of presentiment. In three years' time, the Nobel Prize will be perceived by both Camus and his detractors as the ultimate act of interment.

Quilliot incorporated many of the working notes for his book into his Pléiade commentary a decade later, including Camus's thoughts about his book, which he welcomed as both a comprehensive appraisal of his work to date and a very timely form of closure. To that last end, Camus had advised Quilliot to omit any reference to his future projects and to end the book with *Summer,* the collection of lyric essays he had completed in 1953, his fortieth year, "since, by pure chance, these dates obviously coincide with a sort of turning point in my work and my life."[25] *Summer,* with its early essays on Algeria, the confessional "Enigma," and its final ode to the sea, was in itself a sort of summation—"closing the chapter that began with *Nuptials,*" Camus explained. Quilliot saw in its last entry the "haunting memories of a man who has turned forty," adding that "the poetic vein in [Camus] was certainly not dead."

Quilliot's book *La Mer et les Prisons* came out in 1956, wearing a dark *policier* cover that Camus disliked—a rather alluring photo of him taking a deep drag on a cigarette, above an image of the sea behind bars—although he judged the work "an excellent essay." It is an engaged and at times exalted tribute to Camus and his work—"forty years of age; soon twenty years of literary production; ten years of glory" is the way Quillot leads into his conclusion. This conclusion makes a case for change, which he sees as a sign of vitality. To someone who is sensitive to the circumstances and aware of Quilliot's unusual sympathy for his subject, it also has the tender subtext of a tête-à-tête. It is almost as if, in an hour of need, Quilliot is explaining Camus to Camus, supporting him in the vicissitudes of his profession, urging him on. "In literature, as in life, nothing is ever sure. It's always necessary to begin again and first of all, to watch out for adulation," he writes. He quotes Montaigne on turning forty and learning to grow old: "One steals away every day and faces himself." And then he notes, "It is the paradox of the celebrated writer that he is expected to act his age—if not more—and yet has to remain forever young. It is never good to grow up."[26]

On paper, the years 1953 and 1954 move by at a strange, uneven pace, like a series of episodes without any particular cohesion, momentum, or reason beyond Camus's private hopes and ambitions. They are steeped in an atmosphere of solitude that emerges in occasional outbursts in the journal. "Lost afternoon," "Terrible morning," "Dead day," he enters repeatedly during August 1954 as he wanders alone through art galleries in an empty Paris. I am saddened to see him like this, aimless, in a state of inertia. To the world, nonetheless, Camus is more than ever a celebrated writer, and the odd jobs roll in as if to prove that fame is a self-propelling engine. They seem unlikely for Camus, perhaps because I was unaware of these entries on his résumé—the translation of a small book by James Thurber, *The Last Flower;* a brief text for a Walt Disney volume, "The Living Desert"—although they are also the sort of assignments that characterize interregnums in a writer's life. There are also radio appearances, including his recorded reading of the complete text of *The Stranger* and *Caligula,* and a cultural mission to Italy that had followed an earlier one to the Netherlands, where it was cold and rainy. About Amsterdam, which will be the setting for *The Fall,* he recorded only "always wet."

It seemed to be a time of beginnings and endings. Mamaine died during that second summer; Camus's immeasurable sadness came at a very lonely time and is not expressed in the record. Like a finale to the postwar and post-postwar years, Beauvoir's *The Mandarins* was published in November and won the Prix Goncourt. The transparency of its famous protagonists and the ruthlessness of some of the portrayals made it a source of amusement and exquisite gossip for a few months, but Camus was in Italy and removed from the scene for several weeks during this time. "It seems that I'm its hero. . . . Even better: the dubious acts of Sartre's life have been generously piled on my back. Other than that, garbage," he writes of the book from Rome, sounding more casually ironic than he would later when all its distortions, indiscretions, and slanderous details had registered, and when it seemed clear to everyone that this work amounted to a settling of scores as well as "a desperate exercise in denigration."[27] Despite Beauvoir's disclaimer, there was no question that Camus was Henri Perron, editor of the leftist but anticommunist paper *L'Espoir,* an acclaimed author who no longer has anything to say. (Perron is also a woman-chaser; he is having an affair with a famous actress and no longer loves his wife, a pianist, who is beautiful and sick.) Sartre, the character, was the wise, indeed omniscient, Robert Dubreuilh, who is admired by Henri like a son. As with Mamaine's death, the timing of *The Mandarins* seems cruel to me, but Camus, who showed more anger and disgust than hurt, had already distanced himself from the "comedy of Paris." When asked why he didn't respond to Beauvoir, he said simply, "Because you don't discuss things with a sewer."[28] Nonetheless, he was addressing her and her false accusations in his portrayal of judgment and the *juges-penitents* in *The Fall.*

As I can sense it in the air, change was also real. Sometime during that winter, at the insistence of his in-laws, Camus had moved out of the family apartment on rue Madame; he then lived in a series of small hotels and borrowed flats before he settled into a pied-à-terre in the nearby rue de Chanaleilles, on the floor above René Char. The arrangement seemed to be more of an accommodation than an estrangement—he remained actively engaged in Francine's recovery and was soon giving her manuscript pages of his work to read—but it was also part of a concerted effort to take control of his life and diminish his pain. If his family life was in flux, so was life in Algeria. On November 1, war was effectively declared there when a young new militant faction of the nationalist movement synchronized a dozen bomb attacks around the country, although the governor-general called the events "*préoccupants*" but not "*dramatiques*," and even Camus, who had been following developments in the region, didn't recognize them as more than another crisis. The following spring, however, though it seemed antithetical to his vow to repair and retreat, Camus agreed to write for Jean-Jacques Servan-Schreiber's liberal weekly *L'Express,* largely as a way of addressing the Algerian situation, and to that end, of returning the former premier Pierre Mendès-France to power. Camus knew Mendès-France to be a reformer, pledged to a policy of reconciliation in Algeria.

That Camus inhabits a different place now from two or three years earlier is obvious. As my subject, he seems different, too, and even his isolation has a different cast, a deeper shadow. But that perspective may be small, its measure relative. In character and thought, Camus has remarkable constancy. He is still talking about solitude and solidarity—"I am solitary in my times. I am also, as you know, in solidarity with it—and strictly so," he said to Jean Daniel, then one of the directors of *L'Express*. He refers to himself as *"ce vieux maniaque de bonheur,"* "this old maniac for happiness," although he admits that he has lost his star. The very ups and downs in Camus's life have their own rhythm and meaning, and in the end, they amount to what Quilliot calls "a sort of living dialectic." Nonetheless, Camus's uncertain new direction creates uneasiness that is not usual with him. "After working and producing for twenty years, I still live with the idea that my work has not even begun," he writes in the new preface for *The Wrong Side and the Right Side,* making it seem as if his last decade of engagement with history has been only an unexpected interlude.[29]

10

Pursuing Char

I decided to take a trip to L'Isle-sur-la-Sorgue partly as an excuse to visit the Luberon, for I was still waiting for an interview with Catherine Camus in Lourmarin, which lies only twenty miles to the southeast. I thought it would be enlightening to see where Camus had first escaped from Paris and where he had spent happy summers with his family. I found myself thinking constantly about Camus's recent troubles, whose effects were not to be dispelled for years, if ever, and it seemed like an appropriate moment to experience a part of Provence that he had found restorative. At the same time, I was interested in Camus's friendship with Char, which was crucial to his surviving that period in the 1950s when his life was coming apart, and which had been played out here. It was Char who had shared and nurtured Camus's ideas about revolt, who had supported and publicly defended his book—and to whom *The Rebel* was privately dedicated as sincerely as it was officially inscribed to Jean Grenier. On the working manuscript that Camus offered Char on its completion, he wrote, "To you, dear René, the first draft of this book, which I wish could be *ours* and which, without you, could never have been a book of hope."[1] It was also Char who, in the autumn of 1946, had introduced Camus to the part of Provence that would become a sort of halfway house relative to Algeria, a stay against his *mal de pays,* a resource during crises, and eventually, in Lourmarin, a permanent sanctuary. As caught in a large photographic book, *La Posterité du Soleil,* which was also a product of the Camus and Char friendship—explicitly *theirs,* they said—it was a quiet, unsuspecting place of fruit farms and vineyards, meandering streams and defining rivers, a long plain surrounded by the distant specter of mountains.

L'Isle-sur-la-Sorgue and its skirt of hamlets—Lagnes, Saumane, Costellant—was Char's native ground, the land of his forefathers (who, like the character Jean de Florette in Marcel Pagnol's novel, fought their neighbors for access to water), and the land that nourished his poetry—*mon pays,* he always said. In the only photograph I have found of Char with Camus, he stands before his house at Les Buschats, hands on hips and a cigarette on his lip, a big, broad, imposing Provençal wearing shorts, espadrilles, and an expression of almost defiant confidence. He has the head of a gladiator, as someone once said. Camus stands next to him, also in shorts (and, rather disconcertingly, white socks and street shoes), and by contrast looks thin, rangy, and awkwardly posed. In the photo, there is only the mildest suggestion of the magnitude of Char's presence and the depth of the friendship between Camus and Char, something they both came to think of as *destinée,* "inevitable." From the beginning, Char had said, he knew they had a road to take together.

The photograph nonetheless gave a warning about Char, about his seductive powers and his big presence. One danger lurking in biography seems to be getting too caught up with your subject's friends. In the case of Char, he arrives on the scene—a legendary Resistance fighter, an erstwhile surrealist, an intimate of famous painters, a beguiling storyteller, a poet's poet—with such magnetic force and inherent interest that for a while he disrupts the narrative. Like Camus, he is a man of action with a habit of solitude, a grave intellectual with a love of play. (There is an often recounted tale about Char and Camus being taken, quite happily, for the gangsters Dédé le Mitraille and Pierrot le Fou; and another one, reported in the journal, about Char's wooing a lioness in the Jardin des Plantes.) In ways different from Camus, Char seems eccentric, enigmatic, at times mystical, and of an intensity that is sometimes described as violent, passionate to the point of obsession, and creative to the point of a sort of madness. Add to this Camus's effusive feelings about the writer Char, the greatest living poet in France, the heir to Rimbaud, a poet of revolt, the "poet of our tomorrows," as Camus said in a preface to one of Char's books. My initial reaction to Char may not have been very different from the *coup de foudre* Camus describes, when he reports that three days earlier he has met "*un adorable-épatant-consolant beau garçon,*" "an adorable-amazing-comforting gorgeous guy."

Once I was distracted by Char, it was almost impossible for me not to wander off into the byroads of his biography, into his early antics with the surrealists and his close friendships with Breton, Georges Braque, and others (Matisse, Picasso, Heidegger, and Salvador and Gala Dalí also appear in his story) and into his poetry almost as a reference tool, as a reflection of everything he was. There was always a prospect of cross-over material—well-known literary figures such as Breton and Paul Éluard also had a place in Camus's life—and an understanding that Char's character reflected on Camus's and that Char's life illuminated contemporary times. But the story of his life was for its own sake, too, and it brought other detours and further distractions. The nature of the course I was following, once again a game of endless connections, became clear one afternoon at a large retrospective of the work of Nicolas de Staël at the Pompidou, where I learned from the correspondence on display that the painter, who committed suicide in 1955 at the age of forty-one, had an intense relationship with Char in the last years of his life. Quite overwhelmed by the power and ardor of Staël's canvases, and the intimacy in the letters, I purchased both the exhibition catalog and a biography of Char.

As it happened, the diversion to Staël brought me back to the Luberon, where Char had found a house for him, too, and introduced him to the extended Mathieu family, whose members were already significant intimates of Camus's. Rural patricians, farmers and poets, of an old clan that seemed to be connected to the heart of old Provence, a bulwark of its culture and its hospitality, the Mathieus—Marcelle the matriarch who attracted the company of artists and painters, Henri the poet son, the beautiful daughter Jeanne and her husband Urbain Polge, who became Camus's close friends, and their children Jacques and Gérard—were themselves a story. I did not learn for certain whether Staël and Camus ever met, although the nature of that small rustic community and the centrality of the Mathieus and their expansive domain—Les Camphoux, a prosperous fruit farm—suggest that they crossed paths. Camus, at least, knew a lot about Staël, and had been to one of his shows in Paris, a collaboration with Char called "Poèmes." Stael was also a distraction because it was the Polges who were Camus's mainstay in L'Isle, particularly during the tumult of Francine's illness. Their friendship was easy, happy, and blessedly constant.

Different from Char but connected to Char, who had introduced them, Urbain Polge, a pharmacist in Saint-Rémy-de-Provence and a cultured man rather than an intellectual, was an integral part of the Luberon that sustained Camus. Polge's fundamental humanity reassured Camus and put him at ease. There is a scent of summertime in most of the stories about their times together during the years Camus rented a house called Palerme. These stories describe picnics, fishing, *corridas,* soccer matches, wives off on shopping excusions, and a band of devoted children (all this is a welcome counterpoint to the gravity of moral responsibility and professional stress)—but there is also a more momentous sense of downtime fostered by love and trust. Like North Africans, the Polges were loyal and nonjudgmental, and Camus responded accordingly, confiding in them as he did in few others. Throughout 1954, he submitted almost daily reports on Francine's condition and his own deteriorating state of mind, and they effectively shared his life and troubles, helping to stabilize the family, taking care of his son Jean while Catherine went to stay with her grandmother Faure in Oran. "You must to love them twice as much," Camus counseled his children about the Polges, their second family, called Maman Deux and Papa Deux, "because they are good and intelligent, and good and intelligent people are rare."[2]

Knowing about the Polges warms up and normalizes Camus's life. They are not a constant presence, for they were essentially summer people in L'Isle, and Camus, especially after his separation from Francine, was sometimes absent during the summer months; but they are still important references for Camus, the man behind the fame. More than many of the better-known characters who show up in Camus's story, whose own eminence and reputation constitute part of the message, the Polges convey something basic about how Camus lived; about his nature; about his need for warmth, support, and simplicity; and in that regard about what he needed that was missing in Paris. This was my sense, anyway; later, in Paris, when I met Jacques Polge, the older son—*le génie,* the genius, Camus called him—who came to serve as a sort of reality check on my emerging story, I knew that I was right. Jacques, who had known Char, too, was the source of many small tales and useful bits of information—Camus always seeking out a timid Italian worker at the Mathieus' Les Camphoux for conversation; Camus flirting with their Spanish nanny; Char's power and sense of power—as well as an inside perspective. He had also encouraged me to see the landscape of L'Isle-sur-la-Sorgue for myself and, as a preview, had pulled out his copy of *La Postérité du Soleil*. It had been a wedding present to him from Catherine Camus.

Char completed *La Postérité du Soleil* by himself in 1965, nearly twenty years after its inception. By then it was a memorial to his friend as well as to the land of his childhood. To the gallery of simple arcadian photographs taken by the local photographer Henriette Grindal, for which Camus had written an introduction, Char added a "testimonial" he called *"Naissance et Jour Levant d'une Amitié,"* "Birth and Dawn of a Friendship," in which he recalled the day he had first met Camus and driven him down to L'Isle, watching his eyes light up at a landscape in which he could see Algeria. Their friendship happened under the best conditions, Char said; its slow, happy maturation was a promise of its duration and depth. In 1949, Char had composed for their book a poem called *"De Moment en Moment,"* in which their sense of comradeship and destiny is already clear: "Why this path more than another? Where is it leading to pull us so strongly? What trees and what friends live beyond the horizon of these rocks, in the distant miracle of heat? We have come this far because out there where we were wasn't a possibility any longer."[3]

Most of what bound Camus and Char together—principles, politics, their belief in revolt, and their love of life—are implied in this poem, which continues, rather elliptically, for another eight lines. Before he met Char, Camus did not turn to poetry for sustenance the way he did during the early days of the cold war, when he discovered Char's *Fureur et Mystère,* published by Gallimard in 1948. "The most beautiful book of our unhappy era. With you, the poem becomes courage and pride. In the end, it helps one to live," he wrote to Char that fall, and by then he had begun to love the man, who was becoming inseparable from his poetry, and in a different way from the Luberon.[4] By then they had spent two summers together, shared road trips and endless discussions, and made plans to create the literary magazine *Empèdocle,* named after the Greek philosopher who was a favorite of theirs, and of Nietzsche's. Camus had published

The Plague, which Char declared "a very big book," although he was not usually a fan of the contemporary novel. Camus was also settling into *The Rebel,* beginning to articulate the concept of revolt that was central to each man's thinking.

Camus and Char resembled each other, Camus said; they were "brothers in pain and joy."[5] "A brother chosen by me," Char said of Camus, speaking, too, in his homage in *Postérité,* of the absolute clarity of their friendship. Camus, writer of conscience, and Char, poet of conscience, were both Mediterranean men who shared a belief in limits and found something essential in the tragic optimism of ancient Greece, which Char called "*la sagesse aux yeux pleins de larmes,*" "wisdom with eyes full of tears," a phrase that Camus would quote. But in many respects, the two men were very different, and they led separate lives. Char, six years older, unfettered by the responsibilities of family and domestic life, shuttled between a simple life in L'Isle and his sophisticated, art-centered world in Paris. He was a big dramatic ego who needed disciples, a man made of dynamite, in Stael's words. His assurance impressed Camus, and Camus's quieter ways—his natural measure, his sensitivity, "the beauty and the goodness of his silence"—impressed Char.

For a few years, after the drama surrounding *The Rebel* recedes, there are only random sightings of Camus and Char together, but it is clear from Char's letters that the relationship had not faltered. The letters fill in the gaps and illustrate the style of the intimacy between the two: notes of concern about Francine (and a verse for her) or about the Hungarian revolution (with a newspaper clipping showing Stalin's statue being pulled to the ground in Budapest); worries about Camus's level of stress; a few lines on a postcard—"Yes, Monday lunch" or "The place is dead without you." Char regularly dispatches new poems or lines of poems and makes a gift of two of his early manuscripts and a treasured relic from the Resistance.

In the later 1950s, when it seems that they met only rarely, despite sharing an apartment house in Paris, Char sounds forlorn, even bereft, missing Camus, fearful that he has lost him, or been forgotten by him. In the fall of 1958, just before Camus found his house in Lourmarin, the two men met in L'Isle and walked along the back roads as they used to do, and as they would do again a year later, when Camus returned to Lourmarin to work in isolation on *The First Man*. On parting that final time, Char gave Camus the manuscript of a recent poem, *"La Faux Relevée"* (which, like a presentiment, is about death), and Camus presented Char with a page from a new tribute that he had undertaken, which begins, "Char is in a class by himself, alone, but not apart. Nothing is like him at all."[6] The working manuscript of his tribute was among the papers found in Camus's briefcase when it was recovered from the accident site the next afternoon.

Both Camus and Char had times of solitude—Char's was more hermetic—but each had an extraordinary capacity for friendship and a generous heart. They admired each other greatly. "To admire was one of my great joys, which, having become a man, I no longer hoped for until I met you," Camus says in a letter, and this thought brings to mind, fleetingly, his final disappointment with Pia.[7] "You are one of the rare men, Albert, whom I love and admire from instinct and knowledge simultaneously," Char wrote to Camus during the spring of 1953; his expression of esteem was a form of encouragement at a difficult time. As the letters indicate, the two men helped each other through professional struggles, personal crises, and an era that was in itself a cause for despair. They always used the formal *vous* to address each other, as an expression of absolute respect, but they were never distant. According to their friends, they never overshadowed each other, either. They seemed to need each other, to be warmed and reassured by each other's presence in the world. In the end, that tender symbiosis makes their friendship seem important to know about. Char provided a strong model for Camus, and Camus encouraged Char and affirmed who Char was. As Char said, they were *compagnons*—companions, sidekicks—and this was one of the words he used to describe Camus in his epitaph, the poem *"L'Éternité à Lourmarin,"* which was so painful to write that it took him seven weeks.

Several days passed before I began to feel the effects of being in the Luberon, because it doesn't make a dramatic first impression. The mountains keep their distance; the fields lie green and flat on either side of the road; there are no clues as to where properties with names like Palerme, Les Camphoux, Le Rebanqué, Les Buscats, or Névons might lie. Driving through *centre ville* in L'Isle-sur-la-Sorgue, I noticed a hotel named Névons, like Char's beloved ancestral property; a school and a foundation named for Char; and a square named for his father, Émile. The town was bustling because the annual antiques fair began that day, and traffic moved slowly, the old streets filling with tourists and vendors taking over the main quays of the river that effectively encircles the town and accounts for its name. In a quiet backwater sat a single old wooden paddle wheel, a relic from an era that had already ended when Char and Camus began to compile *La Postérité,* which offers a similar image. To evoke and commemorate a vanishing place—*un temps perdu et un pays perdu* in Char's words, "a lost time and a lost country"—had been the raison d'être of the book, which reflected not only their love of the local landscape but also their shared feelings about its connection to the innocence and happiness of childhood. By the time of its publication Char, the native son, was close to despair over changes being wrought, "the ugliness piling up year after year for the pleasure of new fortunes," as he wrote to a friend. "I don't know how to relate to my country anymore. More and more, I don't recognize myself in what it has become."[8]

Given Char's distress almost half a century earlier, it seemed unlikely that I would fall under the spell of the landscape that Camus had loved, because it no longer existed as it was. Nonetheless, I clung to the romantic notion of following in his footsteps, which I had come to accept as largely an adventure in imagination, and which by then had also become something of a habit. Although it was mainly by chance and serendipity that I stumbled upon a connection to Camus in L'Isle—more exactly, in a hamlet on the road to Apt, where I had reserved a room at Le Mas des Grès—I also think that it was in part simply because I was there on the terrain of his experience. That *mas,* for example, which I had plucked from an outdated Michelin Guide Rouge because it was described as a true Provençal farmhouse, turned out to be next door to Les Camphoux, the Mathieu property. The young proprietress of the inn not only knew the poet son, Henri Mathieu, who lived in nearby Lagnes and liked the food in the hotel dining room, but promptly introduced me to a local woman, Paulette, who had known all the Mathieus and insisted on driving me to Lagnes to meet Henri. Paulette had her own stories, which she told in a happy running chatter as we made our way along dusty back roads—about the fat red peppers she grew that Camus loved; about the wonderful Marcelle Mathieu, "mistress of all"; about the magic of Le Rebanqué, an old stone barn in the hills above Lagnes where Marcelle staged poetry readings and held picnics; about Char and his travels by bicycle. Each story was a germ of the larger story about a way of life and its landscape.

In a more focused way, as I talked with Henri I also stepped directly into a narrative. Henri was in his late eighties when I met him, a few years younger than Camus would have been, still big and solid in the Provençal way, and with a warmth and culture that gave a clue to the spirit of the long-ago summers at Les Camphoux. From the nature of his memories and his frame of reference, I could sense the authenticity of his friendship with Camus and, perhaps more deeply, his friendship with Char, to whom he was already tied by both historic family interactions (the dispute over water rights) and the practice of poetry, and who had introduced them that first summer. (Char, he mentioned by way of background, wrote a text about Henri's mother that was included in the Pléiade edition of his work. Char also wrote several poems about Henri's sister Jeanne—with whom he, like Stael, fell in love.) Henri didn't offer any dramatic new information, but everything he said was corroborative and direct—he sold his first piece to *Empèdocle,* he mentioned with pride—and in a quiet and unexpected way, his utter credibility had a strong impact on me. He recounted conversations with Camus about literature and philosophy and later about his writer's block, which he referred to as "*passages vides,*" "empty periods." He described how relaxed Camus and Char were with each other, and how seductive they were, each in his own way. Camus was capable of charming anyone, he said—servant girls, shopkeepers, socialites—whereas Char preferred the company of more cultivated types. At Les Camphoux, Camus systematically shook hands with all the workers when he came by. Sitting in the parlor of Henri's quiet stone house above Lagnes, I felt that all the members of his family were implicated in his presence, and I knew why Camus had so readily liked and trusted them. In the hope of preserving that presence, on parting I took a picture of Henri at the heavy wooden table where we had talked. He was reluctant to be photographed, but in the snapshot he looks very natural; his blue eyes behind rimless glasses are direct and very clear.

I never got to see the beautiful old barn at Le Rebanqué, the site of so many summer gatherings, although where there used to be only a steep footpath—Camus reportedly rigged up some sort of moving chain to bring up water—there is now a paved road that winds up through the almond trees and olive groves and provides easy access to its quiet meadow high above the valleys. Nor did I attempt to find Palerme, the house that Camus rented for three summers, described by Henri as closer to town and yet still remote and rather grand, a *belle maison* on a property rather than a rudimentry *mas*. That was where Henri met Camus's mother the year she came—she had great beauty, he said, but she was very shy—and also his brother Lucien, who had Camus's profile. But on my way back to my room at Le Mas des Grès on my third and last day, I did turn off at Les Camphoux, and I drove down the road through the rows of apple trees that supply the family's international fruit business, hoping to see or feel something that I could relate to the stories. The air was sweet, the sky was high and blue-gold, and there was a house in the distance that might have been the one I associated with Marcelle's legendary hospitality, but I suddenly felt presumptuous, like a trespasser, and without serious misgivings I turned back.

Despite their seeming aimlessness, my travels around L'Isle-sur-la-Sorgue had their rewards. Even if I was not visiting exactly the same places Camus had integrated into his personal geography, I could at least project him into a living landscape—sitting under *that* old oak tree with a book, swimming in *that* lazy river, taking *that* rocky road down to the village of Fontaine-de-Vaucluse (just pleasantly touristy the day I was there, as it might have been years ago)—and this made him seem familiar, like someone I actually had once known. As the landscape grew on me—*doux et dur*, "sweet and tough," is how the locals describe it; lavender and honey; the mistral and the chalky hills—I could see why Camus might have found it a surprising oasis. The prospect of mountains, the unabashed sunlight, and the vineyards would remind him of Algeria; the men and their machines working the fields would be a comforting sight; the simplicity and honesty of the lifestyle would be a testimony to its humanity. In this new understanding, there was a new sense of kinship.

There was also a small, unexpected moment of truth that affects me even in the retelling. It came when Henri told me that he had been the last person to shake Camus's hand when Camus left the Luberon for Paris on the morning of January 3, 1960. They had all been down for the Christmas holidays, he recounted; Camus had come to say good-bye and was standing outside with the car running. Henri spoke in a quiet way that conveyed old emotions, and in a sudden jolt of Camus's presence I also felt the weight of his absence. Henri was with his parents and Char at Les Camphoux the next day when the call came telling them about the crash. Char had stepped back from the phone and let out a heartrending cry, he said. At Francine's request, Char took charge of the arrangements for a funeral in Lourmarin, but at the cemetery he was overcome with grief and had to leave before the end of the ceremony.

I read Char's letters to Camus in the Bibliothèque Méjanes in Aix-en-Provence. This is where Catherine Camus transferred the Camus estate from its former home in Paris in 2000. Given his feelings about Paris—he was practically *écologiste,* as one friend put it, longing for nature and hating urban stress—Camus would have approved of the change. He probably would also have liked the Centre de Documentation Albert Camus that is now the hub of Camus studies—a small Provençal building set under trees in a quiet courtyard—although the idea of opening his sundry manuscripts and papers to the public would have been another matter. Yet as I leafed through the fat loose-leaf album that contains the working inventory of his archives, skimming through the entries—political essays, letters to editors and organizations, texts of assorted speeches and tributes, and some thirty pages of political inventions (in Spain, Algeria, Hungary, Greece, Tunisia)—I was struck by how determinedly public a man Camus was, even as he was struggling to maintain his privacy. I was also mindful of how much more of his work has been made available to readers as well as scholars in recent decades. With his first writing, the early novel called *The Happy Death, The First Man,* the pieces for *Combat* and *Express,* and the notebooks now in print, Gallimard has been putting together a new Pléiade edition of Camus's collected work that could run to four or five volumes. It may be that there is enough primary source material on record to let us figure out who Camus was without trying to read between the lines of Char's correspondence or ponder the nature of his friendships.

However, even in this scholarly place, home to Camus's oeuvre, multiple versions of manuscripts, and undated texts, I seemed to be drawn to the extraneous or the unusual: his adaptation of *The Stranger* for an opera, a few pages devoted to Ulysses, a cache of humdrum materials—calculations of costs, formal proposals, a copy of "An Inquiry into the Economics and Administration of Theater Companies in Europe"—that illuminated a very businesslike Camus trying to found a theater. Before I had read Char's letters, also in a way extraneous, Marcelle Mahasela, the energetic curator of Camus's archives, had suggested to me that the correspondence was very warmhearted but not particularly informative—a little of this, a little of that, she indicated with a wavy motion of her hands. Yet almost as much as the more serious exchanges, I was affected by Char's emotional New Year's cards, by the black-banded announcement of his mother's death, by the mere sight of his smooth and classical handwriting, so different from Camus's tight, cramped hand, which seemed to sum up one aspect of their friendship. If the ultimate question was about significance, then privately I took heart from Camus's own fondness for odd details and incidental stories, because this fondness was my instinct and my pleasure, too.

I was nonetheless impressed and humbled by the dedication and professionalism of Marcelle Mahasela, who had lived with Camus and his papers every day since the inception of the new center (and had consulted with Catherine Camus on most of those days). Speaking offhand, from a workaday point of view, she had her own vital tidbits of information to offer during the time I was there. Camus was always tearing pages out of his notebooks to use somewhere else, and then failing to put them back, or putting them back in the wrong order, she said with almost wifely familiarity. It was a photograph of Nietzsche, rather than (as I had read) the revolutionary Kaliayev, that Camus hung in his study. Char, whom

Camus had meant to be one of his literary executors (but had not yet written a will), worked hard on the unfinished fourth volume of *Actuelles,* which has not yet been published. When I asked Marcelle Mahasela about Camus's notes on Ulysses, which, given his own odyssey, interested me, she nodded and shrugged. "In a life like his, there are so many tributaries, so many things that are important, but part of something bigger, and therefore less important," she said in a way that offered both advice and a perspective.[9]

After library hours, I walked along the Cours Mirabeau like everyone else in Aix and yielded to its easy, gregarious springtime life. Sitting in a trattoria on a side street, rue Clemenceau, I picked up the conversation at the next table between two lovelorn local girls, who were discussing a strategy of marriage in a heavy, dragging accent that gave their ambitions the same inflection. I watched as a very wide garbage truck began its turn into our very narrow eighteenth-century street, and the waiters hurried out to move aside a stand of welcoming potted plants as it passed, something they must have done every night at about nine. At this hour, the sky was still blue, and a flock of seemingly crazy birds was making a big noise high in the plane trees. Some six or eight blocks away, in the complex of the Bibliothèque Méjanes, not far from the bus terminal and the train station, filling the doorway of the Centre de Documentation, there was a larger than life-size photograph of Camus, who was part of the scene.

11

The Company of Women

Several years ago, I was given a large, spectacular screen print of one of Cartier-Bresson's portraits of Camus, which now hangs on the wall in my study. It is a dramatic contrast to the ordinary little reproduction I pinned up in college. The image is very familiar to me—Camus in a street in wartime Paris, smoking, wearing a heavy overcoat and an expression that is both challenging and inviting—and I no longer consult it for information as I used to do. This morning, however, casting a glance over my shoulder in its direction, I was suddenly struck by all the maleness that has been caught by the camera, and I was reminded of an obvious but critical fact: that Camus's good looks and sex appeal were a primary part of his identity. That he had a famous way with women is not surprising, and this, too, can be inferred from the image.

It was widely known that there were many women in Camus's life. He had good looks, charm, and intelligence; he was serious, responsible, playful, and passionate; and like the legendary Spanish libertine Don Juan, whom he singled out for praise in the *The Myth of Sisyphus,* he also loved to love. In addition to his two marriages and his long affair with Maria Casarès, he had significant shorter affairs with Patricia Blake, the actress Catherine Sellers, and the young art student named in the biographies only as Mi, and close friendly relationships with *copines* such as Janine Gallimard and Mamaine—or Jeanne Sicard and Marguerite Dobrenn, enduring friends from his student days in Algiers. There were unnamed others, too: flirtations, amorous adventures, the countless conquests and brief

213

encounters that are testimonies to a Mediterranean libido and a natural desire for pleasure—to what his friend Jean Daniel called simply Camus's preoccupation with women. Camus quite simply loved women. It was not that he was a *séducteur,* Daniel was careful to explain, but that he was utterly and effortlessly *séduisant.* Men felt that as well as women, he added.

The subject of Camus's relationship to women is itself tantalizing, because of its intimate, slightly forbidden nature, because of his marriage and the circumstances of Francine's illness, and because Camus had so little to say in his work about women except for the misogynistic portrayals in the novels. With a man as famously conscientious as Camus was, it is almost impossible not to be interested in the *voyou* in him, the roguish, libertine side that Daniel speaks of as the counterpoint to his puritanical nature. Being a tough guy modifies the saintliness that was his crown of thorns. In the same way, his moral gravity and humility give his machismo an unusual edge. Camus, it seems, liked it when someone such as Sartre or Beauvoir referred to him as a *voyou,* a tough, just as he liked the comparison to Bogart. He made it clear that he identified personally with Don Juan, although he also made it clear that he suffered considerably from guilt.

There is more to the subject of women than Camus's Don Juanism, or what Germaine Brée called his infinite capacity for sensuality or his obvious eye for beauty. (In the photographs that illustrate the biographies—Francine with her long legs and dazzling smile, Maria intense onstage, Catherine Sellers demure in rehearsal, the very young and beguiling Pat Blake and Mi—the women all appear to have been unusually beautiful.) In the women in his life (the incidental attractions and one-night stands are not in this category), Camus seemed to seek intense friendship as much as passion. More open and more forthcoming with women than with men, he made women his confidantes and confessors, and they, in return, offered the understanding and allegiance he seemed so urgently to need, what Maria Casarès called *"une complicité chaude et claire,"* which was heartfelt approval.[1] Loosening his protective coat of *pudeur* (in a way he rarely did), he talked with women about the most private matters—his work, his ambitions, his illness, his fear of death, his fear of failure—revealing, even dramatizing, his insecurities and anxieties, exposing the vulnerability that always seemed to be present. In moments of despair, as in the aftermath of *The Rebel,* Camus turned to women like a warrior seeking refuge and renewal.

The early photograph of Camus surrounded by three young women on the beach comes to mind again, a recurring and suggestive image. It was taken with his housemates at Tipasa in the idyllic days at the Maison Devant le Monde above Algiers, after his marriage to Simone had ended and before the serious romance with Francine had begun, in an interval when Camus first discovered the pleasures—the affection, the "*simplicité et fidelité*"—of feminine friendship. Much of the ease and joy of that time is recorded in Camus's later letters to Marguerite Dobrenn, Jeanne Sicaud, and Christiane Galindo, who were then his housemates. It shows up in a journal entry—"*L'amitié douce et retenue des femmes,*" "the sweet and lasting friendship of women"—and it is also transposed directly into the pages of *A Happy Death,* his transparently autobiographical first novel, which was not published until after his death, and into the characters of Rose, Claire, and Catherine. *Enfants-soeurs-amies,* "kids-sisters-friends," or *petites filles,* "little girls," is the way Camus addresses these women, with whom he experiences *une amitié vraie.* In the novel, they are an ensemble, "the girls," with whom he lives in unusual harmony and trust, perched as they are in a breathtaking site, a gondola suspended above the panorama of Algiers, joined together daily by a sense of happiness. Read in retrospect, these documents seem invaluable for their revelations, and the words ring true, because they foretell what will become habitual behavior for Camus: his gratitude and protectiveness toward the women in his life, his multiple and simultaneous liaisons, his discomfort with solitude ("curious for me, who so loves society," he writes to Marguerite about a week spent alone and without friends), his "need to withdraw into friendship and confidence and to taste an apparent security before beginning his thing."[2]

In his first attempt at a novel, Camus writes almost compulsively about love and marriage, subjects that he will henceforth refrain from even intimating until his ironic confession in *The Fall,* the novel he published in 1956. Because the writing in *A Happy Death* is so youthful and unguarded, (the relentless flow of the prose seems automatic), this, too, gives the impression of raw, inadvertent truth, offering, at the very least, attitudes and thoughts to be filed away for further consideration. "It's good . . . to have had an unhappy passion—it gives you an alibi for the vague despairs we all suffer from," his alter ego Patrice Mersault (almost the same last name as the protagonist Meursault in *The Stranger*) confesses."[3] "Later on, when you're old and impotent, you can love someone. At our age, you just think you do."[4] Obviously, Camus's recently failed marriage sits heavily on his mind—there are searing descriptions of sexual jealousy and the shame and betrayal of infidelity, and there are lyric passages about love and desire. Marriage is a chain, Camus writes to Marguerite; friendship is freedom.[5] His female friends are a respite from sadness. "That's what I call happiness, little girl," he writes again to Marguerite, "to talk about sausages when the others are interested in the soul's destiny."[6]

As in the private corridors of illness, Camus comes into closer range when he is in the private company of women, which for practical purposes now means in his letters. The letters have the immediacy of conversation, and there, again and again in one way or another, Camus explains and annotates himself. Hundreds of letters to women are listed as source material in the books on Camus, for Camus's relationships were unusually long-lived and constant, like companion pieces to his life. Francine and Maria were the *grands amours,* coexisting as such for almost fifteen years, and both sometimes received two letters a day when Camus was away. But the other affairs had longevity, too, evolving, almost as a pattern, from a first impatient ardor into the more enduring intimacy of friendship. To be loved by Camus was to remain in his story. Long after Koestler's friend Mamaine had left Paris, and until her death, Camus wrote regular, confessional letters to her. Before leaving Lourmarin in January 1960 (he had spent Christmas with his family there), he wrote tender letters about imminent reunions to four women who were constants in his life—Pat Blake, Catherine Sellers, Maria, and Mi. To Mi, who was his new passion and an essential source of renewal, he spoke directly about the pain of their separation and his incessant need for her. "I bless my need," he wrote.[7] In *The Fall,* Jean-Baptiste Clamence, Camus's sardonic, libertine narrator, was also a lover of women. "When I examined . . . the trouble I had separating definitively from a woman—a trouble which used to involve me in so many simultaneous liaisons—I didn't blame my soft-heartedness," he explains, "but merely the desire to be loved and to receive what in my opinion was due me."[8]

Camus, A Romance

The Fall, a rambling, biting monologue that Camus described as a "calculated confession," is a treasure trove of pointed remarks about love, sex, and women, along with the larger issues of guilt, judgment, and the condition of modern man. As Clamence, its main character—once a well-known lawyer in Paris but now a French expatriate drinking gin in a seedy bar in Amsterdam—begins to explain himself and then proceeds to bare his soul, it is impossible not to feel that Camus is implied in all this troubled talk. At times, the self-portrait of this man who specialized in noble causes, who loved women and was courteous, popular, successful, a "tireless dancer and an unobtrusively learned man," seems almost comically transparent. "You would have thought that justice slept with me every night," Clamence says. "In particular the flesh . . . in short the physical . . . brought me steady joys. I was made to have a body." Often, standing on the sidewalk in a passionate discussion with friends, Clamence has lost the thread of an argument because a devastating woman was crossing the street. He tried to renounce women, but it came down to renouncing a game. There are countless similarities between Camus and his antihero, and in some ways these are a source of fun. Camus's friends, too, were gleeful to find such instances of double portraiture and recognized the book as autobiographical, even though Camus publicly denied that he was the hero. In other ways, however, the idea of Clamence as Camus is disturbing, for even as an ironic voice Clamence raises questions of humility and moral gravitas.

Unmistakable, and a far darker matter, is the figure of Francine. She is at the heart of the book, represented in the cry of a young woman who throws herself into the Seine and drowns, a cry that "would continue to await me . . . everywhere, in short, where lies the bitter water of my baptism."[9] Francine herself understood the underpinnings of the book, which came out a year and a half after her recovery, and she recognized it as Camus's effort to confront his guilt. "You owe it to me," she was able to joke about the immediate success of the book, and her comment discloses something about her spirit and their relationship, too. A trusted reader since *The Stranger* was in progress, Francine knew Camus and his work as intimately as anyone—she had even been given early pages of *The Fall* to read—and as their letters over the years reveal, Camus turned to her as a natural ally, almost as an extension of himself. She knew his nature and had long ago accepted his need to philander, but she also had never expected him to fall in love. That development threw her into a state of anguish, which the doctors categorized as an emotional and psychological disorder. During Francine's recuperation, Camus reflected on their relationship, which he described as an "*amitié profonde,*" and on his sense of responsibility, which was as strong as his desire to flee. In his way, Camus always remained loyal to Francine, and he might have continued to live in their apartment on rue Madame to ensure her stability if her family had not insisted that he leave. But he also admitted that they probably never should have married. In her way, Francine acknowledged the importance of Maria, who led a quiet life offstage and was always discreet in her relationship with Camus. For the sake of peace, Maria never again acted in one of his plays, and she published her autobiography after Francine's death, writing then, she said, only as much about Camus as was necessary to make up for the painful years of keeping silent. After Camus's death, it is said, Maria and Francine had a warm relationship.

There is other distracting material about women in *The Fall* (for a while called *Le Cri, The Cry,* and before that *Le Héros*), so much that it seems clear Camus was consciously probing the subject. ("It always seemed to me that our fellow citizens had two passions: ideas and fornication," Clamence says by way of introduction to his dissertation.) In startling contrast to the joyful lover of *The Myth of Sisyphus,* Clamence presents for consideration a ragged new version of Don Juan, one who seeks love and happiness with a certain desperation, who struggles through periods of excess, debauchery, and chastity. "You must know that I always succeeded with women—and without much effort," he begins. "I don't succeed in making them happy or even in making myself happy. . . . No, simply succeed." In the course of his recitation, he offers notes on his experience, like aphorisms: to love many women is not to love any of them; seduction can become a habit devoid of desire; bourgeois marriage has put France into slippers.[10] Twenty years have passed since the young Camus wrote a chapter in *The Myth of Sisyphus* on Don Juan as an absurdist hero: a sensual Sisyphus, sage, self-knowing, self-renewing, discovering new ways of being as he discovered new women. The change is significant. Then, before the war, Camus was still living a more carefree Mediterranean life in Algiers, the sort of Eden that Clamence laments when he says, "Yes, few people could have been more natural than I was. My accord with life was complete." "Oh, sun, beaches, the islands in the path of the trade winds, youth whose memory drives one to despair!" he calls out in a fever. And then, near the end of the book, "Yes, we have lost track of the light, the mornings, the holy innocence of those who forgive themselves."[11]

Despite the many leading remarks, however, Clamence is not Camus, and *The Fall* is a witty, elegant, heavily ironic, carefully crafted work of fiction. It was originally meant to be one of the experimental short stories in *Exile and the Kingdom,* but then it took on a life of its own. Camus, nonetheless, always wrote from experience, and *The Fall* is about Camus and his recent life in its preoccupation with judgment, its evocation of guilt, its moral anguish, its focus on women, and its unrelenting self-analysis. In this last respect, it is also about Sartre and the explicitly named "Paris intellectuals," the original *juges-pénitents* that Camus first noted in his journal, whose criticism had caused him so much pain. (This was even more obvious, it seems, before Camus decided to suppress most of the sarcastic allusions to his colleagues on the left in the interest of the book's symbolic character.)[12] Sartre, who called the book brilliant, apparently understood its ingredients and knew that it was, in a small way, a response to Beauvoir's *The Mandarins* and, in a large way, also a response to his own attack on *The Rebel.* He said he liked the fact that Camus was in it and not in it, showing how well he knew his old friend and the way Camus wrote.[13] Readers who were not privy to the personal facts found the book as enigmatic as, decades ago, it was for me, because it was not a sequential or logical part of his well-planned oeuvre, and because it didn't exactly sound like Camus. This, too, may make a case for the importance of its revelations.

Just as *The Fall* was not only about women, Camus was not only about women either. As Mi volunteered in an interview, women were just one compartment in his life, though they took up a lot of his time. (Friends, family, and even erstwhile lovers have objected to the exaggerated portrayals of Camus as Casanova; they point out that his behavior was not unusual in Europe, particularly postwar Europe.) At the same time, the accounts of Camus's physical allure, which even now continue in interviews and retrospectives, make their point. Robert Gallimard remembers a cocktail party at which Camus was literally surrounded by all the women present. Maria, the daughter of the writer Niccolò Tucci, who was five when she was introduced to Camus at their home in New York and sat on his lap, vividly remembers his presence sixty years later. Still wide-eyed with wonder, Gallimard describes Camus in relation to women as simply *"une chose étonnante"*, "an astonishing thing."[14]

As with his other friends, Camus is judged and informed by the women he loved. In their company, he is an intensified version of himself and, one by one, they help to explain him. (Maria talks about the quality of his smile and his need for order; Mi talks about his sense of fun and the unbearable weight of his responsibilities.) All these women were, like Camus, outsiders in Paris—Algerian, Spanish, English, American, Danish —and that fact may reflect his own sense of exile or simply what he identified in *The First Man* as an irresistible attraction to foreigners, going back to his boyhood.[15] As an ensemble, they bring up interesting questions about the needs of his ego, the impact of his illness, the silence of his mother, and his search for understanding and happiness—*le bonheur* in French, a word that crops up frequently with Camus. They also illustrate his sense of loyalty, and its darker side, which Jean Daniel, his friend, colleague, and fellow *pied noir,* identified as his "guilt complex." In many aspects, Camus was surprisingly old-fashioned, a man of good manners and chivalry with a concern for honor, Daniel said, but he was also one of the first generation in his family to be educated and to seek his way in a wider world. Daniel uses the words "very puritan" to describe Camus and also to explain his guilt. In the case of Francine, whom he knew, he emphasized that Camus suffered deeply over her illness. Camus was never cynical, he said, and would have preferred to be a man who could be faithful.[16]

Jean Daniel also knew Maria Casarès, and when I asked him to describe her for me, he seemed amazed that I had to ask such a question. "What can I say?" he began with more than a hint of impatience. "Maria Casarès was a young Spaniard, who was the daughter of the Republican prime minister before the beginning of the Spanish civil war. She was burning with passion for her country, for music, and especially for the theater.

What she had with Camus was an immense and devouring passion. Nothing else mattered for the two of them." Lowering his voice, as if affected by his own testimony, he concluded, "She was very Spanish, very earthy, very theatrical in every sense of the word."

I already had a mental picture of Maria Casarès, because I had seen her in her first screen role in *Les Enfants du Paradis* (*Children of Paradise*), now a classic. I loved the panorama of early-nineteenth-century Paris, so I used to see this film at least once a year. Even in the unrewarding role of Nathalie, the unsuspecting, forsaken young wife of the mime Baptiste (Jean-Louis Barrault), who has fallen helplessly in love with the elegant courtesan Garance (Arletty), she held the screen. I remembered her proud head, her quiet ferocity, her eyes sparkling with tears. Her lines still hung in the air. "Say something to me," she pleads, confronting Baptiste in a cheap hotel room with Garance. "What about me?" Everything about her performance seems to have relevance now, including, ironically, her place in a triangle of love.

After decades of watching *Children of Paradise* without knowing more about Casarès than this role and an equally mesmerizing one a few years later as Death in Cocteau's *Orphée,* I have gone back to see her as a tender version of the great tragedienne she quickly became. Called "*la mystérieuse*" for her enigmatic soul and "*l'unique*" for her ardor and her range of talent and roles, she was to some minds the best dramatic actress in twentieth-century French theater. In late 1943, when *Children of Paradise* was being filmed, Casarès was already a theatrical star, having been cast by Marcel Herrand in Synge's *Deirdre of the Sorrows* at the Théâtre Mathurins even before she had finished studying at the conservatory or perfected her French. After her hasty exit from Spain in 1936 and her first painful years of exile, the Mathurins was where she regained her footing and grew up, Casarès wrote in her autobiography.

More than a prodigy of stage and screen, however, I can now see Casarès as the charismatic and very young woman she was when her romance with Camus began, only months after the filming of *Children of Paradise* ended. It seems miraculous to have her there for a viewing (Herrand is in the movie, too, in the role of the dashing villain), and I am transported back into the world she inhabited for less than a year with Camus. The youth of the couple—Camus was then thirty, Maria twenty-one—the glamour of the two as exiles and new stars, the occupation that ruled their days, the immediacy of danger that made Paris so dark and so small a place and their affair so urgent a matter—all this makes a true drama. With a new sense of reality I think again about their close encounters with the Gestapo, a drunken bicycle ride across town on the night of the Normandy invasion (Maria was on the handlebars), the company of *résistants* and collaborationists who worked side by side on *Children of Paradise,* the blackouts and electrical shortages that made curtain time for *The Misunderstanding* so unpredictable. Camus called Casarès "War and Peace" because of the circumstances under which they were living and the sanctuary that she provided for him. Wartime gave their relationship added intensity, and when liberation came and Francine, who had been trapped in Algiers, could rejoin her husband, that meant the end of the affair, or, as it turned out, an interlude of four years. Maria considered their separation a matter of honor, but she also said that she didn't wish to be part of a triangle. "Night full of tears," Camus wrote in his journal just before their leave-taking.

Camus and Casarès make a very good story, the celebrated exiles whose personal histories were directly influenced by history. In ways beyond their talent and their glamour, they complemented each other and also resembled each other—in their allegiance to Spain and Spanish blood (although he was Spanish only on his mother's side, Camus took that strain very seriously), in their physical nature, in their passionate curiosity about people, and in their desperate appetite for life.[17] Casarès, proud, impetuous, and independent-minded, lived by the rule *Todo o nada,* "All or nothing," she recounts, until Camus taught her about measure. As an actress, she was tempestuous and flamboyant—her voice tremulous and *rauque,* or husky, as it is usually described; her tears were always real ones, and her roles were often risky. But offstage she was vulnerable, and like Camus she was deeply marked by her displacement and exile. Her autobiography, *Résidente Privilégiée,* written after Franco's death and her first return to Spain in forty years, was an attempt to piece together an identity from memories of her Spanish girlhood and her years in the French theater.

Knowing about Casarès fills in and fills out Camus's life for me in useful ways. Prominent theater people—such as Herrand, who was Casarès's intimate and mentor and is described in loving detail in her book; or her close friend Gérard Philipe, who performed with her onstage and in the film of Stendhal's *La Chartreuse de Parme* (*The Charterhouse of Parma*), making Camus jealous—become working presences rather than incidental facts. The plays of Camus's in which Casarès starred when that was still possible, before Francine's illness, take on romantic as well as professional aspects—time together, work shared, a source of mutual esteem and respect. It was in June 1948 that their affair resumed, almost like a force of nature, following an incidental meeting on the street, and so it no longer seems surprising that at this time Camus turned back, with newfound enthusiasm, to the theater. Their weeks together at the festival in Angers in June 1953, and a few extra days of relaxation together elsewhere, now seem a reasonable factor in Francine's breakdown and despair, which began the following autumn.

From the beginning, Camus and Casarès were grounded in theater as solidly as in Spain. They were a romantic couple—playwright and actress, like George Bernard Shaw and Mrs. Patrick Campbell—and were recognized on the street.[18] In her book, Casarès recalls her first impressions of Camus on the night of the fiesta when Picasso's play was staged (she had been invited in order to bring a breath of Spain for Picasso): the haughty profile, the well-modulated voice, the air of casual indifference that made her think he was an actor (and a natural to play Don Juan). She describes his formidable presence at the stage reading of *The Misunderstanding* and conveys the immediate sense of companionship she felt with

him. Camus gave a brilliant, highly nuanced reading that night, she reports, although exhaustion and violent coughing forced him to stop before the end—excusing himself, as she describes, with a look of sheepish
apology, a hint of irony, and a smile. Those who knew Camus, she adds,
could never forget his particular smile, which was that of a child who has
been caught doing something he knew he would be caught at.[19]

This kind of special detail is what the pursuit of Maria Casarès, like
that of the other intimates, is about—an authentic close-up of Camus. If
it is sometimes sentimental or melodramatic, that is part of the context
and part of her personality, and that fact is telling, too. By all accounts the
love between Camus and Casarès was instinctive and deep, although he
also continued to have other affairs, and she accepted them as pragmati-
cally as she accepted her role as the other woman and his refusal to leave
his wife and children. Casarès had her Don Juanism and her independence,
too; more important, she was sensitive to Camus and the conflict of loyalties that came with having two *grands amours:* Francine with her *bonté,*
or goodness; Casarès with her fire. The two women were necessarily cast
in competition, and their coexistence was accepted even by the family in
the end. Camus had always said that he wanted to have *une vie de famille*
and *une vie de passion,* which were separate compartments, but he had not
foreseen the complicating issues of honor, loyalty, and responsibility.

Several photographs of Camus and Casarès are included in her biography, and these are much more evocative of their relationship than most of
the studio shots of them in rehearsal in Paris or Angers. In one series, taken
on vacation in the Luberon, they are shown with Camus's big old Citroën
(Camus in Borsalino and sunglasses, with cigarette); in another, on vacation in the Vosges (Casarès leaning over Camus as he works at the kitchen
table). There is also a rare picture of Camus napping, a book open on his
chest.[20] Beyond their indication of familiarity and ease, the photographs
are descriptive of the pattern of Camus and Casarès's life together: the sto-
len days or weeks here and there between her theatrical runs and road tours
and his work and family obligations, and, for sustenance, the letters (or when
Camus was with Francine in L'Isle-sur-la-Sorgue in July 1949, the would-
be letters Casarès recorded in her journal for him to read later.)

As the only one of Camus's important lovers to have written a book,
Casarès is a singular source. She provides unique details of Camus's life in

the theater, of Camus on vacation, and of Camus when he was angry about his illness, the same one that killed her father. Her greatest value as an inside informant, however, comes when she tries to pin down exactly who Camus was. He took the place of her father as the anchor and animator in her life, and she idealizes him as "father, brother, friend, lover, and sometimes son," but she also tries to see him clearly for his own sake, and also for the sake of posterity. Speaking from years of being privy to his uncertainties and deepest thoughts, she reinforces much that has been recorded about Camus—his pride, energy, irony, capacity for passion, and attachment to his star. She describes his infidelities as a form of vitality and a desire to live in the present and says that he identified with Don Juan. Casarès remembers Camus the young exile, the African who was discovering a new world while trying to keep the old one intact, as well as an older Camus who was caught in a dilemma about truth and justice in the Algerian war. What she loved most about him, she writes, referring pointedly to the wide criticism of his thinking on the war, was his loyalty to his principles, even in moments when the complexity of his circumstances or his own contradictions made it difficult.

Despite all the ways she knew Camus, Casarès is most revealing when she says that she could never really know him. Even when he was relaxing with her, she saw his guard, "the signs of alert" and his "tireless vigil." She tells of his "taste for the secret," which was as much an ingredient in his taste for romantic adventures as it was in his *pudeur* or his reluctance to speak about his work. Casarès knew all about exile, about the periodic *douleurs,* or sorrows, that came with being a permanent emigrant, and the feeling of otherness that didn't go away; she shared her exile with Camus. What she saw as an unbridgeable distance in him came from something deeper—it was a form of self-defense, she suggests, a protective zone of silence. Many of Camus's Algerian friends, too, spoke of the distance that was present even in his measured voice. He was always cordial and warm, they said, but he established a space between them, much as he did with his public. It seemed to be a way for him to keep his balance.[21]

I was uncomfortable with, even disturbed by, Camus as a libertine. But because of my own *pudeur* and sense of privacy, and perhaps because I was trying to understand, I was reluctant to judge him. I was also impressed by the women with whom he had long relationships, all of whom appeared to be intelligent, lively, and sympathetic as well as very beautiful. In addition, I was encouraged by the fact that Camus intended to write about women in the near future—with sincerity, he specified in his journal. As he confided to his Algerian friend Jean-Claude Brisville about *The First Man,* he wanted to show what his formation owed to women. Previously, his women, as they existed in his work, had a mythic nature, he admitted. Now, after years of warming up, he wanted to create his first important female characters in a work about love.

Francine's response to Camus's new cycle of work was justifiably harsh: "How can you talk about love if you are incapable of it?" Camus's own comments on love over the years—sometimes reflective, sometimes anecdotal, sometimes quite cynical—indicate that it was at least complicated territory for him. Camus has been called a misogynist because of his depiction of women like Marie, Meursault's pleasant but faceless girlfriend in *The Stranger*—as he has been called racist for his depiction of Arabs as incidental, knife-wielding characters in this same novel. In both cases, he has been criticized for a lack of character development and for the rare or passing appearance of women and Arabs in his work. The charges about women are not mitigated by offhand journal entries like this one: "A woman, outside of love, is boring. She doesn't know it. You have to live with one and keep quiet. Or sleep with others and make do. Other things are more important."[22] When thoughts like these reappear in *The Fall,* the reiteration makes them objectionable.

Yet Camus had deep, enduring, loving relationships with women. And it is easy, even quite thrilling, to imagine how richly, and perhaps erotically, he might have written on the subject of love, given the lyricism with which he invokes the physical and sensual world, and the tenderness and emotion that spill over into his love letters. In other entries in his journal, notes for future work, he deconstructs love and records experience in sensitive detail, speaking of identifiable lovers, particularly the later ones, such as Catherine Sellers and Mi, with compassion: "Novel. Mi: in love she breathed like a swimmer and smiled at the same time, then swam faster and faster . . . mouth opened . . . still smiling, as if . . . water had become her element and the earth the arid place where, as a dripping fish, she cheerfully choked."[23] In fact, Camus had already created a new version of a female character in the short story *"La Femme Adultère"* ("The Adulterous Woman"), a languorous, erotic, deeply felt portrait of a woman communing with the desert and the night. Camus began the story sometime in late 1952, not long before he confided to Quilliot that he felt imprisoned as much by the structure and moral strictures of his work to date as by the reputation that the public had invented for him.

Trying to fit Camus's remarks on love to his life brings some insights, although this is territory in which to tread lightly. But as a practical matter, by now his friends and biographers have already opened the window on his private life, offering their own opinions and privileged information—saying that the failure of Camus's first marriage affected him deeply, or that Camus had never intended to marry Maria Casarès, or that for him, women were like a playful addiction.[24] Camus himself offered a startling new perspective on his time with Simone Hié in a letter to her mother, who had sought his advice on Simone's enduring problem with drugs. "I have thought about it and I really don't know what to tell you," he writes to her. "Seventeen years ago, with an intuition that was ahead of my young years, I realized that there was no way out of this situation. That's why I ended it so abruptly, even though that cost me more than I have ever admitted to anyone."[25] After a long silence about his first marriage, this confession has the effect of an exposé. Suddenly even the despair in *Caligula,* which Camus began less than a year after his separation from Simone, has more resonance. "Love, Caesonia! I have learned that it was nothing."[26]

Whether or not Camus's failed marriage accounts for his zeal for sexual conquest, or for his jealousy and possessiveness with women, cannot be known, but it is clear that an early experience of deception and hurt took a considerable toll on a proud, vulnerable young Mediterranean who already had secrets, a protective coat of *pudeur,* and a variety of *malheurs* to transcend. To the tragedy of Simone's addiction was later added the tragedy of Francine's illness. It was difficult for him to love, Camus wrote to the Gallimards, after Francine's ordeal was over, but he did love. Similarly it was difficult for him to write, but he wrote.[27] By then he was at work on *The First Man,* and both those issues were in play.

In late 1959, on the last page of his last journal, Camus took up the subject of his heart at greater length, speaking again of Simone but without mentioning her name. In a *mea culpa* that appears to be the draft of a letter to an intimate, perhaps Catherine Sellers, he attempts to explain his behavior with women to her as well to himself. While his directness and distress make the entry compelling and convincing, his conclusions about himself are saddening. "All my life, as soon as a person got attached to me, I did everything to distance them," he says, blaming in part his pessimistic view of himself. "The first person whom I loved and I was faithful to escaped me through drugs, through betrayal. Maybe many things came from this, from vanity, from fear of suffering further, and yet I have accepted so much suffering. But I have in turn escaped from everyone since and, in a certain way I wanted everyone to escape from me." Excusing himself for any "injustice" on his part, Camus ends with an avowal of tenderness. "I sometimes accuse myself of being incapable of love. Maybe this is true, but I have also been able to select a few people and to take care of them, faithfully, with the best of myself, no matter what they do."[28]

As Camus becomes a more intimate subject for me and his life acquires depth, I understand more fully why he decided to write *The First Man*—in which he will say, under the guise of fiction in a sweeping nine-hundred-page saga: here is what my times have been like, and here is how I became who I am. I am surprised but gratified to find that he is planning to write specifically about the women he has loved—F, C, and Mi as well a mysterious X who appears frequently in his notations—and about his mother, who is, in both simple and complicated ways, the center of his life. Even with only a few hundred pages of an early, unpolished draft in print, *The First Man* has a potential importance that is almost painful to contemplate.

Camus had spoken of making his mother the centerpiece of a novel on love as early as 1951, when he began to put down his thoughts for a preface to a new edition of *The Wrong Side and the Right Side,* his first work, published in Algeria when he was not yet twenty-four. That book, too, was organized around the theme of his mother, which implicated

the whole circle of his experience up till then—his family, his illness, his life in poverty and light. As he explained in his preface, after twenty years of work, his greatest ambition was effectively to write that book again. He wanted to tell the story of a man who came back to rediscover his first truths, to remember how his heart had first opened up.[29] He wanted to be guided by a certain kind of love.

Camus's mother, who was born Catherine Hélène Sintès, has been a visible figure in his private thoughts for as long as he has been keeping a journal. She is the embodiment of the qualities that are most important to him: innocence, compassion, endurance, loyalty, love. The word *bonté,* which combines kindness and goodness, is frequently used to describe her—and to describe Francine—often in contrast to his own "monstrosity." Catherine, partly deaf and nearly mute, illiterate, quite helplessly ignorant and capable of only limited expression, is of a rare simplicity, isolated from world affairs by her disabilities and disposition, cut off even from newspapers and the radio, forever naive, like a character in a fable. Camus describes her quiet patience at the airport in a world of machines that is beyond her comprehension, her childlike responses to events. "Mama and history: someone tells her about Sputnik: 'Oh, I wouldn't like it up there.'"[30] In his book, he will contrast her to the modern universe of cars, planes, and technology, he notes. He makes it clear that his mother's life and nature have had a profound effect on him; her silence, her reserve, her natural sense of pride have provided his "most lofty lessons." Over the years, he has come to understand their symbiotic relationship, how his defiance of fate resulted from her acceptance of it, and his desperate desire for happiness from her lack of it. There is every kind of difference between them, he says, but at the same time, he loves her as he loves no other. He could not live her patient and static life, but no one else has filled his heart. She is his only object of loyalty. She is, he says, the greatest cause that I know in the world.[31]

Without the early chapters of *The First Man* that are now in print—chapters that give intimate details about Camus's first eight years of life—the information on his mother would seem sparse. There are some biographical facts on record—about her grandparents, from Minorca, Spain; her tyrannical mother; her widowhood; her work as a domestic; her infirmities—and there is the provocative portrait drawn in *The Wrong Side and the Right Side*. There is also a fragment from that essay included in the complementary material in the Pléiade, even though Camus cut it from his final draft, which is more forthcoming about the hurt she unconsciously inflicted with her indifference to his illness. "Even more surprising in reflection," he writes there, "was the fact that he had never dreamed of reproaching her for it."[32] Only when I read *The First Man*, however, did Camus's early words in *The Wrong Side and the Right Side* emerge as more than painful memories; then, the full importance of his mother's presence in his life came through to me.

In a familiar photograph of Camus's mother, her head is tilted at an angle, her mouth is set in a faint smile, and she is dressed up, with a bow at her neck, as if, perhaps at her son's request, she had posed for a studio portrait. Middle-aged, both pretty and plain, with a sweet squarish face and big round dark eyes, she projects everything Camus has talked about—kindness, sadness, resignation, and something else he described as not only fatigue but an air of absence and gentle distraction. Except perhaps for her wavy hair, she bears no particular resemblance to him, but then she would always say that he was the spitting image of his father, but without the little mustache.

I have seen some other photographs too: a newspaper print of the widow Camus looking at a picture of her son after he won the Nobel Prize; a sunny snapshot from one of her visits to Provence, in which she wears a shy, disarming smile. More indelible than any of these, however, is the image of her sitting alone on the balcony of her apartment in Belcourt, silently watching the street scene in the fading daylight. This is one of Camus's abiding memories, recorded first in *The Wrong Side and the Right Side,* and then with tender detail in *The First Man*—the gentle distant figure he came upon after school, who twenty years later awaited his returns in the same room, sitting in the same uncomfortable chair. It is hard to get beyond this portrait, for it sums up her life and her enforced solitude, which was also part of Camus's solitude.

Looking back on his childhood, Camus could connect his awareness of his singular attachment to his mother to "the deep and tender image of a *solitude à deux.*" "*Seuls contre tous,*" "alone against everyone," he says about them in reference to a night in his childhood when she was frightened, and he slept beside her to protect her and first realized that she was part of his destiny.[33] In notes and retrospectives, Camus uses other provocative, emotionally charged phrases to try to explain "the bizarre sentiment the son carries for his mother," speaking of her as the immense pity of his heart or of loving her with desperation.[34] Even if he found her silence in the face of adversity admirable, he could never find a way to reach her. He had always thought his mother very beautiful, but he never dared to tell her, he writes as his alter ego Jacques Cormery in *The First Man*. He wanted to tell her, he says, but it would have meant crossing the invisible barrier behind which he had always seen her entrenched.[35] Of Jacques, he also writes: "What he desired most in the world . . . was for his mother to read everything that was his life and being, [and] that was impossible. His love, his only love would be forever speechless."[36] For the end of *The First Man,* which was dedicated to his mother, he inserts in his notes a passage asking for her forgiveness of all the things she could not know about his life. That Camus's primary experience with love had a crucial, complicated impact on his psyche, and probably on his attitude toward women, doesn't seem to be in question; nor does his complete, unalterable devotion to his mother.

In a life as full as Camus's, it is striking how steady a presence his mother maintained, even though she was isolated in her own strict little universe, and even though his every book, refinement, new thought, or new friend increased the distance between them. That was part of it, he said: that she served as a symbol of where and who he had been and also as a counterpoint to where he was and who he had become. In this, and in other ways, she was unchanging and constant—accepting her life without envy or complaint, never passing judgment, in her simple and uneducated point of view capable of a sort of rudimentary wisdom that could be disarming. When Camus announced to her that he had been invited to lunch with the president of France but had declined, her response was, "That's right, son, these people aren't for us."[37] Despite his ever more fervent wishes, she never wanted to live in Provence; it was pretty, she said, but there were no Arabs. (Looking out the window down the tranquil rue Madame during her visits to Paris, she said the same thing.) In *The Wrong Side and the Right Side,* Camus had remarked on his mother's faculty for seeing things in her unique way; in his new novel, he wanted to give her a voice in alternate chapters, to provide a commentary on the same facts with her vocabulary of four hundred words.[38]

There is reverberating irony in the fact that just as Camus was reaffirming his Algerian identity and returning to his sources in Algeria, he, as a *pied noir,* was losing his place there. As the war for independence moved into ever more bloody and desperate phases, his sense of impending loss was one of his motivations for *The First Man,* fueling his desire to record the experience of his community before it was erased, to recount the history of French Algeria before it vanished. Dating back to the first settlement in the 1850s, it was the history of his family, too, for his great-grandfather had been in the first wave of French immigrants. Camus's feeling for his mother had always been intimately bound up with his feeling for Algeria, and now these feelings were virtually inseparable. She was his childhood, Belcourt, the streets teeming with life, the poverty and passion, the sunlight and silence, and she was also the present danger and the uncertain future, the everyday bloodshed and terrorism and his consuming fear for her safety. In the existing chapters of *The First Man,* which move back and forth between childhood and adulthood, Camus slips in a small scene that depicts his mother, rigid and pale, after another bomb has exploded in a nearby street. "You see . . . I'm old. I can't run any more," she says against screams from an ambulance she can't hear. "Like all her people, she had grown up with danger

. . . but she would endure it as she did everything else." It was he, Camus points out, who couldn't bear the look of agony on her face.[39]

In the memory of Parisian intellectuals, Camus is forever linked with his mother on the subject of terrorism, because of a statement he made during a session with students in Stockholm the day after the Nobel Prize ceremonies. Challenged by an angry young Arab about his failure to do anything significant for his country in recent years, he spoke of his feelings about a just Algeria and the equality of its two populations, and also of his reluctance to speak out in public for fear of aggravating a critical situation. "I have always condemned terrorism," he went on to say, "and I must condemn a terrorism that works blindly in the streets of Algiers and one day might strike at my mother and my family. I believe in justice, but I will defend my mother before justice."[40] Only the last sentence of his quite lengthy response struck readers of *Le Monde* the next day, and to eyes that were already critical of Camus and his politics, it read like a rejection of justice rather than a rejection of the justice of terrorism. By late 1957 Camus, who had continued to hope for a multicultural future in Algeria, had already been marginalized, and few people took the time to try to understand his meaning. Widely regarded as scandalous, his remark served to deepen his isolation. Many decades later, it still comes up in discussions of the Algerian war, and it remains puzzling to people who don't know its full context, or who don't know much about Camus.

War in Algeria

On a recent trip to France I was surprised to encounter essays by four well-known North African writers, three of them Algerian, who described an intimate connection to Camus. Since Algeria is still struggling with the idea of its French ancestry and has been anything but sympathetic to its former *pied noir* population, and particularly to a controversial figure like Camus, this expression of fraternity seemed significant. Referring to Camus as his mentor, "the writer I want to resemble," the novelist Yasmina Khadra (the pseudonym of a former Algerian army officer, Mohammed Moulessehoul, who took it to avoid military censorship), says that he chose French over Arabic as his written language as a result of reading *The Stranger*.[1] Marissa Bey remembers that walking through Belcourt on her way to school was the beginning of a feeling of *proximité* to Camus, which to an indigenous Muslim woman, as she describes herself, ran contrary to the history that separated them. "In Algiers, it is with you that I cross our quarter, one of the most bustling in the capital, that I listen to the noise of the crowd returning from the stadium," she writes almost tenderly, using the familiar *tu,* in a hypothetical letter to Camus.[2] In the end, and in different ways, all these writers tie their connection to Camus to the land they shared with him like a heritage— *"belle et effrayante,"* Camus called it, "beautiful and frightening" —the streetscape, the poverty, the heat, the dance halls on the beach, the bleached light, the winds off the plateau of Djémla. More directly, they tie their connection to Camus to his own feelings about that land and the unforgettable way he expressed them. No one wrote more eloquently about Algeria than Camus did, they say; no one better described what it meant to live there.

It is one of the hottest summers on record in the eastern United States, and this may be the perfect weather to be thinking about Algeria. Day after day the sky is cloudless, the sun blazing, the temperature rising, the air heavy, wet, and still. Even at the beach, there is only a poor whisper of wind, which is helpless against the heat. The sand burns underfoot; the ocean has flattened out and gone glassy; the gulls are languid. At mid-day, there is almost no one around, as in Mediterranean countries or in *The Stranger*—a scene of sun and silence. My study, which is half a mile back from the sea and sits under the eaves of the house, is baking and airless. An old fan, almost useless, buzzes and flaps in a way that takes me back to the steamy summers of my childhood around the Great Lakes. I had learned to live with the heat then, and now I don't really mind my situation, although I often emerge from work dazed and dripping. It is another unexpected form of connection, a lesson in the oppressiveness of heat, the sort of heat that can be crushing, can act like a vise on the spirit, making men like Meursault and Caligula crazy.

It is not safe to visit Algeria now; nor has it been safe since the early 1990s, when the government denied the leading Islamic party its victory in the first free multiparty election since independence and set off a state of violent siege that has only recently eased. So I have had to learn about Algeria from elsewhere, trying to draw a sense of place from photographs, movies, music, and books—anything Algerian that has come my way. There is so much to know, particularly for Americans, to whom the country remains distant, distinctly foreign, and threatening. I see the movies in offbeat theaters in New York or in Paris, and they are for the most part expressions of the difficult and still transitional life since independence—a narrative about the aggressive Muslim youth movement in Algiers, for example (*Bab-el-Oued City*), or three emancipated Algerian women in search of a future (*Viva Laldjérie*). I buy CDs of popular stars, such as Souad Massi, who is well known in France and sings in sonorous Arabic and sometimes in flirty, more intimate French. I read novels almost indiscriminately as long as they are set in Algeria or written by past or present Algerians. I have found a collection of reminiscences from French and Arab authors about life before independence, *C'Était Leur France* (*It Was Their France*), and an album of old photographs assembled by a friend of Camus's, *Mon Algérie*. I go back to the early works of Assia Djebar—now Algeria's most acclaimed author, the first from the former North African colonies to be elected to the Académie Française—because these writings came out of her experience in the war and have a haunting, primal authority.

What is clear in all these sources is that Algeria is so strong an experience that it leaves a permanent imprint on the soul. I can feel this when I look at a map, for it is an astonishing country, rugged and immense, three times the size of France, second in size only to the Sudan in Africa, and utterly distinct from its Maghreb neighbors. In the interior, beyond the Europeanized cities along the coastline and beyond the cultivated pastures and vineyards of the hinterland, Algeria becomes a wilderness of high mountain massifs and plunging gorges, remote villages and brutal seasons; in the south, it is defined by its oasis towns and a fat swath of the Sahara Desert. It is said that during a tour there in the 1950s, the French army found the country intoxicating, the vivid cities and their bougainvillea and beaches in violent contrast to the barren peaks, rock-built houses, and nomad tribes of the inhospitable, relentless *bled*. The country "*montait à la tête,*" one of de Gaulle's emissaries is quoted as saying: "It went to your head."[3]

The Algerian War ended in March 1962 with the declaration of independence, but it still figures, explicitly or implicitly, in any discussions of Algeria. The long, savage conflict, which until recently Algerians called "the revolution" and the French sometimes called "*les événements*" ("the events"), is recognized now as one of the longest and bloodiest of the colonial wars, and the most complex.[4] It has left haunting echoes in France, comparable to those of Vichy, some people say, as they continue to plumb the collective memory and sort out the responsibility and the guilt.[5] In recent decades, poverty and unrest in contemporary Algeria have brought millions of North Africans to live, mostly marginally, in France, and this emigration further complicates the situation. Camus has a prominent place in any discussion of Algeria now, not just because of his insights on terrorism or his still controversial role in the war, but also because of his work, which is about Algeria, his heart.

In March 1954, about eight months before synchronized bombings in a dozen sites in the hinterland turned the unrest in Algeria into a war, Camus, in collaboration with a painter and a printer, both friends in Paris, issued a special folio edition of his short story "The Adulterous Woman." It was one of the first stories he had completed for the collection *Exile and the Kingdom,* and it drew upon what he had seen during his trip to the outback of Algeria a year earlier, particularly on his visit to Laghouat, a walled oasis town perched on the edge of the Sahara Desert. That was all I knew about this obscure issue until I actually saw the volume, which on an extravagant impulse I bought online from a rare book dealer in Stockholm. (As the seat of the Nobel Prize in literature, Stockholm was a logical place for such a find, I now realize.) Despite the considerable cost, the color lithographs, and the personal autographs of author and artist that had been advertised, I had not expected the edition to be such an indisputable treasure. Turning its pages was like breathing in Algeria.

In his trip to the south in the winter of 1952, following a visit to his mother and Algiers, Camus was venturing into the Muslim interior, a primitive country hundreds of miles from the glorious coastline he knew— the kingdom of rocks that burn by day and freeze at night and eventually break down into sand, as he described it in his journal.[6] After the public turmoil with Sartre and others, he was content to be alone and on his own, absorbing the stony landscape and the mysterious light with a mixture of gratitude and relief, seeing everything with eyes that were as fresh to the scene as mine were to the details he put into the story.

I read the story slowly, as was natural given the heavy velum pages and the distracting watercolor illustrations. These illustrations were simple, almost naive views of Laghouat and the desert: the former in its typical primary colors, with red walls and yellow minarets against white houses; the latter in the ochres and beiges of sand against the bleached blue of the sky—dromedaries resting at a water hole and the black tents of the nomads minuscule against the immense horizon. The story itself moves slowly in a low key. A lonely forty-year-old woman, Janine, has accompanied her husband on a trip to sell yard goods to the Arabs, and they are idly touring the town. As details accumulate—the white night of a sandstorm, the shepherds who behind their hooded burnooses or veils are only pairs of dark eyes, the cold winter wind, the desolate plateau—they gather force and begin to cast on the reader a spell that resembles the hypnotic spell being cast on Janine. In the final pages, as Janine steals out alone into the icy, starry night and experiences a moment of reunion with the world and her deepest self, the prose becomes urgent and breathless, and like the sky and the earth, begins to spin, conveying a sense of Janine's rapture before she dissolves into tears. "*Ce n'était rien, mon chéri*," "It was nothing, dear," she says to her husband on her return.

"The Adulterous Woman" is a lyrical tour de force, but also a highly sensual version of the basic Camus, a lesson in solitude, life and death, and redemption, transposed to a new, exotic locale in the desert. Janine, like other characters created by Camus, is filled with a nameless anguish, a fear of dying, and a need to be delivered, and her moment of joy is a release from her ordinary life and a rebirth, however fleeting. Even more important, the story turns out to be a lesson on Camus in Algeria: on the way he takes in the landscape, on his passion for the physical place (a "passion without brakes" is a literal translation of his French), and on the power of this place to provoke such a profound attachment. Camus writes about Algeria as he feels it, Yasmina Khadra said, in appreciation of the quality on display here. The dry, vast, sparsely populated Sahara is not the part of Algeria with which Camus is usually associated, but in this story it is a fierce and haunting place. Jean Grenier, who had spent years in the country, was so moved by "The Adulterous Woman," by something beyond the intensity of the evocation and the purity of the language, as he wrote in a letter to Camus, that praise was beside the point.[7] (And Camus wrote back that the joy he experienced reading Grenier's letter made him realize how much he needed encouragement then.)

The simplicity and the wildness, or *démesure,* of the desert may be what Camus was instinctively seeking as an escape from Paris in 1952. He needed to strip down to the basics to recover a sense of who he was, he often said. "In these desolate dried out landscapes . . . I have always been able to find a lesson about poverty and bitterness that almost always takes me back to myself. Which is to say close to an awareness of what I wanted to be," he had written to a girlfriend in the late 1930s, several years before he left Algeria.[8] The setting of "The Adulterous Woman" describes such a place—primitive, poor, a land where men struggle for survival "possessing nothing but serving no one," as Camus writes, a land outside time and the history of men.[9] This last phrase might describe the early scene of *The First Man,* the long-ago, unsettled Algeria of the nine-teenth century, a lonely, rude new frontier. But it has other, eerie rever-berations. Even in 1952 the Sahara was not as forgotten a place as Camus described. Although Camus does not mention it, his trip to Laghouat had been delayed by reports of guerrilla activity in the mountains. In re-mote areas like this, the revolution was being organized and would begin to take shape.

There is another story in the collection *Exile and the Kingdom* that is set in the desolate territory Camus visited in 1952 and relates more di-rectly to the war. "*L'Hôte*" ("The Guest") tells of a schoolteacher, Daru, in a remote village in the high plateau. Daru is unexpectedly assigned by the local gendarme to take a Muslim who has murdered his cousin to a jail across the mountains. En route, having come to know the harshness of life in the *bled,* and feeling compassion for his prisoner, Daru gives him bread and dates and lets him go free, only to notice later, across the rocky plains, that the young Muslim is making his way toward the jail on his own. Returning to his classroom, Daru finds scrawled on the blackboard a message indicating that he and his humanitarian act have been misunder-stood: "You handed over our brother. You will pay for this."[10] Presum-ably written sometime after the beginning of FLN terrorism in November 1954, but conceived soon after his trip, the story catches Camus's own troubled state of mind in the face of the despair in Algeria and the bur-geoning revolution. His setting evokes a cruel, famine-stricken landscape where everyone is poor and unhappy and the sheep are dying by the thou-sands. His character is a reminder of the young instructors who were the first victims of the guerrilla attacks in this area in 1954, and of Camus's own early plans for a career in teaching. Already, Camus seems to be aware of the moral dilemma he is facing in supporting the nationalist move-ment while opposing its use of violence. "Daru looked at the sky, the plains, and, beyond, the invisible lands stretching all the way to the sea," he writes in conclusion. "In this vast landscape he had loved so much, he was alone."[11]

It has taken me a long time and extensive reading to begin to understand the tragedy of the Algerian war, which had been real to me only in the fading graffiti I saw scrawled on walls in Paris and the Midi. Over the years, the war has generated an enormous number of studies in France—according to one estimate, some 3,000 books, fifty films, and twenty documentaries—largely intensely partisan. But perspective comes slowly. It was a war that the French government didn't consider a war, because Algeria constituted three *départements* and was an integral part of France; a war that was long referred to as "the war without a name"; a faraway war of unspeakable atrocities that did not affect the daily lives of most Frenchmen outside the army until the end, when the far-right-wing Organisation Armée Secrète (OAS) brought terrorist bombs to the mainland and planned to invade Paris. Only recently have generals, Arab dissidents, and victims of the violence begun to talk about the power struggles, the torture, the executions, and the miscarriages of justice, and only recently have historians begun to critique the standard narrative of the war.[12]

Now more than ever, its complexity describes this war that involved far more than the issue of independence for 9 million Muslims, and contained within it many other wars—a civil war between the extremist Front de Libération Nationale (FLN) and rival nationalist groups, a guerrilla war between the FLN and the French army, and a political war among the French, at the very least. During the seven and a half years of bitter conflict, the war brought down six prime ministers and the Fourth Republic, and when the rebel generals attempted an invasion of Paris in 1961, it almost toppled General de Gaulle and his new Fifth Republic. The war cost an estimated 500,000 lives, preponderantly among Muslim Algerians (including tens of thousands of *harkis,* the Algerians who fought with the French and were slaughtered by the FLN after the war), and it caused 1 million European settlers to leave Algeria.[13] Its legacy is the memories and the questions that still trouble both France and Algeria. Almost half a century after its end, it remains a war that seems difficult to sum up with any authority beyond its lessons about the relationship between repression and violence and the horrors of terrorism and counterterrorism. The lessons are one reason that Camus figures prominently in the retrospectives.

"The question of Albert Camus" is the way Camus is often introduced in histories now. The phrase is more resonant than it was during the war, when it meant, essentially, Why doesn't Camus take a hard position on the war? Later, after early 1956, when his public appeal for a civilian truce had failed and his series of articles in *L'Express* had abruptly ended, the phrase meant, Why has the best-known French Algerian in the world fallen silent in the heat of a war in which his voice is desperately needed? These days, because it involves hindsight and is informed by the still uncertain status of the new Algeria, the question has become bifurcated and bigger: Might Camus have been prescient in his refusal to negotiate with terrorists and in his belief in reconcilation? And might his silence ultimately have been the voice of morality and reason? There is also a coda, which is a variation on a famous remark of Sartre's in which he admitted that he was wrong to support Stalinism in the 1950s but said that he had been right to be wrong. Given the ensuing decades of demagoguery and repression in Algeria, a younger generation is asking if Camus could have been simply wrong to be right about his country at that time. In Algeria, people such as the writer Marissa Bey are saying that after a lifetime of resenting Camus and branding him as the "other," they now want to know more about him.

The Algerian war spread over the remaining years of Camus's life like an incurable illness. Reading about this last chapter of his life is heavy going, and even with the great success of *The Fall* and, later that year, the honor of the Nobel Prize, it is sad and depressing. Camus's troubles seemed to come together in a rush: the storm over *The Rebel,* Francine's illness, then writer's block and the war, and always, involuntary but inevitable, like a physical reflex, illness and insecurity, each setback seeming to collude with the next one. Sometimes Camus's fate seems almost Shakespearean, and Camus, without dramatizing his situation but with an appreciation of myth, seemed to sense this too. Yet even at the bottom he had his street fighter's strength and always the force of his morality. In all his adversity, Camus never seemed to be more himself or more constant. This is both admirable and sad, but knowing how and why Camus feels as he does, I know too that he cannot change.

It was an increasingly lonely time for Camus after January 1956, when he traveled to Algiers to present his initiative for a civilian truce. Such a truce seemed to be the only way to stop the killing of innocent people and begin a dialogue about the future, "to prevent the worst."[14] After that, as the FLN's terrorism continued to radicalize the French and the French repression served to consolidate the Muslim population, and the FLN became a mass movement, everything began to fall apart. More than ever, I am sensitive to the gap between Camus the private person, who is in increasing turmoil, and Camus the famous writer, who in the next four years will publish seven more books, adapt and direct two major plays in Paris, and win the Nobel Prize. Such is the outside view of a life that plays very differently on the inside, where it moves day to day and sometimes hour by hour, "*hagarde*" and "*angoissée*," as he regularly describes it. It hangs in mind as no small irony that the Nobel Prize will crown Camus as the conscience of his generation at a moment when he is out of sync with that generation as regards a critical war. That he will be embraced by an ever larger readership around the world at a time when he is at his most isolated in France is another irony.

As the spokesperson for justice in Algeria, Camus wasn't on the public stage very long. In the spring of 1955, urged by his Algerian-born friend Jean Daniel, who had promised him complete artistic freedom, he had been persuaded to return to journalism and write twice a week for *L'Express,* Jean-Jacques Servan-Schreiber's smart, seductive new publication, at center left and recently a daily. It was a way to engage, "to speak for Algeria and the Algerians," and—not incidentally—to help Pierre Mendès-France, who had recently been removed from power and was committed to reform in the country, to win the coming election. Uneasy even before writing his first column, and anticipating criticism from both the left and the right, Camus had called on his old friends in Algiers to keep him informed and up to date. As new insurrections and a second massacre of civilians intensified the fear that summer, his responsibility to write weighed ever more heavily, and he could think of nothing but Algeria. "You may be able to prevent me from saying stupid things," he wrote in an anguished letter to Charles Poncet, who was the leader of a band of liberal intellectuals in Algiers that included intimates like Maisonseul and Roblès. "I will also feel more confident about what I can say."[15]

The idea that Camus should come back to Algiers to initiate a dialogue among the warring parties had come from Poncet, who heard in his letter from Camus a voice of hope. The need for a confrontation, a *table ronde*, was what Camus had been preaching in *L'Express*, as he addressed himself directly to the French of Algeria and the militant Arabs, carefully analyzing the responsibilities of each group, condemning the terror and repression, the politics of *"tuer ou fuir,"* "kill or flee," condemning in turn the lassitude and blindness of the French government and the indifference of the mainland French. There were no longer any innocents in Algeria except those who were dying, he said. The distance between mainland France and Algeria had never been greater, he repeated often, using the word *fossé,* or "moat," to describe the distance. Without intervention, Algeria was a land of bloodshed and prisons. Despair was not an alternative, because despair was the name of the war.[16] As he wrote on the eve of his departure for Algiers, in what would be his penultimate editorial for *L'Express,* he saw the crisis in Algeria as tantamount to the Spanish civil war and the defeat of France in 1940 in its far-reaching political and historical ramifications.[17]

The narrative of the afternoon of Sunday, January 22, 1956, when Camus took the stage to read the fifteen-page text of his appeal for a *trève civile* (civilian truce), still reads as an extraordinary drama. Even the building in which the public meeting was held, the Muslim-owned Cercle du Progrès, on the Place du Gouvernement, with its equestrian statue of the duke of Orléans, next door to the French governor-general's office and a stone's throw from the labyrinthine Casbah, populated by Muslims and the FLN, was theatrical. Several thousand people, equal numbers of French Algerians and Muslims, were present at the event, which for security purposes was by invitation, and is remembered as fervently fraternal—the last such gathering in Algiers in recent history. Among these people were all the leading Muslim nationalists as well as Sheikh El Okbi, whom Camus had defended against a murder charge and befriended in his days at *Alger*

Républicain (and who, because he was ailing, had been brought to the event on a stretcher), and a large representation of students and workers. Outside, in the square, a crowd of more than 1,000 predominantly right-wing European *ultras* angrily protested Camus's message, filling the air with cries of "*Camus au poteau*" ("Camus to the stake"), "*Camus à mort*," and "*Mendès à mort*," and sounding the party chant *Al-gér-ie fran-çaise*. A force of some 1,000 Muslim foot soldiers from the Casbah, as arranged by the FLN—"a human sea," Camus said—stood by to contain the demonstrators.[18] The "Marseillaise" was sung, a bonfire was lit near the statue, rocks shattered windows in the hall, and there were fascist salutes.

On the scene, Camus is described as "pale and worried," earnest, determined to finish his address, but also increasingly aware of real danger in the taunts, the rocks, the recent death threats; shocked at the hatred coming from the Europeans; and inwardly convulsed at the thought that an initiative for peace might result in further bloodshed. In content his speech resembled his pieces for *L'Express,* focusing on the importance of showing that an exchange of views was still possible, of agreeing on the single definitive point of saving lives. In tone, his speech was more intimate and beseeching, and in the situation it had a different kind of eloquence, which came from its urgency and its barely muted despair. He painted terrible and knowing pictures of an alternative future in which "because they could not manage to live together, two populations, similar and different at the same time but equally worthy of respect, are condemned to die together, with rage in their hearts."[19] Camus read his remarks purposefully, his voice sometimes husky, pausing once to embrace his old friend Ferhat Abbas, who arrived late on the dais to represent the moderate nationalists, and also managing a weak grin when the crowd outside began to chant "*Ca-mus-ta-gueule,*" rude argot telling him to shut up. He finished to great and heartfelt applause and exited the hall quietly, surrounded by the bodyguards his brother Lucien had assigned to him. The next day he met briefly with the governor-general, who was vaguely supportive of the initiative, and at length with his mother, and then left for the airport amid a cavalcade of friends. They were all armed, he would learn. "Everyone wanted to kill you" was the explanation.[20]

At the beginning of his speech, Camus had made a point of insisting that neither his intervention nor the action of the French and Arab organizers had anything to do with politics. To be political would "merely add to the weight of insults and hatreds under which our country is stifling and struggling," he said. Yet politics was evident in the tense meetings preparatory to the evening, and it was reflected in the Muslim contingent of sponsors for the truce: Mohamed Lebjaoui and Amar Ouzegane (both Camus's friends), and Bouralem Moussaoui and Mouloud Amrane. All four were secretly leaders of the FLN's clandestine movement, as they admitted to Camus on the eve of the appeal, and all four men would later have prominent positions in an independent Algeria. Camus had selected them, along with Abbas, as part of his broad humanitarian front, but they had their own strategic thoughts about the truce: they supported it but knew it to be an illusory goal, though useful in advancing their political credibility. In his book about the revolution, Lebjaoui remembered that Camus was precise and lucid in his judgments, "but still very far, especially, from the reality of the moment."[21]

Following the developments, I have a keen sense of watching Camus in real time, an awareness of what is happening to him as it is happening. Perhaps because he had so much to learn about the situation into which he has been drawn, his idealism seems naive, his honesty a form of innocence. Every day the air seems more charged, the truce less likely, the FLN more cold-blooded in purging its ranks of dissidents, the *pied noir* community more radicalized. (*Pied noir,* or "black foot," was once a neutral term for the French and other European settlers, who wore black boots when they arrived, but during the war it became increasingly politicized, and eventually it designated those who didn't want to end colonialization.)[22] On arriving in Algiers, Camus had taken the time to commit his state of mind to his journal. Away from Paris, with its resignation and nastiness, and no air to breathe, the anguish had left him, he said, and at least he was engaged in the struggle, where, in the end, he had always found peace of mind. "Yes, I arose happy, for the first time in months. I've recovered the star."[23] Three days later, on January 21, there is only a bulletin: "Threats for this evening and tomorrow."[24]

Being on the streets of Algiers, seeing places and faces that are familiar from Camus's youth, brings on an uncomfortable nostalgia for simpler times. The tram stop where Camus descended en route to the lycée is in front of the Cercle du Progrès. The cafés and restaurants where meetings take place are redolent of student life. Many of Camus's friends from these days are still on the scene: Roblès was the chosen moderator of the event; Yves Deschezelles is now the lawyer for Messali Hadj and other centrist nationalists; Maisonseul, the mild-mannered painter, architect, and urban planner, was the liberal chosen to be arrested and imprisoned in the aftermath of Camus's speech on January 22, a clear warning to the group to desist. Some of them were also Camus's bodyguards, when he realized that he needed to have bodyguards.

More significant in the scheme of things is the shift of position that has occurred among Camus's old Muslim friends: Ouzeman, who in the 1930s was Camus's superior in the Communist Party; Abbas, who had long been the French-loving archapostle of moderation, supporting assimilation, patiently waiting for democratic reform. Abbas's appearance on the dais with Camus marked his last stand as a moderate, for within weeks, his final disillusion led him to meld his own movement into the FLN. To his readers, Camus's own disillusion was apparent in the cautious, heavy-hearted piece that he filed in *L'Express* on January 28, in which he stated that he still believed in the free association of French and Arabs and held out for the possibility of a civilian truce but also admitted that he had no idea of how to achieve it.

With the exception of his two letters to *Le Monde* to protest Maisonseul's arrest at the end of February, and his resounding remarks about terrorism the following year in Stockholm, Camus did not speak out or write directly about the Algeria war until the spring of 1958, when he published *Actuelles III*, subtitled *Chroniques Algériennes*. This was his way of filling in, explaining, and justifying his silence for all those who had been waiting. In this volume, he collected about a dozen pieces on Algeria, beginning with his early reporting on Kabylia and including essays from *Combat* and *L'Express* and the texts of the *trève civile* address and his intervention in Maisonseul's case. He ended with a carefully articulated plan for a future Algerian-French federation, in which the Arab and European communities would have equal voices in Algerian society and work together in union with France. This was the only sort of rule that he thought could do justice to the different groups and keep the country strong.

The work was a retrospective, spanning the years from 1939, when, he noted, almost no one was interested in Algeria, to the present, when the whole world was talking about it. Thus *Actuelles III* was a résumé of his own thinking during the last twenty years. In the long foreword, Camus referred to his experience in Algeria as "the long confrontation between a man and his situation, with all the errors, contradictions and hesitations such a confrontation suggests"—a quiet reminder of the personal dimension in his engagement.[25] He could approve neither a policy of oppression in Algeria nor one that would abandon the Arab people to even greater misery and tear the French settlers from their age-old roots, he explained. He sounded both current about the changing consensus on the war and desperate for recognition as the voice of reason, even though, as he said at the outset, by then he knew that his position would not satisfy anyone. "I sincerely regret that," he wrote, "but I can't force what I feel and believe. But then no one satisfies me on the subject either."

As Camus formally withdrew from the fray—"*le jeu publique,*" "the public game," he called it with well-merited cynicism—his words had the intonation of a painful abdication, and this offered some measure of the disappointment, disillusion, anger, hurt, and resolve that had been building over the past two years. Unable to join either of the extreme camps and faced with the progressive disappearance of the "third force," Camus explained further, "doubting too my convictions and my beliefs, convinced finally that the true cause of our madness lies in the ways and workings of our political and intellectual society, I have decided to no longer participate in the unending polemics, the only effect of which has been to fix the intransient in their positions and divide even further a France already poisoned by sectarianism and hate."[26] Until this reality changed, he was resigned to working for Algeria's future in private ways; he said he would not add another word to this last testimony, and in effect he never did.

In February 1956, Camus resigned from *L'Express,* as much because of his uneasiness at the magazine as because of Mendès-France's defeat and his own disgust with what he called the new premier Guy Mollet's "sideshow in Algeria"—and, more specifically, because he did not want to add to the unhappiness of Algeria or the foolishness being written about it. Beginning then, Camus moved offstage. Silence was a form of action, he had resolved, and the private ways that had to substitute for spoken language were exemplified in his ceaseless interventions of the next years, mainly for Muslim nationalists condemned to death; these interventions were another way to stop the shedding of innocent blood. In hindsight, the events of January 22 seemed to have marked the end of the beginning of the war, when there was still a faint prospect of accord, and the beginning of the rest of the war, when positions hardened, the killing intensified, and the only points of convergence between the French and Muslim communities were violent.

Camus seemed rarely to utter the word independence, as if he would not honor that possibility with language and thereby abandon hope. This set him apart from most of his colleagues, who came to accept that inevitability quite early. He kept in touch with the remarkable Germaine Tillion, a liberal, intellectual French sociologist who had earned the trust of FLN leaders and worked tirelessly for French-Muslim reconciliation. In September 1959, when de Gaulle proclaimed Algeria's right to self-determination, promising to offer its citizens a choice between independence or either association or integration with France, Camus was heartened, for in private meetings with the president, he had come to believe that de Gaulle's concept of association matched his own vision of federalism in Algeria. He had new hope for Algeria, he wrote to Chiaromonte, and was sure that de Gaulle's declaration had indicated the right course. To another friend, who asked if this was not the moment to break his silence, Camus replied that if there was a referendum on the Algerian affair, he would write against independence in the Algerian press. Only a few months later, a few weeks after his death, the rage among the *ultras* and the renewed terror by the FLN made it clear that no referendum would ever take place.

It took considerable sifting and sorting of memoirs, histories, and interviews, and required considerable patchwork and projection, for me to get any sense of what Camus was thinking during the downward spiral of events. It often seemed as if he had withdrawn from my view, much as he had withdrawn from public life (preferring to keep his interventions quiet, to meet off the record with President Coty and General de Gaulle). The letters sometimes helped. To Poncet, after the public appeal: "I had the impression (false perhaps because I was tired) of having let down my French and Arab friends a little. Is it because my speech came off as the point of the gathering, without calling for action, without alluding to the injustice of so many years . . . ?"[27] A month later to another Algerian friend (who will later join the radical OAS): "There is presently inside me

De Gaulle in Algiers, June 1958

someone who is dying of shame. If I saw a possible action, no matter how crazy, I would try it. But we are hurtling toward the abyss, we are there already." At the time of the Nobel Prize, he expressed his feelings of fraternity to his friend the Muslim writer Mouloud Ferraoun, and said that he was not yet resigned to the separation of the French and Arab communities.[28] Ferraoun, who continued to work throughout the war for Franco-Muslim solidarity in Algeria, was assassinated by the OAS, along with five other liberal educators, in Algiers in February 1962.

In addition to the letters, the notebooks—although always unpredictable and now noticeably scant in revelations—give an occasional glimpse inside, which can be searing. "Algeria obsesses me this morning," Camus writes in July 1958. "Too late, too late. . . . My land lost, I would be worth nothing."[29] The friends confirm Camus's obsession, speaking of his being consumed, "torn in two," or "too divided." "Algeria was in his mind all the time," Miriam Chiaromonte said to me quietly. That truth is reflected in the work that Camus produced during these last years, which is like a running commentary on the war and its moral repercussions, a calendar of deadly events. *Letter to an Algerian Militant,* first published in a new liberal Algerian magazine launched by his friend Aziz Kessous, came on the heels of a massacre at Philippeville, where the FLN savagely butchered about 100 European men, women, and children in the surrounding villages, and the army responded by shooting thousands of Muslims.[30] The essay begins with a line often quoted to suggest Camus's personal anguish over Algeria: "You will easily believe me if I tell you that I now am hurting about Algeria the way others hurt in their lungs."[31] *Reflections on the Guillotine,* in 1957, his entreaty against capital punishment, which had haunted him since childhood and the story of his father's terrible reaction to a hanging, had been fueled by his helping to defend Muslim militants sentenced to death. His adaptation of Faulkner's *Requiem for a Nun,* which included the murder of a child, a black woman's death sentence, and the importance of truth as a message, seemed like another piece of his mind. *Actuelles III,* published after the war had turned, was a last call to reason. His adaptation of Dostoyevsky's *The Possessed,* which opened to mixed reviews in Paris in January 1959, was to many critics the ultimate story about terrorism.

I examined Camus's every action and every word in the heat of the war and in light of the pressing narrative at hand. As he addresses—again and again, directly and indirectly—the question of an artist's responsibility to his times, he may be at his most revealing. It has been his abiding concern since the days of the Théâtre de Travail, showing up in essays, interviews, speeches, letters, and the journal—"How tempting it is to turn away. But the epoch is ours and we can't leave it hating ourselves," he wrote as he embarked on *The Rebel*—but now it is attached to the context of Algeria and the painful issue of his silence. However resolute at heart, Camus sounds increasingly self-conscious as he insists to friends and the public alike that he "has not separated himself from his times," as he keeps bringing up his early activism like a validation of his true heart and strong record. Occasionally he waxes defiant. "My job is to do my books and to fight when the freedom of my own and my people is threatened. That's all," he inscribes in the journal.[32] "My feeling is that people expect too much of a writer in these matters," he says in the preface to *Actuelles III.*"[33] In his Nobel lecture in Stockholm, entitled "Creating Dangerously," when he talks about the "dangerous implications" of silence and "an age that forgives nothing," his pain and his quandary show through clearly. In publishing *Actuelles III,* Camus was giving in to his critics and making a last effort to give a public voice to his silence, but beyond a few attacks from the doctrinaire left it passed without discernible notice.

As Camus withdrew from the debate about the war, the intellectual establishment in Paris tightened its own engagement, which is a measure of Camus's plight in these last years. From almost the beginning, the left in France—like the left all over the world—had taken on the issue of anticolonialism in Algeria as a legitimate cause, and like the army it developed a powerful and independent voice that affected the course of the war. Camus's old antagonists were familiar faces in the crowd. Sartre, who had delivered a powerful lecture urging self-government for Algeria on the eve of Camus's appeal for a civil truce, became one of the most conspicuous spokesmen for Algerian independence. François Mauriac, who always enjoyed confrontation, regularly challenged or ridiculed Camus in his column in *L'Express*—"Reflections on the Guillotine," he said, made him "feel sick."[34] Francis Jeanson, the most radically avant-garde of the group and the most deeply sympathetic to the Algerian nationalists' cause, assembled a Resistance-like underground network of support for the FLN.[35] Jeanson also wrote an introduction to the first big book by the Algerian nationalist Frantz Fanon, and Sartre wrote one for Fanon's third book, now a classic, *The Wretched of the Earth*.

At times, it seemed as if the attacks on Camus were only a continuation of the polemics of 1952, with the opposed parties still acting out the original drama. In some substantive ways this was true, for the thinking at the heart of *The Rebel*—against totalitarianism, against revolutionary violence, and against history as an end—was fundamental to Camus's position on the war and the FLN. It also seems clear and maybe poignant that Camus, given the recent *mano à mano* with the left—"this Left of which I am a part, in spite of myself and in spite of it"—was all the more sensitized and all the more vulnerable to attack.[36] But by 1957, in the aftermath of the Battle of Algiers and the massacre of Arabs at Mélouza, most of metropolitan France was growing skeptical about the possibility of reconcilation. Not only Camus's ideology but also his idealism could be seen to be at fault. As more and more intellectuals—Sartre in *TM* and many of Camus's friends and colleagues at Gallimard—felt compelled to speak out against the excesses of the army and the "gangrene" of torture on one side and the reprehensible tactics of the FLN on the other, Camus's silence came to seem louder and more irresponsible, "undistinguished," "baffling," "hypocritical," even "immoral," in the words of his critics.[37] At the very least, there was anger or disbelief.

Camus remained essentially unbowed by Parisian intellectuals until the end, stoicism being one of his distinctively Algerian traits, even though, as an Algerian friend put it, he had been "hurt to the point of injury." Notes of bitterness creep into some of his commentary, and there are a few complaints about persecution and betrayal in his letters, but the hurt showed most in his increasing solitude and isolation in Paris, and in the panic attacks and claustrophia that plagued him for months after the Nobel Prize and the new fires it ignited. Not until the following spring did Camus emerge from a state of anguish, exhaustion, and a confessed "sort of madness" to address the process of healing in his journal. "Letting volition sleep. Enough of 'you must,'" he instructed himself. "Wouldn't it be that I have suffered from the excess of my responsibilities?" His prescriptions are impressively self-knowing. "Return as often as possible to personal happiness. Not refusing to recognize what is true even when the truth happens to thwart the desirable." "Recognize the necessity of enemies. Love that they exist."[38]

After the Nobel Prize and the "Stockholm incident," Camus could count some good friends as well as prominent journalists among his adversaries. He had not anticipated, nor did he ever really seem to understand, the clamor over his remark about terrorism and justice, and it is enlightening to discover that he had said essentially the same thing several times before in private company as well as in *The Just Assassins*. "If a terrorist throws a bomb into the Belcourt market where my mother shops and it kills her, I would be responsible in the case where, in order to defend justice I would at the same time have to defend terrorism. I love justice but I also love my mother," he is quoted as saying to Roblès soon after the truce proposal in Algiers.[39]

Camus's fellow *pied noir* Jean Sénac, a poet, disciple, and friend since Camus published Sénac's early work in his Gallimard series *Espoir,* issued the most violent of the responses to Stockholm, a two-pronged attack delivered in the form of a letter and a companion piece for *France Observateur,* which amounted to character assassination. He had already crossed swords with Camus over the "injustice" of the message on justice in *The Just Assassins*. Now a confirmed supporter of independence, Sénac ridiculed Camus's attitude toward his mother (his own mother joined him in the struggle) and assaulted not only his silence but also his Eurocentric paternalism, his distrust of the Arab-Berber universe, his humanism (which Sénac equated with pacification), and his refusal to negotiate for peace. In reply, Camus was hurt and angry at the public nature of Sénac's attack and sardonic about the end of their long friendship, closing with a cool and simple, "Good luck."[40] For eleven years the two writers had exchanged thirty-seven letters, a correspondence that has now been published as a telling story from a tragic war: *Albert Camus–Jean Sénac or the Rebel Son.* Sénac, who returned to Algiers immediately after liberation, was brutally murdered there in the turbulent 1970s.

Other friends distanced themselves as a matter of course, of politics, of principle, of impatience, or of dismay. Among the more admiring and enduring of Camus's Muslim colleagues there was a new sense of reality, a recognition of the culture and experience that necessarily separated them, with the inevitable polarization. Even in the early days of the war, the poet Jean Amrouche had noted that, however perceptive, Camus was weak on solutions. "*Le mal est beaucoup plus profond,*" he had said then of Camus's assessment: "The trouble is much deeper."[41] Ferraoun said essentially the same thing in 1958: "His pity is immense for those who suffer, but he knows, alas, that pity or love has no power over the evil that kills, that demolishes, that would like to wipe the slate clean and create a new world. . . ."[42] Ahmed Taleb Ibrahimi, the future minister of education, who was in prison in 1959, remained outraged about the silence of "Camus, the Algerian," his anger betraying the daunting expectations that were behind his disappointment. Algerians had hoped that Camus would work not only for a rapprochement between Europeans and Muslims, but also to create a vast movement in France for the settlement of the whole colonial problem, he said.[43] Camus could have been the eloquent spokesman for Algerian resistance that he had once been for the French under the occupation.

As they diverged from Camus and began to prepare for a new Algeria, longtime *pied noir* friends like Jean Daniel and Jules Roy may have inflicted the most pain. Poncet, Maisonseul, and the old liberals in Algiers were ready to negotiate with the FLN too, while Camus continued to hold out hope that de Gaulle could negotiate federalism in Algeria—"*une idée farfelu,*" "a crazy idea," the friends had come to think. Camus still had admirers, and a few old *copains* in Algiers held the same loyalties and hopes that he did. Germaine Tillion, too, was dedicated to keeping a bridge open between the two communities and believed that independence would push poverty-stricken Algeria into destitution. But Camus was effectively alone by now, speaking only for himself, and often to himself, standing up even against a fait accompli.[44] Robert Gallimard, like others, looks back ruefully on those days, wishing that he had talked more with Camus, "had explained to him that I understood very well what was in his head." They had spoken "very very little" at the end, he said, because Camus was so torn apart by the situation and yet understood that Algeria would have its independence. "What he wanted—the plebiscite, the original French-Algerian community and the Arab community side by side— was perfectly good, but it was no longer possible, and he was alone, absolutely alone in his thing."[45]

Almost everything Camus did and said in his last years indicates that as he remained unshakable in his position on the war, he was also aware that Algeria would never again be the country he knew and that he would be disenfranchised. It was too late for Algeria, he wrote to Jean Grenier the summer after he published *Actuelles III*. "I did not say so in my book because . . . one doesn't write to say that everything is screwed up. In that case one remains silent. I am preparing myself for that."[46] He also seemed to know that his view of Algeria might have been "myopic," meaning that his feelings about the country could be wrong in the present but might hold true in the future. In an odd, drifting little piece, "*Petit Guide pour les Villes Sans Passé*" ("Little Guide for Cities without a Past"), which was one of his prewar "sun essays" and a love letter to Algiers and Algeria, "my true country," Camus had written, like an alert: "I have a long liaison with Algeria that will undoubtedly never end and which prevents me from being clear-sighted in this respect."[47] A few years later, from Paris, he added to that thought in his notebooks. "Algeria. I don't know whether I can make myself understood, but I have the same feeling on returning to Algeria as I have on looking at the face of a child. And yet I know that all is not pure."[48]

Camus was also undeniably of a particular era in Algeria, which, as time passed, became—in great and unpredictable gulps—ever more defining. It was the era of *The Stranger* and his series on Kabylia for the *Alger*

Republicain when he came of age, when he was in full residence, an era before the war, when Arab nationalism was in its adolescence, its leaders still predominantly moderate and assimilationist, when France was still accepted as the *mère protectrice*. After that, he had only his brief sojourns once or twice a year and his old friends to keep him in touch with a country in dramatic evolution. In April 1945, when he returned to see his mother for the first time since his departure in August 1940, his trip came only weeks before the insurrection and bloody repression at Sétif that changed the face of nationalism and henceforth of his native land. Camus's subsequent front-page articles in *Combat* on the crisis attempted to show the complexity of the situation, to explain the goals of Ferhat Abbas and his new party, and to rally forces for a "justice that would save Algeria from hate." In hindsight, these articles would be seen as too timid, although they were also the only ones to attempt full and informed coverage and, in Abbas's judgment, "the only ones, in that era, in the French press, to tell the truth."[49]

Camus always respected and relied on his experience, which when distilled figured in his moral guidelines. He was also very clear about who he was. He described himself as French-Algerian, a *petit blanc,* the son of an illiterate house cleaner. He was someone who was more at ease with a shopkeeper in the workers' quarter of Algiers than with a professor at the Sorbonne. He was careful to make a distinction between *le petit blanc* and *le grand colon,* because, as he said in *L'Express,* certain Parisians seemed to see all the million *colons* in Algeria as rich vintners and oilmen with ties, cigars, and big Cadillacs, whereas 80 percent of French-Algerians were of the working class, poorly paid, living in villages or the *bled,* struggling to make ends meet, and becoming the first victims of terrorism, like his own family. Being a *petit blanc* was one reason that he could not accept the idea of expulsion from Algeria, because being so poor, his family, like other *petits blancs,* had never exploited or oppressed anybody, and they did not see themselves as colonialists.

Camus was also from the coast, and Algiers and Oran were distinctly French, with their grand boulevards, nineteenth-century imperial architecture, cafés, lycées, and pastry shops. He had visited only for the purpose of research the rugged, famine-stricken Muslim outback, where the revolution was incubated. He was accused of not portraying Muslims in his work, or of portraying them as caricatures (and also of using the old-fashioned and inexact term *Arabs*); and in fact he didn't know many Muslims before he became involved with a circle of nationalists and writers such as Mohammed Dib or Mouloud Mammieri, whom he helped to get published, and he spoke no Arabic. In the 1930s the two communities led separate lives and accepted their cohabitation, a sort of *fraternité souterraine,* with both ties and barriers. That he identified with the Arabs, believed in and fought for their equality, and honored their culture has never been in question. It was his humanism at work, his commitment to liberty and justice, and also his romantic feelings about his country. For Camus, Algeria was not only the sun, the sea, and the light, but also *les indigènes* and the rhythms, sounds, and colors of their daily life. This was true for his mother, too. One of the things Camus said that he was fighting for in its future was a true wedding of cultures, a showcase of harmony between East and West.

Camus has never seemed as vulnerable as he did in these war days, and in almost every way he was vulnerable: removed from his once iconic status among intellectuals; the "whipping boy" of the left; "living a contradiction," as Quilliot describes his inability to take either side in his community; torn between his Algerian self and his French self and in his way loyal to both. Friends say that Camus became quite Parisian during his twenty-year stay in the capital, but that he always retained a slight Algerian accent. I can hear it in his recordings of his work, an odd little inflection in a voice that always surprised me because it was so measured. However deeply Algerian, Camus never forgot that he was French by birth and an orphan of the French state, and he was unflinchingly grateful to the system and the teachers who had shaped him into a writer and thinker. He could love Algeria only as a Frenchman, he said, not a military man or a settler, but a Frenchman who loved Arabs, who would feel like a stranger in the land if it were not their home, too.[50]

13

Fans

I try to picture Camus now, the way he looks, Camus the person, not Camus the historical character. It is an antidote to the research, which is exacting and confining—a responsibility. Sometimes the research seems to take away Camus's mobility, his freedom to be funny or scrappy (sometimes suddenly covered with *épines* like a porcupine, as Roblès once described him), to think about swimming, to have lunch at Le Petit Pavé or couscous at one of the neighborhood establishments in the 8th or the 15th *arrondissement*. There are many things about Camus that don't necessarily connect to events, to other people, or to his books—to the scaffolding of his life. He liked stone, for example, and said that he could have been a sculptor. (Also, like many people who are intimate with illness, he said he could have been a doctor.) He liked Mozart, Edith Piaf, John Wayne, Marlon Brando, ping-pong, fishing, simple hotel rooms, pot-au-feu, oysters, *boudin noir,* Marcelle Mathieu's carrot-zucchini soup. In the months after winning the Nobel Prize, when he suffered from panic attacks, he did some yoga. He once took dancing (or maybe relaxation) lessons from Céline's third wife, Lucette, a dancer, who ran a rather chic movement salon. Two weeks were about as long as he ever managed to give up cigarettes. He never locked his car. He loved his cars and gave them names—Desdemona, Penelope. This is real material, to which it is easy to relate. It is evidence of how much there is to know about Camus, about how complicated he was, and also about how normal he was.

By now, I have a mental gallery of photographs of Camus, in addition to the 1944 Cartier-Bresson on the wall, the commemorative albums on the bookshelf, and a fat folder of clippings from magazines. His features are as familiar as those of close friends. The signs of aging are perceptible: a higher forehead, deepening frown lines, and heavier eyelids. In the photographs, I see moods, dress, experience. There is a young Camus playing the recorder on a rooftop in Algiers, Camus as a journalist at Pétain's trial, Camus in a flannel shirt on the lawn with his children, Camus in tails and white tie in Stockholm, Camus on his terrace overlooking a long stretch of rue Madame. (To annotate this last photo, which, rather inexplicably, appeared on the cover of a playbill for a production of *The Misunderstanding,* Camus had scrawled on its back: "Paris is beautiful from my terrace, but I prefer other terraces and the sun." Inside the playbill, also inexplicably, there is a close-up of Camus's long, elegant hands at rest on his desk.[1]) The photographs are invaluable though unpredictable windows on Camus, and they are also pieces of a giant, impossibly detailed jigsaw puzzle. They once brought Camus closer, but now that I know more about him they assert his distance. Mi said to me that the photos were difficult for her, because they were memories of Camus without what she called the *atmosphère* and the presence. For me, they are memories of someone I never met.

In one of the Canal Plus television specials that I have on tape, there is footage of Camus accepting the Nobel Prize. He is glamorous and very gracious in manner, but much more momentously, for twenty or thirty seconds he is there as he was in life. Nothing unusual happens during the brief sequence—he approaches the stage, bows his head, shakes the hand of King Gustav VI, and is handed a large medal—but as I watched him moving across the floor, lithe and lean, eyes lowered, smiling shyly, looking both humble and proud, I was so overcome with emotion that my eyes began to fill with tears. For a long time I thought it was simply the sight of the real-life Camus—the charm, the boyishness, the feeling of underlying gravitas—that affected me so strongly, and of course it was. But I also know too much about Camus and empathize too readily with him to see him simply anymore. Sometimes I feel almost like his wife or his sister as well as his reader, student, and Boswell, watching over him, worrying about his health or his spirits. Confronted with the clip, I couldn't help thinking about where he had been and where he was going, about his writer's block, his dislike of public honors, his sense of unworthiness, his fears about his future. It was a terrible time to be forty-three years old and in trouble with your new book and receiving an award that in many minds "crowned a finished work," as his critics immediately crowed. It was a poignant and painful time to be a French Algerian in the limelight, the first North African writer to be so highly honored. All this, I think, was what I read on Camus's face and what touched me. At the same time, I could see that he was pleased and quite happy—one of the Gallimards said that he looked like a schoolboy who wasn't sure that he deserved an award for excellence but was enjoying it nonetheless. That puckish look was what really got to me, because it was so young and transcendent.

Camus had thought about refusing the Nobel Prize, or accepting it in absentia and sending a speech. He considered Malraux the proper recipient, and the prize was, in any case, a disaster for him. (Flanner, in her column for the *New Yorker,* said that his statement about Malraux deserving the award was another example of his "insistent truthfulness.") Patricia Blake, with whom he was having lunch in Paris when he was notified of the distinction, reported that he appeared to be "suffocating." Rather than feeling ennobled, he felt defensive. He would have more enemies than ever, he commented knowingly to Jean Grenier a few days later.[2] To

others, he said that he felt mortified or castrated and full of dread. Nonetheless, Camus was elegant and gracious at the receptions, lunches, dinners, press conferences, and photo sessions that filled the week before the official ceremonies in December. He made a compelling young laureate and performed well in Stockholm, with a beautiful wife in attendance, too—he had invited Francine to accompany him because, as he said, she had suffered through the pain of his work and should be present at the honors. His acceptance speech, which delighted the king, was, as his friend Roger Martin du Gare, an earlier Nobel Prize winner, had advised, grave, confidential, very personal, and accessible to all, and it was also unusually modest.

In that speech, under the cover of modesty, but also speaking very personally and often transparently, Camus acknowledged his predicament, even using the word *panique*. Every man, and especially every artist, wants to be recognized, he said. Yet it wasn't possible for him to hear of the decision without comparing the implications with who he really was. "How could a man, relatively young, rich in his private doubts and with books still in the works, accustomed to living in the solitude of work or in the oases of friendship, not experience other than a sort of panic when learning of a decision that suddenly thrust him, and him alone, into the spotlight?" he asked, articulating what he called the disarray and disquiet inside him.[3] His only source of calm in these circumstances, he went on to say, was his own belief that the artist could not isolate himself from society and was obliged to understand rather than to judge. A writer engaged by "refusing to lie about what he knows." Personally, he could not live without his art, Camus said, but art was not a solitary celebration.

To himself, Camus found justification for accepting his award in its recognition of Algerian literature, and in that regard he thanked the Nobel committee for distinguishing first his country and then himself as a French Algerian. His initial thoughts were of his sources; of his childhood teacher Louis Germain, to whom he dedicated his speech when it was published as *Discours de Suède;* of his mother, to whom he immediately sent a telegram, "Maman, I have never missed you as much"; of his old and loyal friends.[4] But it was unavoidable that in selecting Camus the Swedish Academy was thinking about Algeria as a place in crisis, too, and of Camus as a liberal French Algerian who was seeking a peaceful solution, Alfred

Nobel having specifically sought to reward literary work that was "remarkable in an idealistic sense." It was equally unavoidable that the award would have political overtones, and that the Algerian war would be very much in the air at Stockholm.

If Camus enjoyed a few moments of celebration or an occasional rush of pride after winning the Nobel, there are only brief notations and faint intimations in the record. That he was widely and sincerely feted was to be expected, for he had many friends and deep allegiances. Faulkner's letter particularly pleased him, as did a tribute from Spanish Republicans and his warm receptions in Algiers the following spring. (Kindly, in his own letter of appreciation, Mouloud Ferraoun had warned Camus not to take to heart Muslims' silence about his award.) The expressions of support seemed to have little effect on the feelings of entrapment and despair that descended during the first months: "October 19. Frightened by what happens to me, what I have not asked for. And to make matters worse, attacks so low that they pain my heart. . . . Desire once again to leave this country. But for where?" Back in the city in late December, he records his physical and mental disarray in disconcerting detail: "3 p.m. Another panic attack. It was exactly four years ago, to the day, that X [Francine] became unbalanced. . . . For a few minutes a feeling of total madness. Then exhaustion and trembling. Sedatives. I write this an hour later." Three months later, he was breathing more easily; the big crises were over. "Only a dull and constant anxiety now."[5]

During the winter of 1957–1958, Camus seems as low and defenseless as he has ever been. This state is a sad irony at a time of perceived accomplishment and glory, and it will linger until late summer of 1959, when his new novel finally begins to take on a life. His disaffection shows up in bleak melancholy, flashes of irascibility, and an occasional hint of self-pity or bitterness, which is rare for him. According to close friends, in the worst of these times, he struggled with claustrophobia, feelings of suffocation, and thoughts of suicide. His doctors were worried about his diminishing lung capacity, so they had forbidden air travel. (Camus and Francine and an extended party—Janine and Michel Gallimard, his editor Claude Gallimard and Claude's wife Simone, as well as Alfred and Blanche Knopf—took the train to Sweden.) Roblès remembers an afternoon when Camus had to rush to a doctor for oxygen. As much as possible,

Camus kept to himself, to his intimates, and to the theater, where he did not feel isolated or canonized—"*statufié*," as he put it—and where he was full of creative energy. (It was reported that he wrote the first half of his Dostoyevsky adaptation in a day.)

Returning from Sweden, as yet unaware of the repercussions of his statement about his mother and justice, Camus had not anticipated a new round of polemics and ridicule. He immediately sent a long explanatory letter to *Le Monde,* but this note may have made things worse. Only a few months earlier he had pronounced himself *vacciné* and no longer susceptible to the abuse of his intellectual contemporaries, which he declared almost endemic to the species. He had survived the first barrage of criticism, which came almost as soon as the news of his designation was out —criticism disparaging the choice and belittling his works, some of it venomous enough to have been a warning. Rather than honoring a young writer, a prominent critic suggested, the Swedish Academy was "consecrating a precocious sclerosis." His former newspaper *Combat,* taking deadly aim, noted that small countries like Sweden always admired *parfaits petits penseurs polis,* "perfect little polished thinkers."[6] The new assaults were different, more directly damning and double-barreled, because their content was both personal and political. Camus's critics had found in the remark at Stockholm a perfect excuse to address all of his shortcomings, with particular attention to his silence and what was called his "hypocrisy" on the subject of Algeria. Jean Sénac's letter was one of the most scathing.

For Camus, the most devastating aspect of the new offensive may have been a distinct sense that his critics were enjoying the combat, thought that it served him right, and relished his pain. It was not only his unfortunate remark, his unrealistic politics, and his lofty moralism that made him such a satisfying target, but also his elevation to international renown. Even among loyal old friends like Poncet, there was an unspoken disappointment in Camus because despite his imposing new podium and new, eminent status, he didn't use the moment to break his silence and take sides in the war. Instead, he remained ever more determinedly behind the scenes, bringing his new authority to bear with political interventions and petitions, and in unpublicized talks with President Coty and then President de Gaulle about the future of Algeria. He had only disdain for the *ultras* and the military who had helped to return the general to power, and he worried about de Gaulle's commitment to democracy, but he still hoped that de Gaulle would somehow be able to save French Algeria. De Gaulle (whom the Muslims called *le très haut,* "the very tall one") fascinated Camus, as he did many other Frenchmen, with his stature, his almost sacred sense of destiny, and his devotion to France. In his journals, Camus quotes de Gaulle as saying during one of their conversations, "After all, no one has come up with anything better than France."[7]

The fact that Camus's name now carried more weight in the cause of justice and freedom was one of the few positive aspects of his deadly honor, which otherwise only added to his sense of entrapment. Buried in mail (he had to hire a second secretary), pursued on the street, solicited for money as well as for interviews and lectures, he was coming to resemble his portrait of Jonas. "It isn't pleasant to think that when I write now I'll have people looking over my shoulder," he said to friends.[8] The other aspect of the Nobel that served Camus well was the prize money, 18,776,593.80 *anciens* francs or approximately $42,000 dollars (the equivalent today would be about $1 million). Camus, quite characteristically, had never cared about money, disparaged its increasing importance in the world, remained resolutely frugal, and never seemed to submit to its influence. A life directed toward money was a death, he had declared in the early 1940s.[9] In this case, however, the sudden windfall allowed him at last to purchase a country house in the Luberon, in the picturesque ancient village of Lourmarin, not far from Char and the Polges, which provided, almost providentially, a sanctuary and a retreat from life in Paris. Camus also commemorated his award with donations to some causes important to him—such as new equipment for a local sanatorium—and bought gifts for all his colleagues at Gallimard.

As Camus's reputation was falling precipitously among intellectuals in Paris, who liked to say that the Nobel Prize had consecrated him as a "classical" writer, by which they meant passé, sales of his books were booming. New foreign publications and special editions appeared, his readership expanded, and fans cropped up around the world. After the Nobel, Knopf published *The Myth of Sisyphus* and a first theater collection as well as *Discours de*

Suède, his speech accepting the Nobel Prize for literature.[10] Other countries, too, ventured further into Camus's work, beyond the novels that had seemed easier to read. Camus was very popular in India, Germany, parts of South America, Japan, and Israel, and covertly in the Soviet Union. In America, there was also a flurry of interest in Hollywood, where there was talk of making movies of *Caligula* and *The Plague* (with Lillian Hellman and William Wyler developing productions of the latter) and plans for a production by Sidney Lumet of *Caligula* on Broadway (Camus was offered the lead). This stardom was time-consuming, however fickle it might be. (Wyler ultimately had to choose between *The Plague* or *Ben-Hur;* Hellman apparently got only as far as the translation. Lumet produced *Caligula* on Broadway in the 1960s.) At this time, with an introduction from Maria, Camus acquired a theatrical agent, Micheline Rozan, now perhaps best known for her long association with Peter Brook, She greatly improved the quality of Camus's life by taking over the negotiations for rights, options, and road tours, as well as his own numerous plans for productions, and helping him in his quest for a theater. (In late 1959, Brook offered Camus a role in his film *Moderato Cantabile;* the part went to Jean-Paul Belmondo after Camus's death. "A marvelous face and unexpected personality," Brook recalls about Camus from their meeting.)[11]

Like his adversaries, Camus's fans are part of his story. They are a measure not only of his success but also of his particular and unusual appeal. Susan Sontag attributed Camus's appeal to his "moral beauty," which is what the Nobel Prize recognized and what his Parisian critics (*"ennemis,"* as he was calling them by then) were tired of and quick to disparage. Camus's ethics, and his desire to be ethical—his "noble feelings in search of noble acts"—are in large part what continues to draw a wide and unpredictable diversity of readers, particularly in America, where he has more or less escaped criticism, certainly of his person, and where intellectual politics are not the force they are in France.[12] Shortly after Camus's death, describing the unusual outpouring of sorrow and the depth of feeling that he had encountered here, a French writer teaching in the United States remarked, "It would scarcely be a paradox to say that [Camus] is a great American writer even more than a French one, inasmuch as the public makes the writer."[13]

For a while I conducted my own informal survey of Camus's fans in America, taking note of medical students who read *The Plague* as a matter of course; judges who consider *Reflections on the Guillotine* an essential tract on capital punishment; writers who have been affected by Camus in unpredictable ways. William Styron, for instance, said that *The Stranger* influenced his book *The Confessions of Nat Turner* and that, at least semiconsciously, Nat Turner was his version of an existential hero; Czeslaw Milosz, has honored the fact that Camus was unafraid to be simple.[14] (Styron, who had been traveling to France with plans to meet Camus in January 1960, still talked about his sudden death with intense feeling.) I was impressed by the number of people who read Camus's notebooks without knowing much about Camus, and I became accustomed to the way lines of his prose surface in unexpected places, often unattached to any sense of context or meaning, like all-purpose aphorisms. ("Every leaf's a flower," a Source Perrier catalog announced over a setting of leaf-inspired dinnerware.) I was amused to find that Camus was such a malleable and useful hero, but it was unsettling too. I felt more than a little proprietary about him, and protective of my own personal experience. I couldn't help thinking about Catherine Camus, whom by then I had met. She had recalled that at the time of her father's death, when she was fourteen, she had known little about his fame; she knew only that he was her beloved father. She had never expected to share him with so many people, she said, and it had been shockingly painful.

In any roundup of fans, Roger Quilliot had an early preeminence. That was why I had been trying to meet him since my college years. For a month or so, it seemed tragic that I never did get to see him, despite agreeable and promising letters and an arrangement to meet in his office in Clermont-Ferrand on an early September morning. Quilliot's last words to me, as they appeared on the familiar *Sénat* stationery, were: "I hope to be *en mesure* to receive you then." In his choice of words—"up to receiving you"—I had not sniffed out any augury of his death, which was a suicide and occurred a few weeks before our scheduled interview. In his memoirs, published several years later and guided into print by his wife, Claire, who had also taken an overdose of sleeping pills that night but survived, Quilliot describes their preparations for death with happy equanimity. Quilliot had long been suffering from heart and lung failure; Claire had signs of Alzheimer's disease; they were a singularly devoted couple. As Claire said later, unknowingly alluding to me, "We enjoyed ourselves like crazy kids. We photocopied our farewell letters on the sly. We lied. When people asked Roger for a rendezvous in September, he said yes."[15]

My first reaction to the news, which I heard on the radio in a taxi,[16] was disbelief, followed by a sense of outrage and then loss. Not only had my list of questions for Quilliot grown long during my wait, but I had also come to think of him as a trump card, and I had been sincerely excited about our talk, which offered the rich prospect of an insider's retrospective view. But by then I had also been schooled in the unpredictability of interviews, in the way important sources sometimes have fuzzy memories or offer canned stories whereas incidental sources can sometimes provide insight with a mere image. I knew that even in the best of circumstances and health, Quilliot, despite his kind face and solid reputation, might have been cranky, impatient, distracted, or resistant, as Jean Daniel, immersed in editing a breaking story for *Le Nouvel Observateur,* was on the day I met with him. One of the recurring lessons in any form of research or reporting seems to be the inherent difficulty of gathering good information. Nonetheless, I was shocked by Quilliot's death, and I still am. It has made me all the more mindful of how few people are still around to remember Camus as he was in life, of how all the memories of Camus will soon be on the bookshelf. His old friend Édouard Charlot, who had run the bookstore Les Vraies Richesses in Algiers and first published *Nuptials,* had died recently. Young actors in the first big theatrical productions, such as Michael Bousquet and Sergio Reggiani in *The Just Assassins,* were now in their eighties. Quilliot was part of the last roundup.

Quilliot was also a story within a story within a story, and it reflected intimately on Camus. In fact, the whole tale was so perfectly ironic and absurd that I could imagine Camus jotting it down in his notebook. "A man devotes his life to a writer whose work is founded on the rejection of suicide, and then he plots a double suicide with his wife. He is joyous."[17] In a more painful way, Quilliot must have had similar thoughts, for in the letter that was dispatched posthumously to the local newspaper, he seemed to be writing to Camus as directly as to his former constituents and friends. Acknowledging that suicide was generally an act of despair and a "reprehensible" weakness, he explained his decision as an exception. "Will people understand if I say that our mutual choice of a voluntary death is an act of both liberty and the love of life in the fullest?" he asked.[18] In the obituaries, Quilliot was described as Camus's friend as well as his scholar, but in his own memoirs he was more modest. They were *lié,* "bound together," he said, and Camus had enriched his vision of life. It was Camus himself who convinced him that it was a duty to be happy, he said, not to give in to inevitability, whatever face it took.[19]

After Quilliot's death, I dug out my old copy of *La Mer et Les Prisons* as a sort of retrospective on both author and subject. Its pages were the color of café au lait and crumbling and its cover was held together with tape, but as in an encounter between old friends after a long separation, within a matter of minutes the book was the same beloved text of years earlier, but more settled. Quilliot's perspective on Camus still seemed instinctively knowing, and his portrait of the writer as a younger man remained remarkably just. His sympathy for Camus shone through like a beacon, and I could now connect it with his own struggles with illness and despair, the personal identification that is the making of a fan. Quilliot's assessment of Camus never changed, even after his five years of immersion in the life and works. My Camus has not changed significantly either, although he is more weathered, more explicit, and more complex. Quilliot admired Camus's continuity—his fidelity to himself, his poverty, his childhood, and his country—which was part of his staying power. Quilliot also remembered how taken he was when he first read Camus's work, like a *coup de foudre* or a bolt out of the blue.[20]

14

Le Premier Homme

I t strikes me often how bizarre it is to spend so much time thinking about someone you can never know. Days, months, and years of imagining, puzzling, projecting, hypothesizing, sympathizing—trying to follow his course, figure out what he was like, who he was. There are times when my family and friends seem like interlopers, when I am oblivious to the onward pull of my own life. I might be walking down Broadway talking on my cell phone when the hulking frame of Char comes to mind, or I suddenly find myself pondering a war that officially ended almost fifty years ago. Now, curiously, as Camus's death and the end of my research approach, I feel excitement and a sense of imminent reward, almost as if after all my work I not only would come to understand Camus but would get to meet him, too. It is the same delusion that I experienced as I prepared for certain interviews, or as I was traveling to Lourmarin. This is probably quite sad, but the feeling is triumphant and unshakable.

It is difficult to give full attention to Camus's activities in the years after he won the Nobel Prize, because of the insistent and overshadowing fact that he is going to die soon. The tragedy of his death colors everything—the new work in the theater, the joyous new relationship with Mi, the new country house, the new novel that was the first work in his new cycle about love and measure. Everything about Camus seems to be about recovery and renewal now, about his preparations for the future. Everything is thus coated with terrible, heavy irony. Reading about his life, I drag my feet, the way one does nearing the end of a good book, but a hundred times magnified. I think of something Jean Daniel said recently about the Nobel Prize—that however heavy a burden it was for Camus, it turned out to be fortunate that the honor came when it did.[1]

It took most of the two remaining years for Camus to recover his equilibrium and connect with his *amour de vivre* again. Not until the middle of August 1959 would he write, with palpable relief, about caring again, addressing particularly his relationship with Mi: "Absence, painful frustration. But my heart is alive, my heart is finally alive. So it was not true that indifference had overcome everything."[2] And only late the previous fall, when he was rehearsing *The Possessed,* had he begun to shake off the feelings of persecution and rejection that had closed in on him after Stockholm. The increasing talk of an independent Algeria, the shifting attitude toward the FLN, the stony silence that greeted the publication of *Actuelles III, Exile and the Kingdom,* and the new edition of *The Wrong Side and the Right Side*—all served to confirm the fear that he no longer had a voice, or a place, in either France or Algeria.

In the theater, at least, Camus felt like himself, relaxed, spontaneous, generous, comradely, *solidaire.* As the search for a theater of his own stumbled along uncertainly—he was calling it simply Le Nouveau Théâtre —he threw himself into the production of *The Possessed,* as he had done earlier in the year with *Requiem for a Nun.* Both plays were decisive steps into the future. Dostoyevsky was one of his heroes, whom he read and reread (and quoted in the notebooks) almost as frequently as he read Tolstoy and Nietzsche; and *The Possessed,* the most Dostoyevskian of Dostoyevsky's novels, had been in his mind for a long time. He had been "nourished and educated" by *The Possessed,* he explained in his program notes, and ever since writing his chapter on Kirolov for *The Myth of Sisyphus,* he had imagined its characters onstage.[3] Written in an age of terror, the work seemed prophetic, he said, with characters "who resemble us" and a contemporary hero.

Camus's adaptation, which called for twenty-three actors and seven sets and ran three and a half hours, opened in late January 1959. The audience consisted of *tout Paris,* including Malraux, de Gaulle's new minister of culture. The reviews were respectful but mixed, seemingly divided along the lines of cold war politics, and although the show ran for six months it lost money. (Some of the financing had come from Seven Arts in the United States, which had thoughts of a subsequent American production.) Camus expressed no disappointment, but he had invested an enormous amount of work—*"un travail gigantesque"*—in his adaptation and he cared about his cast, which included Catherine Sellers. At that moment, a big success would have been particularly reassuring.

In the spring, in part to give the flagging run of *The Possessed* a boost, Camus agreed to appear on the television program *Gros Plan* to talk about his reasons for working in the theater. These turned out to be not only a celebration of the profession but also a deeper meditation on his whole artistic life and credo. He was alone onstage, speaking directly to the camera, pausing at intervals for video clips from *The Possessed,* which gave his monologue the weight of a heart-to-heart talk. (Nervous about the medium of television and trying to avoid stage fright, he had memorized his long text, which added gravity to his talk, but also a certain stiffness.) With rare candor, he spoke of his discomfort among intellectuals, "who are rarely likable [and] don't succeed in liking each other"; the difficult lot of a writer who "works in solitude and is judged in solitude"; and his own need for the "powerful feeling of hope and solidarity" that comes with a production. He called the theater his convent and his paradise. He discussed his belief in *le spectacle totale,* a production conceived, written, and staged by the same man, and also the prospect of dual careers in theater and literature, "which nourish and sustain one another." In both cases, he seemed to be addressing the question of his future.[4]

In 1958–1959, there were other things about Camus that may be important to know: two more trips to Algeria, a variety of political interventions, a sailing trip to the Aegean with the Gallimards and Maria (so soon after the generals' coup in Algiers and de Gaulle's return to power that he was criticized for being out of the country, and he admitted that he had misgivings in this regard), the purchase of a house in Lourmarin, an intensifying relationship with Mi. Each had its significant details, its implications, its place in the journal, and its impact on his life. Yet with death looming, these biographical facts don't seem to call for the same investigation or scrutiny that they might have commanded earlier. They are what they are, or were. This doesn't mean that the pages of euphoric entries about Greece don't register (with thoughts of Camus's longtime desire to retrace Ulysses's voyage) or that Mi doesn't begin to emerge as a source of rejuvenation, or that Algeria does not become an almost terminally lost cause. But in the perceived race against time, which is all the more dramatic because Camus is oblivious of it, the eye keeps scanning the calendar and the mind keeps jumping ahead. The only thing that still seems to count, because the retrospective eye is fully engaged and knows something, is *The First Man,* which will carry Camus into the future and in a sense give him another life.

In the last pages of Camus's journal, the notes about writing, which are scattered and infrequent, are about his inability to write, his efforts to organize, his feeling of emptiness, the tender feelings he holds for Boris Pasternak after reading *Jivago,* which is also a "book of love," and waiting —waiting "*stupidement,*" as he says. To Chiaromonte, he had written earlier that he was helpless to continue his work and was waiting for "a sort of interior revolution." In August, he wrote to Char that he was waiting to accomplish even the slightest activity. In September, calmer, he seemed to be reminding himself to be patient: "Before writing a novel, I will put myself in a state of darkness for years. Test of daily concentration, intellectual asceticism and extreme lucidity."[5] By then, after some false starts relegated to the wastebasket, Camus had more or less launched his book. Even if still underground, it was more concrete than a bundle of notes, because he was talking about it as he had not done before, out of both *pudeur* and superstition. To Urbain Polge he announced that he was writing a book about his family. To others, he talked of a novel about his "education," a work of the scope of *War and Peace.* A month or so later, quite miraculously deep into the grinding and exhilarating process of writing a book, Camus even agreed to talk to university students about being a writer, and this seemed to mean that he was close to a full recovery.

Camus, a Romance

In November, when Camus writes to friends—Francine, Maria, Mi, Catherine Sellers, Jean Grenier—about his new working life in Lourmarin, he strikes all the familiar chords about writing: the solitude is cruel but necessary; his eye to self-discipline is vigilant; his ambition is strong. But there is also a clear sense of relief in the return to routine, and his joy in reconnecting to the creative life shows through even in his complaints, in this case to Mi, now the most intimate of his correspondents. "I have worked almost all day, but it's true that the solitude is hard. I love life, laughing and pleasures, and you, who are like that plus a little more," he writes, describing the distress of being chained up and cloistered, which is nonetheless the only way to come to terms with his terrible anarchy. "Having lounged about idly for a good half-hour yesterday, I insulted myself aloud for five minutes. Then I behaved well by going back to work with my tail between my legs."[6] I must be almost as relieved as Camus that he is back at work, because I am charmed by his self-depreciation, which is comic and antic, and I find myself smiling.

If Camus's self-doubts remain constant, perhaps greater than ever with the magnitude of his subject, the directness of his approach, and the pressure, they, too, are expressed with a bright new energy. "It isn't that I'm pleased with what I am doing. I lose heart sometimes before the enormity of what I've started. I tell myself that it's impossible, I am writing only foolish things, and I call for a tiny bit of genius that will allow me to work in joy instead of this endless illness, and finally I carry on," he writes in that same letter, self-mockingly. The process of writing itself engendered renewal, and writing about Algeria allowed him a point of view that was longer and more optimistic than current events could afford, bringing him a sort of peace, together with the sense of purpose. In these first pages of his many-layered, multigenerational story—"a fresco," he once called it—he was writing without worrying about his perceived voice, with moments of inspiration and hours of blind, dogged work. He described occasional flashes of excitement, sensing that he was on to something new, a new *épaisseur*, or depth, that for the first time in twenty years of searching and working he was touching on the "truth of art." Five years earlier, Camus had said that he felt he had not really begun his work. To Maisonseul, he stated forthrightly that he was beginning his work *véritablement* with *The First Man*.[7]

Because it was never finished—in fact it was barely begun—*The First Man* remains a promise and a puzzle. Camus had said that he envisioned a work of 900 pages and potentially two volumes, and left behind 144 handwritten pages. These begin with a series of chapters entitled "Looking for a Father" that introduce forty-year-old Jacques Cormery, who has returned home to Algiers during the violent days of the Algerian war to search for his heritage, and they end with a second part called "The Son or the First Man" that follows Cormery through his youth and early education. According to Camus's notes, the next part, "The First Man," would have covered adolescence—subdivided into illness, sports, and morale—and then the man: political action in Algeria and the Resistance. This would be followed by "The Mother," which would encompass lovers, friends, and the Arab question. In his work, Camus said, the real would be treated with imagination. No one can know exactly what that meant, because like the existing text the notes as preserved—which range provocatively over wars, politics, morality, farmers, terrorists, friends, affairs, children, Paris, and Provence and are indisputably fascinating—seem to be inseparable from the reality that has become so familiar as Camus's life. The text itself, because it was never edited or polished, has the eloquence that comes with honesty and spontaneous recollection, which can also be painful.

At its most dramatic, *The First Man,* which is not yet a novel, is a retrospective of heartrending clarity. It is Camus's last look at himself, and his last attempt to make his own quest for identity a part of his art, for whatever truth it might offer. "Forty years of a man's life and the times in which he lived" was the simple view. But "*at the same time* it should be the history of the ending of a world . . . with regret for those years of light running through it," he elaborated in the notes, bringing to mind both Algeria as his childhood and French Algeria as a place. It seems eerily appropriate now that *The First Man* as it stands ends with a chapter entitled "A Mystery to Himself," and that in the last sentence of his last work, Camus or Jacques Cormery contemplates his own death—"he, like a solitary and ever-shining blade of a sword, was destined to be shattered with a single blow and forever."[8]

There are many parallel stories running through *The First Man* and many versions of the First Man himself: Camus or Cormery, the son of a deceased soldier and an illiterate mother, who felt like "the first conqueror"; the French Algerian; one of the poor, "who in order to bear up well . . . must not remember too much."[9] The lost world of French Algeria is at the heart of all the stories—in the life of the child; in the family of *petits blancs;* in the streets of Belcourt, where Arabs pass by as part of the scene. It is interesting to see that Camus, after all the years of criticism, did not change the portrayal of the Arab presence that he had presented in the 1920s and 1930s—passing encounters in the street, "the hard and impenetrable faces around the kiosk"—although in notes and sketches he speaks intimately of individuals and records long conversations with the militant Ben Saddok. In his text, in the voice of a *colon* farmer, he says of the Arabs: "We were made to get along. They are just as stupid and brutal as we are, but we have the same human blood. We're going to kill each other some more, cut off each other's balls and torture each other a bit longer. And then we'll go back to living together as men. It's what the country wants."[10]

The First Man is the opening book of a forthcoming saga, but it is also complete as it stands, just as Camus's life and oeuvre, however abruptly interrupted, are, too. Given the long hesitation about releasing the manuscript, for fear that it would further damage Camus's already ragged reputation, it is at least ironic that he in fact succeeded, thirty-five years after the fact, at what would have been the age of eighty-one, in engineering a new beginning. Published when it was, *The First Man* is responsible for what most critics call the renaissance of Camus and what Catherine Camus prefers to see as a reevaluation. It has had particular resonance among writers and students in Algeria, which would have been very significant to Camus.

Camus's death remains "*une mort imbécile,*" as he called the fate of dying in a car crash, and the ultimate absurdity for the man who named the absurd. Camus had in his pocket a round-trip ticket to travel by train with his family, but he had been persuaded at the last moment to drive to Paris with the Gallimards, their daughter Anne, and their dog, taking a leisurely route north that included meals in two two-star restaurants and a night at an inn. The afternoon of the accident, the Facel-Vega, with Michel Gallimard at the wheel and Camus in the passenger seat, was moving along a straight, wide stretch of the N5 approaching the village of Petit-Villeblevin in Burgundy, when according to witnesses the car suddenly zigzagged off the road, bounced off one plane tree, and crumpled against another, breaking Camus's neck and killing him instantly and gravely wounding Michel, who died several days later. Excessive speed, which Camus was always said to dislike, mechanical failure, and a sudden swerve were considered possible causes for a still inexplicable accident. Camus lay in state in a nearby town hall and then at home in Lourmarin, watched over by Francine, his brother Lucien, Char, Jean Grenier, Roblès, and a few other close friends. Virtually the whole village gathered at the house on the morning of the funeral to join the long procession down through the winding streets to the tiny cemetery on the edge of town.

In the biographies and memoirs, Camus's final months are measured out in a heavy litany of "lasts"—his last days in Paris; his last interview; his last literary essay; his last public appearance; his last letters to Maria, Catherine, and Mi, which all anticipated a tender reunion in Paris. After that, Camus had assigned himself eight monastic months back in Provence to finish a draft of his novel before returning to the city to begin a first season of theater, perhaps on his own stage, and then, the following summer, going to Lourmarin for revisions and a second new book. It was a plan of *mesure*. Combing through their own last moments with Camus, a few friends picked up strange bits of premonition. In an interview early in November, Camus had spoken of hating highways and speed and waved his train tickets to Lourmarin in the air as the proof. He had sobbed despondently when taking leave of Maria later that week. Uncharacteristically, over Christmas he had spoken with Francine about his wish to be buried in Lourmarin. No national funeral, he had advised, but not a shabby one, either. Stories like this, as Lottman points out, are the beginning of mythmaking.[11]

In the last dream I had of Camus, he was full of ordinary life. I had joined him walking down a crowded city street, and as we ducked around people trying to keep abreast of each other, we laughed at ourselves. It seemed that we had decided to go to the movies and were headed that way, but had to figure out how to smuggle my large old dog, with whom Camus had immediately made friends, into the theater with us. This is not a significant dream, just a silly one, spontaneous, happy. But it later made me think of something intimately revealing that Camus wrote in *The First Man* about warmth and his own dog. In one of those long, sweeping, lyrical sentences so characteristic of the book (and this one gathered momentum for two pages, ending with his dog), he was addressing "this night inside him . . . like a second life, truer perhaps than the everyday surface of his outward life, [whose] history could be told as a series of obscure yearnings and powerful indescribable sensations." Slipping into Proustian memories of the scent of books, classrooms, a friend's sweater, his mother's laundry, an aunt's lipstick, he speaks, too, of his love of bodies, their beauty, "which made him laugh with bliss on the beaches"; their warmth and of his longing "to immerse himself in the greatest warmth this earth could give him, which was what without knowing it he had hoped for from his mother." "He did not get it," he said, "or dare to get it, but he found it with the dog Brillant when he stretched out alongside him, and breathed in his strong smell of fur . . . where the marvelous heat of life was still preserved for him who could not do without it."[12]

Dogs were one of the thin but nevertheless connective threads to Camus, and when I finally walked up the steps for my interview with Catherine Camus in her father's old country house in Lourmarin, I was greeted with the aggressive barking of two dogs. Throughout that first meeting, which took place in an informal salon—I on a sofa, Catherine in a chair across a table piled with books—the dogs, Ballou and Chupah, were present and in motion, usually in tandem with a cat. They were so present, in fact, that they dominate the tape I made of our conversation, sometimes obscuring crucial thoughts. "Papa, who was someone very fraternal, who respected others, was only afraid of—," my machine recorded, cutting suddenly to furious barking, scuffling, and then Catherine's attempts to restore order, "*Mais non, Ballou. Mais non. Arrête!*" A little later: "I am confidant that *The First Man*"—bark, bark, bark—"*Alors, tu va t'asseoir. Oh, c'est pénible,*" then sounds of settling. This struck me as tragic at first— I almost wept playing the tape back in my hotel room that night—then as ironic, even comical, and in the end typical.

That first afternoon my notes were not as consequential, anyway, as they would be during other visits, when the conversations were less introductory—less careful, more informed, bolder. The rendezvous was more about place than content, about Camus's personal geography and physical presence, and about my having succeeded in drawing this close. The old stone Provençal house, a onetime silk farm built into the bend of a steep, winding street just below the tranquil place de l'Église, one of the highest points in the village, had suited him and given him peace. It had a narrative to offer in his residence there, however brief that proved to be—in the study he fashioned in the attic, the roses and fruit trees he liked to tend out back, the small stable where he kept a donkey sent from Algeria by a friend. The broad terrace off the salon where we were sitting, which had a sweeping view of the Durance valley—beyond the cemetery and its cypresses, the château, and the vineyards to the silhouettes of mountains—is where Camus stood when he said that he felt as if he could almost touch Algeria. "Almost," Catherine said, because the landscape is not wild enough to be Algerian, and there is no sense of Africa breathing down your neck.

I was not offered a tour of the house as I thought I might have been, although I took a long look over the valley, which reminded me of Tuscany. The prospect had seemed promising, because Camus had taken particular pleasure in furnishing the house himself, from the Algerian lithographs and flea-market antiques down to the casseroles, but at the same time, it was hard to imagine him in these rooms because they were so clearly lived in at present. Catherine had also mentioned that the number of tourists who had knocked on her door the previous summer had been "*terrifiant,*" and this made my own curiosity about his domestic life seem aggressive, too. The success of *The First Man,* which she had painstakingly transcribed from the tiny script, edited, and almost single-handedly brought into print, with a thoughtful introduction, has brought her as well as Camus into the public eye, and at times this prominence has been difficult. But it has also been liberating for her, and has prompted what she described as something of a coming-of-age.

Speaking quite freely, Catherine, who is tall and blond, with big inquiring eyes like her mother's, had an air and a manner that were both sad and brave, *fragile et fort.* She had loved her glamorous, playful, serious father, who died when she was barely an adolescent, and her love showed through in the soft way she talked about him and the fierce way she honored his thought. There is a very tender picture of the two of them in one of the magazine pieces about Catherine I found, which, judging from her size, was taken two of three years before he died: looking happy and a little puckish, he holds her hand as she looks into the camera, sweetly, but also immensely proudly and possessively. Camus's death had been doubly devastating to her, because she had always been sheltered from his public life—"Char came by, Louis Guilloux came by, life was tranquil"—and didn't know of his celebrity until the worldwide mourning seemed to take him away, to deny his very existence as her father. "If he was famous, you have to accept that," she says now, "but at the same time celebrity was so much not him. You feel a chagrin that lasts a lifetime."[13]

As caretaker of Camus's work, Catherine has accepted not only her father's fame but also her own identity as a dutiful daughter, "*la fille d'Albert-Camus,*" or "the Catherine behind the Camus," which, she points out—taking a new perspective—is not exactly the same as "*la fille de mon père,*" "my father's daughter." She had long fled that role and was practicing law when she agreed to succeed her mother as literary executor, a task that had fallen to the family in the absence of a will. (Jean remained in the law, and she "ceded," she says with some obvious resentment toward a brother who has consistently complicated their affairs.)[14] In addressing her decision, Catherine spoke of "revolt" and "humility, the underbelly of truth," phrases that probably meant going against the trend. She is thoroughly steeped in her father's thought and language and can sound just like him in discussing his life, too. "It's that one feels solidarity in a situation of happiness, but this solidarity doesn't exist in unhappiness," she said in attempting to explain Camus, and this remark reminded me of thoughts in his first notebook. She was thirteen, Catherine remembered, when she decided to read *Caligula* to see what her father's work was like. She found it comical, and it made her laugh, she said, again amused, but he had a very different opinion.

During our visits, Catherine was necessarily both *la fille d'Albert-Camus* and *la fille de Camus,* her professional self and her personal self, explicating Camus's work at one moment, sorting through family memories the next. During her tenure as executor—more accurately, a watch—she has had an unpredictable impact on Camus's literary longevity, overseeing the release of his third notebook, volumes of journalism, various essays, *A Happy Death,* and other early work as well as *The First Man,* all of which has impelled forward a new multivolume edition of collected work from the prestigious Bibliothèque de la Pléiade. The first two volumes appeared in 2006, bringing new attention to Camus. The timing, so critical an issue, has been exquisite.

Seeing Catherine was, in a way, coming full circle. As gatekeeper to the Camus estate—all those entries cataloged on all those pages in the fat notebook that I had first seen at IMEC so many years ago—she was the beginning, the permission giver, and now, as she effectively reviewed Camus's work with me, the end. The fact that she was only a few years younger than I, and therefore of my generation, had the curious effect of making me part of Camus's second generation. I could identify with her and her desire to hold on to her father. This may have been presumptuous of me, but it brought Camus down to a very accessible and recognizable life-size. The same was true when I talked with Jean Camus and with Mi.

I went to see Jean, who is reclusive, is reputedly difficult, and rarely grants interviews, in part to actually *see* him, because he is said to resemble his father. Only on confronting this tall, lean, gray-haired figure did I realize—with an outsider's version of the overwhelming compassion Jacques Cormery feels in visiting his young father's grave at the beginning of *The First Man*—that Jean was then more than a decade older than his father had lived to be. He occupied the same apartment house on rue Madame in which he had grown up, and his mother's glossy ebony grand piano, which he plays very seriously, and the shelves of his father's books were part of the continuity. He, like Catherine, was an authentic connection to a very real, everyday Camus, and his memories had almost painful immediacy. Unlike Catherine, he did not have to take a professional perspective; nor did he have to be "vigilant," as she described herself, not to betray Camus's work and perceived wishes. His version of his father was more severe, more precise, more critical, and more convoluted, but no less loving. It seemed to be almost entirely subjective and unfiltered, and this made it at times electrifying.

Although I asked some questions, Jean also talked at will, for despite his reluctance to assume a public role as Camus's son he also seemed eager to have an audience. He sat in a chair across from me, and at one point in our conversation he moved next to me on the sofa, and the very proximity of this man who might or might not look like his famous father suddenly startled me. Discreetly, I tried to study his face, but this only made me more aware of the fact that I had never seen Camus in person. There was an unexpected ease and sense of comradeship between us, which came from my being unusually familiar with Camus's life—knowing all about the Polges, the house called La Palerme, Camus's women, and Francine's illness—so that I occasionally had to remind myself that I had never actually been there on the scene. My advantaged situation also meant that I was very sensitive to minutiae, innuendo, and the wider context of certain remarks. Jean had learned important lessons from his father's example, he said—uninterest in money, a preference for the spiritual over glory—but he also said that he had suffered from his father's "*dureté*," or harshness, toward him. Revisiting the terror of the Wednesday nights when he would present his *cahiers* and Camus would mercilessly criticize his schoolwork, or the moments when Camus's attention to his manners or the way he dressed was humiliating, he said that he could not yet pardon these. ("Crying will not change anything," Camus always said in response to his desperate sobs.)

Later, after Camus had died and Jean first began to investigate his work, he came to understand why the father, who became who he was through the grace of a schoolteacher, had been so tough about his son's education; and why the Mediterranean man, who honored the ways of Don Juan, had tried to correct his son's reticence and introversion. Camus had always judged himself mercilessly, too. Jean is very smart about Camus's work and recites passages by heart with obvious emotion. He sees his father very clearly in the last notebooks and in *The First Man*, although he finds this last work self-conscious and wonders whether Camus would have even retained the existing text in the end. Jean also likes to quote Grenier, whom he adored—"We're going to see *mon maître*," he remembers Camus saying as he piled the kids into the car—and who singled out *pudeur* as his student's most significant trait. "*Pudeur*, which no one can name and everyone feels, is the indispensable companion to the blossoming of our ideas," Jean recites from Grenier's memoir.[15] Jean, too, finds Camus's essence in his *pudeur*, although he knows that his sister speaks first of their father's sense of fraternity. "Perhaps she is right," he said quietly. "But each of us has a sense of our father, like the way we feel things, she with her temperament and I with mine."[16]

Jean and his memories haunted me long after the interview, because his feelings about his father were still so raw and intense, and the hurt of childhood was not yet quelled. Yet in explaining Camus's severity to me, Jean had also been coming to his defense. I continue to be surprised at the things that affect me, that imperceptibly and incrementally have changed my own version of Camus. They could be testimonies as important as the Pia letters, or a moment as small as the spontaneous ovation I drew from a group of villagers in Lourmarin when I went to meet Suzanne Ginoud, Camus's caretaker and friend. "*Oh, là, là, là,* Camus," the woman who ran the *boucherie* cried, throwing her hands into the air. "We lost him, he loved everyone, he spoke to everyone, *il portait la douceur sur le visage,*" "he had kindness in his face."

Perhaps because Mi occupied the end of Camus's life, or perhaps because we were contemporaries, and I could almost imagine myself in her place (about the time she met Camus at the Deux Magots, I was falling for him in his books), her thoughts about Camus remained with me as indelibly as Jean's. The impact of our meeting was enhanced by its setting —the apartment into which Camus had helped her to move in 1959, a warm, graceful, quite bohemian atelier with big greenhouse windows against which a spring rain was pounding. Mi bore a close resemblance to the portrait of the fair, beautiful nineteen-year-old included in the biographies. A small round pedestal table next to me had been Camus's donation to her furnishings. I was conscious of the sway of these perceived connections.

Mi had known Camus for only three years before he died, but her recollections and appraisals were farther-reaching, perhaps because, in the way of lovers and mourners, she had for many years been thinking over their time together. She spoke in fully developed thoughts, as if in the intervening decades she had had the time to give Camus coherent form, even in his mysteries. She was amazed at all he took on, his many lives, the many sides of his personality; she was cognizant, too, of his conflicts, his guilt, his sense of privacy. She understood that in the battered, depressed state of his last years, Camus needed the shelter of kindness, tranquillity, and gaity that she brought him; and she sensed, too, that the depth of his suffering was one of the elements that had allowed him to write more openly and more naturally at the end. In a letter sent from Lourmarin just before the accident, he said he was happy, she recalled: "but you know, it was combat every day" (laughing gently at his habit of writing in long-hand at a standing desk as if the habit was an integral part of the combat).

Thinking back, in a worried way, Mi questioned the very possibility of tranquillity in Camus's life. He had his comic side, she said, but he was a profoundly serious man. His fierce sense of responsibility and his utopian notion of fidelity meant that he would carry the world on his back all his life. He knew his value, but he also realized that he was not perfect. "It was a great paradox—this very moral man, who saw himself incompatible with his desires and his vision of life. These were his contradictions. The only way to sustain all these burdens was a sort of elegance, which he had."

Despite her clarity of thought, Mi often ended a sentence with a trailing, "Oh, I don't know . . ." and she, too, raised the intractable issue of subjectivity. "It is impossible to get all of him," she said, "and then each of us has a vision that is so personal, so intimate, so unique that it is effectively incommunicable." For her, as it is for anyone who tries to catch a glimpse of Camus in life, his presence is elusive; it comes and goes as unpredictably as dreams. "There is no single image of Camus for me now," Catherine had said. "It is all mixed up." Camus's presence was in his charm, which resided in countless small gestures, movements, and manners—his way of putting a glass on a table, of picking up a newspaper, of tilting his head, as Mi began to list them. These are not retrievable; they are bits of ephemera, "the things that can't be found in any book," she said. Earlier in my search, when I had asked Robert Gallimard what was missing in all the biographies and memoirs, he said that it was a sense of Camus the charmer. It was the way he walked, the way he danced, the way he liked to kick a pebble down the street.

I had always expected that I would end my sojourn with Camus logically, at the cemetery. I actually made two trips, one prior to my first meeting with Catherine, and another after the last interview, some years later. Nothing had changed much in the interlude, except that my knowledge of Camus had deepened, and the tall cedars rising up here and there along the rows of tombs seemed more majestic. I had immediately felt very comfortable in the small, simple graveyard, nestled into a hill, drenched in sunlight and "*l'odeur du soleil,*" and visible from Camus's terrace in town. It suited Camus, and this was true of even the more frivolous tombs nearby, with ceramic flowers and enameled portraits: they seemed like good company. His tomb, which now lies next to Francine's, is of great simplicity, an ancient stone deeply incised with his name and dates. It is surrounded with mounds of lavender and irises and, typically, stones, candles, or jars of flowers left by fans. I had only a small pinecone that I had picked up to offer the last time, but I marked it with an E and nestled it amid the lavender. I took a few photographs, too, and, because the sun was behind me, my shadow was imposed on the site—a very nice touch.

I didn't have any particular thoughts as I stood before the grave, but I was content just to be there in Camus's proximity. Eventually, I sat down in the gravel path next to him. In the spring, the sun is already hot in Provence, and I was having my first sunbath of the year, which brought Meursault to mind, and for Camus's sake I wished that the sea were closer, as it is in Tipasa. It occurred to me that it was absurd to be sitting there in the gravel, watching ants make their way around my feet and waiting for something like a visitation or an emanation, and then I remembered Camus's renunciation of the word *absurd* in conversation, which made me smile. Two women came by to leave flowers and take their own pictures, and I thought of Catherine saying that even her father's tomb didn't belong to her.

The happy *eh bien* quality of my communing that day signaled a sort of epiphany. I was calm, not because I knew everything there was to know about Camus, but because I knew once and for all that I would never come close. At the very least, there was his *pudeur,* which Catherine had once described as his "secret garden," and behind that, there would always be "*la part obscure de l'être,*" which he evokes in *The First Man:* the secret part of a being, so intimately connected to creation. I accepted that, as I accepted the fact that I could never really keep up with his busy life. More deeply than before, I had my Camus, and I had his work. The rest was only elaboration and illustration. As Catherine had said of her own years of combing through the estate, Camus was clear and consistent, so the surprises came only in seeing the ways in which he was consistent. She had just learned, for example, that after he won the Nobel Prize, he had sent a large sum of money to the wives and children of men killed in the Hungarian revolution. His work was like that, she said. His work resembled him.

As for my projected rendezvous with Camus, I realize now that it happened, and that I have been in his company for years. I laugh at his jokes, sometimes out loud, even if I already know the lines. I consult him about politics, about how to navigate the morally appalling times that describe my era, too. I admire again and again his honesty, which I have come to recognize as a show of confidence in who he was. Together with his sense of responsibility, it is the most important thing to know about Camus. That and his sense for fun. More and more, I like Camus. I think of him as a friend.

Epilogue

About six months too late, I realized that I wanted to see Camus's car. Catherine had once mentioned that it resided down the street in a garage belonging to his mechanic, a friend. Camus had loved his cars and loved to drive—he used to borrow his uncle's car to drive around with Simone on Sundays—and his big black Citroën seemed to go with his preferred image as a tough guy. I remembered pictures of Camus with his last car, a 1955 Citroën 11 Léger. Catherine had also produced his driver's license for my inspection, green, with fuzzy worn edges and now safely encased in plastic. Camus had named this car Penelope, presumably for the loyal and patient wife of Ulysses and mother of Sisyphus, two heroes of great significance to him. Judging from the way he identified with the Greeks, it seems likely that one day Camus would have written, too, about Ulysses and the voyage that seemed to evoke his own. But he left behind only fragmentary notes and a few journal entries. I never succeeded in seeing the car, because by the time I returned to the rue Albert Camus it had been moved to some inaccessible location out of town.

Acknowledgments

This volume has taken nine years to write, although it could also be said that it was launched years earlier when I was a college student with a special passion for Camus. It is the product of a decade of extensive research, but it is also a purely subjective endeavor to portray a man I sensed I already knew.

There is a legion of people who have helped me in the pursuit of Camus, to whom I can never express the full depth of my gratitude. My first debt is reserved for Catherine Camus, who granted me entry into her father's archives, housed originally at IMEC in Paris and now at the Camus center at the Bibliothèque Méjanes in Aix-en-Provence. At IMEC, Albert Dichy and Sandrine Sansom guided my earliest research; in Aix, Marcelle Mahasela offered me tireless assistance with expertise and kindness. I am also indebted to the librarians of the Beinecke Rare Book and Manuscript Library at Yale University and the Harry Ransom Humanities Center at the University of Texas at Austin for giving me access to Camus's letters to Nicola Chiaromonte and the Knopf papers, respectively.

The interviews I conducted with Catherine Camus, her brother Jean, and others close to Camus were of inestimable value in evoking his presence. To Catherine and Jean, Mi, Roger Grenier, Robert Gallimard, Jean Daniel, Miriam Chiaromonte, Nicole Chaperon, Jacques Polge, Henri Mathieu, Micheline Rozan, André Belamich, Suzanne Ginoud, William Phillips, Lionel Abel, William Styron and Maria Tucci, I express profound thanks. Many others helped me immeasurably with gifts of perspective and knowledge: Herbert Lottman and Olivier Todd, whose fine biographies were indispensable to my understanding of Camus; John Murray, who briefed me exhaustively on the history of TB; Jon Randal on Algeria and its war. Fernando Bo recalled working with Maria Casarès on the stage, Judith Jones described Blanche Knopf at work.

In many ways, this book took shape spontaneously, driven not only by my reading and research, but also by fortuitous encounters, incidental conversations and unforeseen contacts. I allowed this to happen, because it made me feel connected, and it produced a story instead of a study. In ways great and small, friends, family, other writers and Camus fans have contributed to the book and in so doing became an important part of the process: Sarah Catchpole and Ward Just, Walter Stovall, Fran Kiernan, Bruce Davidson, Robert Brustein, George Cooper, Jed Devine, Pat Thompson, Peter Adam, Michael Vinaver, Sylvie Bresson, Diane Johnson, Arthur Hall Smith. Geneviève Chevalier and Jane Kramer made invaluable introductions for me in Paris. Dorcy Erlandson and Mary Blume were uncommon friends and alert scouts there, providing leads and unearthing treasures. Peter Sacks created and presented me with an extraordinary book of paintings inspired and accompanied by the text of Camus's *First Man*. Jean Strouse first urged me to do Camus. Wendy Gimbel was always there, supportive with passion and thought. My readers, Robert Gottlieb, Nancy Nicholas, Wendy Gimbel, Sissela Bok, Jane Kramer, Honor Moore, Nicholas Weinstock and Davis Weinstock, who critiqued various drafts of my manuscript, deserve special thanks, for they offered me precious guidance, encouragement and strength.

I am also very grateful for the work of my research assistant Jessica Leigh Tanner, my technical savior Stephen Mack, and at Grove/Atlantic, the wonderful resources of Alex Littlefield, Sue Cole, Michael Hornburg, and Charles Rue Woods. The enthusiasm and dedication of my agent Flip Brophy and my editor Joan Bingham have sustained me in the uncertain days of writing a book. The love, patience and support of my sons Nicky, Jake and Luke, my daughters-in-law Amanda and Leanne, and, in truly heroic fashion, of my husband, adviser and best friend, Davis, have been the most important thing of all.

Permissions

Grateful acknowledgment is made to Alfred A. Knopf for permission to reprint excerpts from *Albert Camus: A Life,* by Olivier Todd, translated by Benjamin Ivry, copyright © 1997 by Alfred A. Knopf, Inc.; and from the following works by Albert Camus: *The Fall,* translated by Justin O'Brien, translation copyright © 1956 by Alfred A. Knopf, Inc.; *The First Man,* translated by David Hapgood, translation copyright © 1995 by Alfred A. Knopf, a division of Random House, Inc.; *Lyrical and Critical Essays,* translated by Ellen Conroy Kennedy, translation copyright © 1967 by Hamish Hamilton Ltd and Alfred A. Knopf, a division of Random House, Inc.

I also acknowledge with gratitude permission from Herbert Lottman to quote from his book *Albert Camus: A Biography;* from Annie Cohen-Solal to quote from her book *Sartre: A Life;* from Ivan R. Dee to quote from *Notebooks 1951–1959* by Albert Camus, translated from the French by Ryan Bloom, copyright © 1989 by Editions Gallimard, Paris, English translation copyright © 2008 Ivan R. Dee, Inc.; from Humanity Press to quote from *Sartre and Camus: A Historic Confrontation,* translated and edited by David A. Sprintzen and Adrian van den Hoven copyright © 2004; from the University of Nebraska Press to quote from *Correspondence, 1932–1960* by Albert Camus and Jean Grenier, translated by Jan Rigaud, copyright © Editions Gallimard, 1981, translation copyright © 2003 by the University of Nebraska Press; from Princeton University Press to quote from *Camus at Combat: Writing 1944–1947,* copyright © 2006 Princeton University Press.

Catherine Camus and the Fonds Camus have graciously given me permission to quote from Camus's letters to Nicola Chiaromonte and Blanche Knopf. Florence Giry at Gallimard has always been generous and considerate in her response to my book.

Photograph Credits

Camus at his uncle's workplace (p. 19); Camus with Francine at Canastel, near Oran, in 1942 (p. 45); Camus on the ship for New York, March 1946 (p. 99); Camus watching a theatrical rehearsal (p. 181); Camus with friends at Tipasa (p. 213); Camus in 1957 (p. 271): © Collection Catherine and Jean Camus, Fonds Camus, Bibliothèque Méjanes, Aix-en Provence. Droits Réservés.

Camus with Pascal Pia (p. 91); Camus with cigarette in 1946 (p. 125); Camus with cast of *State of Siege* (p. 136); Camus and Michel Gallimard in the country (p. 149); Maria Casarès (p. 221): Roger-Viollet/The Image Works.

A young Camus (p. 15); Catherine Sintès, mother of Camus (p. 129): Lucien Camus Collection.

Camus's *Alger-Républicain* press card (p. 25): Agnely Collection.

Le Panelier (p. 60); © Jean-Jacques Arcis.

Rehearsal of *Désir Attrapé par la Queue*, chez Picasso, 1943 (p. 69): © Estate Brassaï-RMN.

Camus at *Combat* (p. 73): Rue des Archives/The Granger Collection.

Jean-Paul Sartre in 1947 (p. 163): The New York Times Co./ Hulton Archive/Getty Images.

Camus with René Char (p. 199): © collection Petit/DR/Opale.

The Casbah, Algiers (p. 235): © Photothèque Hachette.

De Gaulle in Algiers, June 1958 (p. 250): © Erich Lessing/Magnum.

Camus at the Nobel Prize ceremony, 1957 (p. 261): © Reportagebild, Stockholm.

All efforts have been made by the author to identify copyrights and secure permission to reproduce these photographs.

Notes

Prologue

1. Evan Thomas, *Robert Kennedy: His Life* (New York: Simon and Schuster, 2000), 368.

2. Albert Camus, *The Stranger,* trans. Matthew Ward (New York: Alfred A. Knopf, 1988), 122–3.

3. Albert Camus, *The Myth of Sisyphus and Other Essays,* trans. Justin O'Brien (New York: Vintage International, 1991), 123.

4. Albert Camus, *Lyrical and Critical Essays,* trans. Ellen Conroy Kennedy, (New York: Alfred A.Knopf, 1968), 169.

1   Young in Algeria

1. The term *Zouave* was derived from the name of a Berber tribe from which the French first recruited soldiers early in the settlement of Algeria.

2. Albert Camus, *The First Man,* trans. David Hapgood (New York: Alfred A. Knopf, 1995), 51.

3. *Ibid.,* 39.

4. *Ibid.,* 41.

5. *Ibid.,* 289.

6. *Ibid.,* 310.

7. First published in the April 15, 1953, Bulletin of the R.U.A. (*Racing universitaire d'Alger*), then in "Oui, j'ai joué plusieurs années au RUA," *France-Football,* no. 613 (December 17, 1957). Quoted in Herbert Lottman, *Albert Camus* (New York: Doubleday, 1977).

8. *First Man,* 277.

9. *Ibid.,* 223.

10. *Ibid.*

11. *Ibid.,* 275.

12. Albert Camus,"Hôpital du quartier pauvre," in *Essais*, ed. Roger Quilliot (Paris: Bibliothèque de la Pléiade, Gallimard, 1965), 1216. Also in *Oeuvres completes I: 1931–1944,* ed. Jacqueline Lévi-Valensi (Paris: Bibliothèque de la Pléiade, Gallimard, 2006), 77.

13. See *Le Premier Camus suivi de Écrits de Jeunesse d'Albert Camus* (Cahiers Albert Camus 2), par Paul Viallaneix (Paris: Gallimard, 1973).

14. Camus, Pléiade *Essais*, 1171.

15. Camus, "Sur *Les Iles* de Jean Grenier," Pléiade *Essais*, 1160. Also in "On Jean Grenier's *Les Iles*," *Lyrical and Critical Essays*, 330.

16. From a radio broadcast cited in Albert Camus–Jean Grenier, *Correspondence 1932–1960*, trans. Jan F. Rigaud, annotations Marguerite Dobrenn (Lincoln: University of Nebraska Press, 2003), 260.

17. Camus, "Sur *Les Iles*," 1160. *Lyrical and Critical Essays*, 330.

18. Camus, *The First Man*, 176.

2 Moving On

1. Albert Camus, *Notebooks*, 1935–1942, trans. Philip Thody (New York: Paragon, 1991), 3.

2. *Ibid.*, 6.

3. *Ibid.*,12–13.

4. *Ibid.*, 4.

5. *Ibid.*,10.

6. *Ibid.*, 7.

7. *Ibid.*,15.

8. *Ibid.*, 44.

9. *Ibid.*, 9.

10. *Ibid.*, 10.

11. *Ibid.*, 32.

12. José Lenzini, *L'Algérie de Camus* (Aix-en-Provence: Édisud, 1987), 70.

13. Camus, *Notebooks 1*, 3.

14. Camus, *Le Premier Camus*, 201.

15. *Ibid.*, 258.

16. Camus, *Notebooks 1*, 28.

17. *Ibid.*, 60.

18. *Ibid.*, 31.

19. Camus, "The Wrong Side and the Right Side," *Lyrical and Critical Essays,* 56.

20. *Ibid.*, 58–59.

21. Camus, *Notebooks 1*, 59.

22. Lottman, *Albert Camus*, 130.

23. *Ibid.*, 131.

24. Jean Grenier, *Albert Camus, Souvenirs* (Paris: Gallimard, 1968), 41.

25. Camus–J. Grenier, *Correspondence*, 10–11.

26. Jean Grenier, *Souvenirs*, 46.

27. "Every time, it has always been the great misfortune of wanting to show off which has lessened me in the presence of truth," Camus writes in his long summing up. *Notebooks 1*, 58.

28. Camus, *Notebooks 1*, 44.

29. Lenzini, *L'Algérie de Camus*, 70.

30. Albert Camus, *A Happy Death*, trans. Richard Howard (New York: Alfred A. Knopf, 1972), 89.

31. Olivier Todd, *Albert Camus, A Life*, trans. Benjamin Ivry (New York: Alfred A. Knopf, 1995), 222. Henceforth cited as Todd, *A Life*.

32. *Ibid.*, 70.

33. *Ibid.*, 96.

34. Albert Camus, *Notebooks II 1942–1951*, trans. Justin O'Brien (New York: Alfred A. Knopf, 1965), 142.

35. Olivier Todd, *Albert Camus, Une Vie* (Paris: Gallimard, 1996), 201. Henceforth cited as Todd, *Une Vie*. *Une Vie* was my source for material that was omitted in the English translation of Todd's book, published a year later.

36. Camus, *Notebooks 1*, 105.

37. *Ibid.*, 113.

38. Albert Camus, "Misère de la Kabylie," *Actuelles III: chroniques algériennes. 1936–1958* (Paris: Gallimard, 1958), 50–51. Also in Pléiade *Essais*, 915.

39. *Ibid.*, and Pléiade *Essais*, 938.

40. Camus, *Notebooks 1*, 48.

41. *Ibid.*, 79.

42. Camus, Pléiade *Essais*, 1370.

43. Camus, *Notebooks 1*, 137–38.

44. *Ibid.*, 148–49.

45. Todd, *A Life*, 91–92.

46. Todd, *Une Vie*, 218.

47. Todd, *A Life*, 93.

48. Camus, *Notebooks 1*, 121.

49. *Ibid.*, 72.

50. *Ibid.*, 23.

51. *Ibid.*, 33.

52. Several sources, including a retrospective remark from Camus in the 1950s, suggest that Camus had to leave the country but do not mention any specific move by the government to oust him.

53. Camus, *The Stranger*, 42.

54. *Ibid.*, 85.

55. Jean-Paul Sartre, "Explication of *The Stranger*" in *Camus: A Collection of Critical Essays,* ed. Germaine Brée (Englewood Cliffs, N.J.: Prentice-Hall, 1962), 108.

3   To France

1. Lottman, *Albert Camus*, 539.

2. Janet Flanner, *Paris Journal 1944–1965* (New York: Atheneum, 1971), 456–57.

3. Jules Roy, *Adieu Ma Mère, Adieu Mon Coeur* (Paris: Albin Michel, 1996).

4. Todd, *Une Vie*, 306.

5. Camus, *Notebooks 2*, 54.

6. Todd, *A Life*, 153.

7. Camus, *Notebooks 2*, 41.

8. Camus's chapter on Kafka was reinstated in *The Myth of Sisyphus* in 1947.

9. Todd, *A Life*, 153.

10. Camus, *Notebooks 2*, 61.

11. Albert Camus, *The Plague,* trans. Stuart Gilbert (New York: Alfred A. Knopf, 1948), 231.

12. *Ibid.*, 112.

13. *Ibid.*,113.

14. Camus, *Notebooks 2*, 24.

15. *Ibid.*, 24.

4   Paris 1943

1. Simone de Beauvoir, *The Prime of Life,* trans. Peter Green (New York: World Publishing, 1962), 444.

2. The precise date that Camus became a full participant in the Resistance is not certain. Nor is the exact nature of his informal Resistance work while he was in Chambon, though biographers have described his sheltering Jews and resistants and carrying information.

3. Camus, "Hommage to André Gide," Pléiade *Essais,* 1118.

4. Lottman, *Albert Camus,* 292.

5. Albert Camus, *Camus at Combat: Writing 1944–1947,* trans. Arthur Goldhammer, ed. Jacqueline Lévi-Valensi (Princeton, N.J.: Princeton University Press, 2006), 13.

6. *Ibid.,* 15.

7. *Ibid.,* 17.

8. Camus, *Between Hell and Reason, Essays fom the Resistance Newspaper Combat,* trans. Alexandre de Gramont (Hanover, N.H.: Wesleyan University Press, University Press of New England, 1991), 48.

9. There has always been controversy over which editorials in *Combat* were written by Camus. Some critics accept only the signed ones, others judge according to the language of the pieces or Camus's own references to them. See biographies and *Between Hell and Reason.*

10. Camus, *Notebooks 2,* 147.

11. *Ibid.,* 118.

12. *Camus at Combat,* 119.

13. *Ibid.,* 249–50.

14. *Hell and Reason,* 120, 138.

15. *Ibid.*

16. *Ibid.,* 89.

17. Todd, *Une Vie,* 375.

18. *Camus at Combat,* 83.

19. *Notebooks 2,* 104.

20. *Ibid.,* 106.

21. Beauvoir, *Prime of Life,* 419.

22. *Ibid.,* 445.

23. Herbert Lottman, *The Left Bank: Writers, Artists and Politics from the Popular Front to the Cold War* (Boston: Houghton Mifflin, 1982), 235.

24. Annie Cohen-Solal, *Sartre* (New York: Pantheon, 1987), 252.

25. Simone de Beauvoir, *The Force of Circumstance,* trans. Richard Howard (New York: Putnam, 1965), 39.

26. Cohen-Solal, *Sartre,* 253.

27. Lottman, *Albert Camus,* 371.

28. Camus, *Notebooks 2,* 113.

29. Lottman, *Albert Camus,* 372.

30. Camus also talked about politics with Manès Sperber, a Jewish refugee from Hitler's Germany and a longtime friend of Malraux's. Sperber had been an emissary to the Comintern before denouncing Stalin.

31. Camus, *Notebooks 2*, 121.

32. *Ibid.*, 118.

33. From an interview in the magazine *Caliban* in August 1951, quoted in Pléiade *Essais*, 1166.

34. *Between Hell and Reason*, 143.

35. Roger Grenier, *Pascal Pia ou le droit au néant* (Paris: Gallimard, 1989), 130.

36. Albert Camus–Pascal Pia, *Correspondance, 1939–1947*, ed. Yves Marc Ajchenbaum (Paris: Fayard/Gallimard, 2000), 145.

37. *À Albert Camus, ses amis du Livre* (Paris: Gallimard, 1962), 21–22.

38. Camus-Pia, *Correspondance*, 151.

39. Roger Grenier, personal interview, October 1998.

40. Camus-Pia, *Correspondance*, 152.

41. *Ibid.*, 153–54.

42. *Ibid.*, 145.

43. Quoted in Pléiade *Essais*, 1461.

44. *Between Hell and Reason*, 110.

45. Camus-Pia, *Correspondance*, 144.

46. Camus, *Camus at Combat*, 199–200.

47. There were probably eight articles in all, according to Quilliot and Lottman, but there are questions about the authorship of two of them, which appeared May 23, signed AC, and May 25, unsigned. See Pléiade *Essais*, 1854.

48. Camus, "Crise en Algérie," Pléiade *Essais*, 959.

49. *Ibid.*

50. Beauvoir, *Force of Circumstance*, 107–108.

51. *Ibid.*, 53.

52. *Ibid.*, 110.

5 New York 1946

1. Camus–J. Grenier, *Correspondence*, 116.

2. Lottman, *Albert Camus*, 376.

3. Camus, *American Journals*, trans. Hugh Levick (New York: Paragon, 1987), 32.

4. Hannah Arendt, "French Existentialism," *The Nation*, February 23, 1946, 226–27.

5. Justin O'Brien in *New York Herald Tribune Weekly Book Review*, March 24, 1946.

6. William Phillips, *A Partisan View: Five Decades of the Literary Life* (New York: Stein & Day, 1983), 124.

7. Camus, *American Journals,* 33. The other writer was a Frenchman named Léon Motchane, as yet unknown in America, who had written as Thimerais in the clandestine Éditions de Minuit during the war.

8. This other ms., "*Sommes-Nous des Pessimistes?,*" also bears a penciled note, presumably from Camus's widow as executrix, saying that "perhaps" it was delivered to a gathering of Associated Press reporters.

9. New Yorkers were "a people to whom nothing is impossible," a publicity booklet of the day boasted. See Jan Morris, *Manhattan 1945* (New York: Oxford University Press, 1998), 45.

10. From a manuscript at the Institut Mémoires de L'Édition Contemporaine.

11. *Camus at Combat,* 275–76.

12. Camus, *American Journals,* 42.

13. The apartment had been lent to Camus by a furrier named Zaharo who had heard him speak and called several times to insist that Camus use his place during the months he was away on business.

14. Camus, *American Journals,* 46.

15. *Ibid.,* 54.

16. *Ibid.,* 32.

17. Blake later published a piece on the American "death industry" in *Life* magazine.

18. Some of Camus's experiences in South America were used in the short story "La Pierre Qui Pousse" ("The Growing Stone"), collected in *Exile and the Kingdom.*

19. It appeared in fall 1947 in the magazine *Formes et Couleurs.*

20. Camus, *Lyrical and Critical Essays,* 184.

21. Camus, *American Journals,* 41.

22. Camus, *Lyrical and Critical Essays,* 186.

23. Phillips, *Partisan View,* 131.

24. William Phillips, personal interview, February 5, 1998, in New York City.

25. Todd, *A Life,* 224.

26. Raymond Sokolov, Liebling's biographer, described the review as a eulogy. Sokolov, *Wayward Reporter: The Life of A. J. Liebling* (New York: Harper & Row, 1980).

27. A. J. Liebling, "Absurdiste," *The New Yorker,* April 20, 1946, 22.

28. Sokolov, *Wayward Reporter,* 318.

29. A. J. Liebling, *The Road Back to Paris* (New York: Doubleday, 1944), 217.

30. Liebling, "The Orange Trees" in *The Most of A. J. Liebling* (New York: Simon and Schuster, 1963).

31. Liebling, "Talk of the Town," *The New Yorker,* January 16, 1960, 23–24.

32. Blanche Knopf, "Albert Camus in the Sun," *Atlantic Monthly* (Boston) February 1961, 77.

33. Camus's letter of March 25, 1955, was written by hand.

34. Albert Camus, letter to Blanche Knopf, December 1, 1959. Knopf papers, Harry Ransom Humanities Research Center, University of Texas at Austin.

35. Blanche Knopf, letter to Albert Camus, December 11, 1959, Knopf papers, Ransom Center.

36. *The Library Chronicle* 26 (1, 2) (University of Texas at Austin: Harry Ransom Humanities Research Center, 1995), 81.

37. Camus, letter to Blanche Knopf, October 13, 1949, Ransom Center.

38. Nicola Chiaromonte, *The New Republic,* April 29, 1946.

39. William Styron, *Darkness Visible: A Memoir of Madness* (New York: Vintage/Random House, 1990), 20.

6 Back to Europe

1. Carol Brightman, *Writing Dangerously: Mary McCarthy and Her World* (New York: Harcourt Brace, 1992), 272.

2. Nicola Chiaromonte, "Camus in Memoriam" in Brée, *Camus,* 12.

3. Camus, letter to Nicola Chiaromonte, November 7, 1945, Beinecke Rare Book and Manuscript Library, Yale University, New Haven, CT.

4. Camus, letter to Chiaromonte, September 20, 1946, Beinecke.

5. Camus, letter to Chiaromonte, July 14, 1946, Beinecke.

6. Janet Flanner, *Paris Journal, 1944–1965,* 69.

7. Camus, letter to Chiaromonte, September 20, 1946, Beinecke.

8. Camus-Grenier, *Correspondance,* 93.

9. Nicola Chiaromonte, letter to Andrea Caffi, April 26,1946, trans. Nicholas Weinstock, collection of Miriam Chiaromonte.

10. Camus-Grenier, *Correspondence,* 93.

11. Camus addressed himself directly to European socialists on the need to choose between communist doctrine and a rejection of Marxism as an absolute philosophy.

12. Camus, *Between Hell and Reason,* 128.

13. The editor was the flamboyant Baron Emmanuel d'Astier de la Vigerie, an intimate of both de Gaulle and Stalin.

14. Camus, second letter to Emmanuel d'Astier de la Vigerie, *La Gauche,* October 1948, Pléiade *Essais,* 368.

15. Camus, *The Rebel: An Essay on Man in Revolt*. trans. Anthony Bower (New York: Knopf, 1954), 253.

16. This is the conclusion of Tony Judt, one of Camus's most distinguished and understanding contemporary critics. See *The Burden of Responsibility: Blum Camus and the French Twentieth Century*. (Chicago: University of Chicago Press, 1998), 104.

17. The GLI was the European counterpart of the Europe-America group created by Mary McCarthy and Alfred Kazin in New York a year earlier.

18. Camus, *Notebooks 1942–1951,* 215.

19. *Ibid.,* 216.

20. *Ibid.,* 256.

21. *Ibid.,* 211.

22. Camus-Grenier, *Correspondence,* 151–52.

23. Todd, *Une Vie,* 458.

24. In a typical gesture of admiration and respect, Camus wrote a preface for each memoir.

25. Camus, "Pourquoi l'Espagne (Réponse à Gabriel Marcel)," Pléiade *Essais,* 395–96.

26. Camus, *Notebooks 2,* 182. "Petit fait," he writes, "on croit souvent m'avoir rencontré."

27. The dates come from the bibliography in the Pléiade.

28. Lottman, *Albert Camus,* 427.

29. Camus, *Notebooks 2,* 158.

30. *Ibid.,* 200–201.

31. Lottman, *Albert Camus,* 463.

32. *Ibid.,* 454.

33. *Ibid.,* 433.

34. Camus-Grenier, *Correspondence,* 140, 150.

35. *Ibid.,* 28–29.

36. Camus, *Lyrical and Critical Essays,* 156–58.

37. *Ibid.,* 155.

38. There is also a reference to a smaller work that was a first take on the subject, a mimodrame or play in pantomime called *The Life of the Artist,* about a writer who sacrifices everything, including his family, to his art.

39. Todd, *A Life,* 269.

40. Camus, *Lyrical and Critical Essays,* 16.

41. Camus-Grenier, *Correspondence,* 112.

42. Camus, *Notebooks 2,* 201.

43. *Ibid.*, 246.
44. *Ibid.*, 247–48.
45. *Ibid.*, 217–31.
46. Camus-Grenier, *Correspondence,* 141.
47. Camus, *Notebooks 2,* 230.
48. Beauvoir, *Force of Circumstance,* 196.
49. Camus-Grenier, *Correspondence,* 141.
50. Todd, *Une Vie,* 507.
51. Camus, *Notebooks 2,* 253.
52. Todd, *Une Vie,* 534.
53. Camus, *Notebooks 2,* 238.
54. Camus, "Jonas or the Artist at Work," *Exile and the Kingdom,* 110.
55. Camus, *Lyrical and Critical Essays,* 172.
56. Camus, *Notebooks 2,* 249.
57. *Ibid.*, 270.

7   TB

1. Todd, *A Life,* 260.
2. Mamaine and Koestler married in 1950.
3. Camus, *Notebooks 1,* 71.
4. Camus, *Lyrical and Critical Essays,* 78.
5. Camus, "Fragment Manuscrit pour 'Entre Oui et Non,'" Pléiade *Essais,* 1214.
6. Camus, *Lyrical and Critical Essays,* 5.
7. "Lettre à Jean de Maisonseul," Pléiade *Essais,* 1219
8. *Ibid.*, 1219.
9. Camus, *Lyrical and Critical Essays,* 150.
10. *Ibid.*, 78.
11. Roger Quilliot, *Mémoires II* (Paris: Editions Odile Jacob, 2001), 284.
12. Camus, *Lyrical and Critical Essays,* 77.
13. "Entre Plotin et Saint Augustin," Pléiade *Essais,* 1222.
14. Susan Sontag, *Illness as Metaphor and Aids and its Metaphors* (New York: St. Martin's Press, 2001), 181.
15. *Le Premier Camus,* 242.
16. Pléiade *Essais,* 1668–669.
17. Todd, *A Life,* 153.

18. *Ibid.*

19. Grenier, *Souvenirs,* 9, 14.

20. Todd, *A Life,* 263.

21. This was what Sontag was addressing in her book. See 101.

22. Todd, *A Life,* 264.

23. Todd, *Une Vie,* 502.

24. Camus, *Notebooks 2,* 227.

25. *Ibid.,* 218.

26. *Ibid.,* 246.

27. Camus, *Notebooks 1951–1959,* trans. Ryan Bloom (Chicago: Ivan R. Dee, 2008), 198–99.

28. Pléiade *Essais,* 1895.

29. Quilliot, *Mémoires II,* 268.

30. Todd, *A Life,* 295.

31. Mi, personal interview in Paris, April 4, 2000.

32. Camus, *Notebooks 2,* 267.

33. *Ibid.,* 37. "My youth is fleeing me; that's what it is to be ill."

8   *L'Homme Révolté*

1. Quilliot, *Mémoires II,* 124.

2. Camus, *Notebooks 3,* 22.

3. René Char, letter to Camus, July 16, 1951, in Albert Camus, René Char, *Correspondance 1946–1959,* ed. Franck Planeille (Paris: Gallimard, 2007).

4. Camus had rather bluntly titled his chapter, which appeared first in *Les Cahiers du Sud,* "Lautréamont or Banality," accusing the acclaimed "bard of pure rebellion" of succumbing to "the most absolute conformity"—comformity being "one of the nihilistic temptations of rebellion."

5. Quoted in Lottman, *Albert Camus,* 495.

6. Todd, *Une Vie,* 550.

7. Robert Gallimard, personal interview, May 2006.

8. Camus, *The Rebel,* 3, 4.

9. Beauvoir, *Force of Circumstance,* 231.

10. In 2004 there was *Camus and Sartre: The Story of a Friendship and the Quarrel that Ended It* by Ronald Aronson, followed by *Sartre and Camus: A Historic Confrontation,* by David A. Spritzen and Adrian van den Hoven, which offered the first full-scale inquiries into the matter from this side of the Atlantic.

11. Beauvoir, *Force of Circumstance,* 111.

12. Aronson, *Camus and Sartre,* (Chicago:University of Chicago Press, 2004), 137.

13. For the full text of Sartre's letter to Camus, see *Sartre and Camus: A Historic Confrontation*, ed. and trans. Sprintzen and van den Hoven (Amherst, N.Y.: Humanity Books, 2004), 131–58.

14. Sprintzen and van den Hoven, *Sartre and Camus,* 147.

15. *Ibid.,* 126.

16. Camus, *Notebooks 3,* 38.

17. Todd, *A Life,* 311–12.

18. Jean Daniel, personal interview, April 2002.

19. Sprintzen and van den Hoven, *Sartre and Camus,* 220.

20. Todd, *A Life,* 311.

21. "From 1938 to 1960, they wrote to each other, about each other and in response to each other," as Aronson, who devoted his book to their interaction, puts it. "Sometimes they spoke in code, especially after their break."

22. Sartre, "Tribute to Albert Camus," in Brée, 173.

23. C. D. Lieber, reader's report of November 6, 1951, Knopf papers, Ransom Center.

24. Harry Levin of Harvard University was another reader. Knopf papers, Ransom Center.

25. Konrad Bieber published a very critical article about Anthony Bowers's translation of *The Rebel* in *The French Review* in May 1955, "The Translator: Friend or Foe." See Knopf papers, Ransom Center.

26. H. Stuart Hughes, "Metaphysical Rebellion," *Commentary,* May 1954, 306–8.

9   Friends

1. Camus, *Lyrical and Critical Essays,* 13.

2. Camus, *Notebooks 3,* 98.

3. *Ibid.,* 52.

4. *Ibid.,* 88. A version of this last thought will appear in *The Fall.*

5. Camus, *Notebooks 3,* 63.

6. *Ibid.*

7. *Ibid.,* 42.

8. The quote can be found in "The Growing Stone," in *Exile and the Kingdom,* with "river" substituted for "sea."

9. Camus, *Notebooks 3*, 95.

10. *Ibid.*, 35.

11. Camus, *Lyrical and Critical Essays*, 15.

12. Camus, *Notebooks 3*, 96.

13. Dostoyevsky's 1872 novel *The Possessed*, the basis for Camus's theatrical adaptation, has also been translated as both *The Demons* and *The Devils*.

14. Camus, *Gros Plan*, manuscript copy from the collection of Micheline Rozan.

15. Quoted in Todd, *A Life*, 319.

16. Jean Grenier, *Souvenirs*, 119–20.

17. Camus, letter to Chiaromonte, May 5, 1954, Beinecke.

18. Camus, letter to Chiaromonte, June 25, 1954, Beinecke.

19. Camus, letter to Chiaromonte, May 5, 1954, Beinecke.

20. Camus, *Notebooks 3*, 131.

21. *Ibid.*, 130.

22. *Ibid.*, 115.

23. *Ibid.*, 106.

24. Todd, *Une Vie*, 590.

25. Pléiade *Essais*, 2029.

26. Quilliot, *La Mer et les Prisons*, 23–24.

27. Todd, *Une Vie*, 600.

28. Todd, *A Life*, 325.

29. Camus, *Lyrical and Critical Essays*, 17.

10   Pursuing Char

1. "Notes et Variantes," Pléiade *Essais*, 1635.

2. Todd, *A Life*, 318.

3. René Char, "De Moment en Moment, in *Oeuvres* Complètes (Paris: Bibliothèque de la Pléiade, Gallimard, 1983), 802.

4. "René Char et Camus," Pléiade *Essais*, 1917.

5. Quoted in Lottman, *Albert Camus*, 600.

6. Laurent Greilsamer, *L'Éclair au Front:* La Vie de René Char (Paris: Fayard, 2004), 344.

7. "René Char et Camus," Pléiade *Essais*, 1917.

8. Greilsamer, *L'Éclair au Front*, 361.

9. Conversation with Marcelle Mahasela, Bibliothèque Méjanes, May 18, 2005.

11   The Company of Women

1. Maria Casarès, *Résidente Privilégiée* (Paris: Fayard, 1980), 122.

2. Todd, *A Life,* 129–30.

3. Camus, *A Happy Death,* 114.

4. *Ibid.,* 33.

5. Todd, *A Life,* 154.

6. *Ibid.,* 57.

7. *Ibid.,* 411.

8. Camus, *The Fall,* trans. Justin O'Brien (New York: Knopf, 1957), 66.

9. *Ibid.,* 108.

10. *Ibid.,* 56, 106.

11. *Ibid.,* 144–45.

12. Roger Grenier, *Albert Camus: Soleil et Ombre: Une biographie intellectuelle* (Paris: Gallimard, 1987), 296.

13. Sartre's admiration also showed in his own autobiographical work, *Les Mots* (*The Words*), which appeared seven years later and was also pronounced his masterpiece, ironical, self-critical, puzzling, and seemingly implicating all his contemporaries, but first of all himself.

14. Gallimard talked about Camus on the TV show *Bibliothèque Médicis* on July 22, 2006.

15. Camus, *The First Man,* 192,

16. Jean Daniel, personal interview, April 2002.

17. Casarès, in fact, was a Galacian from La Coruña.

18. At a difficult and dramatic time, several months after Camus's death, Casarès took the lead in Jerome Kilty's play *Dear Liar,* which is the story of Shaw and Campbell; it was an enormous artistic and financial success.

19. Casarès, *Résidente Priviligée,* 232–23.

20. Javier Figuero and Marie-Hélène Carbonel, *Maria Casarès, l'étrangère* (Paris: Fayard, 2005), 165.

21. Lenzini, *L'Algérie de Camus,* 70.

22. Camus, *Oeuvres completes I: 1931–1944,* ed. Jacqueline Lévi-Valensi (Gallimard: Paris, Bibliothèque de la Pléiade, 2006), 970.

23. Camus, *Notebooks 3,* 194.

24. Quilliot, *Mémoires II,* 242.

25. Todd, *A Life,* 316.

26. Camus, "Caligula," *Théâtre, Récits, Nouvelles*, ed. Roger Quilliot (Paris: Bibliothèque de la Pléiade, Gallimard, 1965), 28.

27. Camus, *Notebooks 3,* 259.

28. Camus, *Notebooks 3,* 258–59.

29. Camus, Pléiade *Essais,* 13, or *Lyrical and Critical Essays,* 16, 17.

30. Camus, *First Man,* 305.

31. Camus, "Fragment Manuscrit Pour 'Entre Oui et Non,'" Pléiade *Essais,* 1214.

32. *Ibid.*

33. Camus, *Lyrical and Critical Essays,* 35.

34. Camus, "Commentaires," Pléiade *Essais,* 1176.

35. Camus, *The First Man,* 58.

36. *Ibid.,* 300.

37. Todd, *A Life,* 531.

38. Camus, *The First Man,* 312.

39. *Ibid.,* 76–77.

40. Todd, *A Life,* 378.

12   War in Algeria

1. Although he published many successful novels in Algeria, Khadra, who is well educated and part of the elite of the first generation of independent Algeria, did not reveal his identity until 2001 after leaving Algeria and seeking exile in France. Many of his novels are now published in English.

2. Marissa Bey, "Lettre à Camus," *Le Figaro Littéraire,* May 2006, 43.

3. Alistair Horne, *A Savage War of Peace: Algeria 1954–1962* (New York: Viking, 1978), 49.

4. Portugal's African war was the longest colonial war; the Algerian war was the next longest.

5. Since the 1990s, a surprising array of books have appeared in France on the Algerian war, telling stories about the use of torture and the power of the army, revisiting questions on the justice system, the tactics of terrorism and counterterrorism, and the role of intellectuals in the war.

6. Camus, *Notebooks 3,* 56.

7. Camus–Grenier, *Correspondence,* 167.

8. Lenzini, *L'Algérie de Camus,* 109.

9. Camus, "La femme adultère," *Exile and the Kingdom,* 24.

10. Camus, "L'Hôte," *Exile and the Kingdom,* 109.

11. *Ibid.*

12. Adam Shatz, "The Torture of Algiers," *The New York Review of Books,* November 21, 2002, 53–57.

13. Estimates of the number of casualties in the war and the settlers who fled vary, often dramatically. The Algerians sometimes claim that as many as two million "martyrs" died in the war. See Shatz, "The Torture of Algiers," a careful retrospective on the war and a roundup of recent books on the subject.

14. Camus, *Albert Camus, editorialiste à L'Express mai 1955–février 1956* (*Cahiers Albert Camus 6*), ed. Paul-F. Smets (Paris: Gallimard, 1987), 169. Hereafter cited as *Cahiers*.

15. *Ibid.*, 56.

16. *Ibid.*, 71.

17. *Ibid.*, 165.

18. The numbers in attendance vary widely, depending on the sources. Other details of the event are reconstructed in Lottman, *Albert Camus*, 571–73.

19. Camus, *Resistance, Rebellion, and Death*, trans. Justin O'Brien (New York: Knopf, 1960), 136.

20. Quilliot, "Commentaires," Pléiade *Essais*, 1842.

21. Mohamed Lebjaoui, *Vérités sur la Révolution Algérienne*, quoted in Lottman, *Albert Camus*, 571.

22. Because its origins are uncertain, *pied noir* has many interpretations. In France, having once meant European settlers, it is now often used to mean Algerian Jews, once a large portion of the population.

23. Camus, *Notebooks 3*, 167.

24. *Ibid.*, 167.

25. Camus, Pléiade *Essais*, 900.

26. Camus, *Actuelles III*, 12.

27. *Cahiers*, 172.

28. *Ibid.*, 201.

29. Camus, *Notebooks 3*, 231.

30. Again, according to Alistair Horne's *A Savage War of Peace*, figures vary and may have been as high as 12,000 deaths on the Muslim side, with about 100 European deaths 122.

31. Camus, *Actuelles III*, 125.

32. Camus, *Notebooks 3*, 205.

33. Camus, *Actuelles III*, 27.

34. James D. LeSueur, *Uncivil War* (Lincoln: University of Nebraska Press, 2001), 118.

35. *Ibid.*, see pp. 232–37 for a full discussion of the Jeanson network, the machinations of the left, and Francis Jeanson's trial for treason in 1960.

36. Camus, *Notebooks 3*, 212.

37. LeSueur, *Uncivil War,* see chapter entitled "The Unbearable Solitude of Being: the Question of Albert Camus."

38. Camus, *Notebooks 3,* 203–4.

39. Camus, *Cahiers,* 187.

40. LeSueur, *Uncivil War,* 126–29.

41. Todd, *Une Vie,* 614.

42. Camus, Pléiade *Essais,* 1844.

43. LeSueur, *Uncivil War,* 134. Taleb's disappointment in Camus is expressed here at length.

44. Judt, *The Burden of Responsibility,* 130.

45. Robert Gallimard, personal interview, May 2, 2006.

46. Camus–Grenier, *Correspondence,* 187.

47. "Petit Guide Pour Les Villes Sans Passé," Pléiade *Essaies,* 848–49.

48. Camus, *Notebooks 2,* 89.

49. Camus, *Camus at Combat,* 87.

50. "I am suspect to nationalists on both sides of the fence," Camus explained to a colleague at Gallimard. "I am judged wrong by one group for not being . . . patriotic enough. For the other, I am too much so. I don't love Algeria like a military man or colon does. But can I love it other than a Frenchman? What too many Arabs don't understand is that I love it like a Frenchman who loves Arabs, who would feel like a stranger in the land if it were not their home too." Camus, *Cahiers,* 209.

13   Fans

1. Playbill from Théâtre Gramont, August 1964, private collection.

2. Jean Grenier, *Carnets 1944–1971,* ed. Claire Paulhan (Paris: Seghers, 1991), 240.

3. "Discours du 10 décembre 1957," Pléiade *Essais,* 1071.

4. Todd, *A Life,* 37.

5. Camus, *Notebooks 3,* 197–98.

6. Lottman, *Albert Camus,* 601–2.

7. Camus, *Notebooks 3,* 199.

8. Lottman, *Albert Camus,* 610.

9. Camus, *Notebooks 2,* 70.

10. The English version of Camus's speech, which came out in 1958, translated by Justin O'Brien, was entitled "Speech of Acceptance upon the Award of the Nobel Prize in Literature."

11. Peter Brook, personal interview with Mary Blume, December 2004.

12. Sontag, *Against Interpretation* (New York: Picador, 2001), 57.

13. Serge Doubrovsky, "Camus in America," Brée, 16. Camus, Doubrovsky suggested, was the great writer American literature had waited for, but who never came.

14. William Styron, personal interview, September 19, 2001.

15. Vanessa Schneider, "Histoire d'Amour," *Libération,* January 5, 1999.

16. Quilliot was a nationally known Socialist and a former minister of urban affairs under Mitterrand.

17. The tabloid press called it "un suicide d'amour." Claire had intended to sue the doctors for her resuscitation but later told of receiving hundreds of letters and feeling more love than she had ever known, with no further thoughts of death.

18. Schneider, "Histoire d'Amour."

19. Quilliot, *Mémoires II,* 212, 159.

20. *Ibid.,* 212.

14   *Le Premier Homme*

1. Jean Daniel, *Avec Camus: Comment resister à l'air du temps* (Paris: Gallimard, 2006), 79.

2. Camus, *Notebooks 3,* 251.

3. Todd, *A Life,* 395.

4. Camus, *Gros Plan,* 8.

5. Camus, *Notebooks 3,* 252.

6. Quoted in Todd, *A Life,* 407.

7. *Ibid.,* 744.

8. Camus, *First Man,* 282.

9. *Ibid.,* 193.

10. *Ibid.,* 180.

11. Lottman, *Albert Camus,* 659.

12. Camus, *First Man,* 282.

13. Catherine Camus, personal interview, October 1997.

14. *Télérama,* June 24, 1998, 160.

15. From the introduction to Jean Grenier, *Souvenirs,* 6.

16. Jean Camus, personal interview, April 15, 2005.

Selected Bibliography

Complete Works by Camus

Camus, Albert. *Œuvres complètes I: 1931–1944*. Edited by Jacqueline Lévi-Valensi. Paris: Gallimard (Bibliothèque de la Pléiade), 2006.

——. *Œuvres complètes II: 1944–1948*. Edited by Jacqueline Lévi-Valensi. Paris: Gallimard (Bibliothèque de la Pléiade), 2006.

Camus, Albert. *Théâtre, Récits, Nouvelles*. Edited by Roger Quilliot. Paris: Gallimard (Bibliothèque de la Pléiade), 1962.

——. *Essais*. Edited by Roger Quilliot. Paris: Gallimard (Bibliothèque de la Pléiade), 1965.

Individual Works

Camus, Albert. *Caligula suivi de Le Malentendu*. Paris: Gallimard, 1944.

——. *Caligula and Three Other Plays*. Translated by Stuart Gilbert. New York: Knopf, 1958.

——. *La Chute*. Paris: Gallimard, 1956.

——. *The Fall*. Translated by Justin O'Brien. New York: Knopf, 1957.

——. *Discours de Suède*. Paris: Gallimard, 1958.

——. *Speech of Acceptance upon the Award of the Nobel Prize for Literature, Delivered in Stockholm on the Tenth of December, Nineteen Hundred and Fifty-seven*. Translated by Justin O'Brien. New York: Knopf, 1958.

——. *L'Envers et l'endroit*. Paris: Gallimard, 1958.

——. *The Wrong Side and the Right Side*. In *Lyrical and Critical Essays*. Translated by Ellen Conroy Kennedy. Edited by Philip Thody. New York: Knopf, 1969.

——. *L'État de Siège: Spectacle en 3 parties*. Paris: Gallimard, 1948.

——. *L'Été*. Paris: Gallimard, 1954.

——. *Summer*. In *Lyrical and Critical Essays*. Translated by Ellen Conroy Kennedy. Edited by Philip Thody. New York: Knopf, 1969.

————. *L'Étranger*. Paris: Gallimard, 1942.

————. *The Stranger*. Translated by Matthew Ward. New York: Knopf, 1988.

————. *L'Exil et le royaume*. Paris: Gallimard, 1957.

————. *Exile and the Kingdom*. Translated by Justin O'Brien. New York: Knopf, 1977.

————. *L'Homme révolté*. Paris: Gallimard, 1951.

————. *The Rebel: An Essay on Man in Revolt*. Translated by Anthony Bower. New York: Knopf, 1961.

————. *Les Justes,* Pièce en 5 actes. Paris: Gallimard, 1950.

————. *The Just Assassins*. In *Caligula and Three Other Plays*. Translated by Stuart Gilbert. New York: Knopf, 1958.

————. *La Mort heureuse (Cahiers Albert Camus 1)*. Paris: Gallimard, 1971.

————. *A Happy Death*. Translated by Richard Howard. New York: Knopf, 1972.

————. *Le Mythe de Sisyphe: Essai sur l'absurde*. Paris: Gallimard, 1942.

————. *The Myth of Sisyphus and Other Essays*. Translated by Justin O'Brien. New York: Alfred A. Knopf, 1955.

————. *Noces*. Paris: Gallimard, 1947.

————. *Nuptials*. In *Lyrical and Critical Essays*. Translated by Ellen Conroy Kennedy. Edited by Philip Thody. New York: Knopf, 1969.

————. *La Peste*. Paris: Gallimard, 1947.

————. *The Plague*. Translated by Stuart Gilbert. New York: Knopf, 1948.

————. *Les Possédés*: Pièce en 3 parties, adaptée du roman de Dostoievski par Albert Camus. Paris: Gallimard, 1959.

————. *The Possessed: A Play in Three Parts*. Translated by Justin O'Brien. New York: Knopf, 1960.

————. *Le Premier homme*. Paris: Gallimard, 1994.

————. *The First Man*. Translated by David Hapgood. New York: Knopf, 1995.

Collections, Journals, and Letters

Camus, Albert. *Actuelles: Chroniques 1944–1948*. Paris: Gallimard, 1950.

————. *Actuelles II : Chroniques 1948–1953*. Paris: Gallimard, 1953.

————. *Actuelles III : Chronique algérienne 1939–1958*. Paris: Gallimard, 1958.

————. *Between Hell and Reason: Essays from the Resistance Newspaper Combat, 1944–1947*. Translated and edited by Alexandre de Gramont. Hanover, NH: Wesleyan University Press, 1991.

———. *Albert Camus éditorialiste à L'Express, mai 1955–février 1956 (Cahiers Albert Camus 6)*. Edited by Paul-F. Smets. Paris: Gallimard, 1987.

———. *Camus à Combat: Éditoriaux et articles d'Albert Camus, 1944–1947 (Cahiers Albert Camus 8)*. Edited by Jacqueline Lévi-Valensi. Paris: Gallimard, 2002.

———. *Camus at Combat: Writing 1944–1947*. Translated by Arthur Goldhammer. Edited by Jacqueline Lévi-Valensi. Princeton: Princeton University Press, 2006.

———. *Carnets, mai 1935–février 1942*. Paris: Gallimard, 1962.

———. *Notebooks 1935–1942*. Translated by Philip Thody. New York: Knopf, 1963.

———. *Carnets II, janvier 1942–mars 1951*. Paris: Gallimard, 1964.

———. *Notebooks 1942–1951*. Translated by Justin O'Brien. New York: Knopf, 1965.

———. *Carnets III, mars 1951–décembre 1959*. Paris: Gallimard, 1989.

———. *Notebooks 1951–1959*. Translated by Ryan Bloom. Chicago: Ivan R. Dee, 2008.

———. *Fragments d'un combat: 1938–1940 Alger républicain (Cahiers Albert Camus 3)*. Edited by Jacqueline Lévi-Valensi and André Abbou. Paris: Gallimard, 1978.

———. *Journaux de voyage*. Edited by Roger Quilliot. Paris: Gallimard, 1978.

———. *American Journals*. Translated by Hugh Levick. New York: Paragon, 1987.

———. *Le Premier Camus suivi de Écrits de jeunesse* (Cahiers Albert Camus 2). Introductory essay by Paul Viallaneix. Paris: Gallimard, 1973.

———. *Youthful Writings*. Translated by Ellen Conroy Kennedy. New York: Marlowe & Company, 1976.

———. *Lettres à un ami allemand*. Paris: Gallimard, 1948.

———. *Lyrical and Critical Essays*. Translated by Ellen Conroy Kennedy. Edited by Philip Thody. New York: Knopf, 1969.

———. *Resistance, Rebellion and Death*. Translated by Justin O'Brien. New York: Knopf, 1960.

Camus, Albert, and René Char. *Correspondance, 1946–1959*. Edited by Franck Planeille. Paris: Gallimard, 2007.

Camus, Albert, and René Char. La Posterité du Soleil: Photographies de Henriette Grindal. Itinéraire par René Char. Reliure Inconnue, 1965.

Camus, Albert, and Jean Grenier. *Correspondance: Albert Camus–Jean Grenier, 1932–1960*. Paris: Gallimard, 1981.

———. *Correspondence, 1932–1960*. Translated by Jan F. Rigaud. Annotated by Marguerite Dobrenn. Lincoln: University of Nebraska Press, 2003.

Camus, Albert, and Pascal Pia. *Correspondance, 1939–1947*. Edited by Yves Marc Ajchenbaum. Paris: Fayard/Gallimard, 2000.

Other Works

À Albert Camus, ses amis du Livre. Paris: Gallimard, 1962.

Aronson, Ronald. *Camus and Sartre: The Story of a Friendship and the Quarrel that Ended it*. Chicago: University of Chicago Press, 2004.

Beauvoir, Simone de. *La Force des choses*. Paris: Gallimard, 1963.

———. *The Force of Circumstance*. Translated by Richard Howard. New York: Putnam, 1965.

———. *La Force de l'âge*. Paris: Gallimard, 1960.

———. *The Prime of Life*. Translated by Peter Green. New York: The World Publishing Co., 1962.

———. *Les Mandarins*. Paris: Gallimard, 1954.

———. *The Mandarins*. Translated by Leonard M. Friedman. New York: W. W. Norton, 1991.

Brée, Germaine, editor. *Camus: A Collection of Critical Essays*. Englewood Cliffs, NJ: Prentice-Hall, 1962.

Brightman, Carol. *Writing Dangerously: Mary McCarthy and Her World*. New York: Harcourt/Harvest, 1992.

Brisville, Jean-Claude. *Camus*. Paris: Gallimard, 1959.

Casarès, Maria. *Résidente privilégiée*. Paris: Fayard, 1980.

Cohen-Solal, Annie. *Sartre: A Life*. New York: Pantheon, 1987.

Daniel, Jean. *Avec Camus: Comment résister à l'air du temps*. Paris: Gallimard, 2006.

———. *Avec le Temps: Carnets 1970–1998*. Paris: Grasset, 1998.

Figuero, Javier, and Marie-Hélène Carbonel. *Maria Casarès, l'étrangère*. Paris: Fayard, 2005.

Flanner, Janet. *Paris Journal 1944–1965*. New York: Atheneum, 1971.

Greilsamer, Laurent. *L'Éclair au front: La Vie de René Char*. Paris: Fayard, 2004.

Grenier, Jean. *Albert Camus, Souvenirs*. Paris: Gallimard, 1968.

———. *Carnets: 1944–1971*. Edited by Claire Paulhan. Paris: Seghers, 1991.

———. *Les Îles*. Paris: Gallimard, 1959.

———. *Islands: Lyrical Essays*. Translated by Steve Light. Los Angeles, CA: Green Integer, 2005.

Grenier, Roger. *Albert Camus: Soleil et ombre: Une biographie intellectuelle*. Paris: Gallimard, 1987.

————. *Pascal Pia ou le droit au néant.* Paris: Gallimard, 1989.

Horne, Alistair. *A Savage War of Peace: Algeria 1954–1962.* New York: Viking, 1978.

Judt, Tony. *The Burden of Responsibility: Blum, Camus, Aron and the French Twentieth Century.* Chicago: University of Chicago Press, 1998.

Lenzini, José. *L'Algérie de Camus.* Aix-en-Provence: Edisud, 1998.

Le Sueur, James D. *Uncivil War: Intellectuals and Identity Politics during the Decolonization of Algeria.* Lincoln: University of Nebraska Press, 2005.

Liebling, A. J. *The Road Back to Paris.* New York: Doubleday, 1944.

————. *The Most of A. J. Liebling.* Selected by William Cole. New York: Simon and Schuster, 1963.

Lottman, Herbert R. *Albert Camus: A Biography.* New York: Doubleday, 1979.

————. *The Left Bank: Writers, Artists and Politics from the Popular Front to the Cold War.* Chicago: University of Chicago Press, 1981.

Phillips, William. *A Partisan View: Five Decades of the Literary Life.* New York: Stein & Day, 1983.

Quilliot, Roger. *La Mer et les prisons: Essai sur Albert Camus.* Paris: Gallimard, 1956 (original), 1970 (reprint).

————. *The Sea and Prisons: A Commentary on the Life and Thought of Albert Camus.* Translated by Emmett Parker. University, AL: University of Alabama Press, 1970.

————. *Mémoires.* Paris: Éditions Odile Jacob, 1999.

Quilliot, Roger, and Claire Quilliot. *Mémoires II.* Paris: Éditions Odile Jacob, 2001.

Roblès, Emmanuel. *Camus, Frère de Soleil.* Paris: Éditions de Seuil, 1995.

Roy, Jules. *Adieu ma mère, adieu mon cœur.* Paris: Albin Michel, 1996.

Sebbar, Leïla, editor. *C'était leur France: En Algérie, avant l'Indépendance.* Paris: Gallimard, 2007.

Sokolov, Raymond. *Wayward Reporter: The Life of A. J. Liebling.* New York: Harper & Row, 1980.

Sontag, Susan. *Illness as Metaphor and Aids and its Metaphors.* New York: St. Martin's Press, 2001.

Sprintzen, David A., and Adrian van den Hoven, translators and editors. *Sartre and Camus: A Historic Confrontation.* Amherst, NY: Humanity Books, 2004.

Styron, William. *Darkness Visible: A Memoir of Madness.* New York: Vintage/Random House, 1990.

Thomas, Evan. *Robert Kennedy: His Life.* New York: Simon and Shuster, 2000.

Todd, Olivier. *Albert Camus: Une Vie.* Paris: Gallimard, 1996.

————. *Albert Camus: A Life.* Translated by Benjamin Ivry. New York: Knopf, 1997.